JUDAISM
HISTORY, BELIEF, AND PRACTICE

JUDAISM
HISTORY, BELIEF, AND PRACTICE

EDITED BY MATT STEFON,
ASSISTANT EDITOR, RELIGION

Britannica
Educational Publishing

IN ASSOCIATION WITH

ROSEN
EDUCATIONAL SERVICES

Published in 2012 by Britannica Educational Publishing
(a trademark of Encyclopædia Britannica, Inc.)
in association with Rosen Educational Services, LLC
29 East 21st Street, New York, NY 10010.

Distributed exclusively by Rosen Educational Services.
For a listing of additional Britannica Educational Publishing titles, call toll free (800) 237-9932.

First Edition

Britannica Educational Publishing
Michael I. Levy: Executive Editor
J.E. Luebering: Senior Manager
Adam Augustyn, Assistant Manager, Encyclopaedia Britannica
Marilyn L. Barton: Senior Coordinator, Production Control
Steven Bosco: Director, Editorial Technologies
Lisa S. Braucher: Senior Producer and Data Editor
Yvette Charboneau: Senior Copy Editor
Kathy Nakamura: Manager, Media Acquisition
Matt Stefon: Assistant Editor, Religion

Rosen Educational Services
Heather M. Moore Niver: Editor
Nelson Sá: Art Director
Cindy Reiman: Photography Manager
Nicole Russo: Designer
Matthew Cauli: Cover Design
Introduction by Matt Stefon

Library of Congress Cataloging-in-Publication Data

Judaism: history, belief, and practice / edited by Matt Stefon.
    p. cm.—(The Britannica guide to religion)
"In association with Britannica Educational Publishing, Rosen Educational Services."
Includes bibliographical references and index.
ISBN 978-1-61530-487-5 (library binding)
1. Judaism. I. Stefon, Matt.
BM562.J835 2012
296—dc22

2010044168

Manufactured in the United States of America

On the front cover: The Western Wall, also known as the Wailing Wall, is all that remains of the Second Temple of Jerusalem. The wall is a scared place of prayer and pilgrimage to the Jewish people. *David Sanger/The Image Bank/Getty Images*

On the back cover: The mezuzah is inscribed with scriptural verses (Deuteronomy 6:4–9, 11:13–21) to remind Jews of their obligations toward God. *Shutterstock.com*

On pages 1, 27, 48, 70, 93, 123, 153, 167, 186, 210, 228, 258, 277, 290, 307, 322, 331, 349, 356, 358, 361: *The Four Questions*, illustrated by Arthur Szyk. The Haggadah answers questions posed by children before the seder. *Fotosearch/Archive Photos/Getty Images*

Interior page borders image © www.istockphoto.com/Arkady Mazor

CONTENTS

72

90

95

102

114

130

180

207

214

218

239

260

272

281

286

291

305

329

339

350

Although it is the smallest major religion of the world in number of adherents, Judaism is also one of the oldest. Only Hinduism, the origins of which are diverse and difficult to pin down with historical accuracy, can claim an earlier vintage. Perhaps the oldest monotheistic tradition still in existence, Judaism also influenced two other great monotheistic faiths, both of which trace their lineage to the ancient figure Abraham. Christianity began in the 1st century CE as a movement within Judaism but became increasingly distinct. Arising in the 7th century, Islam claimed to be the culmination of a long train of piety and prophecy that began with Abraham and was fulfilled or "sealed" with the last prophet, Muhammad. Yet alongside these other traditions, Judaism has remained a vibrant expression of the faith of a people and their relationship with the Ultimate.

This book presents a basic introduction to the beliefs, practices, and contemporary forms of Judaism. Jews interpret their relationship with God through history—thus some sense of the historical context within which Judaism arose is necessary for a full understanding and appreciation of how the tradition is practiced today. Textual and archaeological evidence does not perfectly corroborate the biblical account, but the Exodus of the ancient Israelites from Egypt into the Promised Land is considered a foundational event in the sacred narrative that has shaped Jewish identity. Recalling his promise to Abraham that the latter's descendents, collectively called Israel, would remain his chosen people and would become a great nation, YHWH (God) called Moses to lead the people of Israel out of bondage in Egypt and to the land of Canaan. YHWH revealed his law (including the Ten Commandments) to Moses and made through him a covenant with Israel: if the people kept the Law, YHWH would bless them and continue to show them his favour.

This state of favour did not persist, so the Scriptures state, as the people continually turned away from God's covenant. A cycle emerged in which the people turned away, were punished by another nation sent by God, repented, and were saved from destruction and favoured once more, only to turn away from the covenant again—a cycle called the Deuteronomistic history after Deuteronomy, the fifth and final book of the Torah ("law" or "teaching"), which delineated the blessings the Israelites would receive by being faithful to God's Law and the curses they would incur if they strayed. In each time of crisis a tribal leader, or "judge," rose up to save the day and restore the people's fidelity. Yet ultimately, a king was needed—first Saul; then David, a shepherd and poet of the tribe of Judah and the first king

Philo, also known as Philo of Alexandria, is regarded by most as the foremost representative of Hellenistic Judaism. Library of Congress Prints and Photographs Division

to rule over a united Israel; and finally Solomon, David's son, the great city builder renowned for his wisdom, and the builder of the first Temple of Jerusalem. Yet even these kings and, especially, their heirs failed to uphold the utmost piety. Prophets arose—including Amos, who forecast no hope for Israel's redemption, and Isaiah, who declared that Israel would be a light unto all the world's nations—to warn the Israelites of God's displeasure and wrath. Yet David's kingdom split: the north, called Israel, was captured by Assyria in 722 BCE and disappeared from history as a political entity; and the southern kingdom of Judah, where the Temple and, thus, the heart of political and religious life, was captured by Babylon in 587.

After a half century of exile in Babylon, the civic and religious leaders of the Judahim, or "Jews," returned to Israel, their traditions transformed. The Temple was rebuilt, the Scriptures that came to comprise the Hebrew Bible compiled, and YHWH was increasingly viewed as the God of Israel, as well as the God who had created all people and the universe. Two centuries later, Judaism underwent another transformation, as Hellenism, the culture of the classical Greco-Roman world, became the dominant social, cultural, and religious influence not only on Israel but on the ancient Mediterranean. Religious concepts such as the nature of the soul, immortality, and the character of God were given new dimensions as Jewish thinkers including Philo Judaeus

came into contact with Greek thought. Jewish communities outside the land of Israel developed into a flourishing Diaspora. Alexandria, in Egypt, was one of the most prominent Diaspora communities. The Synagogue, or meetinghouse, had its roots in the Diaspora communities. Although Jewish leaders often chafed under Greek and, later, Roman rule and even rose up against it (as in the Maccabean revolt of the 2nd century BCE), the influence of Greco-Roman culture on Jewish thought and life—and then on Christianity and Islam—is indisputable.

With the destruction of the Second Temple by the Romans in 70 CE, and thus the end of the priesthood, Judaism underwent another transformation. Rabbis, men who were educated enough to interpret the Torah, supplanted the old priesthood as the interpreters of tradition. Also, the centre of Jewish life gravitated away from Jerusalem and toward the settlements of the Diaspora. The Talmud (compendium of commentary on the Torah) compiled in Babylon between the 3rd and 7th centuries continues to overshadow that compiled in Jerusalem during that time. Judaism continued to expand throughout the ancient world, with communities established in such countries as Ethiopia (the Falasha), Persia, and, perhaps by the 11th century CE, China (particularly the community at Kaifeng). Its largest branches were, and continue to be, the Sephardi (Jews of Middle Eastern descent who settled in Spain and Portugal) and the

Ashkenazi (Jews of German and Eastern European descent). In some areas, Jews were praised for their contributions—the great thinker Moses ben Maimon, best known by his Greek name Maimonides and also among many Jews as Rambam, was revered by Muslim leaders for his eloquent theological arguments. In other areas Jews were consigned to ghettos, walled-off areas of cities, if they were not expelled altogether, and were subject to violent persecutions. Responses among the Jewish communities of Europe and the Middle East varied. One major response to persecution was rooted in mysticism (Kabbala) and messianic expectation. From the visions of Isaac ben Solomon Luria to the false messiah Shabbetai Zevi—who fuelled hopes throughout a wide swath of the Jewish settlements that the messianic age was at hand, then dashed them when he converted to Islam—mysticism grew into a major aspect of Jewish tradition.

Another response was to find ways to adapt to the broader culture, which for many Jews in Europe entailed embracing the values of the Enlightenment West. The Haskala movement of the 17th and early 18th centuries spawned newspapers, journals, literature, and the first significant Jewish philosophical developments since Maimonides. Also, although it was largely relegated to the margins in the wake of disillusionment over Shabbetaianism, mysticism evolved into a movement called Hasidism, after the charismatic Israel ben Eliezer (also

known by followers as the Besht, short for Ba'al Shem Tov, or "Master of the Good Name") developed a less intellectual, more accessible form of Kabbala. The Hasidim view themselves as having a mission to restore Judaism by bringing all Jews into the Hasidic fold. Zionism, a movement advocating the formation of a Jewish homeland in the land of Israel, emerged as a formidable political force in the late 19th and early 20th centuries.

But equally significant were the impulses toward reform that influenced the formation of what are still the major movements within Judaism. In the mid-19th century, a movement often known as Reform Judaism arose. To varying degrees, Reform Jews place less stress on traditional ritual and dietary practices or on other observances and assume a more accommodating attitude toward secular culture and toward the ordination of women as rabbis. Conservative Judaism, which arose somewhat later, often places greater stress on traditional observances than does Reform Judaism, though it recognizes the ordination of women as rabbis. Orthodox Judaism, whose designation arose in response to Reform and Conservative movements, takes a more stringent view toward tradition, particularly toward ordination of women as rabbis and dietary practices such as abstaining from pork and mixing dairy and meat in the same meal. Yet "Orthodoxy" blurs several variations on practices: there are, for example, Orthodox Jews who uphold a particularly strict observance of tradition, while so-called Modern Orthodox takes a more accommodating stance toward secular culture (e.g., abstaining from eating pork but also eating meat that may not have been prepared according to kosher observances). At the opposite extreme is the Reconstructionist movement, which views Judaism largely as an ethical and cultural tradition rather than a "religion" in the sense of a system of beliefs about the Divine and of rituals that bind people in worship.

Central to Judaism is the tenet of monotheism. In contrast to the traditions of the peoples of neighbouring lands—first the people who inhabited ancient Egypt and the Middle East, and later the Greeks and Romans—Judaism held that there was only one God. The first of the Ten Commandments proclaims that Jews "shall have no other gods before" YHWH, and the Shema, a basic prayer that continues to play a central role in Jewish liturgy and life, exhorts the people of Israel to "Hear [that] the Lord is One." Further, the sacred literature of Judaism contains many examples in which YHWH is proclaimed to be the one and only God who created and sustains the totality of existence. Such biblical narratives as the accounts of the Exodus and the conquest of Canaan demonstrate instances in which God makes known his power, majesty, and sovereignty as the one God—particularly by easily defeating poseurs, including the Egyptian pharaoh, who was esteemed a deity. Even the prophets are humbled by God's unquestioned reign—as was Jonah, who tried to avoid preaching to the wicked denizens of Nineveh the message that would cause them to repent and, thus, bring God's forgiveness. God is transcendent, a personal deity who is supreme and apart from his creation. Thus his presence is not always apparent to human beings, the paramount creatures. The Book of Ecclesiastes illumines the futility of trying to discern God's ways of working within the world. The title character of the Book of Job cries out to the Lord for accountability for his affliction. Job longs for some divine word to explain why God has allowed him, who had always lived an upright life, to suffer and is unsure of what to make of it when he finally gets it.

Yet despite his distance and his silence, God is also a very real presence in Jewish life, which is a manner of making the mundane experience sacred by reflecting upon one's relationship with him. There are several ways of accomplishing this. Observance of certain holy days—especially Pesach, or Passover (a remembrance of the Exodus), and Yom Kippur (the Day of Atonement following the start of the new year)—and of kosher dietary laws is one way of abiding by God's Torah. Keeping the Sabbath each week is a particularly important practice, though Jews of different movements variously interpret the manner of observance. Another way to dwell in God's presence is to study the Scriptures that comprise the Hebrew Bible. It is also known as the Tanakh, a name formed from the first letters of its major divisions: Torah (Law or

Teaching), Nevi'im (Prophets), Ketuvim (Writings). The Bible is considered God's Word—the very characters that record it on the page are sacred and are revered. Thus textual study—learning to read the sacred texts in Hebrew and also studying the commentaries in the Talmud—is important. Mystical reflection has long been an aspect of Judaism. Jewish mysticism always holds that God is an ultimate reality separate from any one aspect of his creation, including individual human beings, yet may come to be known through the emanations or attributes (*sefirot*).

Yet another, crucial way of coming to know the divine presence within human life—one that transcends sectarian boundaries—is ethical and philosophical reflection. Judaism is ethical at its core—it is concerned with one's duties to God and also how the duties one has to other human beings, both within the Jewish community and outside it, relate to one's duty to God. Many great philosophers have arisen from Judaism. Maimonides is well-known for his ethical treatise *A Guide for the Perplexed*. The existentialist thinker Martin Buber was concerned with the parameters for an appropriate, mutual relationship between human beings, which should be patterned on the human relationship with God. Emmanuel Levinas located ethical reflection in loving concern for the Other.

These are but a handful of examples of the richness of Judaism, to which this book can only serve as a humble introduction. This volume hopes to demonstrate that Judaism, like other religious traditions, is more than merely a set of beliefs and practices. It is deeply connected to human society and culture. If it provides you with new knowledge and expands your appreciation for the continued vibrance of Jewish tradition, this volume will have served its purpose.

CHAPTER 1

THE HISTORY OF JUDAISM: BEGINNINGS TO THE SECOND TEMPLE

In nearly 4,000 years of historical development, the Jewish people and their religion have displayed a remarkable adaptability and continuity. In their encounter with the great civilizations, from ancient Babylonia and Egypt to Western Christendom and modern secular culture, they have assimilated foreign elements and integrated them into their own social and religious systems, thus maintaining an

The Western Wall in the Old City of Jerusalem. © *Don Smetzer/Stone*

unbroken religious and cultural tradition. Furthermore, each period of Jewish history has left behind it a specific element of a Judaic heritage that continued to influence subsequent developments, so that the total Jewish heritage at any given time is a combination of all these successive elements along with the adjustments and accretions that have occurred in each new age.

NATURE AND CHARACTERISTICS

The various teachings of Judaism have often been regarded as specifications of the central idea of monotheism. One God, the creator of the world, has freely elected the Jewish people for a unique covenantal relationship with himself. This one and only God has been affirmed by virtually all professing Jews in a variety of ways throughout the ages.

Jewish monotheism has had both universalistic and particularistic features. Along universal lines, it has affirmed a God who created and rules the entire world and who at the end of history will redeem all Israel (the classical name for the Jewish people), all humankind, and indeed the whole world. The ultimate goal of all nature and history is an unending reign of cosmic intimacy with God, entailing universal justice and peace. Between creation and redemption lies the particularistic designation of the Jewish people as the locus of God's activity in the world, as the people chosen by God to be "a kingdom of priests and a holy nation" (Exodus 19:6). This arrangement is designated a covenant and is structured by an elaborate and intricate law. Thus, the Jewish people are both entitled to special privileges and burdened with special responsibilities from God. As the prophet Amos (8th century BCE) expressed it: "You alone have I intimately known of all the families of the earth; therefore I will punish you for all your iniquities" (Amos 3:2). The universal goal of the Jewish people has frequently expressed itself in messianism—the idea of a universal, political realm of justice and peace. In one form or another, messianism has permeated Jewish thinking and action throughout the ages, and it has strongly influenced the outlook of many secular-minded Jews.

Law embraces practically all domains of Jewish life, and it became the principle means by which Judaism was to bring about the reign of God on earth. It is a total guide to religious and ethical conduct, involving ritualistic observance as well as individual and social ethics. It is a liturgical and ethical way constantly expatiated on by the prophets and priests, by rabbinic sages, and by philosophers. Such conduct was to be performed in the service of God, the transcendent and immanent ruler of the universe, the Creator and the propelling force of nature, and the one giving guidance and purpose to history. According to Judaic belief, this divine guidance is manifested through the history of the Jewish people, which will culminate in the messianic age. Judaism, whether in its "normative" form or in its sectarian deviations, never completely departed from this basic ethical and historical monotheism.

PERIODIZATION

The division of the millennia of Jewish history into periods is a procedure frequently dependent on philosophical predilections. The Christian world long believed that until the rise of Christianity, the history of Judaism was but a "preparation for the Gospel" (*preparatio evangelica*) that was followed by the "manifestation of the Gospel" (*demonstratio evangelica*) as revealed by Christ and the Apostles. This formulation could be theologically reconciled with the assumption that Christianity had been preordained even before the creation of the world.

In the 19th century, biblical scholars moved the decisive division back to the period of the Babylonian Exile and the restoration of the Jews to the kingdom of Judah (6th–5th century BCE). They asserted that after the first fall of Jerusalem (586 BCE) the ancient "Israelitic" religion gave way to a new form of the "Jewish" faith, or Judaism, as formulated by the reformer Ezra (5th century BCE) and his school. In *Die Entstehung des Judentums* (1896; "The Origin of Judaism"), the German historian Eduard Meyer argued that Judaism originated in the Persian period, or the days of Ezra and Nehemiah (5th century BCE). Indeed, he attributed an important role in shaping the emergent religion to Persian imperialism.

These theories, however, have been discarded by most scholars in the light of a more comprehensive knowledge of the ancient Middle East and the abandonment of a theory of gradual evolutionary development that was dominant at the beginning of the 20th century. Most Jews share a long-accepted notion that there never was a real break in continuity and that Mosaic-prophetic-priestly Judaism was continued, with only a few modifications, in the work of the Pharisaic and rabbinic sages well into the modern period. Even today the various Jewish groups—whether Orthodox, Conservative, or Reform—all claim direct spiritual descent from the Pharisees and the rabbinic sages. In fact, however, many developments have occurred within so-called normative or Rabbinic Judaism.

In any event, the history of Judaism can be divided into the following major periods: biblical Judaism (*c.* 20th–4th century BCE), Hellenistic Judaism (4th century BCE–2nd century CE), Rabbinic Judaism (2nd–18th century CE), and modern Judaism (*c.* 1750 to the present).

BIBLICAL JUDAISM (20TH–4TH CENTURY BCE)

The Bible depicts the family of the Hebrew patriarchs—Abraham, Isaac, and Jacob (all early 2nd millennium BCE)—as having its chief seat in the northern Mesopotamian town of Harran, which then belonged to the Hurrian kingdom of Mitanni. From there, Abraham, the

Abraham (kneeling) was a Hebrew patriarch and founder of the Hebrew people. SuperStock/ Getty Images

founder of the Hebrew people, is said to have migrated to Canaan (comprising roughly the region of modern Israel and Lebanon), which was a vortex of west Asian, Egyptian, and east Mediterranean cultures throughout the biblical period and later ages. From Canaan, the Hebrew ancestors of the people of Israel (named after the patriarch Jacob, also called Israel) migrated to Egypt, where they lived in servitude; a few generations later, they returned to occupy part of Canaan.

THE ANCIENT MIDDLE EASTERN SETTING

Israelite culture initially resembled that of its surroundings. It was neither wholly original nor wholly primitive. The Hebrews were seminomadic herdsmen and occasionally farmers. Their tribal structure resembled that of the West Semitic steppe dwellers known from the 18th-century BCE tablets excavated at the north-central Mesopotamian city of Mari. Their family customs and law have parallels in the Old Babylonian and Hurro-Semite law of the early and middle 2nd millennium. The conception of a messenger of God that underlies biblical prophecy was Amorite (West Semitic) and also found in the tablets at Mari. Mesopotamian religious and cultural conceptions are reflected in biblical cosmogony, primeval history (including the Flood story in Genesis 6:9–8:22), and law collections. The Canaanite component of Israelite culture consisted of the Hebrew language and a rich literary heritage—whose Ugaritic form (which flourished in the northern Syrian city of Ugarit from the mid-15th century to approximately 1200 BCE) illuminates the Bible's poetry, style, mythological allusions, and religious or cultic terms. Egypt provides many analogues for Hebrew hymnody and wisdom literature. All the cultures among which the patriarchs lived had cosmic gods who fashioned the world and preserved its order, all had a developed ethical system expressed in law and moral admonitions, and all had elaborate religious rites and myths.

Although plainer when compared with some of the learned literary creations of Mesopotamia, Canaan, and Egypt, the earliest biblical writings are so imbued with contemporary ancient Middle Eastern elements that the once-held assumption that Israelite religion began on a preliterate level must be rejected. Late-born amid high civilizations, the Israelite religion had from the start features characteristic of all the known religions of the area. Implanted on the land bridge between Africa and Asia, it was exposed to crosscurrents of foreign thought throughout its history.

THE PRE-MOSAIC PERIOD: THE RELIGION OF THE PATRIARCHS

Israelite tradition identified YHWH (by scholarly convention pronounced Yahweh), the God of Israel, with the creator of the world, who had been known and worshipped from the beginning of time. Abraham did not discover this God but entered into a new covenantal relationship with him, in which Abraham was promised the land of Canaan and numerous progeny. God fulfilled that promise, it is believed, through the actions of the Hebrew leader Moses (14th–13th century BCE): he liberated the people of Israel from Egypt, imposed covenantal obligations on them at Mt. Sinai, and brought them to the Promised Land.

Historical and anthropological studies present formidable objections to the continuity of YHWH worship from Adam (the biblical first man) to Moses. The Hebrew tradition itself, moreover, does not unanimously support even the more modest claim of the continuity of YHWH worship from Abraham to Moses. This lack of continuity is demonstrated in Exodus 6:3, which says that God revealed himself to the patriarchs not as YHWH but as El Shaddai—an archaic epithet of unknown meaning that is not specifically Israelite but is found throughout the patriarchal narratives and in the Book of Job. The epithet El Elyon (God Most High) also appears frequently in the patriarchal narratives. Neither of these epithets is used in postpatriarchal narratives (excepting the Book of Ruth). Other compounds with El are unique to Genesis: El Olam (God the Everlasting One), El Bethel (God Bethel), and El Ro'i (God of Vision). An additional peculiarity of the patriarchal stories is their use of the phrase "God of my [your, his] father." All these epithets have been taken as evidence that patriarchal religion differed

from the worship of YHWH that began with Moses. A relation to a patron god was defined by revelations starting with Abraham (who never refers to the God of his father) and continuing with a succession of "founders" of his worship. Attached to the founder and his family, as befits the patron of wanderers, this unnamed deity acquired various Canaanite epithets (El, Elyon, Olam, Bethel, Qone Eretz ["Possessor of the Land"]) only after their immigration into Canaan. Whether the name of YHWH was known to the patriarchs is doubtful. It is significant that while the epithets Shaddai and El occur frequently in pre-Mosaic and Mosaic-age names, YHWH appears as an element only in the names of Yehoshua' (Joshua) and perhaps of Jochebed—persons who were closely associated with Moses.

The patriarchs are depicted as objects of God's blessing, protection, and providential care. Their response is loyalty and obedience and observance of a cult (i.e., a system of religious beliefs and practices) whose ordinary expression is sacrifice, vow, and prayer at an altar, stone pillar, or sacred tree. Circumcision was a distinctive mark of the cult community. The eschatology (doctrine of ultimate destiny) of their faith was God's promise of land and a great progeny. Any flagrant contradictions between patriarchal and later mores have presumably been censored; however, distinctive features of the post-Mosaic religion are absent. The God of the patriarchs shows nothing of YHWH's "jealousy." No religious tension or contrast with their neighbours appears, and idolatry is scarcely an issue. The patriarchal covenant differed from the Mosaic, Sinaitic covenant in that it was modeled upon a royal grant to favourites and imposed no obligations as conditions of the people's happiness. Evidently not the same as the later religion of Israel, the patriarchal religion prepared the way for the later one through its familial basis, its personal call by the Deity, and its response of loyalty and obedience to him.

Little can be said of the relation between the religion of the patriarchs and the religions of Canaan. Known points of contact between them are the divine epithets mentioned earlier. Like the God of the fathers, El, the head of the Ugaritic pantheon, was depicted as both a judgmental and a compassionate deity. Baal (Lord), the aggressive young agricultural deity of Ugarit, is remarkably absent from Genesis. Yet the socioeconomic situation of the patriarchs was so different from the urban, mercantile, and monarchical background of the Ugaritic myths as to render any comparisons highly questionable.

THE MOSAIC PERIOD

According to Hebrew tradition, a famine caused the migration to Egypt of the band of 12 Hebrew families that later made up a tribal league in the land of Israel. The schematic character of this tradition does not impair the historicity of a migration to Egypt, an enslavement by Egyptians, and an escape from Egypt under an inspired leader by some component of the later Israelite tribes. To disallow these events, it can be argued, would make their centrality as articles of faith in the later religious beliefs of Israel inexplicable.

THE EGYPTIAN SOJOURN

Tradition gives the following account of the birth of the nation. At the Exodus from Egypt (13th century BCE), YHWH showed his faithfulness and power by liberating the Israelites from bondage and punishing their oppressors with plagues and drowning them in the sea. At Sinai he made the Israelites his people and gave them the terms of his covenant, regulating their conduct toward him and each other so as to make them a holy nation. After sustaining them miraculously during their 40-year trek in the wilderness, he enabled them to take the land that he had promised to their fathers, the patriarchs. Central to these events is Moses, who was commissioned by God to lead the Israelites out of Egypt, mediate God's covenant with them, and bring them to Canaan.

Behind the legends and the multiform law collections, it is possible to discern a historical figure to whom the legends and the legislative activity can be attached. And it is precisely Moses' unusual combination of roles that makes him credible as a historical figure. Like Muhammad (c. 570–632 BCE) at the birth of Islam, Moses fills oracular, legislative, executive, and military functions. He shapes the main institutions of Israel: the priesthood and the sacred shrine, the covenant and its rules, and the administrative apparatus of the tribal league. Although Moses is compared to a prophet in various texts in the Pentateuch (the first five books of the Bible), he is never designated as one—the term being evidently unsuited for so comprehensive and unique a figure.

MOSAIC RELIGION

The distinctive features of Israelite religion appear with Moses. The proper name of Israel's God, YHWH, was revealed and interpreted to Moses as meaning *ehye asher ehye*—an enigmatic phrase of infinite suggestiveness, literally meaning "I am/shall be what I am/shall be." The covenant, defining Israel's obligations, is ascribed to Moses' mediation. It is impossible to determine what rulings go back to Moses, but the Decalogue, or Ten Commandments, presented in chapter 20 of Exodus and chapter 5 of Deuteronomy, and the larger and smaller covenant codes in Exodus 20:22–23:33 and 34:11–26 are held by critics to contain early covenant law. From them the following features may be noted: the rules are formulated as God's utterances (i.e., expressions of his sovereign will, directed toward and often explicitly addressed to the people at large, Moses merely conveying the sovereign's message to his subjects) and, publication being of the essence of the rules, the people as a whole are held responsible for their observance.

The liberation from Egypt laid upon Israel the obligation of exclusive loyalty to YHWH. This meant eschewing all other gods—including idols venerated as such—and the elimination of all magical recourses. The worship of YHWH was aniconic (without images). Even figures that might serve in his worship were banned, apparently because their use suggested theurgy (the art or technique of influencing or controlling a god by fixing his presence in a particular place and making him accessible). Although there is a mythological background behind some cultic terminology (e.g., "a pleasing odour to YHWH" and "my bread"), sacrifice is conceived as tribute or is regarded (in priestly writings) as purely a sacrament (i.e., as a material means of interacting with or making a connection to God). Hebrew festivals also have no mythological basis. They either celebrate God's bounty (e.g., at the ingathering of the harvest) or his saving acts (e.g., at the festival of unleavened bread, which is a memorial of the Exodus).

The values of life and limb, labour, and social solidarity were protected in the rules governing interpersonal relations. The involuntary perpetual slavery of Hebrews was abolished, and a seven-year limit was set on bondage. The humanity of slaves was defended: one who beat his slave to death was liable to death; if he maimed a slave, he was required to set the slave free. Murderers were denied asylum and could not ransom themselves from death, and for deliberate and severe

EXODUS

The liberation of the people of Israel from slavery in Egypt under the leadership of the prophet Moses, dated by tradition to about the 13th century BCE, is known as the Exodus and recounted in a biblical book by that name. The English term derives from the Greek term exodus to designate the deliverance of the Israelites from Egyptian bondage and their safe passage through the Sea of Reeds (traditionally mislocated as the Red Sea). The Hebrew title of the work is Shemot ("Names").

Chapters 1–18 narrate the history of the Egyptian bondage, the Exodus from Egypt, and the journey to Mount Sinai under the leadership of Moses. The second half of the book tells of the Covenant that was established between God and Israel at Sinai and promulgates laws for the ordering of Israel's life.

Because Exodus continues the sacred story of the divine promise to Israel begun in Genesis, it must be seen as part of a larger literary unit that is variously understood to include the first four, five, or six books of the Bible.

Scholars have identified three literary traditions in Exodus, designated by the letters J, E, and P. The J strand, so called because it uses the name YHWH (Jahweh in German) for God, is a Judaean rendition of the sacred story, perhaps written as early as 950 BCE. The E strand, which designates God as Elohim, is a version of the sacred story from the northern kingdom of Israel, written in about 900–750 BCE. The P strand, so called because of its cultic interests and regulations for priests, is usually dated in the 5th century BCE and is regarded as the law upon which Ezra and Nehemiah based their reform. Each of these strands preserves materials much older than the time of their incorporation into a written work. Exodus thus conserves extremely old oral and written history.

bodily injuries, the *lex talionis*—the principle of "an eye for an eye"—was ordained. Theft and harm to property were punished monetarily rather than by death.

Moral exhortations called for solidarity with the poor and the helpless and for brotherly assistance to those in need. Institutions were created (e.g., the sabbatical, or seventh, fallow year, in which land was not cultivated) to embody such exhortations in practice.

Because the goal of the Israelites was the conquest of a land, their religion had warlike features. Organized as an army (called "the hosts of YHWH" in Exodus 12:41), they encamped in a protective square around their palladium—the tent housing the ark in which rested the stone "Tablets of the Covenant." When journeying, the sacred objects were carried and guarded by the Levite tribe or clan, whose rivals, the Aaronites, exercised a monopoly on the priesthood. God, sometimes called "the warrior," marched with the army. In war, part of the booty was delivered to his ministers.

Ten Commandments

The Ten Commandments, also called the Decalogue (Greek: deka logoi ["10 words"]), is a list of religious precepts that, according to various passages in the biblical books of Exodus and Deuteronomy, were divinely revealed to Moses on Mt. Sinai and were engraved on two tablets of stone. The Commandments are recorded virtually identically in Exodus 20:2–17 and Deuteronomy 5:6–21. The rendering in Exodus (Revised Standard Version) appears as follows:

I am the Lord your God, who brought you out of the land of Egypt, out of the house of bondage.

You shall have no other gods before me.

You shall not make for yourself a graven image, or any likeness of anything that is in heaven above, or that is in the earth beneath, or that is in the water under the earth; you shall not bow down to them or serve them; for I the Lord your God am a jealous God, visiting the iniquity of the fathers upon the children to the third and the fourth generation of those who hate me, but showing steadfast love to thousands of those who love me and keep my commandments.

You shall not take the name of the Lord your God in vain; for the Lord will not hold him guiltless who takes his name in vain.

Remember the sabbath day, to keep it holy. Six days you shall labor, and do all your work; but the seventh day is a sabbath to the Lord your God; in it you shall not do any work, you, or your son, or your daughter, your manservant, or your maidservant, or your cattle, or the sojourner who is within your gates; for in six days the Lord made heaven and earth, the sea, and all that is in them, and rested the seventh day; therefore the Lord blessed the sabbath day and hallowed it.

Honor your father and your mother, that your days may be long in the land which the Lord your God gives you.

You shall not kill.

You shall not commit adultery.

You shall not steal.

You shall not bear false witness against your neighbor.

You shall not covet your neighbor's wife, or his manservant, or his maidservant, or his ox, or his ass, or anything that is your neighbor's.

In Judaism, the prologue ("I am the Lord your God, who brought you out of the land of Egypt, out of the house of bondage") constitutes the first element, and the prohibitions against false gods and idols the second. Dating the Ten Commandments involves an interpretation of their purpose. Some scholars propose a date between the 16th and 13th centuries BCE because Exodus and Deuteronomy connect the Ten Commandments with Moses and the Sinai Covenant between YHWH (God) and Israel. For those who regard the Ten Commandments as an epitome of prophetic teachings, the date would be some time after Amos and Hosea (after 750 BCE). If the Ten Commandments are simply a summary of the legal and priestly traditions of Israel, they belong to an even later period.

The Commandments contain little that was new to the ancient world and reflect a morality common to the ancient Middle East. They are a description of the conditions accepted by the community of Israel in its relationship to YHWH. The differences found in Exodus and Deuteronomy indicate that the process of transmission from generation to generation brought with it modifications.

THE PERIOD OF THE CONQUEST AND SETTLEMENT OF CANAAN

The conquest of Canaan was remembered as a continuation of God's marvels at the Exodus. The Jordan River was split asunder, the walls of Jericho fell at Israel's shout, the enemy was seized with divinely inspired terror, and the sun stood still to enable Israel to exploit its victory. Such stories are not necessarily the work of a later age. They reflect rather the effect of these victories on the actors in the drama, who felt themselves successful by the grace of God.

A complex process of occupation, involving both battles of annihilation and treaty agreements with indigenous peoples, has been simplified in the biblical account of the wars of Joshua (13th century BCE). Gradually, the unity of the invaders dissolved (most scholars believe that the invading element was only part of the Hebrew settlement in Canaan. Other Hebrews, long since settled in Canaan from patriarchal times, then joined the invaders' covenant league). Individual tribes made their way with varying success against the residue of Canaanite resistance. New enemies, Israel's neighbours to the east and west, appeared, and the period of the judges (leaders, or champions) began.

The Book of Judges, the main witness for the period, does not speak with one voice on the religious situation. Its editorial framework describes repeated cycles of apostasy, oppression, appeal to God, and relief through a champion sent by God. Israel's troubles prior to the institution of the monarchy under Saul (11th century BCE) were caused by the weakness of the disunited tribes and were thus accounted for by the covenantal sin of apostasy. The individual stories, however, present a different picture. Apostasy does not figure in the exploits of the judges Ehud, Deborah, Jephthah, and Samson. YHWH has no rival, and faith in him is periodically confirmed by the saviours he sends to rescue Israel from its neighbours. This faith is shared by all the tribes. It is owing to their common cult that a Levite from Bethlehem could serve first at an Ephraimite and later also at a Danite sanctuary. The religious bond, preserved by the common cult, enabled the tribes to work together under the leadership of elders or an inspired champion in time of danger or religious scandal.

Both written and archaeological testimonies, however, point to the Hebrews' adoption of Canaanite cults—the Baal worship of Gideon's family and neighbours in Ophrah in Judges, chapter 6, is an example. The many cultic figurines (usually female) found in Israelite levels of Palestinian archaeological sites also give colour to the sweeping indictments of the framework of the Book of Judges. But these phenomena belonged to the private, popular religion; the national God, YHWH, remained one—Baal sent no prophets to Israel—though YHWH's claim to exclusive worship was obviously ineffectual. Nor did his cult conform with later orthodoxy. Micah's idol in Judges, chapter 17, and Gideon's ephod (priestly or religious garment) were considered apostasies by the editor, in accord with the dogma that whatever is not orthodoxy is apostasy—heterodoxy (nonconformity) being unrecognized and simply equated with apostasy.

To the earliest sanctuaries and altars honoured as patriarchal foundations—at Shechem, Bethel, Beersheba, and Hebron in Cisjordan (west of the Jordan); and at Mahanaim, Penuel, and Mizpah in Transjordan (east of the Jordan)—were added new sanctuaries and altars at Dan, Shiloh, Ramah, Gibeon, and elsewhere. A single priestly family could not operate all these establishments, and so Levites rose to the priesthood. At private sanctuaries even non-Levites might be consecrated as priests. The Ark of the Covenant was housed in the Shiloh sanctuary, staffed by priests of the house of Eli, who traced their consecration back to Egypt. But the ark remained a portable palladium in wartime, and Shiloh was not regarded as its final resting place. The law in Exodus 20:24–26, which authorized a plurality of altar sites and the simplest forms of construction (earth and rough stone), suited the plain conditions of this period.

THE PERIOD OF THE UNITED MONARCHY

The decentralized tribal league could not cope with the constant pressure of external enemies—camel-riding desert marauders who pillaged harvests annually and iron-weaponed Philistines (an Aegean people settling coastal Palestine *c.* 12th century BCE) who controlled key points in the hill country occupied by the Israelites. In the face of such threats, a central authority that could mobilize the forces of the entire league and create a standing army had to be established. Two attitudes were distilled in the crisis—one conservative and anti-monarchic, the other radical and pro-monarchic. The conservative attitude appears first in Gideon's refusal to found a dynasty in Judges 8:23: "I will not rule you," he tells the people, "my son will not rule over you; YHWH will...!" This theocratic view pervades one of the two contrasting accounts of the founding of the monarchy fused in chapters 8–12 of the First Book of Samuel. The popular demand for a king was viewed as a rejection of the kingship of God, and in response to the demand there appeared a series of inspired saviours, from Moses and Aaron (14th–13th century BCE) through Jerubbaal, Bedan, and Jephthah to Samuel (11th century BCE) himself. The other, more radical account depicts the monarchy as a gift of God, designed to rescue his people from the Philistines (1 Samuel 9:16). Both accounts represent the seer-judge Samuel as the key figure in the founding of Israel's monarchy, and it is likely that the two attitudes struggled within him.

The Benjaminite Saul was made king (c. 1020 BCE) by divine election and by popular acclamation after his victory over the Ammonites (a Transjordanian Semitic people), but his career was clouded by conflict with Samuel, the major representative of the old order. Saul's kingship was bestowed by Samuel and had to be accommodated to the ongoing authority of that man of God. The two accounts of Saul's rejection by God (through Samuel) involve his usurpation of the prophet's authority. King David (10th century BCE), whose forcefulness and religious and political genius established the monarchy on an independent spiritual footing, resolved the conflict.

THE DAVIDIC MONARCHY

The essence of the Davidic innovation was the idea that, in addition to divine election through Samuel and public acclamation, David had received God's promise of an eternal dynasty. A conditional (perhaps earlier) and an unconditional (perhaps later) form of this promise exist in Psalms, chapter 132 and 2 Samuel, chapter 7,

respectively. In its developed form, the promise was conceived of as a covenant with David, paralleling the covenant with Israel and instrumental in the latter's fulfillment—the covenant being that God would channel his benefactions to Israel through the chosen dynasty of David. With this new status came the inviolability of the person of God's anointed (a characteristically Davidic idea) and a court rhetoric—adapted from pagan models—in which the king was styled "the [firstborn] son of God." An index of the king's sanctity was his occasional performance of priestly duties. Yet the king's mortality was never forgotten: he was never deified, and although prayers and hymns might be said on his behalf, they were never addressed to him as a god.

David captured the Jebusite stronghold of Jerusalem and made it the seat of a national monarchy. (Saul had never moved the seat of his government from his birthplace, the Benjaminite town of Gibeah, about three miles north of Jerusalem.) Then, fetching the ark from an obscure retreat, David installed it in his capital, asserting his royal prerogative (and obligation) to build a shrine for the national God and thus at the same time joining the symbols of the dynastic and the national covenants. This move of political genius linked the God of Israel, the chosen dynasty of David, and the chosen city of Jerusalem in a henceforth indissoluble union.

David planned to build a temple to house the ark, but the tenacious tradition of the ark's portability in a tent shrine forced the postponement of the project to the reign of his son Solomon. As part of his extensive building program, Solomon erected the Temple on a Jebusite threshing floor, located on a hill north of Jerusalem, which David had purchased to mark the spot where a plague had been halted. The ground plan of the Temple—a porch with two free-standing pillars before it, a sanctuary, and an inner sanctum—followed Syrian and Phoenician sanctuary models. A bronze "sea" resting on bulls and placed in the Temple court had a Babylonian analogue. The Temple of Jerusalem resembled Canaanite and other Middle Eastern religious structures but was also different from them: notably, in the inner sanctum of the Temple there was no image of God but only the ancient ark covered by the wings of large cherubim. YHWH, who was enthroned upon celestial cherubim, was thus symbolically present in the Temple.

Alongside a brief inaugural poem in 1 Kings 8:12–13, an extensive (and, in its present form, later) prayer expresses the distinctively biblical view of the Temple as a vehicle through which God provided for his people's needs. Because no reference to sacrifice is made, not a trace appears of the standard pagan conception of temple as a vehicle through which humans provided for the gods.

The quality of the preserved narrative of the reign of David, which gives every indication of having come from the hand of a contemporary eyewitness, demonstrates that literature flourished under the aegis of the court. Attached to the royally sponsored Temple must have been a library and a school (in keeping with the universally attested practice of the ancient Middle East), among whose products would have been not only royal psalms but also liturgical pieces intended for the common people that eventually found their way into the book of Psalms.

The latest historical allusions in the Torah literature (the Pentateuch) are to the period of the united monarchy (e.g., the defeat and subjugation of the peoples of Amalek, Moab, and Edom by Saul and David, in Numbers 24:17–20). Conversely, the polity reflected in the laws is tribal and decentralized, with no bureaucracy. Its economy is agricultural and pastoral; class distinctions—apart from slave and free—are lacking; and commerce and urban life are rudimentary. A pre-monarchic background is evident, with only rare explicit reflections of the later monarchy (e.g., in Deuteronomy 17:14–20). The groundwork of the Torah literature most likely crystallized under the united monarchy.

In this period the traditional wisdom cultivated among the learned in neighbouring cultures came to be prized in Israel. Solomon is represented as the author of an extensive literature comparable to that of other sages in the region. His wisdom is expressly attributed to YHWH in the account of his night oracle at Gibeon (in which he asked not for power or riches but for wisdom), thus marking the adaptation to biblical thought of this common Middle Eastern genre. As set forth in Proverbs 2:5, "It is YHWH who grants wisdom; knowledge and understanding are by his command." Patronage of wisdom literature is ascribed to the later Judahite king, Hezekiah (8th–7th century BCE); the connection of wisdom with kings is also common in extra-biblical cultures.

Domination of all of Palestine entailed the absorption of "the rest of the Amorites"—the pre-Israelite population that lived chiefly in the valleys and on the coast. Their effect on Israelite religion is unknown, though some scholars contend that there was a "royally sponsored syncretism" aimed at fusing the two populations. Because popular religion incorporated pagan elements, it is likely that it did not meet the standards of the biblical writers. Such elements may have increased as a result of intercourse with the newly absorbed Amorites. The court itself welcomed foreigners—Philistines, Cretans, Hittites, and Ishmaelites are named, among others—and made use of their service. Their effect on the court religion may be surmised from what is recorded concerning Solomon's many diplomatic marriages: foreign princesses whom Solomon married brought with them the apparatus of their native cults. The king even had shrines to their gods built and maintained on the Mount of Olives. Yet such private cults, while indeed royally sponsored, did not make the religion of the people syncretistic.

Such compromise with the pagan world, entailed by the widening horizons of the monarchy, violated the sanctity of the holy land of YHWH and turned the king into an idolator in the eyes of zealots. Religious opposition, combined with grievances against the organization of forced labour for state projects, led to the secession of the northern tribes (headed by the Joseph tribes) after Solomon's death.

THE PERIOD OF THE DIVIDED KINGDOM

Jeroboam I (10th century BCE), the first king of the north, now called Israel (the kingdom in the south was called Judah), appreciated the inextricable link of Jerusalem and its sanctuary with the Davidic claim to divine election to kingship over all of Israel (the whole people, north and south). He therefore founded rival sanctuaries at the ancient cult sites of Dan and Bethel, and staffed them with non-Levite priests whose symbol of YHWH's presence was a golden calf—a pedestal of divine images in ancient iconography and the equivalent of the cherubim of Jerusalem's Temple. He also moved the autumn ingathering festival one month ahead so as to foreclose celebrating this most popular of all festivals simultaneously with Judah.

The Book of Kings (later divided into two books) remains the almost exclusive source for the evaluation of Jeroboam's innovations and the subsequent official religion of the north down to the mid-8th century. However, this work has severe limitations as a source for religious history. It is dominated by a dogmatic historiography that regards the whole enterprise of the north as one long apostasy ending in a deserved disaster. The culmination of Kings' history with the exile of Judah shows that it came from the northern kingdom. Yet the evaluation of Judah's official religion is subject to an equally dogmatic standard: namely, the royal adherence to the Deuteronomic rule of a single cult site. The author considered the Temple of Solomon to be the cult site chosen by God, according to Deuteronomy, chapter 12, the existence of which rendered all other sites illegitimate. Every king of Judah is judged according to whether or not he did away with all places of worship outside Jerusalem. The date of this criterion may be inferred from the indifference toward it of all persons prior to Hezekiah (e.g., the prophets Elijah and Elisha and Jehoiada, a priest of Jerusalem [all 9th century BCE]).

Another serious limitation is the restriction of Kings' purview: excepting the Elijah-Elisha stories, it recognizes only the royally sponsored cult and pays scant attention to popular religion. In the mid-8th century BCE, the writings of the classical prophets, starting with Amos, first appeared. These take in the people as a whole, in contrast to Kings. However, their interest in theodicy (the problem of reconciling the presumed goodness of God with the existence of evil in the world) and their polemical tendency to exaggerate and generalize what they deem evil must be taken into consideration before accepting their statements as history per se.

Book of Amos

The third of 12 Hebrew Bible books that bear the names of the Minor Prophets is attributed to Amos, a Judaean prophet from the village of Tekoa who was active in the northern kingdom of Israel during the reign of Jeroboam II (c. 786–746 BCE). According to 7:14, Amos was neither a prophet nor the son of a prophet (i.e., he was not a member of a professional prophetic guild). His only credential to prophesy to Israel was a summons by YHWH.

The book is a collection of individual sayings and reports of visions. Whether Amos committed any of his sayings to writing is uncertain. His words may have been recorded by a scribe from Amos's dictation or by a later writer who knew the sayings from oral tradition. The present arrangement of the sayings reflects the activity of someone other than the prophet.

Amos's message is primarily one of doom. Although Israel's neighbours do not escape his attention, his threats are directed primarily against Israel, which, he contends, has defected from the worship of YHWH to the worship of Canaanite gods. This belief prompts his polemic against the feasts and solemn assemblies observed by Israel. He also pronounces judgment on the rich for self-indulgence and oppression of the poor, on those who pervert justice, and on those who desire the day of YHWH on which God will reveal his power, punish the wicked, and renew the righteous. That day, Amos warned, will be a day of darkness for Israel because of its defection from YHWH.

For half a century after the north's secession (c. 922 BCE), the religious situation in Jerusalem was unchanged. The distaff side of the royal household perpetuated, and even augmented, the pagan cults. King Asa (reigned c. 908–867 BCE) is credited with a general purge, including the destruction of an image made for the goddess Asherah by the queen mother, granddaughter of an Aramaean princess. He also purged the qedeshim ("consecrated men"—conventionally rendered as "sodomites," or "male sacred prostitutes").

Foreign cults entered the north with the marriage of King Ahab (reigned 874–853 BCE) to the Tyrian princess Jezebel (died c. 843 BCE). Jezebel was accompanied by a large entourage of sacred personnel to staff the temple of Baal and Asherah that Ahab built for her in Samaria, the capital of the northern kingdom of Israel. Although Ahab's orthodoxy was in every other respect irreproachable, some members of his court may have worshipped the gods of the foreign princess. Jezebel's persecution of the prophets of YHWH—conduct untypical of a polytheist except in self-defense—was probably prompted by the fierce opposition to non-YHWH cults in Israel. Elijah's assertion that the whole country apostatized is a piece of hyperbole based on the view that whoever did not actively fight Jezebel was implicated in her polluted cult. Such must have been the view of the prophets, whose fallen were the first martyrs to die for the glory of God. The quality of their opposition may be gauged by Elijah's summary execution of the foreign Baal cultists after they failed at the contest on Mt. Carmel (Elijah and the priests of Baal appealed respectively to YHWH and Baal to set a pile of wood ablaze to prove whose god was truly God). A three-year drought (attested also in Phoenician sources), declared by Elijah to be punishment for the sin of apostasy, did much to kindle the prophets' zeal.

To judge from the stories of Elisha, devotion to the cult of Baal existed in the capital city, Samaria, but was not felt in the countryside. The religious tone there was set by the popular prophets and their adherents ("the sons of the prophets"). In popular consciousness, these men were wonder-workers—healing the sick and reviving the dead, foretelling the future, and helping to find lost objects. To the biblical narrator, they witnessed the working of God in Israel. Elijah's rage at the Israelite king Ahaziah's recourse to the pagan god Baalzebub, Elisha's cure of the Syrian military leader Naaman's leprosy, and anonymous prophets' directives and predictions in matters of peace and war all served to glorify God. Indeed, the equation of Israel's prosperity with God's interest generated the first appearance of the issue of "true" and "false" prophecy. The fact that prophecy of success could turn out to be a snare is exemplified in a story of conflict between the prophet of doom Micaiah (9th century BCE) and 400 unanimous prophets of victory who lured King Ahab to his death. The poignancy of the issue is highlighted by Micaiah's acknowledgment that the 400 were also prophets of YHWH—but inspired by him deliberately with a "lying spirit."

The Period of Classical Prophecy and Cult Reform

By the mid-8th century BCE, 100 years of chronic warfare between Israel and Aram had finally ended—the Aramaeans having suffered heavy blows from the Assyrians. King Jeroboam II (8th century BCE) undertook to restore the imperial sway of the north over its neighbour, and Jonah's prophecy that Jeroboam would extend Israel's borders from the Dead Sea to the entrance to Hamath (Syria) was borne out. The well-to-do expressed their relief in lavish attentions to the institutions of worship and to their private mansions. But the strain of the prolonged warfare showed in the polarization of society between the wealthy few who had profited from the war and the masses whom it had ravaged and impoverished.

The Emergence of the Literary Prophets

Dismay at the dissolution of Israelite society animated a new breed of prophets—the literary or classical prophets, the first of whom was Amos (8th century BCE), a Judahite who went north to Bethel. The point that apostasy would set God against the community was made in early prophecy. The idea that violation of the social and ethical injunctions of the covenant would have the same result was first proclaimed by Amos. Amos almost ignored idolatry, denouncing instead the corruption and callousness of the oligarchy and rulers. He proclaimed the religious exercises of such villains to be loathsome to God. On their account Israel would be oppressed from the entrance of Hamath to the Dead Sea and exiled from its land.

The westward push of the Neo-Assyrian empire in the mid-8th century BCE soon brought Aram and Israel to their knees. In 733–732, Assyria took Gilead and Galilee from Israel and captured Aramaean Damascus. In 721, Samaria, the Israelite capital, fell. The northern kingdom sought to survive through alliances with Assyria and Egypt. Its kings came and went in rapid succession. The troubled society's malaise was interpreted by Hosea, a prophet of the northern kingdom (Israel), as a forgetting of God. As a result, in his view, all authority had evaporated: the king was scoffed at, priests became hypocrites, and pleasure seeking became the order of the day. The monarchy was godless, putting its trust in arms, fortifications, and alliances with great powers. Salvation, however, lay in none of these but in repentance and reliance upon God.

Prophecy in the Southern Kingdom

Judah was subjected to such intense pressure to join an Israelite-Aramaean coalition against Assyria that its king Ahaz (8th century BCE) instead submitted to Assyria in return for relief. Ahaz introduced a new Aramaean-style altar in the Temple of Jerusalem and adopted other foreign customs that are counted against him in the Book of Kings. It was at this time that Isaiah prophesied in Jerusalem. At first (under Uzziah, Ahaz's prosperous grandfather) his message emphasized the social and religious corruption of Judah, stressing the new prophetic themes of indifference to God (which went hand in hand with a thriving cult) and the fateful importance of social morality. Under Ahaz, the political crisis evoked Isaiah's appeals for trust in God, with the warning that the "hired razor from across the Euphrates" would shave Judah clean as well. Isaiah interpreted the inexorable advance of Assyria as God's chastisement. The "rod of God's wrath," Assyria would be broken on Judah's mountains because of its insolence when God was finished with his purgative work. Then the nations of the world, which had been subjugated by Assyria, would recognize the God of Israel as the lord of history. A renewed Israel would prosper under the reign of an ideal Davidic king, all humanity would flock to Zion (the hill symbolizing Jerusalem) to learn the ways of YHWH and to submit to his adjudication, and universal peace would prevail.

The prophecy of Micah (8th century BCE), also from Judah, was contemporary with that of Isaiah and touched on similar themes (e.g., the vision of universal peace is found in both their books). Unlike Isaiah, however, who believed in the inviolability of Jerusalem, Micah shocked his audience with the announcement that the wickedness of its rulers would cause Zion to become a plowed field, Jerusalem a heap of ruins, and the Temple Mount a wooded height. Moreover, from the precedence of social morality over the cult, Micah drew the extreme conclusion that the cult had no ultimate value and that God's requirement of humanity could be summed up as "to do justice, and to love kindness, and to walk humbly with your God."

REFORMS IN THE SOUTHERN KINGDOM

According to the Book of Jeremiah (about 100 years later), Micah's prophetic threat to Jerusalem had caused King Hezekiah (reigned c. 715–c. 686 BCE) to placate God—possibly an allusion to the cult reform instituted by the king to cleanse Judah of various pagan practices. A heightened concern over assimilatory trends resulted in his also outlawing certain practices considered legitimate up to his time. Thus, in addition to removing the bronze serpent that had been ascribed to Moses (and that had become a fetish), the reform did away with the local altars and stone pillars, the venerable (patriarchal) antiquity of which did not save them from the taint of imitation of Canaanite practice. Hezekiah's reform, part of a policy of restoration that had political as well as religious implications, was the most significant effect of the fall of the northern kingdom on official religion. The outlook of the reformers is suggested by the catalog in 2 Kings, chapter 17, of religious offenses that had caused the fall, the objects of Hezekiah's purge closely resembled them. Hezekiah's reform is the first historical evidence for Deuteronomy's doctrine of cult centralization. Similarities between Deuteronomy and the Book of Hosea lend colour to the supposition that the reform movement in Judah, which culminated a century later under King Josiah, was sparked by attitudes inherited from the north.

Hezekiah was the leading figure in a western coalition of states that joined with the Babylonian king Merodach-Baladan II in a rebellion against the Assyrian king Sennacherib shortly after the Assyrian's accession in 705 BCE. When Sennacherib appeared in the west in 701, the rebellion collapsed. Egypt sent a force to aid the rebels but was defeated. His kingdom overwhelmed, Hezekiah offered tribute to Sennacherib; however, the Assyrian pressed for the surrender of Jerusalem. In despair, Hezekiah turned to the prophet Isaiah for an oracle. While condemning the king's reliance upon Egyptian help, Isaiah stood firm in his faith that Jerusalem's destiny precluded its fall into heathen hands. The king held fast, and Sennacherib, for reasons still obscure, suddenly retired from Judah and returned home. This unforeseen deliverance of the city may have been regarded as a vindication of the prophet's faith and was doubtless an inspiration to the rebels against Babylonia a century later. For the present, although Jerusalem was intact, the country had been devastated and the kingdom turned into a vassal state of Assyria.

During the long and peaceful reign of Manasseh in the 7th century BCE, Judah was a submissive ally of Assyria. Manasseh's forces served in the building and military operations of the Assyrian kings Esarhaddon (reigned 680–669 BCE) and Ashurbanipal (reigned 668–627 BCE). Judah benefitted from the increase in commerce that resulted from the political unification of the entire Middle East. The prophet Zephaniah (7th century BCE) attests to heavy foreign influence on the mores of Jerusalem—merchants who adopted foreign dress, cynics who lost faith in the power of YHWH to do anything, and people who worshipped the pagan host of heaven on their roofs. Manasseh's court was the centre of such influences. The royal sanctuary became the home of a congeries of foreign gods. The sun, astral deities, and Asherah (the female fertility deity) all had their cults alongside YHWH. The countryside also was provided with pagan altars and priests, alongside local YHWH altars that were revived. Presumably, at least some of the blood that Manasseh is said to have spilled freely in Jerusalem must have belonged to YHWH's devotees. No prophecy is dated to his long reign.

With the death of Ashurbanipal, Assyria's power faded quickly. The young king of Judah, Josiah (reigned c. 640–609 BCE), had already set in motion a vigorous movement of independence and restoration, a cardinal aspect of which was religious. First foreign cults were purged in Jerusalem under the aegis of the high priest Hilkiah, then the countryside was cleansed. In the course of renovating the Temple, a scroll of Moses' Torah (by scholarly consensus an edition of Deuteronomy) was found. Anxious to abide by its injunctions, Josiah had the local YHWH altars polluted to render them unusable and collected their priests in Jerusalem. The celebration of the Passover that year was concentrated in the Temple, as it had not been "since the days of the judges who judged Israel," according to 2 Kings 23:22, or since the days of Samuel, according to 2 Chronicles 35:18. Both references reflect the theory of the Deuteronomic (Josianic) reformers that the Shiloh sanctuary was the precursor of the Jerusalem Temple as the sole legitimate site of worship in Israel (as demanded by Deuteronomy, chapter 12). To seal the reform, the king convoked a representative assembly and directed it to enter into a covenant with God over the newfound Torah. For the first time, the power of the state was enlisted on behalf of the ancient covenant and in obedience to a covenant document. It was a major step toward the establishment of a sacred canon.

Josiah envisaged the restoration of Davidic authority over the entire domain of ancient Israel, and the retreat of Assyria facilitated his ambitions— until he became fatally embroiled in the struggle of the powers over the dying empire. His death in 609 was doubtless a setback for his religious policy as well as his political program. To be sure, the royally sponsored syncretism of Manasseh's time was not revived, but

there is evidence of a recrudescence of unofficial local altars. Whether references in the Book of Jeremiah and the Book of Ezekiel to child sacrifice to YHWH reflect post-Josianic practices is uncertain. Yet there is stronger indication of private recourse to pagan cults in the worsening political situation.

The unsettled conditions following Assyria's fall dismayed the devotees of YHWH, who had not been prepared for it by prophecy. Their mood finds expression in the oracles of the prophet Habakkuk in the last years of the 7th century BCE. Confessing perplexity at God's toleration of the success of the wicked in subjugating the righteous, the prophet affirms his faith in the coming salvation of YHWH, tarry though it might. And in the meantime, "the righteous must live in his faith."

Despite these expectations of salvation, the situation grew worse as Judah was caught in the Babylonian-Egyptian rivalry. Some attributed the deterioration to Manasseh's sin of moving toward polytheism. For the prophet Jeremiah (c. 650–c. 570 BCE), the Josianic era was only an interlude in Israel's career of guilt, which went back to its origins. His pre-reform prophecies denounced Israel as a faithless wife and warned of imminent retribution at the hands of a nameless northerner. After Nebuchadrezzar II (reigned c. 605–c. 561 BCE) decisively defeated Egypt at Carchemish (605 BCE), Jeremiah identified the scourge as Babylonia. King Jehoiakim's attempt to be free of Babylonia ended with the exile of his successor, Jehoiachin, along with Judah's elite (597 BCE). Yet the court of the new king, Zedekiah (reigned 597-587/586 BCE), persisted in plotting new revolts, relying—against all experience—on Egyptian support. Jeremiah now proclaimed a scandalous doctrine of the duty of all nations, Judah included, to submit to the divinely appointed world ruler, Nebuchadrezzar, as the only hope of avoiding destruction. A term of 70 years of submission had been set to humiliate all nations beneath Babylonia. Imprisoned for demoralizing the people, Jeremiah persisted in what was viewed as his traitorous message. Judah's leaders, on their part, persisted in their policy, confident of Egypt and the saving power of Jerusalem's Temple to the bitter end.

Jeremiah also had a message of comfort for his hearers. He foresaw the restoration of the entire people—north and south—under a new David. And since events had shown that human beings were incapable of achieving a lasting reconciliation with God on their own, he envisioned the penitent of the future being met halfway by God, who would remake their nature so that doing his will would come naturally to them. God's new covenant with Israel would be written on their hearts, so that they should no longer need to teach each other obedience, for young and old would know YHWH.

Among the exiles in Babylonia, the prophet Ezekiel, Jeremiah's contemporary, was haunted by the burden of Israel's sin. He saw the defiled Temple of Manasseh's

Jeremiah was an early Jewish prophet whose contentious doctrine responded to the turmoil of the Hebrew people. SuperStock/ Getty Images

time as present before his eyes and described God as abandoning it and Jerusalem to their fates. Although Jeremiah offered hope through submission, Ezekiel prophesied an inexorable, total destruction as the condition of reconciliation with God. The majesty of God was too grossly offended for any lesser satisfaction. The glory of God demanded Israel's ruin, but the same cause required its restoration. Israel's fall disgraced YHWH among the nations; to save his reputation, he must therefore restore Israel to its land. The dried bones of Israel must revive, so that they and all the nations should know that he was YHWH (Ezekiel 37). Ezekiel, too, foresaw the remaking of human nature, but as a necessity of God's glorification. The concatenation of Israel's sin, exile, and consequent defamation of God's name must never be repeated. In 587/586 BCE the doom prophecies of Jeremiah and Ezekiel came true. Rebellious Jerusalem was reduced by Nebuchadrezzar, the Temple was burned, and much of Judah's population was dispersed or deported to Babylonia.

THE RELIGIOUS COMMUNITY IN EXILE

The survival of the religious community of exiles in Babylonia demonstrates how rooted and widespread the religion of YHWH was. Abandonment of the national religion as an outcome of the disaster is recorded of only a minority. There were some cries of despair, but the persistence of prophecy among the exiles shows that their religious vitality had not flagged. The Babylonian Jewish community, in which the cream of Judah lived,

had no sanctuary or altar (in contrast to the Jewish garrison of Elephantine in Egypt). What developed in their place can be surmised from new postexilic religious forms: fixed prayer; public fasts and confessions; and assembly for the study of the Torah, which may have developed from visits to the prophets for oracular edification. The absence of a local or territorial focus must also have spurred the formation of a literary centre of communal life—the sacred canon of covenant documents that came to be the core of the present Pentateuch. Observance of the Sabbath—a peculiarly public feature of communal life—achieved a significance among the exiles virtually equivalent to all the rest of the covenant rules together. Notwithstanding its political impotence, the exile community possessed such high spirits that foreigners were attracted to its ranks, hopeful of sharing in its future glory. This moment marks the origin of conversion to Judaism for distinctly religious reasons rather than for reasons of politics, culture, or nationalism.

Assurance of that future glory was given not only by Jeremiah's and Ezekiel's consolations, which were made credible by the fulfillment of the prophecies of doom, but also by the great comforter of the exile, the writer or writers of what is known as Deutero-Isaiah (Isaiah 40–66), who perceived the instrument of God's salvation in the rise and progress of the Persian king Cyrus II (the Great; reigned 550–529 BCE). Going beyond the national hopes of Ezekiel and animated by the

BABYLONIAN EXILE

Also called the Babylonian Captivity, the exile was the forced detention of Jews in Babylonia following the latter's conquest of the kingdom of Judah in 598/597 and 587/586 BCE. The exile formally ended in 538 BCE, when the Persian conqueror of Babylonia, Cyrus the Great, gave the Jews permission to return to Palestine. Historians agree that several deportations took place (each the result of uprisings in Palestine), that not all Jews were forced to leave their homeland, that returning Jews left Babylonia at various times, and that some Jews chose to remain in Babylonia—thus constituting the first of numerous Jewish communities living permanently in the Diaspora.

Although the Jews suffered greatly and faced powerful cultural pressures in a foreign land, they maintained their national spirit and religious identity. Elders supervised the Jewish communities, and Ezekiel was one of several prophets who kept alive the hope of one day returning home. This was possibly also the period when synagogues were first established, for the Jews observed the Sabbath and religious holidays, practiced circumcision, and substituted prayers for former ritual sacrifices in the Temple. The degree to which the Jews looked upon Cyrus the Great as their benefactor and a servant of their God is reflected at several points in the Hebrew Bible, for example, at Isaiah 45:1–3, where he is actually called God's anointed.

universal spirit of the pre-exilic Isaiah, Deutero-Isaiah saw in the miraculous restoration of Israel a means of converting the whole world to faith in Israel's God. Israel would thus serve as "a light for the nations, that YHWH's salvation may reach to the end of the earth." In his conception of the vicarious suffering of God's servant—through which atonement is made for the ignorant heathen—Deutero-Isaiah found a handle by which to grasp the enigma of faithful Israel's lowly state among the Gentiles. The idea was destined to play a decisive role in the self-understanding of the Jewish martyrs persecuted by the Syrian king Antiochus IV Epiphanes (reigned 175–164 BCE)—as recounted in the Book of Daniel—and later again in the Christian appreciation of the death of Jesus.

THE PERIOD OF THE RESTORATION

After conquering Babylonia, Cyrus allowed those Jews who wished to do so to return and rebuild their Temple. Although some 40,000 eventually made their way back, they were soon disillusioned and ceased their rebuilding as the glories of the restoration failed to materialize and as controversy arose with the Samaritans, who opposed the reconstruction. (The Samaritans were a Judaized mixture of native north Israelites and Gentile deportees settled by the Assyrians in the erstwhile northern kingdom.) A new religious inspiration attended the governorship of Zerubbabel (6th century BCE), a member of the Davidic line, who became the centre of messianic expectations during the anarchy attendant upon the accession to the Persian throne of Darius I (522 BCE). The prophets Haggai and Zechariah understood the disturbances as heralds of the imminent overthrow of the Persian empire, as a worldwide manifestation of God, and as a glorification of Zerubbabel. Against the day of the empire's fall, they urged the people to quickly complete the building of the Temple. The labour was resumed and completed in 516, but the prophecies remained unfulfilled. Zerubbabel then disappears from the biblical narrative, and the spirit of the community flags again.

The one religious constant in the vicissitudes of the restored community was the mood of repentance and the desire to win back God's favour by adherence to the rules of his covenant. The anxiety that underlay this mood produced a hostility to strangers and encouraged a lasting conflict with the Samaritans, who asked permission to take part in rebuilding the Temple of the God whom they too worshipped. The Jews rejected the Samaritans on ill-specified but apparently ethnic and religious grounds: they felt the Samaritans to be alien to the Jewish historical community of faith and especially to its messianic hopes. Nonetheless, intermarriage between the two peoples occurred, precipitating a new crisis in 458, when the priest Ezra arrived from Babylon, intent on enforcing the regimen of the Torah. By reviving ancient laws excluding Canaanites and others, and applying them to their own times and neighbours, the leaders of the Jews brought about the divorce and expulsion of several dozen non-Jewish wives and their children. Tension between the xenophobic and xenophilic in postexilic Judaism was finally resolved some two centuries later with the development of a formality of religious conversion, whereby Gentiles who so wished could be taken into the Jewish community by a single, simple procedure.

The decisive constitutional event of the new community was the covenant subscribed to by its leaders in 444, which made the Torah the law of the land. A charter granted to Ezra by the Persian king Artaxerxes I empowered the latter to enforce the Torah as the imperial law for the Jews of the province Avar-nahra ("Beyond the River"), in which the district of Judah (now reduced to a small area) was located. The charter required the publication of the Torah, which, in turn, entailed its final editing—now plausibly ascribed to Ezra and his circle. The survival in the Torah of patent inconsistencies and disagreements with the postexilic situation indicate that its materials were by then sacrosanct, to be compiled but no longer created. But these survivals made necessary the immediate invention of a harmonizing and creative method of textual interpretation to adjust the Torah to the needs of the times. The Levites were trained in the art of interpreting the text to the people; the first product of the creative exegesis later known as Midrash (meaning "investigation" or "interpretation"; plural Midrashim) is to be found in the covenant document of Nehemiah,

BOOKS OF EZRA AND NEHEMIAH

The books of Ezra and Nehemiah constitute a single book in the Hebrew Bible, forming with both books of Chronicles a single history of Israel from the time of Adam. The connection of Ezra-Nehemiah with 1 and 2 Chronicles is clear from the repetition of the closing verses of 2 Chronicles in the opening verses of Ezra. The uniformity of language, style, and ideas of the two books and Chronicles mark the entire work as the product of a single author, known as the Chronicler. He belongs to a period after the Babylonian Exile, probably about 350–300 BCE.

Ezra 1–6 treats the return of the exiles and the rebuilding of the Temple of Jerusalem. The work of Ezra and Nehemiah in reconstituting the life of the people following the Exile is told in Ezra 7 to Nehemiah 13. Textual dislocations raise a question about the chronological sequence of Ezra and Nehemiah to which there is no solid answer.

The activity recounted in Ezra 7 to Nehemiah 13 represents the Chronicler's view of how the life of his people should be organized in the postexilic period with a religious revival in conformity with Mosaic laws.

chapter 9—every item of which shows development, not reproduction, of a ruling of the Torah. Thus, the publication of the Torah as the law of the Jews laid the basis of the vast edifice of Oral Law so characteristic of later Judaism.

Concern over observance of the Torah was raised by the stark contrast between messianic expectations and the harsh reality of the restoration. The contrast signified God's continued displeasure, and the only way to regain his favour was to do his will. Thus, the Book of Malachi, named after the last of the prophets, concludes with an admonition to be mindful of the Torah of Moses. God's displeasure, however, had always been signaled by a break in communication with him.

As time passed and messianic hopes remained unfulfilled, the sense of a permanent suspension of normal relations with God took hold, and prophecy died out. God, it was believed, would some day be reconciled with his people, and a glorious revival of prophecy would then occur. For the present, however, religious vitality expressed itself in dedication to the development of institutions that would make the Torah effective in life. The course of this development is hidden from view by the dearth of sources from the Persian period. But the community that emerged into the light of history in Hellenistic times had been radically transformed by this momentous, quiet process.

CHAPTER 2

HELLENISTIC JUDAISM

Contact between Greeks and Semites goes back to Minoan and Mycenaean times, and is reflected in certain terms used by Homer and other early Greek authors. It is not until the end of the 4th century BCE, however, that Jews are first mentioned by Greek writers, who praise them as brave, self-disciplined, and philosophical.

THE GREEK PERIOD (332–63 BCE)

After Palestine was conquered by Alexander the Great (332 BCE), it became part of the Hellenistic kingdom of Ptolemaic Egypt, the policy of which was to permit the Jews considerable cultural and religious freedom. When in 198 Palestine was conquered by King Antiochus III (reigned 223–187 BCE) of the Syrian Seleucid dynasty, the Jews were treated even more liberally, being granted a charter to govern themselves by their own constitution—namely, the Torah. Greek influence, however, was already apparent. Some of the 29 Greek cities of Palestine attained a high level of Hellenistic culture. The mid-3rd century BCE Zenon papyri, which contain the correspondence of the business manager of a high Ptolemaic official, present a picture of a wealthy Jew, Tobiah, who through commercial contact with the Ptolemies acquired a veneer of Hellenism, to judge at least from the pagan and religious expressions in his Greek letters. His son and especially his grandsons became ardent Hellenists. By the beginning of the 2nd century, the influence of the Hellenistic Age in Judaea was quite strong. Indeed, it has been argued that, if the Seleucids had not forcibly intervened in Jewish affairs, Judaean Judaism would have become even more syncretistic than Alexandrian Judaism. The apocryphal writer Jesus ben Sirach so bitterly denounced the Hellenizers in Jerusalem (*c.* 180 BCE) that he was forced by the authorities to temper his words.

In the early part of the 2nd century BCE, Hellenizing Jews took control of the high priesthood itself. As high priest from 175 to 172, Jason established Jerusalem as a Greek city, with Greek educational institutions. His ouster by an even more extreme Hellenizing faction, which established Menelaus (died 162 BCE) as high priest, occasioned a civil war in which Menelaus was supported by the wealthy aristocrats and Jason by the masses. The Syrian king Antiochus IV Epiphanes, who initially granted exemptions and privileges to the Jews, intervened at the request of Menelaus's party. Antiochus's promulgation of decrees against the practice of Judaism led in 167 BCE to the successful revolt of the priest Mattathias (died 166 BCE) and his five sons—the Maccabees (Hasmoneans). It has been conjectured that one of the Dead Sea Scrolls, *The War of the Sons of Light Against the Sons of Darkness*, mirrors the fierceness of this struggle.

The extreme tactics employed by the Hasmoneans in their struggle with Hellenizing Jews, whose children they forcibly circumcised, indicate the inroads that Hellenism had already made. On the whole, the chief supporters of the Hellenizers were members of the wealthy urban population, while the Maccabees were supported by the peasants and the urban masses. Yet there is evidence that the ruthlessness exhibited by the Hasmoneans toward the Greek cities of Palestine had political rather than cultural origins, and that in fact they were fighting for personal power no less than for the Torah. Indeed, some of the Jews who fought on the side of the Maccabees were idol worshippers. In any event, the Maccabees soon reached a modus vivendi with Hellenism: thus, Jonathan (died 143/142 BCE), according to the Jewish historian Flavius Josephus (*c.* 38–*c.* 100 CE), negotiated a treaty of friendship with Sparta; Aristobulus I (died 103 BCE) actually called himself Philhellene (a lover of Hellenism); and Alexander Jannaeus (died 76 BCE) hired Greek mercenaries and inscribed his coins in Greek as well as in Hebrew. Greek influence reached its peak under King Herod I of Judaea (reigned 37–4 BCE), who built a Greek theatre, amphitheatre, and hippodrome in or near Jerusalem.

King Herod's palace, Herodium, is located south of Jerusalem at a site identified in the 19th century. Getty Images

Social, Political, and Religious Divisions

During the Hellenistic period the priests were both the wealthiest class and the strongest political group among the Jews of Jerusalem. The wealthiest of the priests were the members of the Oniad family, who held the hereditary office of high priest until they were replaced by the Hasmoneans. The Temple they supervised also functioned as a bank, where the wealth of the Temple was stored and where private individuals also deposited their money. From a social and economic point of view, therefore, Josephus is justified in calling the government of Judaea a theocracy. Opposition to the priests' oppressive rule arose among an urban middle-class group known as scribes (*soferim*), who based their interpretation of and instruction in the Torah on an oral tradition probably going back to the time of the return from the Babylonian Exile (538 BCE and after). A special group of scribes known as Hasidim, or "Pietists," became the forerunners of the Pharisees, or "Separatists"—middle-class Jewish scholars who reinterpreted the Torah and the prophetic writings to meet the needs of their times. The Hasidim joined the Hasmoneans in the struggle against the Hellenizers, though on religious rather than political grounds.

Josephus held that the Pharisees and the other Jewish parties were philosophical schools, and some modern scholars have argued that the groupings were primarily along economic and social lines. However, the chief distinctions among them were religious and go back well before the Maccabean revolt. Some modern scholars have sought to interpret the Pharisees' opposition to the Sadducees—wealthy, conservative Jews who accepted the Torah alone as authoritative—as based on an urban-rural dichotomy, but a large share of Pharisaic concern was with agricultural matters. To associate the rabbis with urbanization seems a distortion. The chief support for the Pharisees came from the lower classes, whether in the country or in the city.

The equation of Pharisaic with "normative" Judaism can no longer be supported, at any rate not before the destruction of the Temple in 70 CE. According to the Palestinian Talmud (the annotations and interpretations of the Oral Law compiled by Palestinian Jewish scholars in the 3rd and 4th centuries CE), there were 24 types of "heretics" in Palestine in 70 CE, thus indicating much divergence among Jews. This picture is confirmed by Josephus, who notes numerous instances of religious leaders who claimed to be prophets and who obtained considerable followings.

The chief doctrine of the Pharisees was that the Oral Law had been revealed to Moses at the same time as the Written Law. In their exegesis and interpretation of this oral tradition, particularly under the rabbi Hillel (1st century BCE–1st century CE), the Pharisees were flexible, and their regard for the public won them considerable support. That the Maccabean ruler John Hyrcanus I (reigned 135–104 BCE) broke with them, and that Josephus set their number at merely "more than 6,000" at the time of King Herod indicates that they were less numerous and less influential than Josephus would have his readers believe. The Pharisees stressed the importance of performing all the commandments, including those that appeared to be of only minor significance. Those who were particularly strict in their observance of the Levitical rules were known as ḥaverim ("companions"). They believed in the providential guidance of the universe, in angels, in reward and punishment in the world to come, and in resurrection of the dead, all of which were opposed by the Sadducees. However, in finding a modus vivendi with Hellenism, at least in form and in terminology, the Pharisees did not differ greatly from the Sadducees. Indeed, the supreme council of the Great Synagogue (or Great Assembly) of the Pharisees was modeled on Hellenistic religious and social associations. Because they did not take an active role in fostering the rebellion against Rome in 66–70 CE, their leader, Johanan ben Zakkai, obtained Roman permission to establish an academy at Jabneh (Yavneh, or Jamnia), where in effect the Pharisees replaced the cult of the Temple with a regimen of study and prayer.

The Sadducees and their subsidiary group, the Boethusians (Boethosaeans), who were identified with the great landowners and priestly families, were more deeply influenced by Hellenization. The rise of the Pharisees may thus be seen, in a sense, as a reaction against the more profound Hellenization favoured by the Sadducees, who were allied with the philhellenic Hasmoneans. From the time of John Hyrcanus, the Sadducees generally held a higher position than the Pharisees and were favoured by the Jewish rulers. Religiously more circumscribed than the Pharisees, they rejected the idea of a revealed oral interpretation of the Torah, even though they had their own tradition, the sefer gezerot ("book of decrees" or "decisions"). They similarly rejected the inspiration of the prophetic books of the Bible, as well as the Pharisaic beliefs in angels, rewards and punishments in the world to come, providential governance of human events, and resurrection of the dead. For them Judaism centred on the Temple. About 10 years before the Temple's destruction in 70 CE, however, the Pharisees prevented the Sadducees from entering it, and in effect the Sadducees disappeared from Jewish life.

Not constituting any particular party were the unlearned rural masses known as 'amme ha-aretz ("people of the land"), who were found among both the Pharisees and the Sadducees, and even among the Samaritans. The 'amme ha-aretz did not give the prescribed tithes, did not observe the laws of purity, and were neglectful of the laws of prayer. So great was the antagonism between them and the learned Pharisees that the biblical verse "Cursed be he who lies with any kind of beast" was applied to their daughters. The antipathy was reciprocated, for in the same passage in the Babylonian Talmud (the annotations and interpretations of the Oral Law compiled by Babylonian Jewish scholars in the 5th century CE) are added the words, "Greater is the hatred wherewith the *'amme ha-aretz* hate the scholar than the hatred wherewith the heathens hate Israel." That there was social mobility, however, is clear from the Talmudic dictum, "Heed the sons of the *'amme ha-aretz*, for they will be the living source of the Torah."

Proselytes (converts) to Judaism, though not constituting a class, became increasingly numerous in Palestine and especially in the Diaspora (the Jews living beyond Palestine). Scholarly estimates of the Jewish population of this era range from 700,000 to 5,000,000 in Palestine and from 2,000,000 to 5,000,000 in the Diaspora, the prevailing opinion being that about one-tenth of the population of the Mediterranean world at the beginning of the Christian era was Jewish. Such numbers represent a considerable increase from previous eras and must have included large numbers of proselytes. In a probable allusion to proselytism, in 139 BCE the Jews of Rome were charged by the praetor with attempting to contaminate Roman morals with their religion. The first large-scale conversions were conducted by John Hyrcanus and Aristobulus I, who in 130 and 103 BCE, respectively, forced the people of Idumaea in southern Palestine and the

people of Ituraea in northern Palestine to become Jews. The eagerness of the Pharisees to win converts is attested in The Gospel According to Matthew (23:15), which states that the Pharisees would "traverse sea and land to make a single proselyte." To be sure, some of the proselytes, according to Josephus, did return to their pagan ways, but the majority apparently remained true to their new religion. In addition, there were many "sympathizers" with Judaism (known as *sebomenoi*, "fearers of the Lord"), who observed one or more Jewish practices without being fully converted.

Outside the pale of Judaism in most, though not all, respects were the Samaritans, who, like the Sadducees, refused to recognize the validity of the Oral Law. In fact, the break between the Sadducees and the Samaritans did not occur until the conquest of Shechem by John Hyrcanus (128 BCE). Like the later so-called Qumrān covenanters (the monastic group associated with the Dead Sea Scrolls), they were opposed to the Jewish priesthood and the cult of the Temple, regarded Moses as a messianic figure, and forbade the revelation of esoteric doctrines to outsiders.

Scholars have revised the conception of a "normative" Pharisaic Judaism dominant in Palestine and a deviant Judaism dominant in the Diaspora. On the one hand, the picture of normative Judaism is broader than at first believed, and it is clear that there were many differences of emphasis within the Pharisaic party.

On the other hand, supposed differences between Alexandrian and Palestinian Judaism are not as great as had been formerly thought. In Palestine, no less than in the Diaspora, there were deviations from Pharisaic standards.

Despite the attempts of the Pharisaic leaders to restrain the wave of Greek influence, they themselves showed at least superficial Hellenization. In the first place, as many as 2,500 to 3,000 words of Greek origin are found in the Talmudic corpus, and they supply important terms in the fields of law, government, science, religion, technology, and everyday life, especially in the popular sermons preached by the rabbis. When preaching, the Talmudic rabbis often gave the Greek translation of biblical verses for the benefit of those who understood only Greek. The prevalence of Greek in ossuary (burial) inscriptions and the discovery of Greek papyri in the Dead Sea caves confirm the widespread use of Greek, though it seems few Jews really mastered it. Again, there was a superficial Hellenization in the frequent adoption of Greek names, even by the rabbis; and there is evidence (Talmud, *Soṭa* [a tractate in the Mishna]) of a school at the beginning of the 2nd century CE that had 500 students of "Greek wisdom." At the end of the 2nd century, long after the rabbis prohibited the people from teaching their sons Greek (117), Rabbi Judah ha-Nasi (135–220), the editor of the Mishna, the authoritative compilation of the Oral Law, could still remark,

"Why talk Syriac in Palestine? Talk either Hebrew or Greek." The synagogues of the period are modeled after Hellenistic-Roman basilicas, with inscriptions in Greek and even pagan motifs. Many of the anecdotes told about the rabbis have Socratic and Cynic parallels. There is evidence of discussions between rabbis and Athenians, Alexandrians, Roman philosophers, and even the emperor Antoninus Pius (reigned 138–161). Despite all of these discussions, only one rabbi, Elisha ben Abuyah (early 2nd century), appears to have embraced gnosticism, accepting certain esoteric religious dualistic views. The rabbis never mention the Greek philosophers Plato (428/427–348/347 BCE) and Aristotle (384–322 BCE) or the Hellenistic Jewish philosopher Philo Judaeus (*c.* 15 BCE–*c.* 45 CE), and they never use any Greek philosophical terms. The only Greek author whom they name is Homer. Again, the parallels between Hellenistic rhetoric and rabbinic hermeneutics are in the realm of terminology rather than of substance, and those between Roman and Talmudic law are inconclusive. Part of the explanation of this may be that, although there were 29 Greek cities in Palestine, none was in Judaea, the real stronghold of the Jews.

RELIGIOUS RITES AND CUSTOMS IN PALESTINE

Until its destruction in 70 CE, the most important religious institution of the Jews was the Temple in Jerusalem (the

Second Temple, erected 538–516 BCE). Although services were interrupted for three years by Antiochus IV Epiphanes (167–164 BCE) and although the Roman general Pompey (106–48 BCE) desecrated the Temple in 63 BCE, Herod lavished great expense in rebuilding it. The high priesthood itself became degraded by the extreme Hellenism of high priests such as Jason and Menelaus, and the institution declined when Herod began the custom of appointing high priests for political and financial considerations. That not only the multitude of Jews but the priesthood itself suffered from sharp divisions is clear from the bitter class warfare that ultimately erupted in 59 CE between the high priests on the one hand, and the ordinary priests and the leaders of the populace of Jerusalem on the other.

Although the Temple remained central in Jewish worship, synagogues had already emerged as places for Torah reading and communal prayer and worship during the Babylonian Exile in the 6th century BCE, if not even earlier. In any case, in the following century, Ezra stood upon a pulpit of wood and read from the Torah to the people (Nehemiah). Some scholars maintain that a synagogue existed even within the precincts of the Temple. Certainly, by the time of Jesus, to judge from the references to Galilean synagogues in the Christian Scriptures, synagogues were common in Palestine. Hence, when the Temple was destroyed in 70 CE, the spiritual vacuum was hardly as great as it had been after the destruction of the First Temple (586 BCE).

The chief legislative, judicial, and educational body of the Palestinian Jews during the period of the Second Temple was the Great Sanhedrin (council court), consisting of 71 members, among whom the Sadducees were an important party. The members shared the government with the king during the early years of the Hasmonean dynasty, but, beginning with Herod's reign, their authority was restricted to religious matters. In addition, there seems to have been a Sanhedrin, set up by the high priest, which served as a court of political council, as well as a kind of grand jury.

SYNAGOGUE

The synagogue is a community house of worship that serves as a place for liturgical services as well as assembly and study. Its traditional functions are reflected in three Hebrew synonyms for synagogue: bet ha-tefilla *("house of prayer"),* bet ha-kneset *("house of assembly"), and* bet ha-midrash *("house of study"). The term* synagogue *is of Greek origin (*synagein*, "to bring together") and means a place of assembly. The Yiddish word* shul *is also used to refer to the synagogue, and in modern times, the word* temple *is common among some Reform and Conservative congregations.*

The oldest dated evidence of a synagogue is from the 3rd century BCE, but synagogues doubtless have an older history. Some scholars believe that the destruction of Solomon's Temple in 586 BCE gave rise to synagogues after private homes were temporarily used for public worship and religious instructions. Other scholars trace the origin of synagogues to the Jewish custom of having representatives of communities outside Jerusalem pray together during the two-week period when priestly representatives of their community attended ritual sacrifices in the Temple of Jerusalem. Whatever their origin, synagogues flourished side by side with the ancient Temple cult and existed long before Jewish sacrifice and the established priesthood were terminated with the destruction of the Second Temple by Titus in 70 CE. Thereafter, synagogues took on an even greater importance as the unchallenged focal point of Jewish religious life.

Modern synagogues carry on the same basic functions associated with ancient synagogues but have added social, recreational, and philanthropic programs as the times demand. They are essentially democratic institutions established by a community of Jews who seek God through prayer and sacred studies. The liturgy has no sacrifice, so no priesthood is required for public worship. Because each synagogue is autonomous, its erection, its maintenance, and its rabbi and officials reflect the desires of the local community.

There is no standard synagogue architecture. A typical synagogue contains an ark (where the scrolls of the Law are kept), an "eternal light" burning before the ark, two candelabra, pews, and a raised platform (bimah), from which scriptural passages are read and from which, often, services are conducted. The segregation of men and women, a practice that is still observed in Orthodox synagogues, has been abandoned by Reform and Conservative congregations. A ritual bath (mikvah) is sometimes located on the premises.

RELIGIOUS AND CULTURAL LIFE IN THE DIASPORA

During the Hellenistic-Roman period, the chief centres of Jewish population outside Palestine were in Syria, Asia Minor, Babylonia, and Egypt, each of which is estimated to have had at least one million Jews. The large Jewish community of Antioch—which, according to Josephus, had been given all the rights of citizenship by the Seleucid founder-king, Seleucus I Nicator (died 280 BCE)—attracted a particularly large number of converts to Judaism. In Antioch the apocryphal book of Tobit was probably composed in the 2nd century BCE to encourage wayward Diaspora Jews to return to their Judaism. As for the Jews of Asia Minor, whose large numbers were mentioned by Cicero (106–43 BCE), their not joining in the Jewish revolts against the Roman emperors Nero (reigned 54–68 CE), Trajan (reigned 98–117), and Hadrian (reigned 117–138) would indicate that they had sunk deep roots into their environment. In Babylonia in the early part of the 1st century CE, two Jewish brothers, Asinaeus and Anilaeus, established an independent minor state. Their followers were so meticulous in observing the Sabbath that they assumed that it would not be possible to violate it even to save themselves from a Parthian attack. In the early 1st century CE, according to Josephus, the royal house and many of their entourage in the district of Adiabene in northern Mesopotamia were converted to Judaism. Some Adiabenian Jews distinguished themselves in the revolt against Rome in 66.

The largest and most important Jewish settlement in the Diaspora was in Egypt. There is evidence (papyri) of a Jewish military colony at Elephantine (Yeb), Upper Egypt, as early as the 6th century BCE. These papyri reveal the existence of a Jewish temple—which most certainly would be considered heterodox—and some syncretism (mixture) with pagan cults. Alexandria, the most populous and most influential Hellenistic Jewish community in the Diaspora, originated when Alexander the Great assigned a quarter of the city to the Jews. Until about the 3rd century BCE, the papyri of the Egyptian Jewish community were written in Aramaic. After that, with the exception of the Nash papyrus in Hebrew, all papyri until 400 CE were written in Greek. Similarly, of the 116 Jewish inscriptions from Egypt, all but five are written in Greek. The process of Hellenistic acculturation is thus obvious.

The most important work of the early Hellenistic period—dating, according to tradition, from the 3rd century BCE—is the Septuagint, a translation into Greek of the Hebrew Scriptures, including some works not found in the traditional Hebrew canon. The name of the work (from the Latin *septuaginta*, "70") derived from the belief that 72 translators, 6 from each of the 12 tribes, worked independently on the entire text and produced identical translations. As revealed in the *Letter of Aristeas* and the works of Philo and Josephus, the Septuagint was itself regarded by many Hellenized Jews as divinely inspired. The translation shows some knowledge of Palestinian exegesis and the tradition of Halakhah (the Oral Law); but the rabbis themselves, noting that the translation diverged from the Hebrew text, apparently had ambivalent feelings about it, as is evidenced in their alternate praise and condemnation of it, as well as in their belief that another translation of the Scriptures into Greek was needed. The fact that "Torah" was translated as *nomos* ("law") and *tzedaqa* as *dikaiosynē* ("justice") indicates how deeply the authors of the Septuagint believed that Judaism could be accurately expressed using Greek concepts.

The fact that the temple at Leontopolis in Egypt was established (*c.* 145 BCE) by a deposed high priest, Onias IV, clearly indicates that it was heterodox. As merely the temple of a military colony, it never really offered a challenge to the Temple in Jerusalem. It is significant that the Palestinian rabbis ruled that a sacrifice intended for the temple of Onias might be offered in Jerusalem. The temple of Onias scarcely affected Egyptian Jewry, as can be seen from the silence about it on the part of Philo, who often mentions the Temple in Jerusalem. The temple of Onias, however, continued until it was closed by the Roman emperor Vespasian (reigned 69–79 CE) in 73.

DIASPORA

The word Diaspora comes from a Greek word meaning "dispersion," in this case referring both to the dispersion of Jews among the Gentiles after the Babylonian Exile and the aggregate of Jews or Jewish communities scattered "in exile" outside Palestine or present-day Israel. Although the term refers to the physical dispersal of Jews throughout the world, it also carries religious, philosophical, political, and eschatological connotations, inasmuch as the Jewish people perceive a special relationship between the land of Israel and themselves. Interpretations of this relationship range from the messianic hope of traditional Judaism for the eventual "ingathering of the exiles" to the view of Reform Judaism that the dispersal of the Jews was providentially arranged by God to foster pure monotheism throughout the world.

On the festival of Simḥat Torah, the Scroll of the Law is shown to the congregation of a Tunisian synagogue. *BBC Hulton Picture Library*

The first significant Jewish Diaspora was the result of the Babylonian Exile. After the Babylonians conquered the Kingdom of Judah, part of the Jewish population was deported into slavery. Cyrus the Great, the Persian conqueror of Babylonia, permitted the Jewish leader to return to their homeland, but part of the Jewish community voluntarily remained behind.

The largest, most significant, and culturally most creative Jewish Diaspora in early Jewish history flourished in Alexandria, where, in the 1st century BCE, 40 percent of the population was Jewish. Around the 1st century CE, an estimated 5,000,000 Jews lived outside Palestine, about four-fifths of them within the Roman Empire, but they looked to Palestine as the centre of their religious and cultural life. Diaspora Jews thus far outnumbered the Jews in Palestine even before the destruction of Jerusalem in 70 CE. Thereafter, the chief centres of Judaism shifted from country to country (e.g., Babylonia, Persia, Spain, France, Germany, Poland, Russia, and the United States), and Jewish communities gradually adopted distinctive languages, rituals, and cultures, some submerging themselves in non-Jewish environments more completely than others. While some lived in peace, others became victims of violent anti-Semitism.

Jews hold widely divergent views about the role of Diaspora Jewry and the desirability and significance of maintaining a national identity. While the vast majority of Orthodox Jews support the Zionist movement (the return of Jews to Israel), some Orthodox Jews go so far as to oppose the modern nation of Israel as a godless and secular state, defying God's will to send his Messiah ("Anointed") at the time he has preordained.

The chief religious institutions of the Egyptian Diaspora were synagogues. As early as the 3rd century BCE, there were inscriptions mentioning two *proseuchai*, or Jewish prayer houses. In Alexandria there were numerous synagogues throughout the city, of which the largest was so famous that it is said in the Talmud that he who has not seen it has never seen the glory of Israel.

EGYPTIAN JEWISH LITERATURE

In Egypt the Jews produced a considerable literature (most of it now lost), intended to inculcate in Greek-speaking Jews a pride in their past and to counteract a sense of inferiority that some of them felt about Jewish cultural achievements. In the field of history, Demetrius wrote a work titled *On the Kings in Judaea* near the end of the 3rd century BCE. Perhaps intended to refute an anti-Semitic Egyptian priest and author, it shows considerable concern for chronology. In the 2nd century BCE a Jew who used the name Hecataeus wrote *On the Jews*. Another, Eupolemus (*c.* 150 BCE), like Demetrius, wrote a work titled *On the Kings in Judaea*; an indication of its apologetic nature may be seen from the fragment asserting that Moses taught the alphabet not only to the Jews but also to the Phoenicians and to the Greeks. Artapanus (*c.* 100 BCE), in his own book *On the Jews*, went even further in romanticizing Moses—by identifying him with Musaeus, the semi-mythical Greek poet, and Thoth, the Egyptian god of writing and culture, by asserting that Moses was the real originator of Egyptian civilization, and by claiming that Moses taught the Egyptians the worship of Apis (the sacred bull) and the ibis (sacred bird). Cleodemus (Malchus), in an attempt to win for the Jews the regard of the Greeks, asserted in his history that two sons of Abraham had joined Heracles in his expedition in Africa, and that the Greek hero had married the daughter of one of them. Conversely, Jason of Cyrene (*c.* 100 BCE) wrote a history, of which 2 Maccabees is a summary, glorifying the Temple and violently attacking the Jewish Hellenizers, but his manner of writing history is typically Hellenistic. In addition, 3 Maccabees (1st century BCE) is a work of propaganda intended to counteract those Jews who sought to win citizenship in Alexandria. The *Letter of Aristeas*, though ascribed to the Egyptian king Ptolemy II Philadelphus (308–246 BCE), was probably composed by an Alexandrian Jew about 100 BCE to defend Judaism and its practices against detractors.

Egyptian Jews also composed poems and plays, now extant only in fragments, to glorify their history. Philo the Elder (*c.* 100 BCE) wrote an epic, *On Jerusalem*, in Homeric hexameters. Theodotus (*c.* 100 BCE) also wrote an epic, *On Shechem*; it was quite clearly apologetic, to judge from the fragment connecting the name of Shechem with Sikimios, the son of the Greek god Hermes. At about the same time, a Jewish poet wrote a didactic poem, ascribing it to the pagan

Phocylides, though closely following the Bible in some details. The author disguised his Jewish origin by omitting any attack against idolatry from his moralizing. A collection known as *The Sibylline Oracles*, containing Jewish and Christian prophecies in pagan disguise, includes some material composed by a 2nd-century BCE Alexandrian Jew who intended to glorify pious Jews and perhaps win converts.

A Jewish dramatist of the period, Ezekiel (*c.* 100 BCE), composed tragedies in Greek. Fragments of one of them, *The Exodus*, show how deeply he was influenced by the Greek dramatist Euripides (484–406 BCE). Whether or not such plays were actually presented on the stage, they edified Jews and showed pagans that the Jews had as much material for drama as they did.

The greatest achievements of Alexandrian Judaism were in the realm of wisdom literature and philosophy. In a work on the analogical interpretation of the Law of Moses, Aristobulus of Paneas (2nd century BCE) anticipated Philo in attempting to harmonize Greek philosophy and the Torah. He used allegory to explain anthropomorphisms in the Bible and asserted that the Greek philosophers were indebted to Moses. The Wisdom of Solomon, dating from the 1st century BCE, shows an acquaintance with the Platonic doctrine of the preexistence of the soul and with a method of argument known as sorites, which was favoured by the Stoics. During the same period, the author of 4 Maccabees showed an intimate knowledge of Greek philosophy, particularly of Stoicism.

By far the greatest figure in Alexandrian Jewish literature is Philo, who has come to be recognized as the first Jewish theologian. His use of Greek philosophy, particularly that of Plato, to explicate the ideas of the Torah and his formulation of the Logos (Word, or Divine Reason) as an intermediary between God and the world helped lay the foundations of Neoplatonism, gnosticism, and the philosophical outlook of the early Church Fathers. Philo was a devotee of Judaism neither as a mystic cult nor as a collateral branch of Pharisaic Judaism. With his profound knowledge of Greek literature—and despite his almost total ignorance of Hebrew—he tried to find a way in which Judaism could appropriate Hellenic thought.

There was also a Jewish community in Rome, which numbered perhaps 50,000. To judge from the inscriptions in the Jewish catacombs, it was predominantly Greek-speaking. References by Roman writers, particularly Tacitus (56–120 CE) and the satirists, have led scholars to conclude that the community was influential, that it observed the Sabbath and the dietary laws, and that it actively sought converts.

The Hellenization of the Diaspora Jews is reflected not merely in their literature but even more in various papyri and art objects. As early as 290 BCE, Hecataeus of Abdera, a Greek living in Egypt, had remarked that under the Persians and Macedonians the Jews had greatly modified the traditions of their fathers. Other papyri indicate that at least three-fourths of Egyptian Jews had personal names of Greek rather than Hebrew origin. The only schools mentioned are Sabbath schools intended for adults. This suggests that Jews were extremely eager to gain admittance for their children to Greek *gymnasia*, where quite obviously they would have had to make compromises with their Judaism. Again, there are a number of violations from the norms of Halakha (which precluded the charging of interest for a loan): most notably, 9 of 11 extant loan documents charge interest. There are often striking similarities between Jewish and Greek documents of sale, marriage, and divorce in Egypt, though some of this—as with the documents of the Elephantine Jewish community—may be caused by a common origin in the law of ancient Mesopotamia. The charms and apotropaic amulets are often syncretistic, and the Jews can hardly have been unaware of the religious significance of symbols that were still very much filled with meaning in pagan cults. The fact that the Jewish community of Alexandria was preoccupied in the 1st century BCE and the 1st century CE with obtaining rights as citizens— which certainly involved compromises with Judaism, including participation in pagan festivals and sacrifices—shows how far they were ready to deviate from earlier norms. Philo mentions Jews who scoffed at the Bible, which they insisted on interpreting literally, and others who failed to adhere to biblical laws that they regarded as mere allegory. He writes too of Jews who observed nothing of Judaism except the holiday of Yom Kippur. But despite such deviations, pagan writers constantly accused the Diaspora Jews of being "haters of mankind" and of being absurdly superstitious. Christian writers later similarly attacked the Jews for refusing to give up the Torah. The Jews of Egypt were at least loyal in their contributions of the Temple tax and in their pilgrimages to Jerusalem on the three festivals. Virulent anti-Semitism and massacres perpetrated by non-Jews in Egypt apparently discouraged actual apostasy and intermarriage, which were uncommon.

PALESTINIAN LITERATURE

During this period, literature was composed in Palestine in Hebrew, Aramaic, and Greek. The original language of many of these texts remains disputed by scholars, and the works that have survived were apparently composed by more than one author over a considerable period of time. Of the works originally composed in Hebrew, many—including Ecclesiasticus, 1 Maccabees, Judith, Testaments of the Twelve Patriarchs, Baruch, Psalms of Solomon—existed only in Greek during the remainder of the Hellenistic period. They and many of the Dead Sea Scrolls are generally conscious imitations of biblical books, often reflecting the dramatic events of the Maccabean struggle and often tinged with apocalyptic themes (involving the dramatic intervention of God in history). The literature in Aramaic consists of biblical or Bible-like legends or Midrashic (interpretive) additions (Testament of Job, Martyrdom of Isaiah, Paralipomena of Jeremiah, Life of Adam and Eve, Genesis Apocryphon [from the Dead Sea Scrolls], book of Tobit, History of Susanna, and the story of Bel and the Dragon) and of apocalypses (the First Book of Enoch [perhaps originally written in Hebrew], Assumption of Moses, Syriac Apocalypse of Baruch, Second Book of Esdras, and Apocalypse of Abraham). In Greek the chief works by Palestinians are histories of the Jewish war against Rome and of the Jewish kings by Justus of Tiberias (both are lost) and, by Josephus, *History of the Jewish War*, originally in Aramaic, and *Jewish Antiquities* (both written in Rome).

Of the wisdom literature composed in Hebrew, the book of the Wisdom of Jesus the Son of Sirach, or Ecclesiasticus (c. 180–175 BCE), modeled on the book of Proverbs, identified Wisdom with the observance of the Torah. The Testaments of the Twelve Patriarchs, probably written in the latter half of the 2nd century BCE, patterned on Jacob's blessings to his sons, is thought to belong to eschatological literature related to the Dead Sea Scrolls. The identification of Wisdom and Torah is stressed in the Mishnaic tract *Pirqe Avot* ("Sayings of the Fathers"), which, though edited about 200 CE, contains the aphorisms of rabbis dating back to 300 BCE.

Books such as the Testament of Job, Genesis Apocryphon, the Book of Jubilees (now known to have been composed in Hebrew, as seen by its appearance among the Dead Sea Scrolls), and *Biblical Antiquities* (falsely attributed to Philo; originally written in Hebrew, then translated into Greek, but now extant only in Latin), as well as the first half of Josephus's *Jewish Antiquities*, often show affinities with rabbinic Midrashim (interpretive works) in their legendary accretions of biblical details. Sometimes, as in Jubilees and in the Pseudo-Philo work, these accretions are intended to answer the questions of heretics. But often, particularly in the case of Josephus, they are apologetic in presenting biblical heroes in a guise that would appeal to a Hellenized audience.

Apocalyptic trends, given considerable impetus by the victory of the Maccabees over the Syrian Greeks, were not (as was formerly thought) restricted to Pharisaic circles. They were (as is clear from the Dead Sea Scrolls) found in other groups as well and are of particular importance for their influence on both Jewish mysticism and early Christianity. These books, which have a close connection with the biblical Book of Daniel, stress the impossibility of a rational solution to the problem of theodicy. They also stress the imminence of the day of salvation, which is to be preceded by terrible hardships, and presumably reflected the current historical setting. In the First Book of Enoch there is stress on the terrible punishment inflicted upon sinners in the Last Judgment, the imminent coming of the messiah and his kingdom, and the role of angels.

The sole Palestinian Jewish author writing in Greek whose works are preserved is Josephus. His account of the war against the Romans in his *Life*—and, to a lesser degree, in the *Jewish War*—is largely a defense of his own questionable behaviour as the commander of Jewish forces in Galilee. But these works, especially *Against Apion* and *Jewish Antiquities*, are also defenses of Judaism against anti-Semitic attacks. The *Jewish War* often quite deliberately parallels the *History of the Peloponnesian War* by Thucydides (*c.* 460–*c.* 404 BCE); and the *Jewish Antiquities* quite deliberately parallels the *Roman Antiquities* by Dionysius of Halicarnassus (*c.* 20 BCE), a work that dates from earlier in the same century.

THE ROMAN PERIOD (63 BCE–135 CE)

Under Roman rule a number of new groups, largely political, emerged in Palestine. Their common aim was to seek an independent Jewish state. They were also zealous for, and strict in their observance of, the Torah.

New Parties and Sects

After the death of King Herod, a political group known as the Herodians, who apparently regarded Herod as the messiah, sought to reestablish the rule of Herod's descendants over an independent Palestine as a prerequisite for Jewish preservation. Unlike the Zealots, however, they did not refuse to pay taxes to the Romans.

The Zealots, whose appearance was traditionally dated to 6 CE, were one of five groups that emerged at the outset of the first Jewish war against Rome (66–73 CE), which began when the Jews expelled the Romans from Jerusalem, the client king Agrippa II fled the city, and a revolutionary government was established. The Zealots were a mixture of bandits, insurgents from Jerusalem, and priests, who advocated egalitarianism and independence from Rome. In 68 CE they overthrew the government established by the original leaders of the revolt and took control of the Temple during the civil war that followed. Many of them perished in the sack of Jerusalem by the Roman general (and later emperor) Titus (reigned 79–81) or in fighting after the city's fall. The Sicarii (Assassins), so-called because of the daggers (*sica*) they carried, arose about 54 CE, according to Josephus, as a group of bandits who kidnapped or murdered those who had found a modus vivendi with the Romans. It was they who made a stand at the fortress of Masada, near the Dead Sea, committing suicide rather than allowing themselves to be captured by the Romans (73 CE).

A number of other parties—various types of Essenes, Damascus covenanters, and the Qumrān–Dead Sea groups—were distinguished by their pursuit of an ascetic monastic life, disdain for material goods and sensual gratification, sharing of material possessions, concern for eschatology, strong apocalyptic views in anticipation of the coming of the messiah, practice of ablutions to attain greater sexual and ritual purity, prayer, contemplation, and study. The Essenes differed from the Therapeutae, a Jewish religious group that had flourished in Egypt two centuries earlier, in that the latter actively sought "wisdom" whereas the former were anti-intellectual. Only some of the Essenes were celibate. The

Roman soldiers carrying the menorah from the Temple of Jerusalem in 70 CE; detail of a relief on the Arch of Titus, Rome, 81 CE. Alinari/Art Resource, New York

Essenes have been termed "gnosticizing Pharisees" because of their belief, shared with the gnostics, that the world of matter is evil.

The Damascus sect (New Covenanters) was a group of Pharisees who went beyond the letter of the Pharisaic Halakha. Like the Essenes and the Dead Sea sects, they adopted a monastic lifestyle and opposed the way in which sacrifices were offered in the Temple.

The discoveries of scrolls in the caves of Qumrān, near the Dead Sea, beginning in 1947, focused attention on the groups that had lived there. On the basis of paleography, carbon-14 testing, and the coins discovered in the caves, most scholars accept a 1st-century date for them. A theoretical relationship of the communities with John the Baptist and the nascent Christian groups remains in dispute, however. The sectaries have been identified variously as Zealots, an unnamed anti-Roman group, and especially Essenes. That the groups had secret, presumably apocalyptic teachings is clear from the fact that some of the scrolls are in cryptographic script and reversed writing. Yet, despite the sectaries' extreme piety and legalistic conservatism, apparently they were aware of Hellenism, to judge from the presence of Greek books at Qumrān.

It has long been debated whether gnosticism originated in the apocalyptic strains of Judaism that were prevalent when the Temple was destroyed in 70 CE. Although it is doubtful that there is any direct Jewish source of gnosticism, some characteristic gnostic doctrines are found in certain groups of particularly apocalyptic 1st-century Jews—the dichotomy of body and soul and a disdain for the material world, a notion of esoteric knowledge, and an intense interest in angels and in problems of creation.

EARLY CHRISTIANS AND THE JEWISH COMMUNITY

Although it attracted little attention among pagans and Jews in its early years, the rise of Christianity was by far the most important "sectarian" development of the Roman period. Largely owing to the discoveries at Qumrān, many scholars now regard primitive Christianity, with its apocalyptic and eschatological interests, as part of a broad spectrum of attitudes within Judaism itself, rather than as peripheral to Jewish development or to the norm set by Pharisaic Judaism. Indeed, Jesus himself may now be classified as an apocalyptic prophet whose announced intentions were not to abrogate the Torah but to fulfill it. It is possible to envision a direct line between Jewish currents, both in Palestine and the Diaspora in the Hellenistic Age, and Christianity—particularly in the traditions of martyrdom, proselytism, monasticism, mysticism, liturgy, and theology, and especially with the doctrine of the Logos (Word) as an intermediary between God and the world and as the connection of faith and reason.

The Septuagint in particular played an important role both theoretically, in the transformation of Greek philosophy into the theology of the Church Fathers, and practically, in converting Jews and Jewish "sympathizers" to Christianity. In general, moreover, Christianity was more positively disposed toward Hellenism than was Pharisaism, particularly under the leadership of Paul, a thoroughly Hellenized Jew.

Even after Paul proclaimed his opposition to observance of the Torah as a means of salvation, many Jewish Christians continued the practice. Among them were two main groups: the Ebionites—probably the people called *minim*, or "sectaries," in the Talmud—who accepted Jesus as the messiah but denied his divinity; and the Nazarenes, who regarded Jesus as both messiah and God, yet still regarded the Torah as binding upon Jews.

The number of Jews converted to any form of Christianity was extremely small, as can be seen from the frequent criticisms of Jews for their stubbornness by Christian writers. In the Diaspora, despite the strong influence of Hellenism, there were relatively few Jewish converts, though the Christian movement had some success in winning over Alexandrian Jews.

There were four major stages in the final break between Christianity and Judaism: (1) the flight of the Jewish Christians from Jerusalem to Pella across the Jordan in 70 CE and their refusal to continue the struggle against

SEPTUAGINT

The Septuagint, the earliest extant Greek translation of the Hebrew Bible from the original Hebrew, was presumably made for the use of the Jewish community in Egypt when Greek was the lingua franca throughout the region. Analysis of the language has established that the Torah was translated near the middle of the 3rd century BCE and that the remainder was translated in the 2nd century BCE.

The name Septuagint (from the Latin septuaginta, "70") was derived later from the legend that there were 72 translators, 6 from each of the 12 tribes of Israel, each of whom worked in a separate cell, translating the whole, and all of whom produced identical texts. In fact there are large differences in style and usage between the Septuagint's translation of the Torah and its translations of the later books in the Hebrew Bible. A tradition that translators were sent to Alexandria by Eleazar, the chief priest at Jerusalem, at the request of Ptolemy II Philadelphus (285–246 BCE), a patron of literature, first appeared in the Letter of Aristeas, an unreliable source.

The language of much of the early Christian church was Greek, and it was in the Septuagint text that many early Christians located the prophecies they claimed were fulfilled by Christ. Jews considered this a misuse of Holy Scripture, and they stopped using the Septuagint. In the 3rd century CE, Origen attempted to clear up copyists' errors that had crept into the text of the Septuagint, which by then varied widely from copy to copy. Other scholars also consulted the Hebrew text to make the Septuagint text more accurate. But it was the Septuagint, not the original Hebrew, that was the main basis for the Old Latin, Coptic, Ethiopic, Armenian, Georgian, Slavonic, and part of the Arabic translations of the Hebrew Bible. It has never ceased to be the standard version of the Hebrew Bible in the Greek church, and from it Jerome began his translation of the Vulgate Old Testament.

In addition to all the books of the Hebrew canon, the Septuagint under Christian auspices separated the minor prophets and some other books and added the extra books known to Protestants and Jews as apocryphal and to Roman Catholics as deuterocanonical. The Hebrew canon has three divisions: the Torah (Law), the Nevi'im (Prophets), and the Ketuvim (Writings). The Septuagint has four: law, history, poetry, and prophets, with the books of the Apocrypha inserted where appropriate. This division has continued in the Western church in most modern Bible translations, except that in Protestant versions the Apocrypha are either omitted or grouped separately.

the Romans, (2) the institution by the patriarch Gamaliel II of a prayer in the Eighteen Benedictions against such heretics (c. 100), and (3 and 4) the failure of the Christians to join the messianic leaders Lukuas-Andreas and Bar Kokhba in the revolts against Trajan and Hadrian in 115–117 and 132–135, respectively.

JUDAISM UNDER ROMAN RULE

When Pompey entered the Temple in 63 BCE as an arbiter both in the civil war between John Hyrcanus and Aristobulus I and in the struggle of the Pharisees against both Jewish rulers, Judaea in effect became a puppet state of the Romans. During the civil war between Pompey and Julius Caesar (c. 49–45 BCE), the Idumaean Antipater (died 43 BCE) ingratiated himself with Caesar and was rewarded by being made governor of Judaea. The Jews were rewarded through the promulgation of a number of decrees favourable to them, which were reaffirmed by Augustus (reigned 27 BCE–14 CE) and later emperors. Antipater's son Herod, king of Judaea, an admirer of Greek culture, supported a cult worshipping the emperor and built temples to Augustus in non-Jewish cities. Because he was by origin an Idumaean, he was regarded by many Jews as a foreigner. (The Idumaeans, or Edomites, had been forcibly converted to Judaism by John Hyrcanus.) On several occasions during and after Herod's reign, Pharisaic delegations sought to convince the Romans to end the quasi-independent Jewish government. After the death of Herod's son and successor, Archelaus, in 6 CE, Herod's realms were ruled by Roman procurators, the most famous (or infamous) of whom, Pontius Pilate (died 36 CE), attempted to introduce busts of the Roman emperor into Jerusalem and discovered the intense religious zeal of the Jews in opposing this measure. When the emperor Caligula (reigned 37–41 CE) ordered that a statue of himself be erected in the Temple, a large number of Jews proclaimed that they would suffer death rather than permit such a desecration. In response, the governor of Syria, Petronius, succeeded in getting

FIRST JEWISH REVOLT

The First Jewish Revolt (66–70 CE) was a rebellion against Roman rule in Judaea. It was the result of a long series of clashes in which small groups of Jews offered sporadic resistance to the Romans, who in turn responded with severe countermeasures. In the fall of 66 CE the Jews combined in revolt, expelled the Romans from Jerusalem, and overwhelmed in the pass of Beth-Horon a Roman punitive force under Gallus, the imperial legate in Syria. A revolutionary government was then set up and extended its influence throughout the whole country. Vespasian was dispatched by the Roman emperor Nero to crush the rebellion. He was joined by Titus, and together the Roman armies entered Galilee, where the historian Josephus headed the Jewish forces. Josephus' army was confronted by that of Vespasian and fled. After the fall of the fortress of Jatapata, Josephus gave himself up, and the Roman forces swept the country. On the 9th of the month of Av (August 29) in 70 CE, Jerusalem fell. The Temple was burned, and the Jewish state collapsed, although the fortress of Masada was not conquered by the Roman general Flavius Silva until April 73.

the emperor to delay. The procurators of Judaea, being of equestrian (knightly) rank and often of Oriental Greek stock, were more anti-Jewish than the governors of Syria, who were of the higher senatorial order. The last procurators in particular were indifferent to Jewish religious sensibilities. And various patriotic groups, to whom nationalism was an integral part of their religion, succeeded in polarizing the Jewish population and bringing on the first war with Rome in 66 CE. The climax of the war, as noted earlier, was the destruction of the Temple in 70 CE, though, according to Josephus, Titus sought to spare it.

The papyri indicate that the war against Trajan—involving the Jews of Egypt, Cyrenaica, Cyprus, and Mesopotamia (though only to a minor degree those of Palestine)—was a widespread revolt under a Cyrenian king-messiah, Lukuas-Andreas, aimed at freeing Palestine from Roman rule. In 132–135 CE the same spirit of freedom inspired another uprising, the Second Jewish Revolt, led by Bar Kokhba, who may have had the support of the greatest rabbi of the time, Akiba ben Joseph (40–c. 135). The result was Hadrian's decrees prohibiting circumcision and public instruction in the Torah, though these were soon revoked by Antoninus Pius (reigned 138–161). Having suffered such tremendous losses on the field of battle, Judaism turned its dynamism to the continued development of the Talmud.

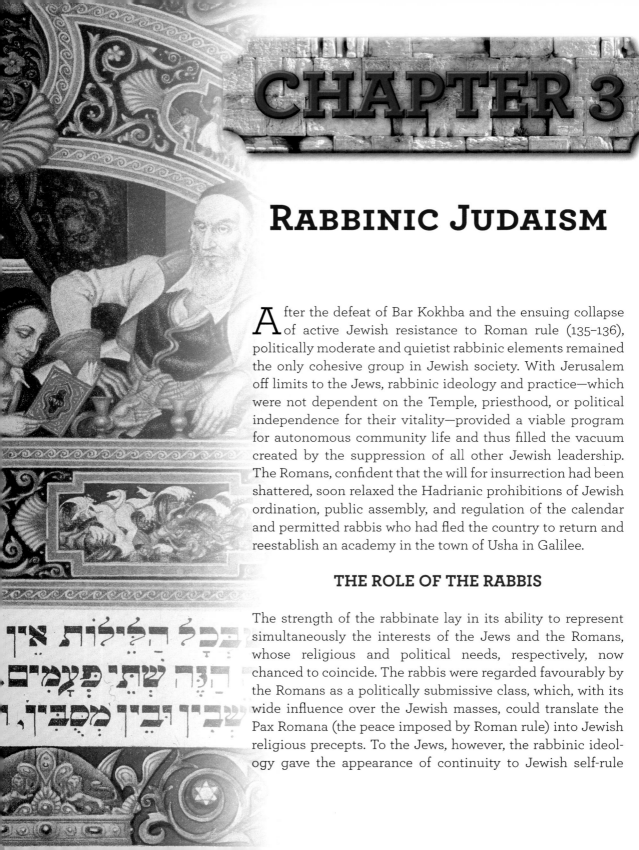

CHAPTER 3

RABBINIC JUDAISM

After the defeat of Bar Kokhba and the ensuing collapse of active Jewish resistance to Roman rule (135–136), politically moderate and quietist rabbinic elements remained the only cohesive group in Jewish society. With Jerusalem off limits to the Jews, rabbinic ideology and practice—which were not dependent on the Temple, priesthood, or political independence for their vitality—provided a viable program for autonomous community life and thus filled the vacuum created by the suppression of all other Jewish leadership. The Romans, confident that the will for insurrection had been shattered, soon relaxed the Hadrianic prohibitions of Jewish ordination, public assembly, and regulation of the calendar and permitted rabbis who had fled the country to return and reestablish an academy in the town of Usha in Galilee.

THE ROLE OF THE RABBIS

The strength of the rabbinate lay in its ability to represent simultaneously the interests of the Jews and the Romans, whose religious and political needs, respectively, now chanced to coincide. The rabbis were regarded favourably by the Romans as a politically submissive class, which, with its wide influence over the Jewish masses, could translate the Pax Romana (the peace imposed by Roman rule) into Jewish religious precepts. To the Jews, however, the rabbinic ideology gave the appearance of continuity to Jewish self-rule and freedom from alien interference. The rabbinic program fashioned by Johanan ben Zakkai and his circle replaced sacrifice and pilgrimage to the Temple with the study of Scripture, prayer, and works of piety, thus eliminating the need for a central sanctuary (in Jerusalem) and making Judaism a religion capable of practice anywhere. Judaism was now, for all intents and purposes, a Diaspora religion, even on its home soil. Any sense of real break with the past was mitigated by continued adherence to purity laws (dietary and bodily) and by assiduous study of Scripture, including the legal elements that historical developments had now made inoperable. The reward held out for scrupulous study and fulfillment was the promise of messianic deliverance (i.e., the divine restoration of all those institutions that had become central in Jewish notions of national independence, including the Davidic monarchy, Temple service, and the ingathering of Diaspora Jewry). Above all these rewards was the assurance of personal resurrection and participation in the national rebirth.

Apart from the right to teach Scripture publicly, the most pressing need felt by the surviving rabbis was for the reorganization of a body that would revive the functions of the former Sanhedrin and

Modern Jews in Israel study the Talmud, which remains the premier introduction to the evolution of rabbinic values and practices. Pedro Ugarte/AFP/Getty Images

pass judgment on disputed questions of law and dogma. Accordingly, a high court was organized under the leadership of Simeon ben Gamaliel (reigned c. 135–c. 175), the son of the previous patriarch (the Roman term for the head of the Palestinian Jewish community) of the house of Hillel, in association with rabbis representing other schools and interests. In the ensuing struggle for power, Gamaliel managed to concentrate all communal authority in his office. The reign of Gamaliel's son and successor, Judah the Prince, marked the climax of this period of rabbinic activity, otherwise known as the "age of the *tannaim*" (teachers). Armed with wealth, Roman backing, and dynastic legitimacy (which the patriarch now traced to the house of David), Judah sought to standardize Jewish practice through a corpus of legal norms that would reflect accepted views of the rabbinate on every aspect of life. The Mishna that soon emerged became the primary reference work in all rabbinic schools and constituted the core around which the Talmud was later compiled. It thus remains the best single introduction to the complex of rabbinic values and practices as they evolved in Roman Palestine.

THE MAKING OF THE MISHNA

Although the promulgation of an official corpus represented a break with rabbinic precedent, Judah's Mishna did have antecedents. During the 1st and 2nd centuries CE, rabbinic schools had compiled for their own use collections of Midrashim (singular Midrash, meaning "investigation" or "interpretation"), in which the results of their exegesis and application of Scripture to problematic situations were recorded in terse legal form. By 200 CE several such compilations were circulating in Jewish schools and were being used by judges. While adhering to the structural form of these earlier collections, Judah compiled a new one in which universally accepted views were recorded alongside those still in dispute, thereby largely reducing the margin for individual discretion in the interpretation of the law. Although his action aroused opposition and some rabbis continued to invoke their own collections, the authority of his office and the obvious advantages of a unified system of law soon outweighed centrifugal tendencies, and his Mishna attained quasi-canonical status, becoming known as "The Mishna" or "Our Mishna." Yet, for all its clarity and comprehensiveness, its phraseology was often obscure or too terse to satisfy all needs, and a companion work known as the Tosefta ("Additions"), in which omitted traditions and explanatory notes were recorded, was compiled shortly thereafter. Neither compilation elucidated the processes by which decisions had been elicited, and various authorities therefore set about collecting the Midrashic discussions of their schools and recording them in the order of the verses of Scripture. During the 3rd and 4th centuries, Midrashim on the Pentateuch were compiled and introduced as school texts.

Fundamentally legal in character, this literature regulated every aspect of life. The six divisions of the Mishna—on agriculture, festivals, family life, civil law, sacrificial and dietary laws, and purity—encompass virtually every area of Jewish experience. Accordingly, the Mishna also recorded the principal Pharisaic and rabbinic definitions and goals of the religious life. One tract, *Pirqe Avot* ("Sayings of the Fathers"), treated the meaning and posture of a life according to the Torah, while other passages made reference to the mystical studies into which only the most advanced and religiously worthy were initiated (e.g., the activities of the *Merkava*, or divine "Chariot," and the doctrines of creation). The rabbinic program of a life dedicated to study and fulfillment of the will of God was thus a graded structure in which the canons of morality and piety were attainable on various levels, from the popular and practical to the esoteric and metaphysical. Innumerable sermons and homilies preserved in the Midrashic collections, liturgical compositions for daily and festival services, and mystical tracts circulated among initiates all testify to the deep spirituality that informed Rabbinic Judaism.

THE MAKING OF THE TALMUDS

The promulgation of the Mishna initiated the period of the *amoraim* (lecturers or interpreters), teachers who made the Mishna the basic text of legal exegesis. The curriculum now centred on the elucidation of the text of the standard compilation, harmonization of its decisions with extra-Mishnaic traditions recorded in other collections, and the application of its principles to new situations.

PALESTINE (*c.* 220–*c.* 400)

Amoraic studies have been preserved in two running commentaries on the Mishna, known as the Palestinian (or Jerusalem) Talmud and the Babylonian Talmud, reflecting the study and legislation of the academies of the two principal Jewish centres in the Roman and Persian empires. (Talmud is also the comprehensive term for the whole collections, Palestinian and Babylonian, containing Mishna, commentaries, and other matter.)

The schools were the primary agencies through which the rabbinic way of life and literature was communicated to the masses. The types of schools ranged from the primary school to the advanced "house of study" and more formal academy (yeshiva), the synagogue, and the Jewish court. Primary schools had long been available in the villages and cities of Palestine, and tannaitic law made education of male children a religious duty. Introduced at the age of 5 or 6 to Scripture, the student advanced at the age of 10 to Mishna and finally in midadolescence to Talmud, or the processes of legal reasoning. Regular reading of Scripture in the synagogue on Mondays, Thursdays, Sabbaths, and festivals, coupled with concurrent translations into the Aramaic vernacular and frequent sermons, provided for lifelong instruction in the literature and the various teachings elicited from it. The amoraic emphasis on the moral and spiritual aims of Scripture and its ritual is reflected in their Midrashic collections, which are predominantly homiletical rather than legal in character.

An amoraic sermon conceded that, of every 1,000 beginners in primary school, only one would be expected to continue as far as Talmud. In the 4th century, however, there were enough advanced students to warrant academies in Lydda, Caesarea, Sepphoris, and Tiberias (in Palestine), where leading scholars trained disciples for communal service as teachers and judges. In Caesarea—the principal port and seat of the Roman administration of Palestine, where pagans, Christians, and Samaritans maintained renowned cultural institutions—the Jews too established an academy that was singularly free of patriarchal control. The outstanding rabbinic scholar there, Abbahu (c. 279–320), wielded great influence with the Roman authorities. Because he combined learning with personal wealth and political power, he attracted some of the most gifted students of the day to the city. About 350 the studies and decisions of the authorities in Caesarea were compiled as a tract on the civil law of the Mishna. Half a century later, the academy of Tiberias issued a similar collection on other tracts of the Mishna, and this compilation, in conjunction with the Caesarean material, constituted the Palestinian Talmud.

Despite increasing tensions between some rabbinic circles and the patriarch, his office was the agency that provided a basic unity to the Jews of the Roman Empire. Officially recognized as a Roman prefect, the patriarch at the same time sent representatives to Jewish communities to inform them of the Jewish calendar and other decisions of general concern and to collect an annual tax of a half shekel, paid by male Jews for his treasury. As titular head of the Jewish community of Palestine and as a vestigial heir of the Davidic monarchy, the patriarch was a reminder of a glorious past and a symbol of hope for a brighter future. How enduring these hopes were may be seen from the efforts to gain permission to rebuild the Temple in Jerusalem. Although reconstruction of the Temple was authorized by the emperor Julian (reigned 361–363), it came to naught because of a disastrous fire on the sacred site and the emperor's subsequent death.

The adoption of Christianity as the religion of the empire had no direct effect on the religious freedom of the Jews. The ever-mounting hostility between the two religions, however, resulted in severe curtailment of Jewish disciplinary rights over their coreligionists, interference in the collection of patriarchal taxes, restriction of the right to build synagogues, and, finally, upon the death of the patriarch Gamaliel VI about 425, the abolition of the patriarchate and the diversion of the Jewish tax to the imperial treasury.

Mediterranean Jewry was now fragmented into disjointed communities and synagogues. But the principles of the regulation of the Jewish calendar had been committed to writing in approximately 359 by the patriarch Hillel II, and this, coupled with the widespread presence of rabbis, ensured the continuity of Jewish adherence. Even the restrictions on synagogal worship and preaching imposed by the Eastern emperor Justinian I (reigned 527–565) apparently had no devastating effect. A new genre of liturgical poetry, combining ecstatic prayer with didactic motifs, developed in this period of political decline and won acceptance in synagogues in Asia Minor as well as beyond the Euphrates.

BABYLONIA (200–650)

In the increasingly unfriendly climate of Christendom, Jews were consoled by the knowledge that in nearby Babylonia (then under Persian rule) a vast population of Jews lived under a network of effective and autonomous Jewish institutions and officials. Steadily worsening conditions in Palestine drew many Jews to Persian domains, where economic opportunities and the Jewish communal structure enabled them to gain a better livelihood while living in accordance with their ancestral traditions. To regulate internal Jewish affairs and ensure the steady flow of taxes, the Parthian, or Arsacid, rulers (247 BCE–224 CE) had appointed in approximately 100 CE an exilarch, or "head of the [Jews in] exile"—who claimed more direct Davidic descent than the Palestinian patriarch—to rule over the Jews as a quasi-prince. About 220, two Babylonian disciples of Judah ha-Nasi, Abba Arika (known as Rav) and Samuel bar Abba, began to propagate the Mishna and related tannaitic literature as normative standards. As heads of the academies at Sura and Nehardea, respectively, Rav and Samuel cultivated a native Babylonian rabbinate, which increasingly provided the manpower for local Jewish courts and other communal services. While the usual tensions between temporal and religious arms frequently existed in Babylonia, the symbiosis of exilarchate and rabbinate endured until the middle of the 11th century.

Paradoxically, Babylonian rabbinism derived its theological and political strength from its fundamentally unoriginal character. As a transplant of Palestinian Judaism, it asserted its historical legitimacy to the Sāsānian dynasty (224–651), who protected Jewish practices against interference from fanatical Magian priests, and to native Jewish officials, who argued for the validity of indigenous Babylonian deviations from Palestinian norms. But ultimately the historical importance of this transplantation lay in Babylonia's serving as the proving ground for the adaptability of Palestinian Judaism to a Diaspora situation. Legal and theological adaptations generated by the new locale and the needs of the times inevitably produced changes in the religious tradition. The laws of agriculture, purity, and sacrifices all of necessity fell into disuse. The principles embodied in these laws, however, and the core of the legal and theological system—consisting of faith in the revelation and election of Israel, the requirement that the individual live by the canons of Jewish civil and family law, and the network of communal institutions modeled on those of Palestinian Judaism—remained intact, thereby ensuring a basic continuity and uniformity among rabbinically oriented communities everywhere. Because historical circumstances made Babylonia the mediator of this tradition to all Jewish communities in the High Middle Ages (9th–12th centuries), the Babylonian version of Jewish religion became synonymous with normative Judaism and the measure of Judaic authenticity everywhere.

"The law of the [Gentile] government is binding"—the principle formulated by Samuel (died 254), head of the academy at Nehardea—summarizes the essential novelty in rabbinic reorientation to life on foreign soil. Whereas Palestinian rabbis had complied with imperial decrees of taxation as legitimate de facto—and this was all that Samuel had in mind—Babylonian teachers now rationalized governmental authority in this respect as legitimate de jure, thus enjoining upon the Jews political quietism and submissiveness as part of their religious doctrine. In all other areas of civil law, the Jews were instructed by their rabbis to file suit in Jewish courts and thus to conduct their businesses as well as their family lives by rabbinic law.

While the rabbis could impose their discipline more effectively in matters of public law than in private religious practice, the density of the Jewish population in many areas of Parthia (northeastern Iran) and Babylonia facilitated the application of moral and disciplinary pressures. The most effective vehicle for the dissemination of their teachings was the academies, where judges and communal teachers were trained. Among these institutions, those of Sura and Pumbedita remained preeminent. Frequent public lectures in the synagogues of the academies on Sabbaths and festivals were capped by public *kalla* (study-course) assemblies for alumni of the schools during the two months, Adar (February–March) and Elul (August–September), when the lull in agricultural work freed many to attend semiannual refresher instruction. These meetings were followed by regular popular lectures during the festival seasons that soon followed. Thus, while rabbis constituted a distinct class within the community, their efforts were oriented toward making as much of the community as possible members of a learned and religious elite. The harmonious relations that obtained with but few interruptions over the centuries between the Sāsānian rulers and their Jewish subjects gave the Jewish population the air of a quasi-state, which the Jewish leadership frequently extolled as superior to the Jewish community of Palestine.

The dissemination of the Palestinian Talmud probably stimulated the Babylonians to follow suit by collecting and arranging the records of study and decisions of their own academies and courts. The Babylonian Talmud, which apparently underwent several stages of redaction (*c.* 500–650) on the basis of the proto-Talmuds—the early collections of commentaries on the Mishna used in the academies—accordingly became the standard of reference for judicial precedent and theological doctrine for all of Babylonian Jewry and all those communities under its influence. Some scholars have postulated a group of anonymous editors of these earlier materials, calling them *stammaim* ("anonymous ones"). As had been the case with the Mishna, the redaction of the Babylonian Talmud was later designated by authorities as marking the end of a period in Jewish history. The scholars who added the finishing stylistic touches, known as *savora'im* ("explicators"), were classified as a transitional stage between the *amoraim* and the *geonim*.

The enduring vigour of Jewish faith during these centuries is graphically demonstrated by the missionary activity of Jews throughout the ancient Middle East, especially in the Arabian Peninsula. Proud Jewish tribes living in close proximity to each other in the vicinity of Yathrib (later Medina, Muhammad's home city) engaged in agriculture and commerce, and proclaimed the superiority of their monotheistic ethos and eschatology. In Yemen (southwestern Arabia) the last of the Ḥimyarite rulers (reigned from *c.* 2nd century CE), Dhu Nuwas, proclaimed himself a Jew and finally suffered defeat in approximately 525 as a consequence of Christian influence on the Abyssinian armies. Jewish missionaries, however, continued to compete with Christian missionaries and thus helped to lay the groundwork for the birth of an indigenous Arabic monotheism—Islam—that was to alter the course of world history.

THE AGE OF THE *GEONIM*

The lightning conquests in the Middle East, North Africa, and the Iberian Peninsula by the armies of Islam (7th–8th century) created a political framework for the basically uniform (i.e., Babylonian) character of medieval Judaism. As a "people of the Book" (i.e., of the Bible), the Jews were permitted by the Muslims to live under the same autonomous structure that had developed under Arsacid and Sāsānian rule.

TRIUMPH OF THE BABYLONIAN RABBINATE

The heads of the two principal academies were now formally recognized by the exilarch, and through him by the Muslim caliphs (the civil and religious heads of the Muslim state), as the official arbiters of all questions of religious law and as the religious heads of all Jewish communities that came under Muslim sway. Known as *geonim* (plural of *gaon*, "excellency"), they conducted high courts manned by scholars of graded ranks, and they received financial support from Jewish communities assigned to them by the exilarch. Religious questions and contributions were solicited from all Jewish communities, and these, along with formal gaonic replies (*responsa*), were regularly publicized at the semi-annual *kalla* convocations. Under the strong leadership of Yehudai, gaon of Sura (presided 760–763), the Babylonian rabbinate made vigorous efforts to replace Palestinian usage wherever it was still in vogue—including the study of Palestinian amoraic legal literature—with Babylonian practice and texts, thus making the Babylonian Talmud the unrivalled standard of Jewish norms. The campaign's success is indicated by the usage of the term *Talmud*, which, when unqualified, has ever since meant the Babylonian Talmud. Indeed, even in Palestine the Babylonian corpus displaced its older rival and caused the study of Palestinian Talmudic literature to be confined to circles of legal specialists.

ANTI-RABBINIC REACTIONS

The firm—and occasionally oppressive—tactics of exilarchs and *geonim* generated anti-rabbinic reactions in the form of sectarian and messianic revolts, especially in outlying areas where enforcement was difficult. Inspired in part by ancient Palestinian sectarian doctrines and in part by Muslim usage, the sects were by and large quickly and forcefully suppressed. In the 8th century, according to the traditional Rabbinite account, Anan ben David, a disaffected member of the exilarchic family, founded a dissident sect, the Ananites, later known as the Karaites (Scripturalists). The exact relationship between the followers of Anan and the later Karaites, however, remains unclear. The term itself first appeared in the 9th century, when various dissident groups coalesced and ultimately adopted Anan as their founder, though they rejected several of his teachings. The new sect advocated a threefold program of rejection of rabbinic law as a human fabrication and therefore as an unwarranted, unauthoritative addition to Scripture; a return to Palestine to hasten the messianic redemption; and a reexamination of Scripture to retrieve authentic law and doctrine. Under the leadership of Daniel al-Qumisi (*c.* 850?), a Karaite settlement prospered in the Holy Land, from which it spread as far as northwestern Africa and Christian Spain. A barrage of Karaite treatises presenting new views of scriptural exegesis stimulated renewed study of the Bible and the Hebrew language in Rabbinite circles as well. The most momentous consequence of these new studies was the invention of several systems of vocalization for the text of the Hebrew Bible in Babylonia and Tiberias in the 9th and 10th centuries. The annotation of the Masoretic (traditional, or authorized) text of the Bible with vocalic, musical, and grammatical accents in the Tiberian schools of the 10th-century scholars Ben Naftali and Ben Asher fixed the Masoretic text permanently and, through it, the morphology of the

Hebrew language for Karaites as well as Rabbinites.

In the face of sectarian challenges, the *geonim* intensified their efforts against any deviation from Rabbinite norms. They began to issue handbooks of Jewish law that set forth in concise and unequivocal terms the standards for correct practice. A number of these codes, notably the *Halakhot gedolot* ("Great Laws"), *Siddur Rav Amram Gaon* ("The Prayer Book of Rav Amram Gaon"; on liturgical practice), and *She'eltot* ("Disquisitions") by Aḥa of Shabḥa (c. 680–c. 752), attained authoritative status in local schools and further unified medieval Judaism.

The *geonim*, however, were powerless to halt several social developments in the 9th century that progressively undermined their hold even on Rabbinite communities. A renaissance of Greek philosophy and sciences in Arabic translation, coupled with the progressive urbanization of the upper classes of all religious and ethnic groups in the centres of political, commercial, and cultural activity, generated a new intelligentsia that cut across religious and ethnic lines. Widespread skepticism concerning basic doctrines of faith such as creation, revelation, and retribution was most poignantly represented by latitudinarianism (the tendency to be flexible and tolerant about deviations from orthodox beliefs and doctrines) and by antinomian gnostic groups that denied divine providence and omniscience. Ḥiwi al-Balkhī, a 9th-century skeptical Jewish

pamphleteer, scandalized the faithful by openly attacking the morality of Scripture and by issuing for schools an expurgated edition of the Bible that omitted "offensive" material (e.g., alleged stories of God acting dishonestly). A mystifying Hebrew tract titled *Sefer yetzira* ("Book of Creation") posited in terse and enigmatic epigrams a novel theory of creation that betrayed Neoplatonic influence. Karaites joined philosophically oriented intellectuals in heaping scorn on popular Rabbinite customs that smacked of superstition and, above all, on Talmudic homilies that referred to God in anthropomorphic terms.

Gaonic difficulties were compounded by the rise in North Africa and Spain of populous and wealthy Jewish communities that, thanks to the development of their own local schools and talent, ignored the Babylonian academies or favoured one over the other with religious queries and, in consequence, with financial contributions. To the delight of dissidents and the chagrin of the faithful, competition between the Babylonian academies turned to internecine hostility. Occasional revolts against exilarchic taxation and administration in outlying areas of Persia had to be quelled with armed force. The Palestinian Rabbinites had revived their own academies, and their presidents now not only appealed for support in other Diaspora lands but challenged the authority of the Babylonians to serve as final arbiters on matters of public import, such as the regulation of the calendar. By 900 the Rabbinite community of Babylonia was in a state of chaos and dissolution.

THE GAONATE OF SA'ADIA BEN JOSEPH

In a bold effort to restore discipline and respect for the gaonate, the exilarch David ben Zakkai (916/917–940) bypassed the families from whom the *geonim* had traditionally been selected and in 928 appointed Sa'adia ben Joseph (882–942) to head the academy of Sura. Of Egyptian birth, Sa'adia had gained wide acclaim for his scholarly retorts to Karaites, heretics, and Palestinian Rabbinites. Politically, Sa'adia's brief presidency was a fiasco and aggravated the chaos by a communal civil war. His gaonate, however, gave an official stamp to his many works, which responded to the ideological challenges to Rabbinism by restating traditional Judaism in intellectually cogent terms. Sa'adia thus became the pioneer of a Judeo-Arabic culture that would blossom fully in Andalusian Spain a century later. His translation of the Bible into Arabic and his Arabic commentaries on Scripture made the rabbinic understanding of the Bible accessible to masses of Jews. His poetic compositions for liturgical use provided the stimulus for the revival of Hebrew poetry. Above all, his rationalist commentary on the puzzling *Sefer yetzira* and his brilliant treatise on philosophical theology, *The Book of Beliefs and Opinions*, synthesized the Torah (understood as the divine law in the Five Books of Moses together with the rabbinic understanding of this revelation) and "Greek wisdom" in accordance with the dominant Muslim philosophical school of *kalām*. His efforts made Judaism philosophically respectable and the study of philosophy a religiously acceptable pursuit.

Far from tightening the gaonic hold over the Jewish communities of the Arabic world, Sa'adia's works actually provided the wherewithal for ever-greater intellectual and religious self-sufficiency. While economic, political, and military upheavals progressively weakened various institutions in the Middle East, concurrent prosperity and consolidation in the West stimulated the maturation of indigenous leadership in Egypt, Al-Qayrawān (Kairouan; in present-day Tunisia), and Muslim Spain. To be sure, able *geonim* such as Sherira and his son Hai (939–1038) exercised enormous influence over the Judeo-Arabic world through hundreds of legal *responsa* issued in the course of their successive terms (968–1038) at Pumbedita. Circumstances beyond anyone's control, however, were gradually undermining the effectiveness of exilarchate and gaonate. But by 1038, the year of Hai's death, the consequences of four centuries of gaonic activity had become indelible: the Babylonian Talmud had become the agent of basic Jewish uniformity; the synthesis of philosophy and tradition had become the hallmark of the Jewish intelligentsia; and the Hebrew classics of the past had become the texts of study in Jewish schools everywhere.

MEDIEVAL EUROPEAN JUDAISM

Developments within the two major Jewish communities of medieval Europe were complicated by their uncertain relationship with the Christian community surrounding them. By all accounts, Christians and Jews had been on relatively good terms until the 11th century. In the early Middle Ages there were frequent contacts between Christians and Jews, who intermarried and shared language and culture. In the Carolingian era some bishops even complained that the Jews were favoured too much by Carolingian rulers. The situation became more complicated after about the year 1000, as Christian society began a process of reorganization that contributed to the marginalization of the Jews and other groups. Although the Jews did not endure unrelenting persecution and even enjoyed a cultural renaissance in the 12th century that paralleled a Christian one, they faced an increasingly hostile community that created a new theological image of the Jews and undermined the place of the Jews in society.

MARGINALIZATION AND EXPULSION

In the opening decade of the 11th century, Jews in various parts of Europe faced violent attacks and forced conversions that led some, according to one account, to commit suicide rather than accept baptism. Attacks against the Jews and full-scale massacres of Jews would occur throughout the rest of the Middle Ages, most notably at Mainz in the Rhineland in 1096, in England in 1198–90, in Franconia in 1298, and in France in 1320. The image of the Jews among Christians worsened, and numerous anti-Semitic stereotypes appeared in the 12th century. The most notorious example of these was the blood libel, which alleged that the Jews killed Christian boys and used their blood to make unleavened bread.

Meanwhile, official legislation of the church confirmed the declining position of the Jews. Pope Innocent III issued a decretal declaring the Jews to be in

Pope Innocent III decreed that Jews should be in everlasting servitude for the killing of Jesus Christ and forced them to wear distinguishing clothing to the 1215 Lateran Council. Time & Life Pictures/Getty Images

perpetual servitude for the killing of Christ, and at the fourth Lateran Council in 1215 the Jews were ordered to wear distinctive clothing, forbidden to hold public office, and prohibited from appearing in public during the last three days of the Easter season. With the discovery and burning of the Talmud by Christians in the 13th century, the church's view of the Jews worsened, because the church thus became aware that contemporary Jews were different from biblical Jews. The acceptance of the Talmud by the Jews was understood as heretical by the church, which had already launched a Crusade and the Inquisition against Christian heretics. The Jews' failure to live up to the Christian understanding of them undermined the contemporary theological justification for their continued existence (i.e., until the end of time, as witness to the truth of Christian revelation).

Challenges also emerged in the economic and social order as economic opportunities were increasingly restricted. Although there were Jewish merchants, artisans, and viticulturists throughout much of the Middle Ages, by the 12th and 13th centuries the Jews were limited to the occupation of money lending, which brought some of them great wealth but also great animosity from borrowers. Moreover, the Jews were often an important source of capital for the monarchs of Europe. As an important source of revenue, the Jews provided a valuable service to the kings and thus received special protection in the law.

This relationship, however, had an ominous side, as the Jews came to be defined in the law as the personal property of the king, to be exploited as he saw fit. Jews also lost their status as individuals and were secure only as long as they were of utility to their lords.

The declining economic usefulness of the Jews and the related deterioration of their social and religious status led to their expulsion from England in 1290 and from France in 1306. Jews were also expelled from the Holy Roman Empire and, most notoriously, from Spain in 1492. In Spain, anti-Jewish riots in the late 14th century had led to the conversion of large numbers of Jews, the so-called conversos. Spanish Christians, however, remained distrustful of the conversos, who were thought to maintain contact with unconverted Jews and to practice the Jewish faith secretly. An inquisition established to deal with the conversos led to local expulsions in the 1480s. By 1492, however, the king and queen, Ferdinand and Isabella, and their inquisitors decided that the only real solution to the problem was the permanent separation of the conversos and the Jews. The Jews were compelled to choose between baptism and exile, and ultimately some 40,000 (estimates range as high as 800,000) departed Spain, never to return. They settled in Navarre (then outside the kingdom of Spain), North Africa, and Portugal. Many of those in Portugal, however, accepted Christianity as a result of an order of expulsion or conversion there in 1497.

THE TWO MAJOR BRANCHES

Despite the fundamental uniformity of medieval Jewish culture, distinctive Jewish subcultures were shaped by the cultural and political divisions within the Mediterranean basin, in which Arabic Muslim and Latin Christian civilizations coexisted as discrete and self-contained societies. Two major branches of rabbinic civilization developed in Europe: the Ashkenazic, or Franco-German, and the Sephardic, or Andalusian-Spanish. Distinguished most conspicuously by their varying pronunciation of Hebrew, the numerous differences between them in religious orientation and practice derived, in the first instance, from the geographical fountainheads of their culture—the Ashkenazim (plural of Ashkenazi) tracing their cultural filiation to Italy and Palestine and the Sephardim (plural of Sephardi) to Babylonia—and from the influences of their respective immediate milieus. While the Jews of Christian Europe wrote for internal use almost exclusively in Hebrew, those of Muslim areas regularly employed Arabic for prose works and Hebrew for poetic composition. Whereas the literature of Jews in Latin areas was overwhelmingly religious in content, that of the Jews of Spain was well endowed with secular poetry and scientific works inspired by the cultural tastes of the Arabic literati. Most significantly, the two forms of European Judaism differed in their approaches to the identical rabbinic base that they had inherited from the East and in their attitudes to Gentile culture and politics.

SEPHARDIC DEVELOPMENTS

In Muslim Spain, Jews frequently served the government in official capacities and, therefore, not only took an active interest in political affairs but engaged in considerable social and intellectual intercourse with influential circles of the Muslim population. Because the support of letters and scholarship was part of state policy in Muslim Spain, and because Muslim savants traced the source of Muslim power to the vitality of the Arabic language, scripture, and poetry, Jews looked at Arabic culture with undisguised admiration and unabashedly attempted to adapt themselves to its canons of scholarship and good taste. The cultured Jew accordingly demonstrated command of Arabic style and the ability to display the beauty of his own heritage through a philological mastery of the text of the Hebrew Bible and through the composition of Hebrew verse, now set to an Arabic metre. Because Arabic philosophers and scientists promulgated the compatibility of Greek philosophy with the revelation to Muhammad, rationalist study of the Jewish classics and defense of rabbinic faith in philosophical terms became dominant motifs in the Andalusian Jewish schools (in southern Spain).

The period of feverish literary creativity in classical Jewish disciplines as well as in the sciences in Spain has been called the golden age of Hebrew literature (c. 1000–1148). Jewish culture of this age was distinguished by the supreme literary merit of its Hebrew poetry, the new spirit of relatively free and rationalist examination of hallowed texts and doctrines, and the extension of Jewish cultural perspectives to totally new horizons—mathematics, astronomy, medicine, philosophy, political theory, aesthetics, and belles-lettres. Noteworthy too was the frequent overlapping of the Sephardic religious leadership with the new Jewish courtier class. The unprecedented heights that the latter attained—Ḥisdai ibn Shaprut (c. 915–975) as counsellor to the caliphs of Córdoba; the Ibn Nagrelas as viziers of Granada; the Ibn Ezras (Moses ibn Ezra, c. 1060–1139; and Abraham ben Meir ibn Ezra, c. 1092–1167), the Ibn Megashs, and the Ibn Albalias as high officials in Granada and Sevilla (Seville)—and the distinctions of these men and their protégés in Jewish and worldly letters restored the ancient integration of culture and practical life and expressed the identification of the Jewish elite with the biblical age of Jewish power and artistic creativity. The effort to recapture the vitality and beauty of biblical poetry stimulated comparative philological and fresh exegetical research that yielded new insights into the morphology of the Hebrew language and into the historical soil of biblical prophecy. Judah ibn Ḥayyuj and Abū al-Walīd Marwān ibn Janāḥ produced manuals on biblical grammar that applied the results of Arabic philology to their own tongue and provided the principles of Hebrew grammatical study down to modern times. The anticipations of modern higher biblical criticism by Judah ibn Bala'am and Moses ibn Gikatilla (11th century) were popularized in Hebrew a few generations later by Abraham ibn Ezra. In the revival of Hebrew poetry, liturgical as well as secular, that translated the new preoccupation with language and beauty into art, Andalusian Jewry saw its greatest achievements. Solomon ibn Gabirol (c. 1022–c. 1058), Moses ibn Ezra, and Judah ha-Levi (c. 1075–1141) were the acknowledged supreme geniuses of a form of expression that became a passion with thousands the length and breadth of Spain. But the most enduring consequence of the new temper was the redefinition of religious faith in the light of Greco-Arabic philosophical theories. The exposition of faith in Neoplatonic terms by Solomon ibn Gabirol, the defense of Rabbinism using Aristotelian categories by Abraham ibn Daud (c. 1110–c. 1180), the attack on the religious inadequacy of philosophy by Judah ha-Levi, and the epoch-making Aristotelian philosophical theology by Moses Maimonides (1135–1204) fixed philosophical inquiry as an enduring subject on the agenda of rabbinic concerns. Beginning in the 13th century, a new class of philosophers sponsored the translation of Arabic literature into Hebrew and of Hebrew and Arabic literature into Latin. They brought Jews and their thought into the mainstream of Western philosophy and gained for them the position of middlemen of culture between East and West.

The salient trends of Sephardic Judaism did not imply relegation of the rabbinic class to a secondary role. Rather, they shaped a fresh approach to rabbinic texts that paralleled in many respects those adopted in biblical exegesis. Strict adherence to consistency, systematization, and philological exactitude yielded new codes that often diverged from gaonic judgments. A digest of Talmudic law by Isaac Alfasi (1013–1103) placed the Sephardic rabbinate on a self-reliant footing and epitomized its method of getting at the essentials of Talmudic law by sidestepping contingent discussions. In this area too, it was Moses Maimonides who brought the Sephardic principles of comprehensiveness, lucidity, and logical arrangement to their apex through his code of Jewish law, *Mishne Torah*. Written in Mishnaic Hebrew, the work remains the only comprehensive treatment of all of Jewish law, including those fields that are not applicable in the Diaspora (agriculture, purity, sacrifices, Temple procedure).

With Maimonides, however, the pure Sephardic tradition came to an end, for the Almohad (Amazigh [Berber] Muslim reformers) invasion of Spain in 1147–48

SEPHARDI

The term Sephardi *refers to a member of the Jews who lived in Spain and Portugal from the Middle Ages until their persecution and mass expulsion from those countries in the last decades of the 15th century and their descendants. The Sephardim initially fled to North Africa and other parts of the Ottoman Empire, and many of these eventually settled in such countries as France, Holland, England, Italy, and the Balkans. Salonika (Thessaloníki) in Macedonia and the city of Amsterdam became major sites of Sephardic settlement. The transplanted Sephardim largely retained their native Judeo-Spanish language (Ladino), literature, and customs. They became noted for their cultural and intellectual achievements within the Mediterranean and northern European Jewish communities. The Sephardim differ notably from the Ashkenazim (German Jews) in preserving Babylonian rather than Palestinian Jewish ritual traditions. Of the estimated 700,000 Sephardic Jews in the world today (far fewer than the Ashkenazim), many now reside in the state of Israel. The chief rabbinate of Israel has both a Sephardic and an Ashkenazi chief rabbi.*

Though the term Oriental Jews *is perhaps more properly applied to Jews of North Africa and the Middle East who had no ties with either Spain or Germany and who speak Arabic, Persian, or a variant of ancient Aramaic, the designation* Sephardim *frequently signifies all North African Jews and others who, under the influence of the "Spanish Jews," have adopted the Sephardic rite.*

wiped out the Jewish communities of Andalusia and drove thousands to northern Spain and Provence (a province of southeastern France) or, as in the case of Maimonides' family, to North Africa and Egypt. Sephardic Jewry suddenly encountered a discrete, mature Jewish culture that for centuries had been developing independently and along quite different lines.

ASHKENAZIC DEVELOPMENTS

The Ashkenazic Jewry, into whose communities the Sephardim had been thrust by political events, regarded their own heritage and the Christian world in which they lived from a perspective shaped exclusively by rabbinic categories. They drew their school texts and the values that determined their judgments from the Talmud and the Midrash. Sensing no intellectual challenge in Christian faith, which they regarded with thinly concealed contempt, they constituted for the most part a merchant class that lived in urban centres under the protection of ecclesiastical and temporal rulers but also under their own complex of laws and institutions. Except for mercantile relations, Christian society was closed to them, thanks largely to age-old ecclesiastical prohibitions forbidding all social intercourse with Jews. With the Arab conquest of Spain and the rise of the Carolingians (the dynasty that ruled western Europe in the 8th and 9th centuries), the 12-decade interlude of suppression by

the Visigoths (589–711) came to an end, and the Roman precedent of toleration and autonomy again became the rule. Merchants and rabbis moved from Italy to France and the Rhineland, and infused new energies into the Jewish communities there. An indigenous religious leadership began to emerge at the very time that Andalusian Jewry was entering its golden age. The First Crusade (1096–99) unleashed a tide of hatred, periodic violence, and progressive restrictions on Jewish activities in the Rhineland, but the communities affected had attained sufficient resilience to reestablish their communal institutions shortly afterward and to continue the cultivation of their deeply ingrained traditions.

By 1150 Ashkenazic Jewry had established a culture of its own, with an indigenous literature that ranged from the popular homily to the esoteric tract on the nature of the divine glory. Study of the Bible and the Talmud was oriented toward a mystical pietism in which prayer and contemplation of the secrets embedded in the liturgy were to lead to religious experience. Significantly, the fathers of the Ashkenazic tradition were remembered as liturgical poets and initiates into divine mysteries, and the early codes of the Franco-German schools were heavily weighted with discussions of liturgical usage. After the Second Crusade (1147–49), the German Jewish mystics (also called Hasidim, or pietists) placed heavy emphasis on the merits of asceticism, martyrdom, and penitence, thus adapting to a Jewish idiom the features of saintliness then current in Christian Europe. For the masses of Jews, the cultural fare consisted principally of biblical tales and instruction as interpreted by rabbinic Midrash, the lives of scholars and saints, and liturgical poetry reaffirming the election of Israel and faith in messianic redemption. The chief vehicle of popular instruction consisted of anthologies from the rabbinic writings and commentaries on Scripture, of which the most popular was that of Rabbi Solomon ben Isaac of Troyes (1040–1105), known as Rashi, the acronym formed from the initials of his name in Hebrew. For the more advanced student, Rashi composed a succinct commentary on the Talmud that achieved an authority approaching that of the text itself.

As living sources of law and values, the Bible and the Talmud had an impact on public and private, as well as secular and religious, affairs. Taking their cue from Talmudic precedent and from Christian ecclesiastical procedures of their own times, the Ashkenazic rabbis occasionally gathered in regional synods to enact legislation on problems of a general nature for which there was no adequate precedent in the literature. Among the most enduring of these measures were the prohibition of bigamy and arbitrary divorce, and severe economic penalties for abandonment of wives. Of far more immediate concern to the average Jew were the circumvention of Talmudic prohibitions against usury,

relaxation of prohibitions regarding traffic with Gentiles in wines, and adoption of severe disciplinary measures, such as excommunication, against informers or those appealing, in cases involving Jews, to the Gentile authorities.

A new religious trend began in Provence in the 13th century with the introduction into the Talmudic academies of a novel form of mystical study known as Kabbala (literally, "tradition"), which soon spread to northern Spain. Expressing gnostic doctrines in rabbinic guise, the devotees of Kabbala devised an esoteric vocabulary that reinterpreted the Bible and rabbinic law as allegories of the various modes in which God is manifested in a spiritual universe, access to which was reserved for initiates. The most renowned literary product of this new circle was the *Zohar* ("The Book of Splendour"), a vast mystical commentary on the Pentateuch by Moses de León (*c.* 1250–1305); with later additions it became the Bible of Jewish mystics everywhere. Although some of the theological notions of the Kabbalists deviated from basic postulates of Jewish monotheism, the insistence of the mystics on unflagging ritual orthodoxy and on a nominal acceptance of the biblical text as divine revelation helped them avert the suspicions aroused by Jewish Aristotelians and Averroists—followers of the 12th-century Arabic Aristotelian philosopher Averroës (1126–98)—and, in time, even won for them the status of a rabbinic elite. Indeed, in the early 13th

ASHKENAZI

The term Ashkenazi refers to any member of the Jews who lived in the Rhineland valley and in neighbouring France before their migration eastward to Slavic lands (e.g., Poland, Lithuania, Russia) after the Crusades (11th–13th century) and their descendants. After the 17th-century persecutions in eastern Europe, large numbers of these Jews resettled in western Europe, where they assimilated, as they had done in eastern Europe, with other Jewish communities. In time, all Jews who had adopted the "German rite" synagogue ritual were referred to as Ashkenazim to distinguish them from Sephardic (Spanish rite) Jews. Ashkenazim differ from Sephardim in their pronunciation of Hebrew, in cultural traditions, in synagogue cantillation (chanting), in their widespread use of Yiddish (until the 20th century), and especially in synagogue liturgy.

Today Ashkenazim constitute more than 80 percent of all the Jews in the world, vastly out-numbering Sephardic Jews. In the late 20th century, Ashkenazic Jews numbered more than 11 million. In Israel the numbers of Ashkenazim and Sephardim are roughly equal, and the chief rabbinate has both an Ashkenazic and a Sephardic chief rabbi on equal footing. All Reform and Conservative Jewish congregations belong to the Ashkenazic tradition.

century, some of the mystics lent their support to a campaign that condemned the study of philosophy as generating skepticism, latitudinarianism, and disrespect for traditional literature.

CONFLICTS AND NEW MOVEMENTS

The conflict between philosophers and anti-philosophers in Provence and northern Spain represented a clash between two mature Jewish subcultures of diverse geographic origins, the Sephardic and the Ashkenazic, each of which had in the course of centuries developed different esoteric doctrines to transcend the legalistic formalism and confining dogmas of normative Judaism. Both forms of speculation sought salvation for exceptional individuals through knowledge and thus provided an immediate substitute for messianic deliverance from exile and servitude. Each group charged the other with distortion of tradition, and each issued apologias and excommunications characteristic of medieval doctrinal controversy. While the rifts between them reached bitter proportions, the common threat posed by ecclesiastical attacks on the Talmud in public disputations and by the expulsion of the Jews from France in 1306 prevented open rupture or resolution of the conflict. Ever since that time, two strands of orthodoxy representing the two forms of medieval metaphysical speculation have lived side by side in an uneasy truce.

Most rabbinic circles of the 14th and 15th centuries displayed a progressive dogmatism and insistence on uniformity of practice. The great legal code of Jacob ben Asher of Toledo (c. 1269–c. 1340), *Arba'a turim* (c. 1335; "Four Rows"), which sought to level differences in usage between Ashkenazim and Sephardim, signified the dominant trend of the rabbinate. The increasing hardening of ideological lines, however, did not eliminate independent thinking. Isaac Albalag (13th century) propounded an Averroist (rationalistic) interpretation of the Bible predicated on a theory of double truth (of reason and revelation), whereas Gersonides (Levi ben Gershom; 1288–1344) gave Jewish Aristotelianism a new and comprehensive formulation. In Muslim areas, the Maimonidean regimen of philosophical contemplation was extended by Maimonides' son Abraham to a quest for pietist ecstasy that seemed to have much in common with Sufism (Islamic mysticism).

The anti-Jewish riots in Spain and their consequences stimulated the anti-intellectualism of the rabbinate. Hasdai Crescas (1340–1410), while conceding the philosophical untenability of traditional belief in free will, launched a scathing attack on Aristotelian approaches to religion, and his disciple Joseph Albo (c. 1380–c. 1444) issued a compendium on dogma that reaffirmed the traditional postulates of divine creation, revelation, and retribution as axioms of Judaism. But these reassertions of traditional faith could not overcome the ideological and social fragmentation that had split the Spanish communities, often leaving them in open conflict with each other. Widespread marranism (ostensible conversion to Christianity) polarized the community and left residues of bitterness toward those returning to the fold. The expulsions from Spain and Portugal drove the leadership into intensified pursuits of mystical escape from, and rationalization of, the endless calamities that befell their flocks. In Italy and the Ottoman Empire (Asia Minor, northeastern Africa, and southeastern Europe)—the two principal centres of refuge for the exiles of the Iberian Peninsula—legalistic Kabbalism, which insisted on strict observance of the law as a precondition of mystical practice and study, became the dominant form of rabbinic leadership. Despite the terrible circumstances, the rabbinate continued to produce works of encyclopaedic proportions and staggering erudition in every field of Jewish learning.

Inspired by the Jewish tradition that the coming of the messiah would be preceded by horrendous catastrophes, a group of rabbis established a community in Zefat (Safed), Palestine, where, in anticipation of the new dawn, every aspect of life was conducted on principles of saintliness and mystical contemplation. Under the leadership of Jacob Berab, the ancient practice of ordination (*semikha*) was reinstituted in 1538 to form the nucleus of a revived Sanhedrin that would administer ritual procedures requiring fully ordained authorities. Although the effort failed because of rabbinic opposition, it reflected the temper of the times and further fanned messianic hopes sparked shortly before by the campaigns of Solomon Molkho (c. 1500–32) and David Reubeni (died after 1532) in Italy; Molkho was burned at the stake by the Christian authorities, and Reubeni died in prison. In Ẓefat itself, Kabbalism soon entered a new phase under the inspiration of Isaac Luria (1534–72) and Ḥayyim Vital (1543–1620), who confided to their disciples that the calamities of Israel were but a mirror of the captivity into which many sparks of the Godhead itself had fallen. Liturgical innovations and a novel mystical theology were formulated to redeem the imprisoned elements of divinity and thus restore creation to the harmony intended for it.

That the Almighty himself was not quite omnipotent, at least with respect to the fate of his chosen people, was cautiously hinted in a Hebrew work of history (1550) by Solomon ibn Verga (1460–1554), who regarded the Jewish problem as a sociopolitical one to which theological answers were futile. Such guarded rationalism was entertained by a number of courageous thinkers in 16th-century Italy, where, despite the policy of ghettoization (the segregation of the Jewish community in a restricted quarter) begun by Venice in 1516 and soon extended to all major Italian cities, the spirit of the Renaissance and the passion for historical criticism had captivated many Jews. Catholic scholars and prelates occasionally employed rabbis to instruct them in the Hebrew language and in the secrets of the Kabbala, which some Christians believed actually verified the postulates of their own faith. Contacts with Christian scholars in turn introduced Jews such as Azariah dei Rossi (c. 1513–78), whose Meor 'enayim ("Enlightenment of the Eyes") inaugurated critical textual study of rabbinical texts, to new bodies of literature that had been lost to the Jewish community, such as the works of Philo and Josephus.

Such phenomena, however, were comparatively rare and isolated. The spread of dogmatic Kabbalism eventually led to the widespread acceptance of the views of the pseudo-messiah Shabbetai Tzevi (1626–76). Most of European and Ottoman Jewry was swept into near hysteria in the belief that the end was now finally at hand. When Shabbetai converted to Islam after being apprehended by the Ottoman government, all but his most faithful followers were despondent, though some tried to explain the apostasy of the pseudo-messiah as a form of voluntary crucifixion for the sake of the Jews. A witch hunt on the part of traditionalists to uncover the remaining cells of heresy unsettled Jewish communities everywhere.

The following century (to c. 1750) was the darkest in the history of Rabbinic Judaism. Scholarship declined and popular religion became mechanical to an extent that Jews had never before experienced. Polish Jews suffered terribly during the Deluge, a period of peasant

Shabbetaianism

In the 17th century, Shabbetaianism—a messianic movement that, in its extreme form, espoused the sacredness of sin—swept through the Diaspora. The leader of the movement was Shabbetai Tzevi, a self-proclaimed messiah and charismatic mystic. Coerced by the sultan of Constantinople to accept Islam, Shabbetai Tzevi shocked and disillusioned many of his followers by proclaiming himself a Muslim.

Other followers, interpreting Shabbetai Tzevi's apostasy as a step toward ultimate fulfillment of his messiahship, also proclaimed themselves Muslims. They argued that such outward acts were irrelevant as long as one remains inwardly a Jew. Those who embraced the theory of "sacred sin" believed that the Torah could be fulfilled only by its seeming annulment.

After Shabbetai Tzevi's death in 1676, the sect continued to flourish. The nihilistic tendencies of Shabbetaianism reached a peak in the 18th century with the false messiah Jacob Frank, who claimed to be Shabbetai Tzevi's reincarnation and whose followers reputedly sought redemption through orgies. The confusion and ill feeling ran so deep among the Jewish communities that a strong aversion to mysticism and active messianic tendencies developed in response.

revolts and war involving Poland, Russia, and Sweden that began in 1648. The Jews were slaughtered by rebels and professional soldiers during the war, which was fought mostly on Polish soil, and many survivors were sold as slaves in Turkey. The massacres and impoverishment of Polish Jewry after 1648 brought a pall over the growing eastern European centres of Jewish life. Antinomian eruptions of extreme Shabbetaians under the leadership of the self-proclaimed messiah and later Catholic convert Jacob Frank (1726–91) alarmed Gentile authorities almost as much as they did Jews. But the fossilization referred to above was only apparent. Beneath the surface many were restlessly searching for new avenues of faith, and the 18th century saw fresh responses that set the history of the Jews and of Judaism in new directions and marked the beginning of a new era.

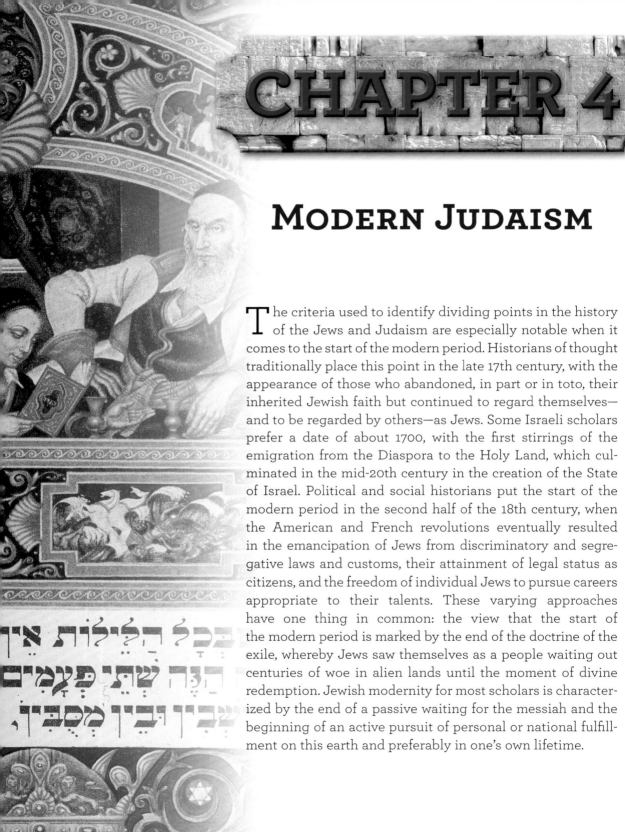

CHAPTER 4

MODERN JUDAISM

The criteria used to identify dividing points in the history of the Jews and Judaism are especially notable when it comes to the start of the modern period. Historians of thought traditionally place this point in the late 17th century, with the appearance of those who abandoned, in part or in toto, their inherited Jewish faith but continued to regard themselves— and to be regarded by others—as Jews. Some Israeli scholars prefer a date of about 1700, with the first stirrings of the emigration from the Diaspora to the Holy Land, which culminated in the mid-20th century in the creation of the State of Israel. Political and social historians put the start of the modern period in the second half of the 18th century, when the American and French revolutions eventually resulted in the emancipation of Jews from discriminatory and segregative laws and customs, their attainment of legal status as citizens, and the freedom of individual Jews to pursue careers appropriate to their talents. These varying approaches have one thing in common: the view that the start of the modern period is marked by the end of the doctrine of the exile, whereby Jews saw themselves as a people waiting out centuries of woe in alien lands until the moment of divine redemption. Jewish modernity for most scholars is characterized by the end of a passive waiting for the messiah and the beginning of an active pursuit of personal or national fulfillment on this earth and preferably in one's own lifetime.

THE HASKALA

Although the 18th century Haskala (Enlightenment) among the Ashkenazim of central and eastern Europe is often taken as the starting point of Jewish modernity, the process of Westernization had begun a good deal earlier among the Sephardim in western Europe and in Italy. The Marranos who went to the Jewish communities of Amsterdam and Venice in the 17th century to declare themselves Jews carried with them the Western education that they had acquired while living as Christians in the Iberian Peninsula, as well as the habits of criticism that had kept them from assimilating into the majority during their Marrano years. Some, such as Benedict (Baruch) de Spinoza (1632–77), a son of Marranos, applied these skills to all of the biblical tradition, including especially their own religion. In Italy there was an older Jewish community that had never been sealed off culturally from the influence of its environment. Some of its figures were influenced by, and participated in, the main currents of the Renaissance.

Increased contact with Western languages, manners, and customs came to the Ashkenazim only in the 18th century, when new economic opportunities created such possibilities. Jewish bankers and brokers in various German principalities, army provisioners in most European countries, capitalists who were permitted to live in places such as Berlin because they opened new factories or were otherwise helpful to the expansion of the economy—all were in increasing contact with Gentile society, and most began to strive for full acceptance. Around this wealthy element there arose a number of intellectuals who agitated for the end of ghettoization as a necessary preamble to the emancipation of the Jews.

In Central Europe

The most outstanding figure of the 18th-century Jewish Enlightenment was the philosopher Moses Mendelssohn (1729–86), a devoted adherent of traditional Judaism who turned away from the historic Jewish preoccupation with the Talmud and its literature to the intellectual world of the European Enlightenment. Mendelssohn did not attempt a philosophical defense of Judaism until pressed to do so by Christians who questioned how he could remain faithful to what they saw as an unenlightened religion. In his response, *Jerusalem*, published in 1783, Mendelssohn defended the validity of Judaism as the inherited faith of the Jews by defining it as revealed divine legislation, and he declared himself at the same time to be a believer in the universal religion of reason, of which Judaism was but one historical manifestation. Aware that he was accepted by Gentile society as an "exceptional Jew" who had embraced Western culture, Mendelssohn's message to his own community was to become

The philosopher and biblical translator Moses Mendelssohn was the most prominent figure of the Jewish Enlightenment. Imagno/Hulton Archive/Getty Images

Westerners, to seek out the culture of the Enlightenment. To that end he joined with a poet, Naphtali Herz (Hartwig) Wessely (1725–1805), in translating the Torah into German, combining Hebrew characters with modern German phonetics in an effort to displace Yiddish, and wrote a modern biblical commentary in Hebrew, the *Be'ur* ("Commentary"). Within a generation, Mendelssohn's Bible was to be found in almost every literate Jewish home in central Europe, serving to introduce its readers to German culture. Through his personal example and his life's work, Mendelssohn made it possible for his fellow Jews to join the Western world without sacrificing their Judaism. Indeed, he convinced them that Judaism is compatible with an intellectual commitment to universal reason.

Mendelssohn's work was carried on by the Berlin Haskala, a group of Jewish intellectuals who had gathered around Mendelssohn during his lifetime. The Haskala was most active in the 20 years following his death. In the pages of their Hebrew-language periodical, *Ha-Me'assef* ("The Collector"), they preached the virtues of secular culture and publicized the need for secular education. In response to the Edict of Toleration promulgated in 1781 by the Holy Roman emperor Joseph II (reigned 1765–90), Naphtali Wessely issued an urgent call for the reform of Jewish education as a prelude to full emancipation. Secular subjects—mathematics, German, and world history and literature—were to take precedence over traditional Jewish studies. The study of the Bible, because it was generally acknowledged to be a fundamental part of Western culture, was to be emphasized at the expense of the customary focus on the Talmud. Following this model, modern Jewish schools were established by Jewish intellectuals and businessmen in several German cities, among them Frankfurt and Hamburg. As its educational activities began to bear fruit in the wide dissemination of secular culture, the Berlin Haskala abandoned the use of Hebrew for German and gradually disintegrated. Unlike Mendelssohn himself, his immediate intellectual descendants, including his own children, were unable to strike a balance between Jewish and secular culture. Their Western education undermined their religious faith, and they saw themselves as Europeans rather than as Jews.

One of Mendelssohn's disciples, David Friedlaender, offered to convert to Christianity without accepting Christian dogma or Christian rites. He felt that both Judaism and Christianity shared the same religious truth but that there was no relation at all between that truth and Judaism's ceremonial law. The offer was refused because Friedlaender would not acknowledge the superiority of Christianity and make an unconditional commitment to it. Unlike Friedlaender, many other followers of Mendelssohn chose to leave the Jewish faith as the only way to win full acceptance in European society.

IN EASTERN EUROPE

Thus, the Haskala was quickly played out in central Europe. As an idea, its further career was to continue in eastern Europe, particularly in the Russian Empire, where it flourished in the middle third of the 19th century until, as a result of the pogroms of 1881, Jews lost faith in the willingness of Russians to accept "enlightened" Jews. It was a tenet of the Russian Haskala that the tsar was a benevolent leader who would bestow emancipation upon his Jewish subjects as soon as they proved themselves worthy of it. A goal of the Russian Haskala, therefore, was for the Jews to transform themselves into model citizens—enlightened, unsuperstitious, devoted to secular learning and productive occupations. Following the example of the Berlin Haskala, a Russian Hebrew-language writer, Isaac Baer Levinsohn (1788–1860), published a pamphlet, *Te'uda be-Yisrael* ("Testimony in Israel"), extolling the benefits of secular education. At the same time, writers such as Joseph Perl (1774–1839) and Isaac Erter (1792–1851), though traditional Jews themselves, attacked in virulent satire the superstitious folk customs of the masses, thereby opening the way to the anticlericalism that became characteristic of the Russian Haskala.

In the 1840s and '50s the group's emphasis shifted from satirical attacks on the cultural parochialism of the Pale of Settlement (the regions to which the Jews were restricted) to romanticization of life outside the Pale, including periods of the Jewish past. Thus, Hebrew poets and novelists in Russia, such as Micah Judah Lebensohn (1828–52) and Abraham Mapu (1808–67), contributed to the creation of a modern Hebrew literature. In the 1860s the Russian Haskala, reflecting the larger political climate, entered a "positivist" phase, calling for practical social and economic reforms. Hebrew-language journals were established, and the Hebrew essay and didactic poetry, calling for religious and cultural reforms, came into their own, particularly in the hands of the poet Judah Leib Gordon (1830–92) and the essayist Moses Leib Lilienblum (1843–1910). Abandoning the original Hebrew and German orientation of the Russian Haskala, a number of Jewish intellectuals—the most prominent of whom were Yoachim Tarnopol (1810–1900), Osip Rabinovich (1817–69), and Lev Levanda (1835–88)—became Russifiers, founding Russian-language Jewish weeklies devoted to "patriotism, emancipation, modernism." Like their contemporary fellow Jews in western Europe, they declared themselves to be Russians by nationality and Jews by religious belief alone. In 1863 a group of wealthy Jews in St. Petersburg and Odessa created the Society for the Promotion of Culture Among the Jews of Russia for the purpose of educating Russian Jewry into "readiness for citizenship." The goal of all segments of the Russian Haskala in the 1860s and '70s was to turn Jews into good Russians and to make their Jewishness a matter of personal choice. But the hopes of the Haskala were upset by the reaction of Russians following the assassination of Tsar Alexander II in 1881. Several Jewish communities were destroyed in pogroms, which often received the tacit approval of the governing authorities. Jewish economic life was severely curtailed, and quotas for Jewish students were put in place in secular educational institutions. The bright optimism of Russian-Jewish intellectuals faded.

RELIGIOUS REFORM MOVEMENTS

One element of Westernization that the Haskala championed was the reform of religion. This movement began in western Europe during the Napoleonic period (1800–15), when certain aspects of Jewish belief and observance were seen as incompatible with the new position of the Jew in Western society. Napoleon convoked a Sanhedrin in 1807 to create a modern definition of Judaism that renounced Jewish nationhood and national aspirations, asserted that rabbinic authority was purely spiritual, and recognized the priority of civil over religious authority even in matters of intermarriage. In countries other than France, the rationale for reform, at least in its early years, was more aesthetic than doctrinal. The external aspects of Jewish worship (i.e., the form of the service) was unacceptable to the newly Westernized members of the Jewish bourgeoisie in both Germany and the United States, whose cultural standards had been shaped by the surrounding society and who desired above all to resemble their Gentile peers.

Thus, the short-lived Reform temple established in Seesen in 1810 by the pioneer German reformer Israel Jacobson (1768–1828) introduced organ and choir music, allowed men and women to sit together during worship, delivered the sermon in German instead of Hebrew, and omitted liturgical references to a personal messiah and the restoration of Israel. A more radical temple established in Hamburg in 1818 adopted all of Jacobson's reforms and published its own much-abridged prayer book, which deleted almost all references to the long-awaited restoration of Zion. Reformers in Charleston, South Carolina, introduced similar changes in the synagogue ritual in 1824. It was apparent to the reformers that in Western society Judaism would have to divest itself of its alien customs and conform to the cultural and intellectual standards of the new "age of reason."

German Reform in the 1840s became institutionalized, a matter of organized formal belief and practice. At a series of synods held at Brunswick (1844), Frankfurt (1845), and Breslau (1846), it created the first theological rationalization for changes introduced to the faith in the previous generation. Judaism, it was declared, had always been a developmental religion that conformed to the demands of the times. Moreover, the reformers maintained, the Jews were no longer a nation and therefore were bound not by their religious and political code of law but only by the dictates of moral law. Rituals that impeded full Jewish participation in German social and political life were no longer considered valid expressions of Jewish religious truth. The use of Hebrew in religious services was limited. Practices such as circumcision, the dietary laws, and all national messianic hopes were questioned in light of the "spirit of the times." Messianism in Reform Judaism was transformed into active concern for social welfare in the present, and the Jewish role in history became Diaspora-centred. Some even thought of it as constituting a mission to the Gentiles.

Although Reform Judaism was initiated in Europe, its success was limited there because many central European governments would not recognize more than one form of Judaism in any one locale. Even in areas where it had taken root, by the middle of the 19th century, European Reform (now usually called "Liberal Judaism") lost much of its early radicalism. Reform was much more successful in the United States, where it was carried by massive numbers of German Jewish immigrants in the 1840s and

REFORM JUDAISM

Reform Judaism sets itself at variance with Orthodox Judaism by challenging the binding force of ritual, laws, and customs set down in the Bible and in certain books of rabbinic origin (e.g., the Talmud). It is a religious movement that has modified or discarded several traditional Jewish beliefs, laws, and practices in an effort to adapt Judaism to the social, political, and cultural conditions of the modern world.

Israel Jacobson (1768–1828), a Jewish layman, established an innovative school in Seesen, Brunswick, in 1801. There he held the first Reform services in 1810, attended by adults as well as children. Jacobson's liturgy was in German rather than Hebrew; organ and choir music were added to the service; and Jacobson instituted confirmation for both boys and girls to replace the traditional boys' bar mitzvah ceremony. The liturgy omitted all references to a personal messiah who would restore Israel as a nation. Jacobson held Reform services in Berlin in 1815, and from there Reform practices spread to Denmark, Hamburg, Leipzig, Vienna, and Prague. Reform worshippers were no longer required to cover their heads or wear the prayer shawl (tallit). Daily public worship was abandoned; work was permitted on the Sabbath; and dietary laws (kashrut) were declared obsolete.

Rabbi Abraham Geiger (1810–74) was one of the leading ideologists of the Reform movement. He concluded that the essence of Judaism is belief in the one true God of all humankind, the practice of eternally valid ethical principles, and the communication of these truths to all nations of the world. Samuel Holdheim (1806–60) rejected Jewish marriage and divorce laws as obsolete, arguing that such codes fell outside the ethical and doctrinal functions of Judaism and were superseded by the laws of the state. He agreed with Geiger that monotheism and ethics are the principal criteria of authentic Judaism. Both felt that Judaism must be a living, constantly developing faith, compatible with the spirit of the times.

where it coalesced with existing American reform movements. Rabbi Isaac Mayer Wise (1819–1900), a German emigrant, was a central figure in the remarkable success of Reform Judaism in the United States, where it had begun in 1841 when a congregation in Charleston, South Carolina, joined the Reform movement. Wise not only issued a widely influential prayer book (1857) but eventually established the Hebrew Union College (1875), for the education of Reform rabbis, and the Central Conference of American Rabbis (1889). Two other emigrants, David Einhorn (1809–79) and Samuel Hirsch (1815–89), provided the theoretical foundations of American Reform. Hirsch was chairman of the first conference of American Reform rabbis, which met in Philadelphia in 1869. It declared that Jews should no longer look forward to a return to Palestine, and it rejected belief in bodily resurrection after death. The question of Zionism, support for an independent Jewish nation, was controversial within the Reform movement until the establishment of Israel in 1948.

By 1880 almost all 200 synagogues in the United States (amalgamated in the Union of American Hebrew Congregations in 1873) were Reform. In 1885 a conference of Reform rabbis formulated what was then the most comprehensive statement of Reform philosophy in the so-called Pittsburgh Platform. This manifesto announced that Judaism was an evolutionary faith and no longer a national one, and it declared that the Mosaic and rabbinical laws regulating diet, purity, and dress were "entirely foreign to our present mental and spiritual state." While the preservation of historical identity was considered beneficial, the maintenance of tradition was not. The Talmud was to be treated merely as religious literature, not as legislation. The principles of the Pittsburgh Platform remained the official philosophy of the American Reform movement until 1937, when a later generation, seeking to meet different emotional and intellectual needs, reintroduced the concept of Jewish personhood into the Columbus Platform. This document also reemphasized Hebrew and traditional liturgy and practices. After World War II, Reform in the United States developed along two tracks. It departed in new ways from traditional Judaism in ordaining women (1972), allowing patrilineal descent (1983), and sanctifying same-sex marriage (2000). On the other hand, some Reform Jews began reintegrating long-discarded rituals into worship services. This neo-ritualism stimulated greater use of Hebrew in prayer books and a more dynamic Zionism.

If Reform was a child of Enlightenment rationalism, Conservative Judaism was a child of historical romanticism. It began in 1845, when Zacharias Frankel (1801–75) and a group of followers seceded from a second Reform synod at Frankfurt over the issue of limiting the use of Hebrew to a small core of prayers. For Frankel, Hebrew represented the spirit of Judaism and the Jewish people,

CONSERVATIVE JUDAISM

Conservative Judaism is a religious movement that seeks to conserve essential elements of traditional Judaism, while allowing for the modernization of religious practices in a less radical sense than that espoused by Reform Judaism.

Zacharias Frankel (1801–75), whose ideology inspired early Conservative ideas, broke with modernizing extremists after a series of Reform conferences in Germany (1844–46). Holding fast to the notion that the Jewish religion is inextricably bound up with Jewish culture and a national identity, he refused to abandon religious customs and traditions as nonessentials.

Frankel felt that historical studies could bring to light those elements of the Written and Oral Law that were merely contemporary expressions of more abiding religious truths. These, then, could be reinterpreted to fit the context of modern life. Frankel's view of Judaism emphasizes the sacredness of the Law as a living force applicable to all generations.

Despite different opinions, Conservative Jews have found a common bond by maintaining continuity with the past. These differences make Conservative Judaism a theological coalition rather than a homogeneous expression of beliefs and practices. These differences also explain why it is all but impossible to enunciate a distinct theology of the movement. Conservative rituals show a like diversity, ranging from Orthodoxy to Reform.

and Judaism itself was not merely a theology of ethics but the historical expression of the Jewish experience. He called this definition "positive-historical Judaism." Although Conservative Judaism conceived of Judaism as a developmental religion, it charted its course through close study of tradition and the will of the people and thus came to largely traditional conclusions about religious observance. Following Orthodoxy, Conservatives insisted on the sacredness of the Sabbath. Dietary laws were respected and observed, but with modifications when necessary. In 1985, Conservative Judaism distinguished itself further from traditional Judaism by ordaining women rabbis. Many Conservatives, stressing Jewish nationalism as inseparable from the culture of the Jewish people, encouraged the study of Hebrew and supported the secular Zionist movement. Conservative Judaism became especially successful in the United States, where it is represented by the United Synagogue of America. Its official body, the Rabbinical Assembly, is headquartered at the Jewish Theological Seminary in New York City.

ORTHODOX DEVELOPMENTS

Although affected by the efforts at religious reform, the bulk of the official Jewish establishment in western and central Europe remained Orthodox (a term first used by Reform leaders to designate their traditionalist opponents).

In Western and Central Europe

Under the leadership of Samson Raphael Hirsch (1808–88) in Frankfurt, a more modern and militant form of Judaism arose. Known as Neo-Orthodoxy, the new movement asserted its right to break with any Jewish community that contained Reform elements. The teachings of Neo-Orthodoxy were profoundly influential, for they indicated the possibility of living a ritually and religiously full life while being totally integrated into Western society. This was accomplished by positing a theoretical division between religion and culture: in religion the Jews were to remain Orthodox (though deferring their messianic aspirations to the unforeseeable future), while in manners and culture they were to become Western. This form of Orthodoxy, which became the intellectual model for Western Orthodoxy, continued into the 21st century in the United States in a variety of religious and academic institutions (such as the Yeshiva University in New York City and the bulk of English-speaking Orthodox synagogues), coexisting in substantial tension with a number of Orthodox groups, most notably the Lubavitcher and Satmar Hasidim and some Talmudic academies that viewed the Western world as the enemy and chose to re-create the ghetto.

In Eastern Europe

By the mid-18th century, Orthodoxy in eastern Europe, having been convulsed by frantic messianism and stifled by the sterility of legalistic scholarship, was ripe for revival. In the mid-17th century the experience of Shabbetaianism, the first messianic movement to excite virtually all of world Jewry, had revealed the pervasiveness of Jewish exhaustion with the Exile and fervent longing for messianic redemption. Later, in the 18th century, the nihilistic sect of Frankists (the followers of Jacob Frank) transformed that longing into a this-worldly hysteria. Talmudic piety and study, sunk in excessive *pilpul* (acute logical distinctions that often became mere hairsplitting), was refreshed by the new critical methods of Elijah ben Solomon (1720–97), the gaon of Vilna. Although essentially a legal rigorist, he was open to more-scientific methods of textual analysis insofar as they helped him to elucidate Talmudic texts. Orthodox religious expression also was raised to a new level with the development of Hasidism (pietism) by Israel Ba'al Shem Ṭov (c. 1700–60) in the mid-18th century. Hasidism contained elements of social protest, being at least in part a movement of the poor against the wealthy communal leadership and of the unlearned against the learned—though many of its leaders, among them Rabbi Dov Baer (1710–72), who was the *maggid* ("preacher") of Mezhirich, and Rabbi Levi Isaac of Berdichev (1740–1810), were well-versed in Talmudic learning. Nevertheless, it was essentially a nonmessianic outcry in the name of piety, emphasizing prayer and personal religious devotion here and now. The major innovation that Hasidism introduced into Jewish religious life was the charismatic leader, the *rebbe*, who served as teacher, confessor, wonder-worker, God's vicar on earth, and, occasionally, atoning sacrifice. The earliest *rebbes* were democratically chosen, but spiritual dynasties formed as the position of leadership passed to the descendants of the first *rebbe*s on the presumption that they had inherited their fathers' charisma. Hasidism spread throughout eastern Europe and was most successful in Poland.

Hasidism made little headway in Lithuania, where the traditional rabbinic class, under the leadership of Elijah ben Solomon, was able to stave off its influence by issuing a ban of excommunication (*ḥerem*, "anathema") against the new movement. The tactic, which involved a complete boycott and cutting off of communication, was widely embraced by non-Hasidic rabbis, who were given the title of Mitnaggedim ("Opponents") by the Hasidim. In areas where the rabbis had lost the respect of the masses, however, the *ḥerem* proved

ORTHODOX JUDAISM

Those Jews who are considered "Orthodox" adhere most strictly to traditional beliefs and practices. They resolutely refuse to accept the position of Reform Judaism that the Bible and other sacred Jewish writings contain not only eternally valid moral principles but also historically and culturally conditioned adaptations and interpretations of the Torah that may be legitimately discarded in modern times. In Orthodox Judaism, therefore, both the Written Law (Torah, the first five books of the Hebrew Bible) and the Oral Law (codified in the Mishna and interpreted in the Talmud) are immutably fixed and remain the sole norm of religious observance.

Orthodox Judaism has resisted modern pressures to modify its observance and has held fast to such practices as daily worship, dietary laws (kashruth), traditional prayers and ceremonies, regular and intensive study of the Torah, and separation of men and women in the synagogue. It also enjoins strict observance of the Sabbath and religious festivals, and does not permit instrumental music during communal services.

Despite such seeming inflexibility, Orthodox Judaism is marked by considerable variety. Neo-Orthodoxy, for example, a late 19th-century development under the leadership of Samson Raphael Hirsch, sanctioned modern dress, the use of the vernacular in sermons, and a more positive view of modern culture.

All Jewish groups—Orthodox, Conservative, and Reform—consider themselves and each other as adherents of the Jewish faith. This fact, however, has not deterred Orthodox rabbis from challenging the legitimacy of certain non-Orthodox marriages, divorces, and conversions on the grounds that they violate prescriptions of Jewish law.

largely ineffective, and it called forth a round of counter-excommunications by the Hasidic rebbes. With the passage of time, Hasidim and Mitnaggedim abandoned their conflict and came to see each other as allies against the threat to all Orthodox Jewish religion posed by Haskala and secularization. The impact of Hasidism on eastern European Jewry cannot be overemphasized; even in Lithuania, where it did not take firm hold, it stimulated the growth of a homegrown pietism in the Musar (ethicist) movement of the mid-19th century, and it renewed the Talmudic energies of its opponents.

DEVELOPMENTS IN SCHOLARSHIP

As the Jews of central Europe moved into mainstream society, a group of young Jewish intellectuals devoted themselves to Jewish scholarship of a type far different from traditional Talmudic learning or medieval philosophy. In 1819 Leopold Zunz (1794–1886) and Moses Moser (1796–1838) founded the Society for Jewish Culture and Learning. The original group quickly dissolved, however, and Zunz became the unofficial leader of a generation of scholars dedicated to the *Wissenschaft des Judentums* ("science of Judaism").

The Wissenschaft movement sought to prove that the Jewish past was intellectually respectable and worthy of study, and hence that the Jews deserved an equal place within European societies.

Jewish scholarship was enlisted as a weapon in the battles for change. Thus, Isaac M. Jost (1793–1860) wrote a general history of the Jews to promote Reform, Zunz's *Gottesdienstliche Vorträge der Juden, historisch entwickelt* (1832; "The Worship Sermons of the Jews, Historically Developed") served to legitimize the modern innovation of the sermon in the vernacular, and Abraham Geiger (1810–74), the outstanding leader of German Reform in the 1840s and '50s, interpreted the Pharisees as the forerunners of the reformers of his own day. In their work, these intellectuals presented archetypes of what modern Jews should become. To support their claims of academic respectability, the Wissenschaft figures highlighted those aspects of the Jewish past that were closely integrated with general fields of study. In particular, Moritz Steinschneider (1816–1907), who owes his fame to towering achievements in bibliography, was concerned above all with the contribution of Jews to science, medicine, and mathematics. These scholars set out to praise Judaism as one of the cofounders of the Western tradition. They argued that, because the Jews produced great culture whenever they were not excluded from European society, they would repeat such accomplishments under conditions of social and political equality.

The Wissenschaft movement stimulated the critical study of the Jewish past, and great works of synthesis written from a variety of perspectives began to appear: the multivolume *Geschichte der Juden von den ältesten Zeiten bis auf die Gegenwart* (1853–76; *History of the Jews*), written from a romantic-national point of view by Heinrich Graetz (1817–91); *Dorot ha-rishonim* (1897–1932; "The First Generations"), by Isaac Halevy (1847–1914); *Toldot Yisrael* (1894; "History of Israel"), written from an orthodox standpoint by Ze'ev Jawitz; and *Die Weltgeschichte des jüdischen Volkes* (1925–30; "The World History of the Jewish People") by Simon Dubnow (1860–1941), reflecting his belief in secular, nationalistic communal autonomy. After the 1920s this tradition of great synthesis was carried on in the United States by Salo W. Baron (1895–1989), who by the early 1980s had produced 18 volumes of his *Social and Religious History of the Jews* (1952–83), and in Israel by Ben-Zion Dinur (1884–1973), whose chief work was *Yisrael ba-gola* (3rd ed., 5 vol., 1961–66; "Israel in the Exile"). Many other first-rank scholars in Europe, Israel, and the United States have made notable contributions to the study of Jewish history, rabbinics, and mysticism.

JEWISH-CHRISTIAN RELATIONS

Jewish-Christian relations in the 19th century were strained at best and often broke down during periods of open conflict. The established Christian churches, particularly Roman Catholicism, were staunch upholders of the old order. They identified the Jews as the major beneficiaries of the French Revolution and as the carriers of liberal, secular, anticlerical, and often revolutionary doctrines. Clerical anti-Semitism allied itself with the anti-Semitism of the traditional right in France, and both forms contended with movements that supported the results of the French Revolution in the great convulsion of the Dreyfus Affair in the last years of the 19th century. In Russia the conflict between the Jews and the Orthodox Church released the most open and virulent manifestation of religious anti-Semitism. In the view of the church, the Jews were seeking to undermine Russian Orthodoxy and the tsar, the very foundations of Russian society. The church and the tsarist authorities condoned—and even encouraged—violent pogroms against the Jews in 1881–82 and again in 1905.

Russian Orthodoxy was also active in spreading the blood libel, a superstitious belief in Jewish ritual murder of Christian children whose blood would be used to make unleavened bread at Passover. The blood libel first emerged in the 12th century and often led to the persecution of Jews. It reemerged in Damascus in 1840 (in which instance the French consul in Syria initiated the accusation) and in Tiszaeszlár, Hungary, in 1882. In both cases, torture was used to obtain false confessions, though the accused were ultimately cleared. The most infamous occurrence of the blood libel in modern times was the case of Mendel Beilis, a Jewish bookkeeper in Odessa who was accused of ritual murder by the tsarist government in 1911. Imprisoned for more than two years, he was eventually acquitted by an all-Christian jury.

From Russian Orthodox circles too arose the *Protocols of the Learned Elders of Zion*, a fraudulent documentation of an alleged international Jewish conspiracy to conquer the world by subverting the social order through liberalism, Freemasonry, and other modern movements. The concoction appeared about the turn of the 20th century and was proved to be a forgery by 1921. Despite this demonstration, the *Protocols* was widely used in anti-Semitic propaganda in Europe, the United States, and the Arab world into the 21st century.

In the 20th century, Jews and Christians moved toward mutual understanding. Although many Christians continued to hold irrational and hostile attitudes toward Jews, some liberal Christian voices were raised against anti-Semitism in the early decades of the century. In the United States the National Conference of Christians and Jews was founded in 1928 in response to the virulent anti-Semitism propagated in Henry Ford's newspaper, the *Dearborn Independent*. Some Christian leaders spoke out during the 1930s against the Nazi persecution of the Jews, but the majority of Christian leaders in Europe remained silent, even during the Holocaust. In 1946, however, the World Council of Churches denounced anti-Semitism, and in 1965 the Second Vatican Council of the Roman Catholic Church adopted the schema on the Jews and other non-Christian religions, which formally revised the church's traditional attitude toward the Jews as the killers of Christ. A growing feeling of ecumenism was shared between Jews and Christians. Indeed, Pope John Paul II made improved relations between Catholics and Jews a hallmark of his papacy. Although there remain many difficulties related to the question of the place that Zionism and the State of Israel hold within Judaism, the older forms of official church anti-Semitism have been radically diminished.

ZIONISM

The most striking of the new phenomena in Jewish life was Zionism, which, insofar as it focused on the return to Zion (the poetic term for the Holy Land), recalled older religious themes. Because it stressed the establishment of a secular state, however, Zionism was yet another example of the secularization of Jewish life and of Jewish messianism. In its secular aspects, Zionism attempted to complete the emancipation of the Jews by transforming them into a nation like all other nations. Although it drew upon the general currents of 19th-century European nationalism, its major impetus came from the revival of a virulent form of racist anti-Semitism in the last decades of the 19th century, as previously noted. Zionism reacted to anti-Semitic contentions that the Jews were aliens in European society and could never hope to be integrated into it in significant numbers. It transformed this charge into a basic premise of a program of national regeneration and resettlement. Zionism has come to occupy roughly the same place in Jewish life as the Social Gospel did in Christian life. Involvement in Israel as the new centre of Jewish energies, creativity, and renewal served as a kind of secular religion for many Diaspora Jews.

AMERICAN JUDAISM

The history of Judaism in the United States is the story of several fresh beginnings. In the colonial period the character of the tiny American Jewish community was shaped by the earliest Sephardic immigrants. The community was officially Orthodox but, unlike European Jewish communities, was voluntaristic, and by the early 19th century much of the younger generation had moved away from the faith. By the mid-19th century a new wave of central European immigrants revived the declining community and remade it to serve their own needs. Primarily small shopkeepers and traders, the new immigrants migrated westward, founding new Jewish centres that were almost entirely controlled by laymen.

Life on the frontier in an open society created a predisposition for religious reform, and it is significant that the greatest American Reform Jewish leader of the 19th century, Isaac Mayer Wise, was based in Cincinnati, Ohio. Wise sought to unite all of American Jewry in the new nontraditional institutions that he founded: the Union of American Hebrew Congregations (1873), Hebrew Union College (1875), and the Central Conference of American Rabbis (1889); but his ever more radical reforming spirit ultimately drove traditionalist elements into opposition.

The head of the traditionalists was Isaac Leeser (1806–68), a native of Germany, who had attempted to create an indigenous American community along the lines of a modernized traditionalism. After his death, Conservative forces became disorganized, but, in reaction to Reform, they defined themselves by their attachment to the Sabbath, the dietary laws, and especially to Hebrew as the language of prayer. Under the leadership of Sabato Morais (1823–97), a traditional Sephardic Jew of Italian birth, Conservative circles in 1886 founded a rabbinic seminary of their own, the Jewish Theological Seminary of America.

The eastern European immigrants who moved in large numbers to American shores from 1881 to 1914 were profoundly different in culture and manners from the older elements of the American Jewish community, and they and their descendants have made American Judaism what it is today. The bridge between the existing Jewish community led by German Jews of Reform persuasion and the new immigrant masses was the traditionalist element among the older settlers. A traditionalist, Cyrus Adler (1863–1940), cooperated with the German Reform circle of Jacob Schiff (1847–1920) in reorganizing the Jewish Theological Seminary (1902) and other institutions for the purpose of Americanizing the eastern European immigrants. Enough eastern European rabbis and scholars had immigrated, however, to create their own synagogues, which reproduced the customs of the Old World. In 1880 almost all of the 200 Jewish congregations in the United States were Reform, but by 1890 there were 533 synagogues, and most of the new ones founded by immigrant groups were Orthodox. The Union of Orthodox Jewish Congregations, which was established in 1898 by elements associated with the

Temple Emmanuel synagogue, New York City, 1896. Library of Congress, Washington, D.C.

Jewish Theological Seminary, was soon taken over by Yiddish-speaking recent immigrants for whom the seminary was much too liberal. In 1902 immigrant rabbis also formed their own body, the Union of Orthodox Rabbis of the United States and Canada (the Agudath ha-Rabbanim), which fostered the creation of yeshivas (rabbinic academies) of the old type. In 1915 two small yeshivas, Etz Chaim and Rabbi Isaac Elhanan Theological Seminary, merged and undertook a program of further growth, adding Yeshiva College of secular studies in 1928 and becoming Yeshiva University in 1945. The eastern European Orthodox elements concentrated primarily on Jewish education, and it was they who introduced the movement for Jewish day schools, analogous to Christian parochial schools. Gradually, an American version of Orthodoxy developed on the Neo-Orthodox model of Samson Raphael Hirsch (1808–88), which combined institutional separatism with a certain openness to general culture.

The immigrants and their children had three desires: to advance socially by joining older congregations or forming their own in an Americanized image, to affirm an unideological commitment to Jewish life, and to maintain their ties to the overseas Jewish communities of their origin. With their strong sense of Jewish personhood, they introduced Zionism into American Jewish life and accepted the basic ideas of the Reconstructionism of Mordecai Kaplan (1881–1983), which was committed to Zionism. A small group of anti-Zionists remained a significant force in the 1930s and '40s, but their central organization, the American Council for Judaism, represented the descendants of earlier German Jewish immigrants. The later immigrants took over all the earlier institutions of the Jewish community and imbued them with their own spirit.

American Jewish religious life is a continuum, from the most traditional Orthodoxy to the most radical Reconstructionism. In theory, all Orthodox groups agree on the revealed nature of all of Jewish law. For Reform groups, the moral doctrine of Judaism is divine and its ritual law is man-made. Conservatives see Judaism as the working out in both areas of a divine revelation that is incarnate in a slowly changing human history. And the Reconstructionists (who also include some Conservative and Reform Jews) view Judaism as the evolving civilization created by the Jewish people in the light of its highest conscience. The role of the rabbi is substantially the same in all three groups: no longer a Talmudic scholar but a preacher, pastor, and administrator, a cross between a parish priest and the leader of an ethnic group. Religious life for the three major Jewish denominations—Orthodox, Reform, and Conservative—revolves around the individual synagogue and the denomination to which it belongs. As religious identification has become increasingly respectable in American life, the Jews have followed the American norm, affiliating in greater numbers with synagogues, though often for ethnic or social rather than religious reasons.

RECONSTRUCTIONISM

Reconstructionism is an American Jewish movement that holds that Judaism is in essence a religious civilization whose religious elements are purely human, naturalistic expressions of a specific culture. Because Reconstructionism rejects the notion of a transcendent God who made a covenant with his chosen people, it does not accept the Bible as the inspired word of God.

The principles of Reconstructionism were first publicly enunciated by Rabbi Mordecai M. Kaplan (1881–1983) in his book Judaism as a Civilization *(1934). Kaplan felt that for Jews to survive in modern times, especially in the United States, it was necessary for them to reconstruct their lives on the cultural foundation of a historical peoplehood. This new covenant would serve to unite all Jews, regardless of individual religious beliefs and practices. Because cultural bonds are more fundamental to Judaism than are religious doctrines, all Jews can live a distinctive Jewish life without necessarily being religiously Jewish.*

To maintain and strengthen their identity, Jews should, according to Kaplan, cherish all elements of their history (e.g., language, arts, ritual) that underscore their common heritage. They must, however, also learn to respect diversity as an enrichment of Jewish life. They must be willing to accept constant change and creativity as normal signs of vitality and growth. In such a context, all Jews can actively participate in Jewish life while freely mingling with other peoples. They can, moreover, inspire others with such traditional ideals as the unity of all humankind and thus promote the cause of universal freedom, justice, and peace. Reconstructionism strongly supports the State of Israel, not as an ideal home for all Jews, but as the cradle of Jewish civilization and as a focal point for Jews throughout the world.

Though Kaplan's views were, in some respects, more extreme than those advocated by Reform Judaism, he was long associated with Conservative Judaism at the Jewish Theological Seminary of America, in New York City, and was highly respected by his colleagues. Orthodox rabbis, however, could not abide his teachings, and the Union of Orthodox Rabbis declared Kaplan's views totally unacceptable.

Reconstructionists, who numbered about 60,000 in the early 21st century, come mostly from the ranks of the Conservative and Reform movements. Their liturgy resembles that of the Conservatives except for the addition of certain supplementary medieval and modern elements. The monthly Reconstructionism Today, *published by the Jewish Reconstructionist Foundation, is the main voice of the movement.*

JUDAISM IN OTHER LANDS

Modernity came first to the Jewish people of Europe. It was therefore within the European context that representatives of important non-Ashkenazi communities—such as the proto-Zionist Sephardi Judah ben Solomon Ḥai Alkalai (1798–1878) of Sarajevo and the Luzzatto family and Elijah Benamozegh (1822–1900) in Italy—participated in variations of Jewish modernity. In England and France more so than in Germany or Russia, the central focus of Jewish experience was *Wissenschaft des*

Judentums, with its Enlightenment ideology. There the "republic of scholarship" became the synagogue of the Jewish intelligentsia. In neither country did Reform Judaism gain a major foothold, for the Orthodox establishment liberalized its synagogue practice while retaining its essentially conservative outlook. In Anglo-Jewish life in the last decades of the 19th century, the two most pronounced modernist tendencies were the moderate, romantic traditionalism of Solomon Schechter (1847–1915) and the "renewed Karaism" of Claude Joseph Goldsmid Montefiore (1858–1938), whose version of religious reform was "back to the Bible."

In South America and Canada, Jewish modernity appeared late, for European Jewry arrived in those places even later than in the United States, attaining significant numbers only in the 20th century. These communities were dependent on immigrant scholars and intellectuals for serious Jewish thought. Jews in the Arab lands in North Africa and the Middle East, living in traditional societies, entered modernity even later than those on the peripheries of Europe. Many of them received their first introduction to the Western world in schools set up by the Alliance Israélite Universelle (a Jewish defense organization centred in Paris), which combined Jewish education with the language and values of French civilization. Yet most of these communities remained traditionalist almost up to the moment when they were expelled or felt compelled to relocate, beginning in 1948, when the State of Israel was created. The ferment of modernity in all its forms is now being felt in their ranks. In Israel, which has received a large segment of Sephardic Jewry, the attention of these communities has turned to gaining equality with the more advanced Ashkenazim rather than to developing forms of modern Jewish thought.

Other groups that may be described as regional or ethnic include the Bene Israel, descendants of Jewish settlers in the Bombay region of India, whose deviation in some Halakhic matters from the present Orthodox consensus has raised problems for those among them who have migrated to Israel. Another such group is the Black Jews of the United States, whose place in and relation to the rest of the Jewish community remains unclear. The Kaifeng Jews of China are Han Chinese descendants of a community

KAIFENG JEW

Kaifeng Jews are members of the former religious community in Henan province, China, who boasted a careful observance of Jewish precepts over many centuries that has long intrigued scholars. Matteo Ricci, the famous Jesuit missionary, was apparently the first Westerner to learn of the existence of Chinese Jews. In 1605 he was visited by a young Chinese man who claimed to be one of many monotheists living in the city of Kaifeng. Three years later a Chinese Jesuit visited the community, confirmed the existence of a large synagogue (with a Holy of Holies accessible only to the chief rabbi), and testified to the authenticity of Jewish observances. The Jewish character of the community was unmistakable, for the Chinese observed the Sabbath and major religious festivals, practiced circumcision, read the Torah, had Hebrew manuscripts, used name tablets rather than pictures in their synagogue, and abstained from eating pork. Their Chinese name, Tiaojinjiao (literally, "pick out the tendons"), refers to practices prescribed by Jewish dietary laws.

An extant stone tablet dated 1512 and found in Kaifeng claims that Judaism entered China during the latter half of the Han dynasty (206 BCE–220 CE), but it is more likely that Jews entered Kaifeng sometime prior to 1127 from India or Persia (Iran). The oldest known synagogue in Kaifeng was built in 1163.

The religious life of the Jewish community in Kaifeng was permanently disrupted by the protracted period of war and social upheaval that accompanied the establishment of the Qing (Manchu) dynasty in 1644. The flooding of the city in 1642 by rebels to prevent its capture destroyed the synagogue as well as Jewish records, books, and burial grounds. Jewish religious education was also severely disrupted at that time, and these factors, combined with the increased tendency of the Kaifeng Jews to intermarry with Han Chinese or to convert to other religions, resulted in a rapid decline in religious fervour that was never rekindled. The strong ties with past traditions were irreparably severed with the passing of the older generation. Though the synagogue was rebuilt in 1653, few members of the community were left who could read Hebrew by 1700. When the last Chinese rabbi died in 1800, the spirit of Judaism in Kaifeng was so enfeebled that Christian missionaries were able to purchase Torah scrolls, Hebrew manuscripts, and records, which eventually were placed in libraries and museums in Europe and the United States.

Efforts by the Portuguese Jews of London in 1760 to contact the Chinese Jews were unsuccessful, as were similar efforts by the Jews of London in 1815. Two Chinese Christian converts, however, dispatched to Kaifeng in 1850 by the Anglican Mission in Hong Kong, visited the synagogue, obtained scrolls and Hebrew manuscripts of the Tanakh (Hebrew Bible), and brought back copies of Hebrew inscriptions. Though few traces of active Judaism remained, the information thus obtained made it possible to reconstruct history. A Protestant missionary visiting Kaifeng in 1866 was told that poverty had forced the Chinese Jews to dismantle their synagogue and sell the stones to Muslims who wished to build a mosque.

In 1870 a letter from Kaifeng arrived in Hong Kong. It was in reply to a letter sent 26 years earlier by a British officer. The reply described the plight of the Kaifeng Jews in pitiful terms. When several attempts by European Jews in China to raise money for the Kaifeng community met with little response, the Chinese Jews were invited to move to Shanghai. An old gentleman and his son arrived in the early 1900s to announce that they were among the last members of the once-flourishing community.

founded sometime before the 12th century by Persian Jewish settlers.

The Falashas of Ethiopia constitute one of the more prominent groups who have developed regionally specific variants of Judaism. The Falashas call themselves House of Israel (Beta Israel) and claim descent from Menilek I, traditionally the son of the Queen of Sheba (Makeda) and King Solomon. Their ancestors, however, were probably local Agew peoples in Ethiopia who were converted by Jews living in southern Arabia in the centuries before and after the start of the Christian Era. The Falasha have a Bible and a prayer book written in Ge'ez, the ancient Ethiopian language. They have no Talmudic laws, but their preservation of and adherence to Jewish traditions is undeniable. They observe the Sabbath, practice circumcision, have synagogue services led by priests (*kohanim*) of the village, follow certain dietary laws of Judaism, observe many laws of ritual uncleanness, offer sacrifices on Nisan 14 in the Jewish religious year, and observe some of the major Jewish festivals. From 1980 to 1992 some 45,000 Falasha fled drought- and war-stricken Ethiopia and emigrated to Israel. The number of Falasha remaining in Ethiopia is uncertain, but estimates ranged to only a few thousand.

Falashas, Ethiopians of Jewish faith, make up a major group of regionally specific variations of Judaism. Jose Cendon/AFP/Getty Images

CONTEMPORARY JUDAISM

As a result of the Holocaust, Judaism has become a non-European religion. Its three major centres, which together include more than three-fourths of world Jewry, are Israel, the Slavic region of the former Soviet Union, and the United States. Although Jews constitute only a small fraction of the population of the United States, Judaism plays an important role in American life. With Roman Catholicism and Protestantism it is regarded as one of the major American faiths. Similarly, in the international realm of Western religion, Judaism has been welcomed as a partner able to deal with other major religions as an equal on issues such as anti-Semitism, human rights, and world peace.

Within its own community, Jewry is faced with the increasing secularization of Jewish identity in its three major centres, each in its own way. In the United States the open society and the "melting pot" ideologies of past generations have fostered among many Jews a sense of Jewish identity increasingly devoid of concrete religious, national, or historical content. In the former Soviet Union, government policy from the 1930s had banned the teaching of Judaism and Jewish culture to the young and had severely discouraged any manifestation of Jewish identity as a sign of the political disloyalty of "rootless cosmopolitans." And in Israel a secular nationalism has taken root, raising questions about the role that Judaism plays in the identity of the average Israeli.

Nonetheless, underneath the external secularization there are signs of a deep and persisting religious fervour, in which the sense of history, community, and personal authenticity figure as the intertwined strands of Jewish religious life, especially as it has been affected by the State of Israel. Some rituals of the Jewish tradition, especially the rites of passage at the crucial stages of individual existence, are almost universally observed. In the United States, for example, more than 80 percent of Jewish children receive some formal religious training. Among Jewish youth there is, in some circles, a quest for tradition. In the United States, Jewish communes have been established that seek new forms of Jewish expression. In Israel, groups such as Mevaqshe Derekh ("Seekers of the Way") have tried to bridge secular Israeli culture and Jewish tradition and to maintain traditional Jewish ethical standards even in wartime. In Russia, thousands of young people gather on several occasions of the year to dance and sing and express solidarity in front of the synagogues in St. Petersburg and Moscow. Still, signs of major weaknesses persist. The rate of intermarriage among Jews in the Diaspora has increased, while regular synagogue attendance, at the very highest 20 percent in the United States, remains far below church attendance.

Despite their lack of traditional piety, there is a general sense among

Jews that they remain Jews not because of the force of anti-Semitism but because of the attractiveness of their tradition and their sense of a common history and destiny. Although in 1945 the world Jewish community, decimated and horrified by the Holocaust, felt in danger of disappearing, there appeared to be no such despair in the last quarter of the century, when there was an expectation that Jewish communal feeling would remain strong—especially, for many or most Jews, in light of the existence of the State of Israel. Judaism enjoyed a heightened dignity in the eyes of the world, not only because of the creation of the State of Israel but also because of Judaism's close relations with other world religions. Although the recurring phenomenon of the alienation of young Jews from their tradition was troubling, it was no more so than in recent past generations. Along with other major religions, Judaism's most disturbing problem was how to deal with secular ideologies and the growth of secularism within its own ranks. Thus, at the beginning of the 21st century, it appeared that Judaism would have to contend with as many problems as the other major religions did, but it would face them with no less confidence—and with more confidence than it had felt at the start of the previous century.

CHAPTER 5

THE LITERATURE OF JUDAISM

A paradigmatic statement is made in the narrative that begins with Genesis and ends with Joshua. In the early chapters of Genesis, the divine is described as the creator of humankind and the entire natural order. In the stories of Eden, the Flood, and the Tower of Babel, humans are recognized as rebellious and disobedient. In the patriarchal stories (about Abraham, Isaac, Jacob, and Joseph), a particular family is called upon to restore the relationship between God and humankind. The subsequent history of the community thus formed is recounted so that God's desired restoration may be recognized and the nature of the obedient community may be observed by his people: the Egyptian servitude, the Exodus from Egypt, the revelation of the "teaching," the wandering years, and finally fulfillment through entrance into the "land" (Canaan). The prophetic books (in the Hebrew Bible these include the historical narratives up to the Babylonian Exile—i.e., Joshua, Judges, Samuel, and Kings) also address the tension between rebellion and obedience, interpreting it within the changing historical context and adding new levels of meaning to the motif of fulfillment and redemption.

From this "narrative theology," as it has been recited throughout the centuries, new formulations of the primal affirmations have been drawn. These have been clothed in philosophical, mystical, ethnic, and political vocabularies, among others. The emphases have been various, the disagreements often profound. No single exposition has exhausted the possibilities of the affirmations or of the relationship between them. Philosophers have expounded them on the highest level of abstraction, using the language of the available philosophical systems. Mystics have enveloped them in the extravagant prose of speculative systems and in simple folktales. Attempts have been made to encompass them in theoretical ethical statements and to express them through practical ethical behaviour. Yet, in each instance, the proposed interpretations have had to come to terms with the spiritual and intellectual demands arising out of the community's experience. The biblical texts, themselves the products of a long period of transmission and embodying more than a single outlook, were subjected to extensive study and interpretation over many centuries and, when required, were translated into other languages. The whole literature remains the basis of further developments, so that any attempt to formulate a statement of the affirmations of Judaism must, however contemporary it seeks to be, give heed to the scope and variety of speculation and formulation in the past.

THE HEBREW BIBLE (TANAKH)

In its general framework, the Hebrew Bible is the account of God's dealing with the Jews as his chosen people, who collectively called themselves Israel. After an account of the world's creation by God and the emergence of human civilization, the first six books narrate not only the history but the genealogy of the people of Israel to the conquest and settlement of the Promised Land under the terms of God's covenant with Abraham, whom God promised to make the progenitor of a great nation. This covenant was subsequently renewed by Abraham's son Isaac and grandson Jacob (whose byname Israel became the collective name of his descendants and whose sons, according to legend, fathered the 13 Israelite tribes) and centuries later by Moses (from the Israelite tribe of Levi). The following seven books continue their story in the Promised Land, describing the people's constant apostasy and breaking of the covenant; the establishment and development of the monarchy in order to counter this; and the warnings by the prophets both of impending divine punishment and exile and of Israel's need to repent. The last 11 books contain poetry, theology, and some additional history.

The Hebrew Bible's profoundly monotheistic interpretation of human life and the universe as creations of God provides the basic structure of ideas that gave rise not only to Judaism and Christianity but also to Islam, which emerged from Jewish and Christian tradition and views Abraham as a patriarch. Except for a few passages in Aramaic, appearing mainly in the apocalyptic Book of Daniel, these scriptures were written originally in Hebrew during the period from 1200 to 100 BCE. The Hebrew Bible probably reached its current form about the 2nd century CE.

Engraving by William Blake for an illuminated edition of The Book of Job, 1825. Courtesy of the trustees of the British Museum; photograph, J.R. Freeman & Co. Ltd.

The Hebrew canon contains 24 books, one for each of the scrolls on which these works were written in ancient times. The Hebrew Bible is organized into three main sections: the Torah, or "Teaching," also called the Pentateuch or the "Five Books of Moses"; the Nevi'im, or Prophets; and the Ketuvim, or Writings. It is often referred to as the Tanakh, a word combining the first letter from the names of each of the three main divisions. Each of the three main groupings of texts is further subdivided. The Torah contains narratives combined with rules and instructions in Genesis, Exodus, Leviticus, Numbers, and Deuteronomy. The books of the Nevi'im are categorized among either the Former Prophets—which contain anecdotes about major Hebrew persons and include Joshua, Judges, Samuel, and Kings—or the Latter Prophets—which exhort Israel to return to God and are named (because they are either attributed to or contain stories about them) for Isaiah, Jeremiah, Ezekiel, and (together in one book known as "The Book of the Twelve") the 12 Minor Prophets (Hosea, Joel, Amos, Obadiah, Jonah, Micah, Nahum, Habakkuk, Zephaniah, Haggai, Zechariah, Malachi). The last of the three divisions, the Ketuvim, contains poetry (devotional and erotic), theology, and drama in Psalms, Proverbs, Job, Song of Songs (attributed to King Solomon),

NEVI'IM AND KETUVIM

The books attributed to the Prophets (navi) comprise the second division of the Hebrew Bible. Known as the Nevi'im, they follow the Torah and precede the Ketuvim, or Writings. In the Hebrew canon the Prophets are divided into (1) the Former Prophets (Joshua, Judges, Samuel, and Kings) and (2) the Latter Prophets (Isaiah, Jeremiah, Ezekiel, and the Twelve, or Minor, Prophets: Hosea, Joel, Amos, Obadiah, Jonah, Micah, Nahum, Habakkuk, Zephaniah, Haggai, Zechariah, and Malachi). The books ascribed to these latter 12 are compiled into one book, "The Book of the Twelve." This canon, though somewhat fluid up to the early 2nd century BCE, was finally fixed by a council of rabbis at Jabneh (Jamnia), now in Israel, at the end of the 1st century CE.

The Ketuvim ("Writings") comprise the third division of the Hebrew Bible. Divided into four sections, the Ketuvim include: poetical books (Psalms, Proverbs, and Job), the Megillot, or Scrolls (Song of Solomon, Ruth, Lamentations of Jeremiah, Ecclesiastes, and Esther), prophecy (Daniel), and history (Ezra, Nehemiah, and 1 and 2 Chronicles).

Thus the Ketuvim are a miscellaneous collection of liturgical poetry, secular love poetry, wisdom literature, history, apocalyptic literature, a short story, and a romantic tale. They were composed over a long period of time—from before the Babylonian Exile in the early 6th century BCE to the middle of the 2nd century BCE—and were not entirely accepted as canonical until the 2nd century CE. Unlike the Torah and the Nevi'im (Prophets), which were canonized as groups, each book of the Ketuvim was canonized separately, often on the basis of its popularity.

Ruth, Lamentations, Ecclesiastes, Esther, Daniel, Ezra-Nehemiah, and Chronicles.

SOURCES AND SCOPE OF THE TORAH

The concept "Giver of Torah" played a central role in the understanding of God, for it is Torah, or "Teaching," that confirms the events recognized by the community as the acts of God. In its written form, Torah was considered to be especially present in the first five books of the Bible (the Pentateuch), which themselves came to be called Torah. In addition to this written Torah, or "Law," there were also unwritten laws or customs and interpretations of them, carried down in an oral tradition over many generations, which acquired the status of oral Torah.

The oral tradition interpreted the written Torah, adapted its precepts to ever-changing political and social circumstances, and supplemented it with new legislation. Thus, the oral tradition added a dynamic dimension to the written code, making it a perpetual process rather than a closed system. The vitality of this tradition is fully demonstrated in the way the ancient laws were adapted after the destruction of the Temple in 70 CE and by the role played by the Talmud in the survival of the Jewish people in exile. By the 11th century, Diaspora Jews lived in a Talmudic culture that united them and that superseded geographical boundaries and language differences. Jewish communities governed themselves according to Talmudic law, and individuals regulated the smallest details of their lives by it.

Central to this vast structure was, of course, the Jewish community's concern to live in accordance with the divine will as it was embodied and expressed in Torah in the widest sense. Scripture, Halakhic and Haggadic Midrash, Mishna, and Gemara were the sources that Jewish leaders used to give their communities stability and flexibility. Jewish communities and individuals of the Diaspora faced novel and unexpected situations that had to be dealt with in ways that would provide continuity while making it possible to exist with the unprecedented.

PROPHECY AND RELIGIOUS EXPERIENCE

Torah in the broad sense includes the whole Hebrew Bible, including the books of the Prophets. According to the Prophets, God was revealed in the nexus of historical events and made ethical demands upon the community. In Rabbinic Judaism the role of the prophet—the charismatic person—as a source of Torah ended in the period of Ezra (i.e., about the time of the return from the Babylonian Exile in the 5th century BCE). This opinion may have been a reaction to the luxuriant growth of apocalyptic speculation, a development that was considered dangerous and unsettling in the period after the Bar Kokhba revolt, or Second Jewish Revolt (132–135 CE). Indeed, there seems to have developed a suspicion that reliance on unrestrained individual experience as a source of Torah was inimical to the welfare of the community. Such an attitude was by no means new. Deuteronomy (13:2–19) had already warned against such "misleaders." The culmination of this attitude is to be found in a Talmudic narrative in which even the *bat qol*, the divine "echo" that announces God's will, is ignored on a particular occasion. Related to this is the reluctance on the part of teachers in the early centuries of the Common Era to point to wonders and miracles in their own time. Far from expressing an ossification of religious experience—the development of the siddur (prayer book) and the Talmudic reports on the devotional life of the rabbis contradict such an interpretation—the attitude seems to be a response to the development of religious enthusiasm such as that exhibited in the behaviour of the Christian church in Corinth—as Paul's First Letter to the Corinthians reveals—and among gnostic sects and sectarians. Thus, even among the speculative mystics of the Middle Ages, where allegorization of Scripture abounds, the structure of the community and the obligations of the individual are not displaced by the deepening of personal religious life through mystical experience. The decisive instance of this is Joseph Karo (1488–1575), who was thought to be in touch with a supernal guide but who was at the same time the author of an important codification of Jewish law, the *Shulḥan ʿarukh*.

Admittedly, there have been occasions when Torah, even in the wide sense, has been rigidly applied. In certain historical situations the dynamic process of Rabbinic Judaism has been treated as a static structure. What is of greater significance, however, is the way in which this tendency toward inflexibility has been reversed by the inherent dynamism of the rabbinic tradition.

Modern Views of Torah

Since the end of the 18th century, the traditional position has been challenged both in detail and in principle. The rise of biblical criticism has raised a host of questions about the origins and development of Scripture and thus about the very concept of Torah, in the senses in which it has functioned in Judaism. Naturalistic views of God have required a reinterpretation of Torah in sociological terms. Other positions of many sorts have been and undoubtedly will be forthcoming. What is crucial, however, is the concern of all these positions to retain the concept of Torah as one of the central and continuing affirmations of Judaism.

MISHNA

The oldest authoritative postbiblical collection and codification of Jewish oral laws is the Mishna, which was systematically compiled by numerous scholars (called *tannaim*) over a period of about two centuries. The codification was given final form early in the 3rd century CE by Judah ha-Nasi. The Mishna supplements the written, or scriptural, laws found in the Torah. It presents various interpretations of selective legal traditions that had been preserved orally since at least the time of Ezra (*c.* 450 BCE).

Intensive study of the Mishna by subsequent scholars (called *amoraim*) in Palestine and Babylonia resulted in two collections of interpretations and annotations of it called the Gemara, or Talmud. In the broader sense of the latter terms, the Mishna and Gemara together make up the Talmud.

TALMUD AND MIDRASH

Second only to the Tanakh in importance and reverence are the commentative and interpretative writings on Torah: the Talmud and the Midrash.

DEFINITION OF TERMS

The Hebrew term *Talmud* ("study" or "learning") commonly refers to a compilation of ancient teachings regarded as sacred and normative by Jews from the time it was compiled until modern times and still so regarded by traditional religious Jews. In its broadest sense, the Talmud is a set of books consisting of the Mishna ("repeated study"), the Gemara ("completion"), and certain auxiliary materials. The Mishna is a collection of originally oral laws supplementing scriptural laws. The Gemara is a collection of commentaries on and elaborations of the Mishna, which in "the Talmud" is reproduced in juxtaposition to the Gemara. For present-day scholarship, however, Talmud in the precise sense refers only to the materials customarily called Gemara—an Aramaic term prevalent in medieval rabbinic literature that was used by the church censor to replace the term *Talmud* within the Talmudic discourse in the Basel edition of the Talmud, published 1578–81. This practice continued in all later editions.

The term *Midrash* ("exposition" or "investigation"; plural, Midrashim) is also used in two senses. On the one hand, it refers to a mode of biblical interpretation prominent in the Talmudic literature; on the other, it refers to a separate body of commentaries on Scripture using this interpretative mode.

OPPOSITION TO THE TALMUD

Despite the central place of the Talmud in traditional Jewish life and thought, significant Jewish groups and individuals have opposed it vigorously. The Karaite sect in Babylonia, beginning in the 8th century, refuted the oral tradition and denounced the Talmud as a rabbinic fabrication. Medieval Jewish mystics declared the Talmud a mere shell covering the concealed meaning of the written Torah, and heretical messianic sects in the 17th and 18th centuries totally rejected it. The decisive blow to Talmudic authority came in the 18th and

19th centuries when the Haskala (the Jewish Enlightenment movement) and its aftermath, Reform Judaism, secularized Jewish life and, in doing so, shattered the Talmudic wall that had surrounded the Jews. Thereafter, modernized Jews usually rejected the Talmud as a medieval anachronism, denouncing it as legalistic, casuistic, devitalized, and unspiritual.

There is also a long-standing anti-Talmudic tradition among Christians. The Talmud was frequently attacked by the church, particularly during the Middle Ages, and accused of falsifying biblical meaning, thus preventing Jews from becoming Christians. The church held that the Talmud contained blasphemous remarks against Jesus and Christianity and that it preached moral and social bias toward non-Jews. On numerous occasions the Talmud was publicly burned, and permanent Talmudic censorship was established.

On the other hand, since the Renaissance there has been a positive response and great interest in rabbinic literature by eminent non-Jewish scholars, writers, and thinkers in the West. As a result, rabbinic ideas, images, and lore, embodied in the Talmud, have permeated Western thought and culture.

CONTENT, STYLE, AND FORM

The Talmud is first and foremost a legal compilation. At the same time it contains materials that encompass virtually the entire scope of subject matter explored in antiquity. Included are topics as diverse as agriculture, architecture, astrology, astronomy, dream interpretation, ethics, fables, folklore, geography, history, legend, magic, mathematics, medicine, metaphysics, natural sciences, proverbs, theology, and theosophy.

This encyclopaedic array is presented in a unique dialectic style that faithfully reflects the spirit of free give-and-take prevalent in the Talmudic academies, where study was focused upon a Talmudic text. All present participated in an effort to exhaust the meaning and ramifications of the text, debating and arguing together. The mention of a name, situation, or idea often led to the introduction of a story or legend that lightened the mood of a complex argument and carried discussion further.

This text-centred approach profoundly affected the thinking and literary style of the rabbis. Study became synonymous with active interpretation rather than with passive absorption. Thinking was stimulated by textual examination. Even original ideas were expressed in the form of textual interpretations.

The subject matter of the oral Torah is classified according to its content into Halakha and Haggada and according to its literary form into Midrash and Mishna. Halakha ("law") deals with the legal, ritual, and doctrinal parts of Scripture, showing how the laws of the written Torah should be applied in life. Haggada ("narrative") expounds on the nonlegal parts of Scripture, illustrating biblical narrative, supplementing its stories, and exploring its ideas. The term *Midrash* denotes the exegetical method by which the oral tradition interprets and elaborates scriptural text. It refers also to the large collections of Halakhic and Haggadic materials that take the form of a running commentary on the Bible and that were deduced from Scripture by this exegetical method. In short, it also refers to a body of writings. Mishna is the comprehensive compendium that presents the legal content of the oral tradition independently of scriptural text.

MODES OF INTERPRETATION AND THOUGHT

Midrash was initially a philological method of interpreting the literal meaning of biblical texts. In time it developed into a sophisticated interpretive system that reconciled apparent biblical contradictions, established the scriptural basis of new laws, and enriched biblical content with new meaning. Midrashic creativity reached its peak in the schools of Rabbi Ishmael and Akiba, where two different hermeneutic methods were applied. The first was primarily logically oriented, making inferences based upon similarity of content and analogy. The second rested largely upon textual scrutiny, assuming that words and letters that seem superfluous teach something not openly stated in the text.

The Talmud (i.e., the Gemara) quotes abundantly from all Midrashic collections and concurrently uses all rules employed by both the logical and textual schools; moreover, the Talmud's interpretation of Mishna is itself an adaptation of the Midrashic method. The Talmud treats the Mishna in the same way that Midrash treats Scripture. Contradictions are explained through reinterpretation. New problems are solved logically by analogy or textually by careful scrutiny of verbal superfluity.

The strong involvement with hermeneutic exegesis—interpretation according to systematic rules or principles—helped develop the analytic skill and inductive reasoning of the rabbis but inhibited the growth of independent abstract thinking. Bound to a text, they never attempted to formulate their ideas into the type of unified system characteristic of Greek philosophy. Unlike the philosophers, they approached the abstract only by way of the concrete. Events or texts stimulated them to form concepts. These concepts were not defined but, once brought to life, continued to grow and change meaning with usage and in different contexts. This process of conceptual development has been described by some as "organic thinking." Others use this term in a wider sense, pointing out that, although rabbinic concepts are not hierarchically ordered, they have a pattern-like organic coherence. The meaning of each concept depends on the total pattern of concepts, for the idea content of each grows richer as it interweaves with the others.

Early Compilations

Ezra the scribe who, according to the Book of Ezra, reestablished and reformed the Jewish religion in the 5th century BCE, began the "search in the Law . . . to teach in Israel statutes and ordinances."

His work was continued by *soferim* (scribes), who preserved, taught, and interpreted the Bible. They linked the oral tradition to Scripture, transmitting it as a running commentary on the Bible. For almost 300 years they applied the Torah to changing circumstances, making it a living law. They also introduced numerous laws that were designated "words of the *soferim*" by Talmudic sources. By the end of this period, rabbinic Judaism—the religious system constructed by the scribes and rabbis—was strong enough to withstand pressure from without and mature enough to permit internal diversity of opinion.

At the beginning of the 2nd century BCE, a judicial body headed by the *zugot*—pairs of scholars—assumed Halakhic authority. There were five pairs in all, between *c.* 150 and 30 BCE. The first of the *zugot* also introduced the Mishnaic style of transmitting the oral tradition.

The Making of the Mishna: 2nd–3rd Centuries

Hillel and Shammai, the last of the *zugot*, ushered in the period of the *tannaim*— "teachers" of the Mishna—at the end

The ancient art of writing the Torah is kept alive even today. Mario Tama/Getty Images

of the 1st century BCE. This era, distinguished by a continuous attempt to consolidate the fragmentary Midrashic and Mishnaic material, culminated in the compilation of the Mishna at the beginning of the 3rd century CE. The work was carried out in the academies of Hillel and Shammai and in others founded later. Most scholars believe that Halakhic collections existed prior to the fall of Jerusalem, in 70 CE. Other compilations were made at Jabneh, a Palestinian town near the Mediterranean, as part of the effort to revitalize Judaism after the disaster of 70 CE. By the beginning of the 2nd century there were many such collections. Tradition has it that Rabbi Akiba organized much of this material into separate collections of Midrash, Mishna, and Haggada, and introduced the formal divisions in tannaitic literature. His students and other scholars organized new compilations that were studied in the different academies.

After the rebellion of the Jews against Roman rule led by Simeon bar Kokhba in 132–135, when the Sanhedrin (the Jewish supreme court and highest academy) was revived, the Mishnaic compilation adopted by the Sanhedrin president became the official Mishna. The Sanhedrin reached its highest stature under the leadership of Judah ha-Nasi (Judah the Prince, or President), and he was also called Rabbi, as the preeminent teacher.

It seems certain that the official Mishna studied during his presidency was the Mishna we know and that he was its editor. Judah aimed to include the entire content of the oral tradition. He drew heavily from the collections of Akiba's pupils but also incorporated material from other compilations, including early ones. Nevertheless, the accumulation was such that selection was necessary. Thus almost no Midrash or Haggada was included. Colleagues and pupils of Judah not only made minor additions to the Mishna but tried to preserve the excluded material, the Baraitot ("Exclusions"), in separate collections. One of these was the Tosefta ("Addition"). Midrashic material was gathered in separate compilations, and later revisions of some of these are still extant. The language of all of the tannaitic literature is the new Hebrew developed during the period of the Second Temple (c. 6th century BCE–1st century CE).

THE MAKING OF THE TALMUDS: 3RD–6TH CENTURIES

The expounders of the Mishna were the *amoraim* ("interpreter"), and the two Talmuds—the Palestinian (or Jerusalem) and the Babylonian—consist of their explanations, discussions, and decisions. Both take the form of a running commentary on the Mishna.

The foundations for these two monumental works were begun by three disciples of Judah ha-Nasi: Johanan bar Nappaḥa, Rav (Abba Arika), and Samuel bar Abba, in their academies at Tiberias, in Palestine, and at Sura and Nehardea in

Babylonia, respectively. Centres of learning where the Mishna was expounded existed also at Sepphoris, Caesarea, and Lydda in Palestine. In time new academies were established in Babylonia, the best known being those at Pumbedita, Mahoza and Naresh, founded by Judah bar Ezekiel, Rava, and Rav Pappa, respectively. The enrollment of these centres often numbered in the thousands, and students spent many years there. Those who no longer lived on the academy grounds returned twice annually for the *kalla*, a month of study in the spring and fall.

Academies differed in their methods of study. Pumbedita, for example, stressed casuistry, while Sura emphasized breadth of knowledge. Students often moved from one academy to another and even from Palestine to Babylonia or from Babylonia to Palestine. This kept open the channels of communication between the various academies and resulted in the inclusion of much Babylonian material in the Palestinian Talmud, and vice versa.

Despite the overwhelming similarity of the two Talmuds, however, they do differ in some ways. The Palestinian Talmud is written in the Western Aramaic dialect, the Babylonian in the Eastern. The former is invariably shorter, and, not having been subject to final redaction, its discussions are often incomplete. Its explanations tend to remain closer to the literal meaning of the Mishna, preferring textual emendation to casuistic interpretation. Finally, some of the legal concepts in the Babylonian Talmud reflect the influence of Persian law, for Babylonia was under Persian rule at the time.

The main endeavour of the *amoraim* was to thoroughly explain and exhaust the meaning of the Mishna and the Baraitot. Apparent contradictions were reconciled by such means as explaining that conflicting statements referred to different situations or by asserting that they stemmed from the Mishnayot (Mishnas) of different *tannaim*. The same techniques were used when amoraic statements contradicted the Mishna. These discussions took place for hundreds of years, and their content was passed on from generation to generation, until the compilation of the Talmud.

The portion of the Palestinian Talmud dealing with the three Bavot ("gates")—that is, the first three tractates of the fourth order of the Mishna (for orders and tractates, see Talmudic and Midrashic literature, in the following section)—was compiled in Caesarea in the middle of the 4th century and is distinguished from the rest by its brevity and terminology. The remainder was completed in Tiberias some 50 years later. It seems likely that its compilation was a rescue operation designed to preserve as much of the Halakhic material collected in Palestinian academies as possible, for by that time the deterioration of the political situation had forced most Palestinian scholars to emigrate to Babylonia.

The Babylonian Talmud was compiled up to the 6th century. Some scholars suggest that the organization of the Talmud

began early and that successive generations of *amoraim* added layer upon layer
to previously arranged material. Others
suggest that at the beginning a stra-
tum called Gemara, consisting only of
Halakhic decisions or short comments,
was set forth. Still others theorize that no
overall arrangement of Talmudic material
was made until the end of the 4th century.

The statement in the tractate *Bava
metzia* that "Rabina and Rav Ashi were
the end of instruction" is most often
understood as referring to the final
redaction of the Talmud. Since at least
two generations of scholars following
Rav Ashi (died 427) are mentioned in
the Talmud, most scholars suggest that
"Rabina" refers to Rabina bar Huna (died
499), and that the redaction was a slow
process lasting about 75 years to the end
of the 5th century.

According to the tradition of the
geonim—the heads of the academies at
Sura and Pumbedita from the 6th to the
11th centuries—the Babylonian Talmud
was completed by the 6th-century
savoraim ("expositors"). But the extent
of their contribution is not precisely
known. Some attribute to them only short
additions. Others credit them with creating the terminology linking the phases
of Talmudic discussions. According to
another view, they added comments and
often decided between conflicting opinions. The proponents of the so-called
Gemara theory noted earlier ascribe
to them the entire dialectic portion of
Talmudic discourse.

TALMUDIC AND MIDRASHIC LITERATURE

Four main genres make up Talmudic
and Midrashic literature: the Mishna, the
Tosefta, the Talmud, and the Midrashim.

MISHNA

The Mishna is divided into six orders
(*sedarim*), each order into tractates
(*massekhtot*), and each tractate into chapters (*peraqim*). The six orders are *Zera'im*,
Mo'ed, *Nashim*, *Neziqin*, *Qodashim*, and
Ṭohorot.

1. *Zera'im* ("Seeds") consists of 11
   tractates: *Berakhot*, *Pea*, *Demai*,
   Kilayim, *Shevi'it*, *Terumot*,
   Ma'aserot, *Ma'aser sheni*, *Ḥalla*,
   'Orla, and *Bikkurim*. Except for
   Berakhot ("Blessings"), which
   treats of daily prayers and grace,
   this order deals with laws related
   to agriculture in Palestine. It
   includes prohibitions against
   mixtures in plants (hybridiza-
   tion), legislation relating to the
   sabbatical year (when land lies
   fallow and debts are remitted),
   and regulations concerning the
   portions of harvest given to the
   poor, the Levites, and the priests.
2. *Mo'ed* ("Festival") consists of
   12 tractates: *Shabbat*, *'Eruvin*,
   Pesaḥim, *Sheqalim*, *Yoma*, *Sukka*,
   Betza, *Rosh Hashana*, *Ta'anit*,
   Megilla, *Mo'ed qaṭan*, and

Ḥagiga. This order deals with ceremonies, rituals, observances, and prohibitions relating to special days of the year, including the Sabbath, holidays, and fast days. Because the half-shekel Temple contribution was collected on specified days, tractate *Sheqalim,* regarding this practice, is included.

3. *Nashim* ("Women") consists of seven tractates: *Yevamot, Ketubbot, Nedarim, Nazir, Soṭa, Giṭṭin,* and *Qiddushin.* This order deals with laws concerning betrothal, marriage, sexual and financial relations between husband and wife, adultery, and divorce. Because Nazirite (ascetic) and other vows may affect marital relations, *Nedarim* ("Vows") and *Nazir* ("Nazirite") are included here.

4. *Neziqin* ("Damages") consists of 10 tractates, the first three of which were originally considered one (the *Bavot*): *Bava qamma, Bava metzia, Bava batra, Sanhedrin, Makkot, Shevu'ot, 'Eduyyot, 'Avoda zara, Avot,* and *Horayot.* This order deals with civil and criminal law concerning damages, theft, labour relations, usury, real estate, partnerships, tenant relations, inheritance, court composition, jurisdiction and testimony, erroneous decisions of the Sanhedrin, and capital and other physical punishments. Because idolatry, in the literal sense of worship or veneration of material images, is punishable by death, *'Avoda zara* ("Idolatry") is included. *Avot* ("Fathers"), commonly called "Ethics of the Fathers" in English, seems to have been included to teach a moral way of life that precludes the transgression of law.

5. *Qodashim* ("Things") consists of 11 tractates: *Zevaḥim, Menaḥot, Ḥullin, Bekhorot, 'Arakhin, Temura, Keretot, Me'ila, Tamid, Middot,* and *Qinnim.* This order incorporates some of the oldest Mishnaic portions. It treats of the Temple and includes regulations concerning sacrifices, offerings, and donations. It also contains a detailed description of the Temple complex.

6. *Ṭohorot* ("Purifications") consists of 12 tractates: *Kelim, Ohalot, Nega'im, Para, Ṭohorot, Miqwa'ot, Nidda, Makhshirin, Zavim, Ṭevul yom, Yadayim,* and *'Uqtzin.* This order deals with laws governing the ritual impurity of vessels, dwellings, foods, and persons, and with purification processes.

TOSEFTA

The Tosefta ("Addition") closely resembles the Mishna in content and order. In its present form it at times supplements the Mishna, at other times comments on it, and often also opposes it. There is no Tosefta on the tractates *Avot, Tamid, Middot,* and *Qinnim.* The Talmud quotes from many other collections of Mishnaiot and Baraitot: some are attributed to *tannaim,* and predate the established Mishna; and others, to *amoraim.* The original material is lost.

TALMUD (GEMARA)

Although the entire Mishna was studied at the Palestinian and Babylonian academies, the Palestinian Talmud (Gemara) covers only the first four orders (except chapters 21–24 of *Shabbat* and chapter 3 of *Makkot*) and the first three chapters of *Nidda* in the sixth order. Most scholars agree that the Palestinian Talmud was never completed to the fifth and sixth orders of the Mishna and that the missing parts of the other orders were lost. A manuscript of chapter 3 of *Makkot* was, in fact, found and was published in 1946.

The Babylonian Talmud does not cover orders *Zera'im* (except *Berakhot*) and *Tohorot* (except *Nidda*) and tractates *Tamid* (except chapters 1, 2, and 4), *Sheqalim, Middot, Qinnim, Avot,* and *'Eduyyot.* Scholars concur that the Talmud for these parts was never completed, possibly because their content was not relevant in Babylonia.

MIDRASHIM

There are two types of Midrashim: Halakhic and Haggadic.

Halakhic

Halakhic Midrashim are exegetic commentaries on the legal content of Exodus, Leviticus, Numbers, and Deuteronomy. The five extant collections are *Mekhilta,* on Exodus; *Mekhilta deRabbi Shim'on ben Yoḥai,* on Exodus; *Sifra,* on Leviticus; *Sifre,* on Numbers and Deuteronomy; *Sifre zuṭa,* on Numbers. (*Mekhilta* means "measure," a norm or rule; *Sifra,* plural *Sifre,* means "writing" or "book.") Critical analysis reveals that *Mekhilta* and *Sifre* on Numbers differ from the others in terminology and method. Most scholars agree that these two originated in the school of Ishmael and the others in that of Akiba. In their present form they also include later additions. Mention should also be made of *Midrash tannaim* on Deuteronomy, consisting of fragments recovered from the Yemenite anthology *Midrash ha-gadol.*

Haggadic

Haggadic Midrashim originated with the weekly synagogue readings and their accompanying explanations. Although Haggadic collections existed in tannaitic times, extant collections date from the 4th–11th centuries. Midrashic compilations were not authoritatively edited and tend to be coincidental and fragmentary.

Most notable among biblical collections is *Midrash rabba* ("Great Midrash"), a composite of commentaries on the Pentateuch and five Megillot (Song

HALAKHAH

In Hebrew, Halakhah literally means "the Way." It is the name for the totality of laws and ordinances that have evolved since biblical times to regulate religious observances and the daily life and conduct of the Jewish people. Quite distinct from the Law of the Torah (the first five books of the Bible), Halakhah purports to preserve and represent oral traditions stemming from the revelation on Mount Sinai or evolved on the basis of it. The legalistic nature of Halakhah also sets it apart from those parts of rabbinic, or Talmudic, literature that include history, fables, and ethical teachings (Haggada). That Halakhah existed from ancient times is confirmed from non-Pentateuchal passages of the Bible, where, for example, servitude is mentioned as a legitimate penalty for unpaid debts (2 Kings 4:1).

Oral traditions concerning Jewish law passed from generation to generation, and eventually it became apparent that they required organization. The work of gathering opinions and interpretations was begun by Rabbi Akiba in the 1st–2nd century CE and carried on by his disciples, such as Rabbi Meïr. Early in the 3rd century, this new compilation, the Mishna, was complete, arranged in its final form by Judah ha-Nasi. Though the Mishna contained the most comprehensive collection of Jewish laws up to that time, it was not meant to settle issues involving contradictory interpretations. Almost immediately, however, Jewish scholars in Palestine and Babylonia began to elaborate extensive interpretations of the Mishna that were called Gemara. When the work was completed several centuries later, the Mishna and the Gemara, taken together, were called the Talmud.

Centuries later, social and economic changes presented new problems of interpretation and required new applications of the law. This gave rise to new compilations of Halakhah by such outstanding scholars as Moses Maimonides in the 12th century, Jacob ben Asher in the 12th and 13th centuries, and Joseph Karo in the 16th century.

Though Judaism acknowledges a continuous development of Halakhah, the law is always viewed as an explication or extension of the original Torah given on Mount Sinai. Conservative rabbis tend to adapt certain Halakhahs to fit conditions in the modern world, as, for instance, the Halakhah regarding observance of the Sabbath. Reform Jews tend to disregard Halakhah, though some of them adhere to certain of its precepts. Interpretations and discussions of law directly related to scriptural texts are referred to as Midrash Halakhah.

of Songs, Ruth, Ecclesiastes, Esther, Lamentations) differing in nature and age. Its oldest portion, the 5th-century *Genesis rabba*, is largely a verse-by-verse commentary, while the 6th-century *Leviticus rabba* consists of homilies and *Lamentations rabba* (end of 6th century) is mainly narrative. The remaining portions of *Midrash rabba* were compiled at later dates.

The *Tanḥuma* (after the late-4th-century Palestinian *amora* Tanḥuma bar

Abba), of which two versions are extant, is another important Pentateuchal Midrash. Additional Midrashic compilations include those to the books of Samuel, Psalms, and Proverbs. Mention should also be made of *Pesiqta* ("Section" or "Cycles") *deRab Kahana* (after a Babylonian *amora*) and *Pesiqta rabbati* ("The Great Cycle"), consisting of homilies on the Torah (Pentateuch) readings that occur on festivals and special Sabbaths.

Haggadic compilations independent of biblical text include *Avot deRabbi Natan, Tanna deve Eliyyahu, Pirqe* ("Chapters") *deRabbi Eliezer,* and tractates *Derekh eretz* ("Correct Conduct"). These primarily deal with ethics, moral teachings, and biblical narrative.

Among the medieval anthologies are the *Yalquṭ* ("Compilation") *Shimoni* (13th century), *Yalquṭ ha-makhiri* (14th century), and *'En Ya'aqov* ("Eye of Jacob," 16th century). The two most important modern Haggadic anthologies are those of Wilhelm Bacher and Louis Ginzberg.

CODES

The Talmud's dialectic style and organization are not those of a code of laws. Accordingly, codification efforts began shortly after the Talmud's completion. The first known attempt was *Halakhot pesuqot* ("Decided Laws"), ascribed to Yehudai Gaon (8th century). *Halakhot gedolot* ("Great Laws"), by Simeon Kiyyara, followed 100 years later. Both summarize

Talmudic Halakhic material, omitting dialectics but preserving Talmudic order and language. The later *geonim* concentrated on particular subjects, such as divorce or vows, introducing the monographic style of codification.

Codification literature gained impetus by the beginning of the 11th century. During the next centuries many compilations appeared in Europe and North Africa. The most notable, following Talmudic order, were the *Hilkhot Harif,* by Isaac Alfasi (11th century), and *Hilkhot Harosh,* by Asher ben Jehiel (13th–14th centuries). Though modelled after *Halakhot gedolot,* the *Hilkhot Harif* encompasses only laws applicable after the destruction of the Temple but includes more particulars. The *Hilkhot Harosh* closely follows Alfasi's code but often also includes the reasoning underlying decisions.

The most important of the topically arranged codifications were the *Mishne Torah, Sefer ha-ṭurim,* and *Shulḥan 'arukh.* The *Mishne Torah* ("The Torah Reviewed") by Maimonides (12th century), is a monumental work, original in plan, language, and order. It encompasses all religious subject matter under 14 headings and includes theosophy, theology, and religion. The *Sefer ha-ṭurim* ("Book of Rows," or " Parts"), by Jacob ben Asher (14th century), the son of Asher ben Jehiel, introduced new groupings, dividing subject matter into four major categories (*ṭurim*) reminiscent of the Mishnaic orders and including only laws applicable after the destruction of the Temple. Finally, the *Shulḥan 'arukh* ("The Prepared Table") by Joseph Karo (16th century), the last of the great codifiers, is structured after the *Sefer ha-ṭurim,* but presents the Sefardic (Middle Eastern and North African) rather than the Ashkenazic (Franco-German and eastern European) tradition, with decisions largely following those of Alfasi, Maimonides, and Rabbi Asher. When the 16th-century Ashkenazic codifier Moses Isserles added his notes, this became the standard Halakhic code for all Jewry.

COMMENTARIES

The interpretive literature on the Talmud began with the rise of academies in Europe and North Africa. The earliest known European commentary, though ascribed to Gershom ben Judah (10th–11th centuries), is actually an eclectic compilation of notes recorded by students of the Mayence (Mainz) Academy. Compilations of this kind, known as *qunṭresim* ("notebooks"), also developed in other academies. Their content was masterfully reshaped and reformulated in the renowned 11th-century commentary of Rashi (acronym of *Rabbi Shlomo Yitzḥaqi*), in which difficulties likely to be encountered by students are anticipated and detail after detail is clarified until a synthesized, comprehensible whole emerges.

The commentaries of Ḥananel ben Ḥushiel and Nissim ben Jacob ben Nissim, the first to appear in North Africa (11th century), are introductory in nature. They summarize the content of Talmudic discussions, assuming that details will be understood once the general idea becomes comprehensible. This style was later followed by the Spanish school, including Joseph ibn Migash and Maimonides. However, as Rashi's work became known, it displaced all other commentaries. (Note its predominant role in the sample page of Talmud.)

A new phase in Talmudic literature was initiated by Rashi's grandchildren, Rabbis Isaac, Samuel, and Jacob, the sons of Meir, who established the school of *tosafot.* (These medieval "additions" are not to be confused with the tannaitic Tosefta previously discussed.) Reviving Talmudic dialectic, they treated the Talmud in the same way that it had treated the Mishna. They linked apparently unrelated statements from different Talmudic discourses and pointed out the fine distinctions between seemingly interdependent statements. This dialectic style was soon adopted in all European academies. Even the writings of Ravad (Abraham ben David), Zerahiah ha-Levi, and Yeshaya deTrani, three of the most original Talmudists (12th century), reflect the impact of Tosafist dialectic.

The works of Meir Abulafia and Menaḥem Meiri, although of the North African genre, include a strong dialectic element. In Spain such dialectic works were known as *ḥiddushim* or *novellae* (because they sought "new insights"), the most famous being those written by four generations (13th–14th centuries) of teacher and pupil: Ramban (Naḥmanides, or Moses ben Naḥman), Rashba (Solomon ben Adret), Ritba (Yomtov ben Abraham), and Ran (Nissim ben Reuben Gerondi).

A major role in establishing Talmudic authority was also played by the *responsa* literature, replies (*responsa*) to legal and religious questions. Beginning in the 7th century, when the Babylonian *geonim* responded in writing to questions concerning the Talmud, it developed into a branch of Talmudic literature that continued to the present. Then, as now, Talmudic authorities were approached for explanations and decisions. Among the *geonim* the best known were Sherira (10th century) and his son Hai. In the Middle Ages the most important were Alfasi, Ibn Migash (Joseph ibn Migash), Maimonides, Ravad (Abraham ben David of Posquières), Ramban, Rashba, Rosh (Asher ben Jehiel), Ran, and Ribash (Isaac ben Sheshet Perfet).

WRITING AND PRINTING THE TALMUDS

Study in the academies was always oral. Hence the question of when the Mishna and Talmud were first committed to writing has been the subject of much discussion. According to some scholars, the process of writing began with Judah ha-Nasi. Others attribute it to the *savoraim*.

The Palestinian Talmud was first printed in Venice (1523–24). All later editions followed this one. Printing of the Babylonian Talmud was begun in Spain about 1482, and there have been more than 100 different editions since. The oldest extant full edition appeared in Venice (1520–23). This became the prototype for later printings, setting the type of page and pagination (a total of close to 5,500 folios). The standard edition was printed in Vilna beginning in 1886. It carries many commentaries and commentaries upon commentaries. In the reproduced here, the Mishna and the Gemara are placed in the centre column of the page and are printed in the heavy type. The commentary of Rashi is always located in the inner column of the page and the *tosafot* in the outer column. Other commentaries and references to legal codes and to scriptural verses surround the major commentaries, in smaller type. Talmudic citations are made by tractate name, folio number, and side of the folio (a or b).

NONLEGAL SUBJECT MATTER

The Talmudic rabbis never formally systematized their beliefs. Nevertheless, their underlying religious concepts are clearly reflected in their decisions, ideas, and attitudes.

MAIN RELIGIOUS DOCTRINES

Preeminent in rabbinic thinking were the concepts of God, Torah, and Israel.

God

The rabbinic God was primarily the biblical God who acted in history, the creator and source of life who was experienced through the senses rather than intellect. In reaction to sectarian teachings (i.e., gnosticism and early Christianity), however, the rabbis stressed God's universality, absolute unity, and direct involvement with the world. His immanence and transcendence (being present in and beyond the universe) were emphasized, and biblical anthropomorphisms (ascribing human attributes to God) were explained metaphorically. The rabbis also stressed an intimacy into the relationship between God and man. God became the father to whom each individual could turn in direct prayer for his needs. To the names YHWH and Elohim, which traditionally were identified with God's mercy and judgment, respectively, the rabbis added new terms reflecting his other attributes—for example, Shekhina ("Presence"), representing his omnipresence, or immanence; and Maqom ("Place"), his transcendence.

Torah

Torah, in the Talmudic sense, refers to all religious and ethical teachings handed down by tradition. According to the rabbis, God created the Torah long before the world. It contained the eternal divine formula for the world's future workings and thus the answers to all problems for all times and all people. God himself is depicted as studying the Torah, for even he cannot make decisions concerning the world that contradict it.

Israel

The people Israel, according to the rabbis, were chosen by God to be the guardian of his Torah, and, just as God chose Israel, Israel chose God. Thus, the concept of Israel as a nation bound together by an irrevocable commitment to bring the Torah to the world, and bearing corporate responsibility for this mission, was formed. No Jew can free himself from this commitment, but anyone accepting it, regardless of race, becomes a full-fledged Jew with obligations binding him and his descendants.

With this in mind, the rabbis repeatedly emphasized the importance of studying Torah. They pointed out that the Torah is not a declaration of religious beliefs. Rather it is a statement of a discipline regulating each detail of life. Any transgression of this discipline hampers the divine plan of establishing God's way of life in this world.

Worship

The intensive rabbinic religious involvement led to the growth of a new concept of worship. While in the Bible worship was usually centred in the sanctuary of the Temple in Jerusalem, the rabbis, particularly after the destruction of the Second Temple (70 CE), attempted to sanctify all of life. Thus, they said that one must bless God upon arising in the morning, before dressing, before and after meals, and in all ordinary daily actions or routines.

Each move in life should be an act of worship glorifying God's name.

Messianic Kingdom

In rabbinic thinking the establishment of God's kingdom was tied to the Messiah, who was to be a descendant of King David—wise, just, a great scholar, a moral leader, and courageous king. He would redeem the Jews from exile and reestablish their independence in the land of Israel. With this the world would be ushered into a new era of righteousness and universal peace. The rabbis referred to this era as "the world to come," portraying it as an immense academy in which the righteous would study Torah without interruption. They refrained from describing it further, saying that human language and fantasy are inadequate to its wonders.

The nature of the Messiah and the time of his arrival raised much speculation. Following the defeat of Bar Kokhba, leader of the revolt against Roman rule (135 CE), the Messiah's coming, in rabbinic thought, faded into the mysterious and distant future, and descriptions concerning his personality assumed supernatural overtones.

DOCTRINE OF HUMANITY

Human fate, achievements and failures, and being and nothingness all occupy an important place in Talmudic literature. The rabbis' concept of humanity was a universal one. While they assumed that Jews are bound by greater religious duties than others, they considered all people equal, all created in the image of God. "Therefore, but a single man was created . . . That none should say to his fellow, 'My father was greater than thy father'" (tractate *Sanhedrin*).

The world, according to the Talmud, was created for the sake of human beings, and it is incumbent upon them to keep it in order. Personal responsibility begins at home. One must care for one's own health, marry, build a family, provide for and educate children, and honour parents, friends, and elders. One also carries social responsibilities and has to be part of the community. A person must learn a trade and work so that he does not become a burden to the community.

The uniqueness of human beings in this world, likened by the Talmud to the uniqueness of God in the universe, lies in their freedom of choice. Nature follows its laws and angels their missions, but an individual is his or her own master. The rabbis considered the human being to be a wondrous and harmonious being. The duality of human nature was explained by the existence of a good and bad impulse, personified by two angels, *yetzer ha-ṭov* (the good inclination) and *yetzer ha-ra'* (the evil inclination), which enter each human after birth. It is one's duty to overcome the evil inclination, and one is rewarded for accomplishing this. Moreover, because there is corporate

A Jewish father, following the Talmud's instruction to educate his children, reads to them at home. Rosebud Pictures/The Image Bank/Getty Images

responsibility, not only is the sinner punished but the community at large also suffers. Yet one can reverse the course of sin and punishment by repentance. Although repentance may be accompanied by formal and ceremonial acts, such as fasting, its basic principle is the renunciation of the sin and the wholehearted decision not to repeat it. When someone transgresses against God, his sin is forgiven by repentance alone, but when he transgresses against other people, he must make good his wrongdoing as well as repent.

Medicine and Science

The Talmud devoted considerable attention to the maintenance of good health, regarding it a religious duty. A keen understanding of the importance of hygiene in preventing illness was reflected in an emphasis upon bodily cleanliness. The rabbis also stressed the necessity for moderation in eating and drinking and the importance of a proper diet. The Talmud prescribed remedies for illnesses and mentioned surgical techniques, such as cesarean section.

Religious concerns surrounding the calendar, prohibitions against planting seeds of different kinds together, dietary laws, and Sabbath-walking limits resulted in an intense rabbinical interest in astronomy, zoology, mathematics, and geometry.

LEGEND AND FOLKLORE

Side by side with the Midrashic Haggada, which was the outgrowth of Bible exegesis and developed in the academies, the Talmuds and Midrashic collections contain a large quantity of Haggadic material with mythological rudiments, allusions to pagan beliefs and customs, and folkloristic elements of a world strange to the rabbis. Folktales and legends, animal lore, and adventure narratives, containing pagan ideas and beliefs, that were told by their Gentile neighbours were no doubt a major attraction to the common Jews, especially those in the countryside (the 'am ha-aretz, or "people of the land"). The rabbis realized the great danger involved in this situation and developed their own folk material. They adopted the dramatic and artistic parts of these stories but rejected the unwanted elements, replacing them with their own ideas. Thus the animals and birds in fables quote the Bible and discuss it in the same manner that the rabbis do.

Ancient mythology seems to have been well known and liked by the Jewish masses. Again, to fight its influence, the rabbis reworked its content in their own spirit. They retained the mythological suspense—the sea tries to drown the earth—but there is no mythological struggle between equal powers; angels try to prevent the creation of man, but they do not possess titanic power. All are subdued by the command of God. Thus, the rabbis

HAGGADA

Those parts of rabbinical, or Talmudic, literature that do not deal directly with the laws incumbent upon Jews in the conduct of their daily life are together called Haggada. The contents of Haggada can be broken down into five classes: (1) interpretations and expositions of Biblical stories and chronicles; (2) ethical teachings in the form of homilies, maxims, parables, similes, fables, riddles, and witticisms; (3) theological works, including religious speculations, apologetics, and polemics; (4) popular science, including medicine, astronomy, mathematics, magic, and astrology; and (5) history, including embellishments of postbiblical Jewish history, legends, sagas, biographical stories, and folklore.

The writing of Haggada began about the 5th century BCE and reached its peak in the 2nd to 4th century CE as a defensive response to the rise of Christianity. Haggada make up about one-third of the Babylonian Talmud and about one-sixth of the Palestinian Talmud. They are also collected in the Midrash. Traditionally, Haggada appealed to the less-educated sections of the Jewish community, in contrast to Halakha (legal literature), which was the province of the learned.

transformed the ancient myths into dramatic evidence against polytheism. (See also Chapter 10: Jewish Myth and Legend.)

Astrology, Magic, and Divination

Astrology was a recognized science in the ancient world. The rabbis could not reject it entirely, and some concluded that the power of the stars is confined to Gentiles. Others made it part of God's order, saying that stars influence this world in the same way that climate influences plants. The rabbis strenuously objected to omens and other forms of divination because they considered them magic. Dreams were considered by some rabbis as meaningless, while others saw in them an element of prophecy.

The rabbis believed in the efficacy of magic but strenuously objected to its practice. They permitted only magic that had been proved effective in healing. They also permitted the use of incantations for the purpose of counteracting the hold of magic. Because of their supposedly protective nature, the use of amulets was also countenanced.

The existence of a demonic kingdom was accepted by the rabbis without question. Evil spirits are invisible and fill the nether world. They avoid sunlight and concentrate in waters and deserted places. They also mingle with people, trouble them, and help them. They have passions and are born and die like people. However, they also have some of the traits and powers of angels. The evil eye was considered as dangerous as evil spirits. It was thought that for mysterious reasons some people have the power to injure others by looking at them and that it is generally jealousy that triggers this effect. The rabbis, however, repeatedly emphasized that all of these strange powers are under the divine government and, moreover, that they cannot hurt the pious.

Talmudic Law and Jurisprudence

Unlike the Romans, who considered ritual law (*fas*) God-given and social law (*lex*) man-made, the rabbis believed all Jewish law to be of divine origin. Thus, for example, unfairness in labour relations was considered a religious sin and caring for the sick a religious obligation. Though familiar with the concept of natural law (ethical principles inherent in the nature of things and apprehensible through human reason), the rabbis objected to making nature the basis of law. Even rabbinic ordinances were regarded as having validity only because the authority of the rabbis is sanctioned by the Torah.

Methods of Arriving at Legal Principle and Decisions

Ancient Halakha knew no controversy. The earliest controversy dates to the pre-tannaitic *zugot*. Hillel and Shammai differed on significant issues, and, with the rise of their schools, Halakhic uniformity began to crumble. Halakha became a scholastic discipline that developed in academic rather than judicial settings, more and more issues remaining unresolved. More than 300 controversies between the schools of Hillel and Shammai (called the House of Hillel and the House of Shammai, respectively) are reported in Talmudic sources. As time passed, disputes proliferated even more and were considered legitimate provided they conformed to the rule of Halakhic discipline.

No attempt was made to restore Halakhic uniformity until the beginning of the 2nd century CE. Controversies were sometimes resolved by citing old traditions, by establishing precedents, or, when the sages could convene, by vote taking.

At Jabneh, Gamaliel II, the president of the revived Sanhedrin (c. 80–c. 115 CE), attempted to suppress diversity of opinion but failed. The right to differ was already established. Moreover, in the Halakhic collection compiled at Jabneh (tractate 'Eduyyot'), the views of individual scholars were preserved. The sages at Jabneh, however, did take a major step toward restoring Halakhic consistency by upholding the generally more lenient views of the House of Hillel over those of the House of Shammai, thus establishing the Hillelite tradition as the main trend of rabbinic Judaism.

The principle that differing opinions should be recorded was followed by Judah ha-Nasi in his Mishna. Modern scholars differ as to whether he meant to compile a code of law or merely a Halakhic collection. The *amoraim*, however, accepted his Mishna as the definitive code and introduced a set of guidelines according to which disputes were decided. Thus, for example, collective (". . . the sages said") and individual opinions stated anonymously were taken as law; Akiba's decisions were upheld over those of his colleagues. Similar guidelines developed also with regard to amoraic controversies.

With the completion of the Talmud, a new phase in Halakhic development began. Not only were there two different Talmuds and a large Haggadic literature but even within each of the Talmuds diversified opinions were reported. The *geonim* laid down rules governing the use of this enormous literature for lawmaking. They designated the Babylonian Talmud the highest authority, taking the Palestinian Talmud into consideration only when it did not disagree with the Babylonian or when the latter expressed no opinion on a subject. They also deprived the Haggadic literature of Halakhic authority and set guidelines for the precedence of opinion among *amoraim*. These geonic rules served as the basis of all future codifications.

After the geonic period, two methods of decision making were applied. The first of these primarily relied on the authoritative codes. The Mediterranean rabbis, for example, made the code of Maimonides the source of all of their lawmaking. The second method relied on the original Talmudic sources for decision making. This method was applied by the Tosafists and their followers, who, though they consulted the older codes, did not accept them as the final authorities. The *responsa* literature represents a synthesis of these two methods. Although it makes use of codes as the main source of law, its decisions are always accompanied by a discussion and analysis of earlier relevant literature. This approach has been used by rabbis to the present day.

Additionally, in particular instances throughout the ages rabbinic authorities promulgated ordinances (*taqqanot*) and edicts (*gezerot*). These were made in response to pressing needs of time and circumstance, and this form of lawmaking was most frequently used by rabbinic synods in the Middle Ages.

ADMINISTRATION OF JUSTICE

A comprehensive judicial system is described in Talmudic sources.

Courts

The highest court was the Great Sanhedrin. It consisted of 71 members and convened daily in one of the Temple halls. It was the highest legal and religious authority in the country and had exclusive jurisdiction over matters of a national and public nature. It also functioned as the court of appeals, dealing with cases that were not resolved by the lower courts.

Next in line of judicial authority was the Lesser Sanhedrin. Each town with a population of 120 or more had a court of this kind. These courts each consisted of 23 members and dealt with cases involving capital punishment.

The members of the Sanhedrins had to be ordained, pious, mature in age, sound in mind and body, of wide knowledge, and of pure Jewish descent. Persons who were too old or who had never had children were ineligible, for it was thought that they might not be merciful.

The lower courts dealt with all remaining cases. Each consisted of three members and convened on Mondays and Thursdays. In cases involving a penalty the three judges had to be ordained, but in those involving ordinary monetary litigation ordination was not required. In the latter type of case, concerned parties were allowed the alternative of setting up ad hoc arbitration bodies.

Rules of Evidence

Jewish law was extremely strict regarding evidence acceptable in court. In cases entailing physical punishment, no circumstantial evidence, confession, or self-incrimination was recognized. The testimony of two eyewitnesses who confronted the defendant was required. In monetary cases documentary evidence and, at times, oaths were acceptable. Any mental or moral defects or self-interest in the case disqualified witnesses. Relatives could not serve as judges or witnesses.

Trial Procedure

Jewish law knows of no lawyers. After the facts were presented, the court investigated, deliberated, and made its decision by voting. Both sides had to be treated equally, even to the point of seeing to it that neither should be dressed more richly than the other. Each side could be heard only in the presence of the other.

In the trial procedure of capital cases, there was a clear tendency toward bias in favour of the defendant. Thus, only the judges could argue for conviction, but all present could argue for acquittal. The most junior judges voted first so that they would not be unduly influenced by their seniors. A majority of one was sufficient for acquittal, but a majority of two was necessary for conviction. A verdict of acquittal could be reached on the same day but one of conviction only on the following day. When the court erred, only its convictions, and not its acquittals, were reversed.

CRIMINAL LAW

In Jewish law, ritual and nonritual transgressions were crimes punishable by court. Each of the 36 most severe transgressions (e.g., adultery, sodomy, idolatry, sorcery, or murder) carried one of four types of death penalty (stoning, burning, beheading, and strangling). Rabbinic law, however, tended to minimize the practice of capital punishment. The rigorous cross-examination of witnesses and the warning of impending punishment that the transgressor had to receive immediately before committing his crime made it almost impossible to reach a death verdict.

If despite all of this a death verdict was reached, every legal effort was made to allow for a last-minute reversal. Execution was expedited and carried out in the most humane manner possible, the accused being given an opiate before dying. To show their compassion the judges fasted on the day of execution. According to tradition the death penalty was abolished 40 years before the destruction of the Temple, when the Great Sanhedrin was exiled from the Temple complex.

The punishment for 207 other transgressions (e.g., perjury, some forms of incest, the eating of forbidden foods) was flagellation. Here, too, the rabbis tended to be lenient. As in capital cases, a rigorous cross-examination and a warning were required. The maximum number of stripes administered was 39. Prior to flagellation the transgressor was examined medically to determine the number of stripes he could withstand.

Side by side with the preceding penalties, the courts also inflicted *makkat mardut* (disciplinary stripes) and excommunication in cases where regular flagellation could not legally be applied. These two punishments were generally used in Babylonia, where ordained courts did not exist. It should be mentioned also that the Mishna includes a few obscure references to a form of imprisonment used instead of capital punishment.

Civil and Social Law

Although the rabbis considered both ritual and nonritual law sacred, they demonstrated great independence in supplementing the relatively brief relevant scriptural comments and regulations with a comprehensive system of civil and social law. In response to variations in social and economic circumstances, certain differences in Palestinian and Babylonian Talmudic law emerged. The Babylonian rabbis, for example, recognized the law of the state as binding in monetary matters, while the Palestinian rabbis did not. In general, however, Jewish civil law developed relatively autonomously. In instances where the rabbis did adopt alien legal concepts, they elaborated upon them until they could be fully integrated into the spirit and structure of Jewish law.

The following are four of the areas covered:

Social welfare: A comprehensive social welfare system was worked out, including obligations to provide for children, educate them, and train them for a profession. Regulations of charity, medical assistance, and burial of the dead were established.

Torts: Included were all damages caused by a person directly or indirectly via his property. The main aim was to compensate for damages. Consequently, no torts were classified as criminal. Even "an eye for an eye" was interpreted to mean financial compensation.

Family law: Included were regulations concerning marriage and divorce procedures and the innovation of the *ketubba* (marriage contract), which spells out the mutual obligations of husband and wife in the areas of finance, medical care, clothing, housework, sexual relations, and child care. According to biblical law, the right to inherit belongs to sons first. To protect the rights of wives and daughters, rabbinic law obligated the sons to maintain the widows and unmarried daughters.

Financial law: Except for Genesis 23:9 ff., Jer. 32:10, and Ruth 4:8, Scripture makes no reference to transaction procedures. The growth of finances, industry, and land estates led the rabbis to develop laws concerning contracts, partnerships, and legal arrangements to circumvent the biblical prohibition against usury. A series of modes of transaction effecting the transfer and acquisition of property evolved. Labour relations, rents, and leases were also carefully regulated.

The Talmud Today

With the rebirth of a Jewish national state (since 1948) and the concomitant revival of Jewish culture, the Talmud has achieved renewed importance.

Role in the Jewish Community

Orthodox Jewry has always focussed upon study of the Talmud and has believed it to be the absolute Halakhic authority. This belief has now become even further intensified. While rabbinic courts in Israel have jurisdiction only in the area of family life, it has become one of the aims of religious (Orthodox) Jewry there to establish Talmudic law as the general law of the state.

It should also be noted that, aside from the special case of Israel, the legal system described in the preceding text has continued to function down to the present day in Jewish communities all over the world. The jurisdiction of rabbinic courts is voluntarily accepted by Orthodox Jews. These courts continue to exert authority, especially in the areas of family and dietary law, the synagogue, and the organization of charity and social activity.

Conservative Jewry, too, has always been committed to rabbinic tradition. It has, however, conceptualized this tradition as an evolutionary process in which Halakha changes to meet the challenge of new conditions. Professional scholarship was considered crucial for understanding the furthering of this process. More recently, however, as a result of revived nationalism, new emphasis has been put upon lay education. Thus, a network of day schools and higher institutions

Students study the Talmud, which Orthodox Jews consider absolute Halakhic authority. Bloomberg via Getty Images

of learning in which rabbinic tradition occupies a major role in the curriculum has been established. Scores of young Conservative Jews now search in the Talmud for answers to crucial problems, such as abortion and civil violence.

Classical (19th-century) Reform Judaism not only disassociated itself from the Talmud but negated it. More recently, however, Reform leaders have been inclined to reestablish some measure of ritual practice and rabbinic climate. Thus, it is now not unusual to find them stating their decisions in the form of *responsa* and using the rabbinic style of argument and even the casuistic type of Talmudic dialectic (*pilpul*) to justify their religious practices.

TALMUDIC SCHOLARSHIP

Although Talmudic scholarship continues to be advanced by individuals in a number of countries, its two main centres are in Israel and the United States. The Israeli centre has tended to focus upon research of a critical nature. Like Bible criticism, this work is divided between source criticism (i.e., discovering the different sources, their dates, and the methods by which Talmudic literature was formed) and textual criticism (i.e., establishing the correct text and reading). Research is also being done on Haggadic concepts and thinking, Talmudic law, and Halakhic development.

Talmudic scholarship in the United States has tended to be more philosophically and historically oriented. There has been great interest in the development of Halakhah and in folklore and custom. Essential work has been done and continues to be done in the areas of source criticism. A work unique in scope and method is S. Lieberman's commentary on the Tosefta.

CHAPTER 6

BASIC BELIEFS AND DOCTRINES

Judaism is more than an abstract intellectual system, though there have been many efforts to view it systematically. It affirms divine sovereignty disclosed in creation (nature) and in history, without necessarily insisting upon—but at the same time not rejecting—metaphysical speculation about the divine. It insists that the community has been confronted by the divine not as an abstraction but as a person with whom the community and its members have entered into a relationship. It is, as the concept of Torah indicates, a program of human action, rooted in this personal confrontation. Further, the response of this particular people to its encounter with God is viewed as significant for all humankind. The community is called upon to express its loyalty to God and the covenant by exhibiting solidarity within its corporate life on every level, including every aspect of human behaviour, from the most public to the most private. Thus, even Jewish worship is a communal celebration of the meetings with God in history and in nature. Yet the particular existence of the covenant people is thought of not as contradicting but rather as enhancing human solidarity. This people, together with all humanity, is called upon to institute political, economic, and social forms that will affirm divine sovereignty. This task is carried out in the belief not that humans will succeed in these endeavours solely by their own efforts, but that these sought-after human relationships have their source and their goal in God, who assures their actualization. Within the community,

Jewish worshippers at King Herod's palace, Herodium. The community is asked to convey its devotion to God in both public and private. Menahem Kahana/AFP/Getty Images

each Jew is called upon to realize the covenant in his or her personal intention and behaviour.

In considering the basic affirmations of Judaism from this point of view, it is best to allow indigenous formulations rather than systematic statements borrowed from other traditions to govern the presentation.

GOD

An early statement of basic beliefs and doctrines about God emerged in the liturgy of the synagogue some time during the last pre-Christian and first Christian centuries. Some evidence suggests that such formulations were present in the Temple cult that came to an end in the year 70 CE. A section of the siddur that focuses on the recitation of a series of biblical passages (Deuteronomy 6:4–9; Deuteronomy 11:13–21; Numbers 15:37–41) is named for the first of these, Shema ("Hear"): "Hear, O Israel! the Lord is our God, the Lord alone" (or ". . . the Lord our God, the Lord is one"). In the Shema—often regarded as the Jewish confession of faith, or creed—the biblical material and accompanying benedictions are

SHEMA

The Shema is the Jewish confession of faith made up of three scriptural texts (Deuteronomy 6:4–9, 11:13–21; Numbers 15:37–41), which, together with appropriate prayers, forms an integral part of the evening and morning services. The name derives from the initial word of the scriptural verse "Hear, O Israel: The Lord our God is one Lord" (Deuteronomy 6:4). The time for recital was determined by the first two texts: "when you lie down, and when you rise." The Shema texts are also chanted at other times during the Jewish liturgy. The biblical verses inculcate the duty to learn, to study, and to observe the Torah. These texts and their appropriate prayers are consequently sacred to Jews because they contain a profession of faith, a declaration of allegiance to the kingship and kingdom of God, and a symbolic representation of total devotion to the study of the Torah.

arranged to provide a statement about God's relationship with the world and Israel (the Jewish people), as well as about Israel's obligations toward and response to God. In this statement, God—the creator of the universe who has chosen Israel in love ("Blessed art thou, O Lord, who has chosen thy people Israel in love") and showed this love by the giving of Torah—is declared to be "one." His love is to be reciprocated by those who lovingly obey Torah and whose obedience is rewarded and rebellion punished. The goal of this obedience is God's "redemption" of Israel, a role foreshadowed by his action in bringing Israel out of Egypt.

UNITY AND UNIQUENESS

At the centre of this liturgical formulation of belief is the concept of divine singularity and uniqueness. In its original setting, it may have served as the theological statement of the reform under Josiah, king of Judah, in the 7th century BCE, when worship was centred exclusively in Jerusalem and all other cultic centres were rejected, so that the existence of one shrine only was understood as affirming one deity. The idea acquired further meaning, however. It was understood toward the end of the pre-Christian era to proclaim the unity of divine love and divine justice, as expressed in the divine names YHWH and Elohim, respectively. A further expansion of this affirmation is found in the first two benedictions of this liturgical section, which together proclaim that the God who is the creator of the universe and the God who is Israel's ruler and lawgiver are one and the same—as opposed to the dualistic religious positions of the Greco-Roman world, which insisted that the creator God and the lawgiver God are separate and even inimical. This affirmation was developed in philosophical and mystical terms by both medieval and modern thinkers.

CREATIVITY

This "creed," or "confession of faith," underscores in the first benediction the relation of God to the world as that of creator to creation. "Blessed art thou, O Lord our God, King of the Universe, who forms light and creates darkness, who makes peace and creates all things." It adds the assertion that his activity is not in the past but is ongoing and continuous, for "he makes new continually, each day, the work of creation." Thus, unlike the deity of the Stoic worldview, he remains actively present in nature. This creed also addresses the ever-present problem of theodicy. Paraphrasing Isaiah 45:7, "I form the light and create darkness; I make peace, and create evil," it changes the last word to "all" (or "all things"). The change was clearly made to avoid the implication that God is the source of moral evil. Judaism, however, did not ignore the problem of pain and suffering in the world. It affirmed the paradox of suffering and divine sovereignty, of pain and divine providence, refusing to accept the concept of a God that is Lord over only the harmonious and pleasant aspects of reality.

ACTIVITY IN THE WORLD

The second and the third benedictions deal with divine activity within the realm of history and human life. God is the teacher of all humanity; he has chosen the people of Israel in love to witness to his presence and his desire for a perfected society; he will, as redeemer, enable humanity to experience that perfection. These activities, together with creation itself, are understood to express divine compassion and kindness as well as justice (judgment), recognizing the sometimes paradoxical relation between them. Taken together, they disclose Divine Providence—God's continual activity in the world. The constant renewal of creation (nature) is itself an act of compassion overriding strict justice and affording humankind further opportunity to fulfill the divinely appointed obligation.

The basically moral nature of God is asserted in the second of the biblical passages that form the core of this liturgical statement (Deuteronomy 11:13–21). Here, in the language of its agricultural setting, the community is promised reward for obedience and punishment for disobedience. The intention of the passage is clear: obedience is rewarded by the preservation of order, so that the community and its members find wholeness in life; while disobedience—rebellion against divine sovereignty—shatters order, so that the community is overwhelmed by adversity. The passage of time has made the original language unsatisfactory (promising rain, crops, and fat cattle), but the basic principle remains, affirming that, however difficult it is to recognize the fact, there is a divine law and judge. Support for this affirmation is drawn from the third biblical passage (Numbers 15:37–41), which explains that the fringes the Israelites are commanded to wear on the corners of their garments are reminders to observe the commandments of God, who brought forth Israel from Egyptian bondage. The theme of divine redemption is elaborated in the concluding benediction to point toward a future in which the as-yet-fragmentary rule of God will be brought to completion: "Blessed is his name whose glorious kingdom is for ever and ever."

OTHERNESS AND NEARNESS

Within this complex of ideas, other themes are interwoven. In the concept of the divine creator there is a somewhat impersonal or remote quality—of a power above and apart from the world—which is emphasized by expressions such as the trifold declaration of God's holiness, or divine otherness, in Isaiah 6:3: "Holy, holy, holy is the Lord of hosts . . ." The development of surrogate divine names for biblical usage, as well as the substitution of Adonai ("my Lord") for the tetragrammaton (YHWH) in the reading of the Bible itself, suggests an acute awareness of the otherness of God. Yet the belief in the transcendence of God is mirrored by the affirmation of God's immanence. In the biblical narrative it is God himself who is the directly active participant in events, an idea that is emphasized in the liturgical narrative (Haggada; "Storytelling") recited during the Passover meal (seder): "And the Lord brought us forth out of Egypt—not

by an angel, and not by a seraph, and not by a messenger . . ." The surrogate divine name Shekhina, "Presence" (i.e., the presence of God in the world), is derived from a Hebrew root meaning "to dwell," again calling attention to divine nearness. The relationship between these two affirmations, otherness and nearness, is expressed in a Midrashic statement, "in every place that divine awesome majesty is mentioned in Scripture, divine abasement is spoken of, too."

SHEKHINA

In Jewish theology, Shekhina (literally "dwelling," or "presence") is the presence of God in the world. The designation was first used in the Aramaic form, shekinta, in the interpretive Aramaic translations of the Hebrew Bible known as Targums, and it was frequently used in the Talmud, Midrash, and other postbiblical Jewish writings. In the Targums it is used as a substitute for "God" in passages where the anthropomorphism of the original Hebrew seemed likely to mislead. Thus, belief in the transcendence of God was safeguarded. In many passages Shekhina is a reverential substitute for the divine name.

In rabbinic literature the Shekhina is associated with several other religious and theological terms. It is said that the Shekhina descended on the tabernacle and on Solomon's Temple, though it is also said that it was one of the five things lacking in the Second Temple. The glory of God that filled the tabernacle (Exodus 40:34) was thought of as a bright radiance, and the Shekhina is sometimes similarly conceived.

Closely connected with these ideas is the concept of divine personhood, most particularly illustrated in the use of the pronoun "thou" in direct address to God. The community and the individual, confronted by the creator, teacher, and redeemer, address the divine as a living person, not as a theological abstraction. The basic liturgical form, the *berakha* ("blessing"), is usually couched in the second person singular: "Blessed art thou..." This relationship, through which remoteness is overcome and present-ness is established, illuminates creation, Torah, and redemption, for it reveals the meaning of love. From it flow the various possibilities of expressing the divine-human relationship in personal, intimate language. Sometimes, especially in mystical thought, such language becomes extravagant, foreshadowed by vivid biblical metaphors such as the husband-wife relation in Hosea, the "adoption" motif in Ezekiel 16, and the firstborn-son relation in Exodus 4:22. Nonetheless, although terms of personal intimacy are used widely to express Israel's relationship with God, such usage is restrained by the accompanying sense of divine otherness. This is evident in the liturgical "blessings," where, following the direct address to God in which the second person singular pronoun is used, the verbs are with great regularity in the third person singular, thus providing the requisite tension between nearness and otherness, between the personal and the impersonal.

MODERN VIEWS OF GOD

The Judaic affirmations about God have not always been given the same emphasis, nor have they been understood in the same way. This was true in the Middle Ages, among both philosophers and mystics, as well as in modern times. In the 19th century, western European Jewish thinkers attempted to express and transform these affirmations in terms of German philosophical idealism. Later thinkers turned to philosophical naturalism, supplemented with the traditional God language, as the suitable expression of Judaism. In the first half of the 20th century the meaningfulness of the whole body of such affirmations was called into question by the philosophical school of logical positivism. The destruction of six million Jews in the Holocaust raised the issue of the validity of concepts such as God's presence in history, divine redemption, the covenant, and the chosen people.

ISRAEL (THE JEWISH PEOPLE)

The concluding phrase of the second benediction of the liturgical section—"who has chosen thy people Israel in love"—clearly states that God's choice to establish a relationship with Israel in particular was determined by divine love.

CHOICE AND COVENANT

The patriarchal narratives, beginning with the 12th chapter of Genesis, presuppose the choice, which is set forth explicitly in Deuteronomy 7:6–8 in the New Jewish Version:

> For you are a people consecrated to the Lord your God: of all the peoples on earth the Lord your God chose you to be His treasured people. It is not because you are the most numerous of peoples that the Lord set His heart on you and chose you—indeed you are the smallest of peoples; but it was because the Lord loved you and kept the oath He made with your fathers that the Lord freed you with a mighty hand and rescued you from the house of bondage, from the power of Pharaoh king of Egypt.

BOOK OF DEUTERONOMY

The fifth book of the Hebrew Bible, written in the form of a farewell address by Moses to the Israelites before they entered the Promised Land of Canaan, presents the terms of the Covenant between the people of Israel and YHWH. The speeches that constitute this address recall Israel's past, reiterate laws that Moses had communicated to the people at Horeb (Sinai), and emphasize that observance of these laws is essential for the well-being of the people in the land they are about to possess. The title Deuteronomy, derived from Greek, thus means a "copy," or a "repetition," of the law rather than "second law," as the word's etymology seems to suggest.

Although Deuteronomy is presented as an address by Moses, scholars generally agree that it dates from a much later period of Israelite history. An early edition of Deuteronomy as it exists today has been identified with the book of the Torah discovered in the Temple of Jerusalem about 622 BCE (2 Kings 22:8; 2 Chronicles 34:15). This early edition, corresponding roughly to chapters 5–26 and 28 of Deuteronomy as it now stands, expresses a cultic liturgy. Chapters 5–11 contain an introductory speech by Moses, largely hortatory. In chapters 12–26 laws are reiterated that the people are exhorted to obey. The section closes with a report of the formulation of a Covenant between God and his chosen people. Chapter 28 recounts in elaborate detail the blessings or curses that will come upon the people, depending on their response to laws that explicate their covenantal obligations. This arrangement of materials corresponds to the liturgy of Covenant renewal festivals that were celebrated in Israel's premonarchic period. Within this cultic context extremely ancient laws were preserved and transmitted.

The principles governing the Deuteronomistic historian's presentation of Israel's history are set forth in the book of Deuteronomy: faithfulness to YHWH and obedience to his commands bring blessings; the worship of foreign gods and negligence of YHWH's statutes bring a curse; YHWH can be worshiped in only one sacred place (Jerusalem) by all Israel; priests, prophets, and kings are subject to YHWH's law granted through Moses. Thus, the attribution of Deuteronomy to Moses tends to place Israel in an advanced stage of its history—when kings and a centralized cult were contemporary concerns—under the requirements of renewed ancient traditions.

Later rabbinic traditions on occasion sought to base God's choice upon some special merit of Israel, and the medieval poet and theologian Judah ha-Levi suggested that the openness to divine influence originally present in Adam continued only within the people of Israel.

The background of this choice is the recurring disobedience of humankind narrated in Genesis 2–11 (the stories of Adam and Eve, Cain and Abel, Noah, and the Tower of Babel). In the subsequent chapters of Genesis, Abraham and his descendants are singled out not merely as the object of the divine blessing but also as its channel to all humanity. The choice, however, demands a reciprocal response from Abraham and his lineage. That response is obedience, as exemplified in the first instance by Abraham's readiness to leave his "native land" and his "father's house" (Genesis 12:1). This twofold relationship was formalized in a mutually binding agreement, a covenant between the two parties. The covenant, thought by some modern biblical scholars to reflect the form of ancient suzerainty treaties, indicates (as in the Ten Utterances, or Decalogue) the source of Israel's obligation—the acts of God in

The Tower of Babel, *oil painting by Pieter Brueghel the Elder, 1563; in the Kunsthistorisches Museum, Vienna.* Courtesy of the Kunsthistorisches Museum, Vienna

history—and the specific requirements those acts impose. The formalization of this relationship was accomplished by certain cultic acts that, according to some contemporary scholars, may have been performed on a regular basis at various sacred sites in the land before being centralized in Jerusalem. The content of the covenantal obligations thus formalized was Torah. Israel was bound in obedience, and Israel's failure to obey provided the occasions for the prophetic messages. The prophets, as spokespersons for God, called the community to renewed obedience, threatened and promised disaster if obedience was not forthcoming, and sought to explain the covenant's persistence even when it should have been repudiated by God.

The choice of Israel is expressed in concrete terms in the requirements of the precepts (*mitzwot,* singular *mitzwa*) that are part of Torah. The blessing recited before the public reading of the Pentateuchal portions on Sabbath, festivals, holy days, fasts, and certain weekdays refers to God as "He who chose us from among all the peoples and gave us His Torah," thus emphasizing the intimate relationship between the elective and revelatory aspects of God.

Israel's role was not defined solely in terms of its own obedience to the commandments. Abraham and his descendants, for example, were seen as the means by which the estrangement of disobedient humankind from God was to be overcome. Torah was the formative principle underlying the community's fulfillment of this obligation. Israel was to be "a kingdom of priests and a holy nation" (Exodus 19:6) functioning within humanity and for its sake. This task is enunciated with particular earnestness in the writings of the Prophets. In Isaiah 43–44, Israel is declared to be God's witness and servant, who is to bring the knowledge of God to the nations, and in 42:6–7 it is described as a "covenant of the people, to be a light of the nations, to open the blind eyes, to bring out the prisoners from the prisons, and them that sit in darkness out of the prison house." This double motif of a chosen people and a witness to the nations, joined to that of the righteous king, developed in the biblical and postbiblical periods into messianism in its several varieties.

The intimate relation between choice, covenant, and Torah determined the modality of Israel's existence. Religious faith, far from being restricted to or encapsulated in the cult, found expression in the totality of communal and individual life. The obligation of the people was to be the true community, in which the relationship between its members was open, in which social distance was repudiated, and in which response to the divine will expressed in Torah was called for equally from all. One of the important recurring themes of the prophetic movement was the adamant rejection of any tendency to limit divine sovereignty to the partial area of "religion," understood as the realm of the priesthood and cult. Subsequent developments continued this theme, though it appeared in a number of other forms. Pharisaic Judaism and its continuation, Rabbinic Judaism, resolutely held to the idea of the all-pervasive functioning of Torah, so that however the various Jewish communities over the centuries may have failed to fulfill this idea, the self-image of the people was that of a "holy community."

ISRAEL AND THE NATIONS

The double motif of "treasured people" and "witness" was not without its tensions as it functioned in ongoing history. Tensions are especially visible in the period following the return from the Babylonian Exile at the end of the 6th and the beginning of the 5th century BCE. It is, however, doubtful whether the use of such terms as nationalism, particularism, or exclusivism are of any great help in understanding the situation. Emphasis has, for example, been laid upon Ezra 9:2 and 10:2, in which the reestablished community is commanded to give up wives taken from "the peoples of the land." This is taken as an indication of the exclusive and nationalistic nature of Judaism, without reference to the situation in which a harassed contingent of returning exiles sought to maintain itself in a territory surrounded by politically unfriendly if not hostile neighbours. Nor does this recognize that foreigners were admitted to the Jewish community. In the following centuries, some groups engaged in extensive missionary activities, appealing to the individuals of the nations surrounding them to join themselves to the God of Israel, the one true God and the creator of heaven and earth.

A more balanced view recognizes that, within the Jewish community, religious universalism was affirmed by the same people who understood the nature of Jewish existence in politically particularistic (i.e., nationalistic) terms. To neglect either side is to distort the picture. In no case was the universalism disengaged from the reality of the existing community, even when it was expressed in terms of the ultimate fulfillment of the divine purpose, the restoration of the true covenantal relationship between God and all humankind. Nor was political particularism, even under circumstances of great provocation and resentment, misanthropic. The most satisfactory figure in describing the situation of the restored community, and one that continues to be useful in dealing with later episodes, is that of the human heartbeat, made up of two functions, the systole, or contraction, and the diastole, or expansion. There have been several periods of contraction and of expansion throughout the history of Judaism. The emphasis within the abiding tension has been determined by the historical situation in which the community has found itself. To generalize in one direction or the other is fatal to an understanding of the history and faith of the "holy community."

THE PEOPLE AND THE LAND

Closely related to the concept of Israel as the chosen, or covenant, people is the

role of the land of Israel. In the patriarchal stories, settlement in Canaan is an
integral part of God's fulfillment of the
covenant. The goal of the Israelites who
escaped from Egypt and of those who
returned from the Babylonian Exile is
the same land, and entry into it is understood in the same fashion. As there was
the choice of a people, so there was the
choice of a land—and for much the same
reason. It was to provide the setting in
which the community could come into
being as it carried out the divine commandments. This choice of the land
contrasts significantly with the predominant ideas of other peoples in the ancient
world, in which the deity or divinities
were usually bound to a particular parcel
of ground outside of which they lost their
effectiveness or reality. Although some
such concepts may very well have crept
into Israelite thought during the period
of the kings (from Saul to Jehoiachin),
the crisis of the Babylonian Exile was met
by a renewal of the affirmation that the
God of Israel was, as Lord of all the earth,
free from territorial restraint, though he
had chosen a particular territory for this
chosen people. Here again the twofold
nature of Jewish thought becomes apparent, and both sides must be affirmed or
the view is distorted.

Following the two revolts against
Rome (66–73 CE and 132–135 CE), the Jews
of the ever-widening dispersion continued, as they had before these disasters,
to cherish the land. Once again it became
the symbol of fulfillment, so that return to
it was looked upon as an essential part of
messianic restoration. The liturgical patterns of the community, insofar as they
were concerned with natural phenomena (e.g., planting, rainfall, harvest, and
the annual cycle) rather than historical
events, were based on geography, topog-
raphy, and agricultural practices of the
land. Although some Jews continued to
live in the land, those in the distant dispersion idealized it, viewing it primarily
in eschatological terms—their destina-
tion at the end of days, in the world to
come. The 11th-century poet Judah
ha-Levi not only longed for it in verse but
also gave it a significant role in his theological interpretation of Judaism and
eventually sought to return to it from his
native Spain.

It was not, however, until the 19th
century that the land began to play a
role other than the goal of pilgrimage
or of occasional settlement by pietists
and mystics. At the end of the 19th century the power of the territorial concept
was released in eastern Europe in a cultural renaissance that focused, in part,
on a return to the land and, in western
and central Europe, in a political movement coloured by nationalist motifs in
European thought. The coming together
of these two strains of thought gave rise
to Zionism. This predominantly political
movement reflected a dissatisfaction with
the overall status of the Jewish people in
the modern world.

The political emphasis of Zionism
aroused considerable opposition from
three competing views of the status of
the Jewish people. The first opposition

came from some traditionalist Jews (now called "Orthodox" or "ultra-Orthodox") who were convinced that the Jewish nation must remain a solely religious community in the Diaspora and even in the land of Israel. They accepted the political rule of the Gentiles until the time when God will send his messiah to redeem the Jewish people by supernaturally returning all of them to the land of Israel to rebuild the Temple in Jerusalem.

The second opposition came from acculturated Jews in western Europe and North America who believed that Jews are part of larger secular polities and that their role in them should be that of a communion of like-minded religious believers, similar to that of the Catholic and Protestant denominations.

The third opposition came from some eastern European Jews who maintained that the Jewish people should seek their own national status in the territories in which they were presently living, similar to the resurgence of nationalism among a number of smaller nations living under the Austro-Hungarian or Russian empires. It was not until the Nazi Holocaust in the middle of the 20th century that the vast majority of Jews regarded Zionism, if not as the solution to the "Jewish question," then as something the Jews could not very well survive without. After this time, Jewish opposition to Zionism was confined to peripheral groups on the right who still saw Zionism as pseudo-messianism and to peripheral groups on the left who still saw Zionism as isolating Jews from more important universalist goals.

Modern Views of the People Israel

The nature of the people Israel and of the land of Israel has been variously interpreted in the history of Jewish thought. In modern times some interpretations have been deeply influenced by contemporary political and social discussions in the general community. Thus, for example, Zionist theoreticians were influenced by concepts of political nationalism on the one hand and by socialist ideas on the other. Further, the challenge to traditional theological concepts in the 19th century raised issues about the meaning of the choice of Israel, and Jewish thinkers borrowed from romantic nationalism ideas such as the "genius" of the people. In the 20th century, attempts were made to approach the question sociologically, dismissing the theological mode as unhelpful. The concept of the chosen people was accordingly understood as indicating a specific role deliberately undertaken by the Jewish people and similar to that espoused by other groups (e.g., manifest destiny by the American people). The establishment of the State of Israel motivated some thinkers to call for a repudiation of the idea, in keeping with the position that normal existence for the Jews requires the dismissal of such concepts. Although only a small minority of Jewish thinkers espoused this position, the concept of the choice of Israel was not without theological difficulties. In the late 20th century there were also some important attempts by Jewish thinkers to develop a theology of election.

The most important scholarship on the concept of "chosenness" was Michael Wyschogrod's *The Body of Faith* (1983) and David Novak's *The Election of Israel* (1995). Wyschogrod held that the people of Israel were elected because of God's exceptional love for them and that God's love existed prior to the revelation to Moses on Mount Sinai. Novak also accepted the traditional belief that God formed a unique relationship with Israel but maintained that God extends his covenant to the world and that the particularity of Israel's election is implicated in the general covenant with the world and vice versa.

HUMANITY

In Genesis 1:26, 27; 5:1; and 9:6, two terms occur, "image" and "likeness," that seem to indicate clearly the biblical understanding of essential human nature: humans are created in the image and likeness of God. Yet the texts in which these terms are used are not entirely unambiguous. The idea they point to does not appear elsewhere in Scriptures, and the concept is not too prominent in the rabbinic interpretations. What the image and likeness of God, or the divine image, refers to in the biblical texts is not made explicit, and, in light of the fact that the texts are dominated by psychosomatic conceptions of the nature of humanity (i.e., involving both soul and body), it is not possible to escape entirely the implication of "bodily" similarity. What the terms meant in their context at the time and whether they reflect mythological usages taken over from other Middle Eastern thought are by no means certain. However, according to Akiba, the most prominent 2nd-century CE rabbi, the "image" of God seems to mean the unique human capacity for a spiritual relationship with him. This interpretation thus avoids any suggestion of a physical similarity between God and humans.

THE EARTHLY-SPIRITUAL CREATURE

A dualistic interpretation of humanity was offered in parts of the ancient Jewish community that were deeply influenced by Greek philosophical ideas. In this understanding, the divine likeness is identified with the immortal, intellectual soul as contrasted to the body. Other ancient and modern thinkers have understood the likeness as ethical, placing particular emphasis on freedom of the will. Clearly, no doctrine of humanity can be erected on the basis of these several verses alone—a broader view must be taken. A careful examination of the biblical material, particularly the words *nefesh*, *neshama*, and *ruaḥ*—which are often too broadly translated as "soul" and "spirit"—indicates that these terms must not be understood as referring to the psychical side of a psychophysical pair. A human being does not possess a *nefesh* but rather is a *nefesh*, as Genesis 2:7 says, "wayehi ha-adam le-nefesh hayya" (". . . and the man became a living being"). Humans are, for most of the biblical writers, "a unit of vital power," not a dual creature separable into two distinct parts of unequal importance and value. While this understanding of human nature dominated biblical thought, in apocalyptic literature (2nd century BCE– 2nd century CE) the term *nefesh* was viewed as a separable psychical entity with existence apart from the body. This conception of human nature was not entirely divorced from the unitary biblical view, but a body-soul dualism was effectively present in such literature. In the Alexandrian version of Hellenistic Judaism, the orientation toward Greek philosophy, particularly the Platonic view of the soul imprisoned in the flesh, led to a clear-cut dualism with a negative attitude toward the body. Rabbinic thought remained closer to the biblical position, at least in its understanding of the human being as a psychosomatic unit, even though the temporary separation of the components after death was an accepted position.

The biblical view of the human as an inseparable psychosomatic unit meant that death was understood to be human dissolution. Although a human being ceased to be, this dissolution was not utter extinction. Some of the power that functioned in the unit may have continued to exist, but it was not to be understood any longer as life. The existence of the dead in sheol, the netherworld, was not living but the shadow or echo of living. For most biblical writers this existence was without experience, either of God or of anything else; it was unrelated to events. To call it immortality is to empty that term of any vital significance. The concept of sheol, however, along with belief in the possibility of the miraculous restoration of dead individuals to life and even the idea of the revival of the people of Israel from the "death" of exile, provided a foothold for the development of belief in the resurrection of the dead body at some time in the future. The stimulus for this may have come from ancient Iranian religion, in which the dualistic cosmic struggle is eventually won by life through the resurrection of the dead. This idea appeared in sketchy form in postexilic writings (Isaiah 26:19; Daniel 12:2). In this view there is life only in the psychosomatic unit now restored. This restoration was bound up with the eschatological hope of Israel and was limited to the righteous. In subsequent apocalyptic literature, a sharper distinction between body and soul was entertained, and the latter was conceived of as existing separately in a disembodied state after death. Although at this point the doctrine of the resurrection of the body was not put aside, the direction of thinking changed. The shades of sheol were now thought of as souls, and real personal survival—with continuity between life on earth and in sheol—was posited. Greek ideas, with their individualistic bent, influenced Jewish thought, so that the idea of a resurrection that was in some way related to a final historical consummation began to recede. True life after death was now seen as release from the bondage of the body, so that in place of or alongside of the afterlife of physical resurrection was set the afterlife of the immortal soul.

It was not the status of the soul, however, that concerned the biblical and rabbinic thinkers. Instead, the latter's discussions of biblical themes emphasized the ethical import of the composite nature of human beings. Humans are in a state of tension or equilibrium between the two foci of creation, the "heavenly" and the "earthly." They necessarily participate in both. But this means that they are the only creatures who can truly serve their creator, for they alone, partaking of both sides of creation, may choose between them. It is this ability to make an ethical choice that is the distinguishing mark of humans. It is not derived from the "heavenly" side but resides in the dual nature of human existence. This view is clearly not a type of body-soul dualism in which the soul is the source of good and the body the basis of evil. Such an attitude, however, did appear in some rabbinic material and was often affirmed in medieval philosophical and mystical speculations and by some of the later moralists. An important development of

biblical-rabbinic ideas, these later commentaries represent authentic attempts to come to terms with other currents of thought and with the problems and uncertainties inherent within the earlier materials themselves.

THE ETHICALLY BOUND CREATURE

Humankind is then viewed as ethically involved. The central theme of the first 11 chapters of Genesis focuses on this responsibility, for the implicit assumption of the pre-patriarchal stories is the human ability to choose between obedience and disobedience. Rabbinic Judaism, taking up the covenant-making episode between God and Noah (Genesis 9:8–17), developed it as the basis of humanity's ethical obligation. All humanity, not merely Israel, is engaged in a covenant relationship with God, which was spelled out in explicit precepts—variously enumerated as 6, 7, or even 10 and occasionally as many as 30—that reflect general humanitarian behaviour and are intended to assure the maintenance of the natural order by the establishment of a proper human society. The covenant with Israel was meant to bring into being a community that would advance the development of this society through its own obedience and witness.

Human nature, viewed ethically, was explained in Rabbinic Judaism not only as a tension between the "heavenly" and "earthly" components but as a tension between two "impulses." Here again, fragmentary and allusive biblical materials were developed into more comprehensive statements. The biblical word *yetzer*, for example, means "plan," that which is formed in human minds. In the two occurrences of the word in Genesis (6:5; 8:21), the plan or formation of the human mind is described as *ra'*, perhaps "evil" in the moral sense or maybe no more than "disorderly," "confused," "undisciplined." Other occurrences in the Bible do not have this modifier. Nonetheless, the Aramaic translations (Targumim) invariably replaced it with *bisha* ("wicked") wherever it occurred. Rabbinic literature created a technical term, *ha-ra'* ("the evil impulse"), to denote the source within humans of their disobedience, and subsequently the counter-term *yetzer ha-ṭov* ("the good impulse") was used to indicate humans' obedience. These terms more clearly suggest the ethical quality of human duality, while their opposition and conflict point to human freedom and the ethical choices humans must make. Indeed, it is primarily within the realm of the ethical that Judaism posits freedom, recognizing the bound, or determined, quality of much of humans' natural environment or physiological makeup.

This ethically free creature stands within the covenant relationship and may choose to be obedient or disobedient. Sin, then, is ultimately deliberate disobedience or rebellion against the divine sovereign. This is more easily observed in relation to Israel, for it is in this connection that the central concern of Judaism is most

evident and discussed in greatest detail. The covenant relationship is not limited to Israel, because, according to Judaic tradition, all humankind stands within a covenant relation to God and is commanded to be moral and just. Therefore, the same choice is made universally. In technical language, the acceptance of divine sovereignty by the people of Israel and by individuals within that community is called "receiving the yoke of the kingship." This involves intellectual commitment to a basic belief, as expressed by the Deuteronomic proclamation: "Hear, O Israel, the Lord, our God, the Lord is one!" It also imposes obligations regarding communal and individual behaviour. These two responses are understood to be inextricably bound, so that rejection of the divine sovereign is manifest as denial of God both intellectually and practically. It amounts to "breaking the yoke of the kingship." In more specific terms, sin is sometimes summed up under three interrelated headings: idolatry, murder, and illicit sexual behaviour, each of which involves rebellion, for it involves activities that deny—if not God's existence—his commanding relationship and the requirement of human response. Such behaviour destroys the community and sets individual against individual, thus thwarting the ultimate purpose of God, the perfected human society.

If humans are free to choose rebellion and to suffer its consequences, they are also able to turn back to God and to become reconciled with him.

The Bible—particularly the prophetic writings—is filled with this idea, even though the term *teshuva* ("turning") came into use only in rabbinic sources. Basically, the idea grows out of the covenant: the opportunity to return to God is the result of God's unwillingness—despite human failures—to break off the covenant relationship. Rabbinic thought assumed that even the direst warnings of utter disaster and rejection imply the possibility of turning back to God, motivated by remorse and the desire for restoration. Divine readiness and human openness are the two sides of the process of reconciliation. What was expressed in prophetic literature in relation to the immediate historical and political situation was stated in the synagogal liturgy in connection with Pentateuchal and prophetic lessons and the homilies developed from them. Thus, the divine invitation was constantly being offered. Humans are called upon to atone for their rebellion by positive action in the other direction and are summoned to reconstitute wholeness in their individual and communal life.

Jewish existence, as it developed under rabbinic leadership following the two disastrous rebellions against Rome, was an attempt to reconstitute a community of faith expressed in worship in an ordered society in which the individual would live a hallowed life of response to the divine will. Although this plan was not spelled out in detail, it was probably understood to be the paradigm for the eventual reconstruction of humanity.

MEDIEVAL AND MODERN VIEWS OF HUMANITY

Although the Jewish view of human nature was centrally concerned with ethics, metaphysical issues, however rudimentary in the beginning, were also included in the developing discussion. Medieval philosophers, for example, sought an accommodation between the doctrine of the resurrection of the body and the concept of the immortality of the soul. The greatest of them, Moses Maimonides (1135–1204), propounded an extremely subtle position that equated immortality with the cleaving of the human intellect to the active intellect of the universe, thus limiting it to philosophers or to those who accepted a suitable philosophical theology on faith. Little or no consensus was evident in the modern period, though the language of resurrection or immortality was still used, even when its content was uncertain. Alongside this lack of agreement, however, Judaism's basic affirmation about human nature remained the same: a human being is to be understood, however else, as a creature who makes free ethical choices for which he is responsible.

ETHICS AND SOCIETY

Jewish affirmations about God and humans intersect in the concept of Torah as the ordering of human existence in the direction of the divine. Humans are ethically responsible creatures who are responsive to the presence of God in nature and in history. Although this responsiveness is expressed on many levels, it is most explicitly called for within interpersonal relationships. The Pentateuchal legislation sets down, albeit within the limitations of the structures of the ancient Middle East, the basic patterns of these relationships. The prophetic messages maintain that the failure to honour these demands is the source of social and individual disorder. Even the most exalted members of society are not free of ethical obligations, as is seen in the ethical confrontation of David by Nathan ("Thou art the man") for seducing Bathsheba and arranging to have her husband killed (2 Samuel 12).

THE ETHICAL EMPHASIS OF JUDAISM

What is particularly striking about Jewish ethical concerns is the affirmation that God is not only the source of ethical obligation but is himself the paradigm of it. In the so-called Code of Holiness (Leviticus 19), imitation of divine holiness is offered as the basis of human behaviour in both the cultic-ceremonial and ethical spheres. The basic injunction, "You shall be holy, for I, the Lord your God, am Holy," underlies the concern for economically vulnerable members of the community; obligations toward neighbours, hired

An Israeli charity distributes food to needy community members, following the Code of Holiness: "You shall be holy, for I, the Lord your God, am Holy." David Silverman/Getty Images

labourers, and the physically handicapped; interfamilial relationships; and attitudes toward strangers (i.e., non-Israelites). Acceptable human behaviour was therefore "walking in all His ways" (Deuteronomy 11:22). The dialectical relation between God and man in the literary prophets also exhibits divine righteousness and divine compassion as patterns to be emulated in the life of the community.

This theme, *imitatio Dei* ("imitation of God"), is expressed succinctly in a commentary on Deuteronomy 11:22 that answers the question of how it is possible to walk "in all His ways": "As He is merciful and gracious, so be you merciful and gracious. As He is righteous so be you righteous. As He is holy, strive to be holy" (*Sifre* Deuteronomy 85a). Even more daringly, God is described as clothing the naked, nursing the sick, comforting the mourners, and burying the dead, so that human beings may recognize their own obligations.

INTERPENETRATION OF COMMUNAL AND INDIVIDUAL ETHICS

What stands out in the entire development of Jewish ethical formulations is the constant interpenetration of communal and individual obligations and concerns. A just society requires just people, and a just person functions within a just society. The concrete expression of ethical requirements in legal precepts takes place with both ends in view, so that the process of beginning the holy community and the process of forming the *ḥasid* ("pious"), the person of steadfast devotion to God, are concomitant. The relationship between the two is, of course, often mediated by the historical situation, so that in some periods one or the other moves to the centre of practical interest. In particular, the end of the Judaean state (70–135 CE) truncated the communal aspect of ethical obligations, often limiting discussion to apolitical responsibilities rather

BOOK OF LEVITICUS

The Book of Leviticus is a manual primarily concerned with the priests and their duties. Although Leviticus is basically a book of laws, it also contains some narrative (chapters 8–9, 10:1–7, 10:16–20, and 24:10–14). The book is usually divided into five parts: sacrificial laws (chapters 1–7), the inauguration of the priesthood and laws governing their office (chapters 8–10), laws for ceremonial purity (chapters 11–16), laws governing the people's holiness (chapters 17–26), and a supplement concerning offerings to the sanctuary and religious vows (chapter 27).

Scholars agree that Leviticus belongs to the Priestly (P) source of the biblical traditions. This material is dated according to one theory in the 7th century BCE and is regarded as the law upon which Ezra and Nehemiah based their reform. Older material, however, is preserved in P, particularly the "Code of Holiness" (chapters 17–26), dating from ancient times.

than to the full range of social involvements. The reestablishment of the State of Israel in the 20th century therefore reopened for discussion areas that for millennia were either ignored or treated as mere abstractions. This implies that the full ethical responsibility of Jews cannot be carried out solely within the realm of individual relationships but must include involvement in the life of a fully articulated community.

This double involvement is most vividly apparent in the biblical period, when both were equally present as divine command and demand. In the rabbinic period, because of the new political context, the communal aspect receded, so that discussion was mainly oriented toward relationships between members of the Jewish community or between individuals as such and away from political responsibilities. Nonetheless, the virtues that were understood to govern these relationships were, in their biblical setting, communal as well. Righteousness and compassion had been obligations of the state, governing the relationship between political units, as the first two chapters of Amos make evident. At the same time, as Micah 6:8 shows, doing justly, loving mercy, and walking humbly with God were obligations of the individual as well. Given the situation of the Jewish Diaspora following the revolts against Rome in the 1st and 2nd centuries CE, the individual pattern became the primary object of concern. Theoretical ethical systems were not developed until the Middle Ages, but even in the early period it was understood that the dynamic of ethical theory stood behind the practical system of Halakha, the enumeration of legal precepts. This meant that the law assumed an ethical core that existed prior to revelation and that the laws were just and merciful because God was just and merciful. Thus an attempt was made to reduce the hundreds of precepts to a small number expressing the ethical essence of Torah.

The Key Moral Virtues

In keeping with the rabbinic understanding of Torah, study also was viewed as an ethical virtue. Passages from the Mishna, which are repeated in the traditional prayer book, enumerate a series of virtuous acts—honouring parents, deeds of steadfast love, attendance twice daily at worship, hospitality to wayfarers, visiting the sick, dowering brides, accompanying the dead to the grave, devotion in prayer, peacemaking in the community and in family life—and conclude by declaring that the study of Torah is the premier virtue. The extracts enumerated in the Mishna and the prayer book exhibit the complex variety of ethical behaviour called for within the Jewish tradition. To parental respect and family tranquillity are added the responsibility of parents for children, the duties of husband and wife in the establishment and maintenance of a family, and ethical obligations that extend from the conjugal rights of each to the protection of the wife if the marriage is dissolved. The biblical description of God as upholding the cause of the fatherless and the widow and befriending strangers, providing them with food and clothing (Deuteronomy 10:18), remained a factor in the structure of the community. Ethical requirements in economic life are expressed concretely in passages such as Leviticus 19:35–36: "You shall do no wrong in judgment, in measures of length or weight or quantity. You shall have just balances, just weights, a just *ephah*, and a just *hin*" (*ephah* and *hin* are units of measure). Another example is Amos's bitter condemnation of those who "sell the righteous for silver, and the needy for a pair of shoes" (Amos 2:6). Such injunctions, together with many other specific precepts and moral requirements, established the basis for a wide-ranging program that sought to govern, both in detail and in general, the economic life of the individual and the community.

Relations within the human sphere are not the only object of ethical concern; nature also is so regarded. The animal world, in the biblical view, requires merciful consideration, so that on the Sabbath not only humans but also their domestic animals are required to rest (Exodus 20:10; 23:12). Mistreatment of beasts of burden is prohibited (Deuteronomy 22:4), and wanton destruction of animal life falls under the ban (Deuteronomy 6–7). In the rabbinic attitude toward creation, all of nature is the object of human solicitude. Thus, the food-yielding trees of a city under siege may not be destroyed, according to Deuteronomic legislation (Deuteronomy 20:14–20). The enlargement of this and other biblical precepts

resulted in the generalized rabbinic prohibition, "You shall not destroy," which governs human use of the environment.

THE RELATION TO NON-JEWISH COMMUNITIES AND CULTURES

Although the end of the Jewish state reduced the scope of ethical judgments in the political sphere, relations between the Jewish community and other polities—particularly the Roman and Christian empires and the Islamic states—provided opportunities for the exploration of the ethical implications of such encounters. Because most of these situations were characterized by gross disparities of power, with the Jews the weaker party, prudential considerations were dominant. Despite this, Jewish authorities sought to bring to bear upon these external arrangements the ethical standards that governed the internal structures.

The problem of the relationship between the Jewish community, in whatever form it has existed, and other social units has been vastly complicated. The relation is ideally that of witness to the divine intent in the world. Practically, it has swung between the extremes of isolation and assimilation, in which the ideal has, on occasion, been lost sight of. Culturally, from its earliest beginnings, the people of Israel have met and engaged the ideas, forms, behaviours, and attitudes of their neighbours constructively. Israel reformulated what it received in terms of its own commitments and affirmations. On more than a few occasions, as in the period of settlement in Canaan, it rejected the religious and cultural ideas and forms of the indigenous population. On other occasions—as in Islamic Spain from the 8th to the 15th century—it actively sought out the ideas and cultural patterns of its neighbours, viewing them from its own perspective and embracing them when they were found to be of value. Indeed, the whole history of Israel's relationship with the world may be comprehended in the metaphor, used previously, of the heartbeat with its systole and diastole. No period of its existence discloses either total rejection of or abject surrender to other cultural and political structures but rather a tension, with the focal point always in motion at varying rates. Judaism's adjustment to and relation with other social and political units has involved larger aspects of communal and individual life. Whether or not under such circumstances it is helpful to describe Judaism as a civilization, it is important to recognize that, viewed functionally, much more must be included than is usually subsumed under the term *religion* in modern Western societies.

THE FORMULATION OF JEWISH ETHICAL DOCTRINES

The ethical concerns of Judaism have frequently been expressed in literary works. Not only were rabbinic writings constantly directed toward the establishment of legal patterns that embody such concerns, but in the medieval period the issues were dealt with in treatises on morals; ethical wills, in which a father instructed his children about their obligations and behaviour; sermons; and other forms. In the 19th century, the traditionalist Musar ("Moral Instructor") movement in eastern Europe and the philosophical discussions of the nascent Reform movement in the West focused upon ethics. Indeed, since the political and social emancipation of the Jews, ethical and social rather than theological questions have been given priority. Often the positions espoused have turned out to be "Judaized" versions of ethical theories or political programs. In some instances, as in the case of the distinguished German Jewish philosopher Hermann Cohen (1842–1918), the result has been a compelling restatement of a secular philosophical ethics in Jewish form. In others it has resulted in no more than a pastiche. More crucial, however, is the question of the uniqueness and authority of Jewish ethics. The reestablishment of the Jewish state renewed the possibility that the full range of ethical decisions, communal and individual, may be confronted. In such a situation the ethical task of the people moves out of the realm of speculation to become actual again.

THE UNIVERSE

Although Genesis affirms divine creation, it does not offer an entirely unambiguous view of the origin of the universe, as the debate over the correct understanding of Genesis 1:1 discloses. (Was there or was there not a preexisting matter, void, or chaos?) The interest of the author, however, was not in the mode of creation—a later concern perhaps reflected in the various translations of the verse, "In the beginning God created," which could signify what medieval philosophers designated *creatio ex nihilo* ("creation out of nothing"). He was concerned rather to affirm that the totality of existence—inanimate (Genesis 1:3–19), living (20–25), and human (26–31)—derived immediately from the same divine source. As divine creation, the universe is transparent to the presence of God, so that the Psalmist said, "The heavens declare the glory of God, and the expanse proclaims [that it is] the work of his hands" (19:1). Indeed, the repeated phrase, "And God saw how good it was" (Genesis 1:4, 10, 12, 18, 25, 31), may be understood as the foundation of this affirmation, for the workmanship discloses the workman.

CREATION AND PROVIDENCE

The observed order of the universe is further understood by the biblical author as the direct result of a covenantal relationship between the world and God: "So long as the earth endures, seedtime and harvest, cold and heat, summer and winter, day and night, shall not cease" (Genesis 8:22). This doctrine of the providential ordering of the universe, reaffirmed in Rabbinic Judaism, is not without its difficulties, as in the liturgical change made in Isaiah 45:7 to avoid ascribing evil to God. Despite the problem of theodicy, Judaism has not acquiesced to the mood

reported in the Palestinian Targum to Genesis 4:8: "He did not create the world in mercy nor does he rule in mercy." Rather, Judaism has affirmed a benevolent and compassionate God.

God's creation, the physical world, provides the stage for history, which is the place of the human encounter with the divine. An early Midrash, responding to the question of why Scripture begins with the story of creation, asserts that it was necessary to establish the identity of the Creator with the giver of Torah, an argument basic to the liturgical structure of the Shema. This relationship is further emphasized in the Kiddush, the prayer of sanctification recited at the beginning of the Sabbath. That day is designated "a remembrance of creation" and "a recollection of the going-forth from Egypt." Thus, creation (nature) and history are understood to be inextricably bound, for both derive from the same divine source. This being so, redemption—the reconciliation of God and man through and in history—does not ignore or exclude the natural world. Using the imagery of an extravagantly fecund world of nature, rabbinic thought expressed its view of the all-inclusive effects of the restored relationship.

HUMANITY'S PLACE IN THE UNIVERSE

The human creature is, of course, subject to the natural order. Humans carry on their relationship with God in the world and through the world. The commandments of Torah are obeyed not solely as observances between humans and God but as actions between humans themselves and between humans and the world. The creation story describes the human as ruler over the earth and its inhabitants (Genesis 1:26–28; Psalms 8:5–9). Nonetheless, far from being an arbitrary master, human dominion is limited by Torah. The regulations in the Torah are concerned not only with transactions between humans but also with human responsibilities to cultivated land, to the produce of the soil, and to domesticated animals. Bound in the network of existence, humans as moral creatures are responsible for creation in all its parts.

Even the destruction of the Jewish commonwealth in the 1st and 2nd centuries CE did not alienate Jews from these responsibilities, as the elaborate system of Mishna and Gemara reveals. The gradual but consistent exclusion of the Jews from immediate connection with large segments of the natural world, through legislation in Christendom and Islam, tended to dull their awareness of it. The recurring references to the natural world in the religious calendar, however, and the observation of harvest festivals even by city dwellers continued to remind the community of its ties. Thus, at the end of the 19th century, the nascent Zionist movement recognized that the regeneration of the Jewish people involved, among other requirements, a responsible relation to the natural order expressed in its attitude toward and treatment of the land.

If nature as the place of divine disclosure has, during long periods of Jewish existence, assumed a somewhat subordinate role, it has never been rejected or been seen to be irrelevant to the divine purpose. Indeed, in Jewish eschatology, its restoration is part of the goal of history.

INTERMEDIARY BEINGS: ANGELS AND DEMONS

The exact nature of nonhuman beings mentioned in Scripture—angels, or messengers (*angel* is derived from the Greek word *angelos*, which is the equivalent of the Hebrew word *mal'akh*, "messenger")—is not altogether clear, and their roles seem ephemeral. In the postexilic period, perhaps under Iranian influence, and in the late biblical and postbiblical literature, these beings emerge as more complete and often as clearly identifiable individuals with their own personal names. The unfocused biblical view gave way to an elaborate hierarchy of functionaries who acted, in some apocalyptic visions, as a veritable heavenly bureaucracy. Despite a consensus concerning their existence, there was little agreement about their role or importance. In some Midrashim God takes counsel with them, whereas in other sources the rabbis urge Jews not to involve them but to approach God directly.

Like their counter-figures the demons, angels have a residual existence rooted in various layers of the Jewish experience and interpretation of the universe.

At some times they are highly individualized and sharply realized, and at others they are much more imaginary. The medieval philosophers and the early mystics saw them through Aristotelian or Neoplatonic categories. The Kabbalists continually invented new angels and fitted them into their complicated network of cosmic existence. Their role, however, even in periods of considerable emphasis, was peripheral, and they were outside the great movements and meanings of Jewish thought.

Contemporary philosophical speculation about the nature of the universe has, of course, required a response from Jewish thinkers. But, given the particular temper of a period in which metaphysics has not been central to much of theological discussion, no major statement has developed that has taken hold of the dominant positions and attempted to view them from the Jewish creationist perspective. The attempt within Reconstructionism to provide a naturalistic framework for Judaism, while courageous, seems to be based on a philosophical naturalism that many consider outmoded.

ESCHATOLOGY

The choice of Israel, according to the Bible, occurred because of humankind's continual failure, by rebellion against its creator, to fulfill its divine potential. The subsequent inability of Israel to become the holy community and thereby a witness to the nations gave rise to the prophetic movement that summoned the people to obedience. An integral part of prophetic summoning, side by side with threats of punishment and warnings of disaster, was the vision of a truly holy community, a society fully responding to the divine imperative. This kingdom of the future was conceived of as entirely natural, functioning as any normal social and political unit. The future kingdom would be governed by a human ruler, who would carry out his tasks within the sphere of divine sovereignty, serving primarily to exhibit his own obedience and thus to stimulate the obedience of the entire people. This future monarch was often, though not always, portrayed in terms of an idealized David, using features of his life and reign that would emphasize submission to God, social stability, economic satisfaction, and peace. During the period of the monarchy, the prophetic demand was directed toward each succeeding king, with the hope—or even the expectation—that he would be or become the new David, the ideal ruler.

THE FUTURE AGE OF HUMANKIND AND THE WORLD

The Babylonian Exile added a new measure of urgency to this expectation, but it was not expressed in any uniform fashion. The later chapters of the Book of Ezekiel provide the constitution for the new commonwealth but do not describe the peculiar characteristics of the ruler, while the later chapters of the Book of Isaiah focus on several figures—including Cyrus II the Mede, who conquered the Babylonian Empire and freed the Jews from Babylonian captivity—who are seen as the divine instruments ushering in a new era. Although the virtues ascribed to these figures are extraordinary, they are neither superhuman nor suprahuman. Indeed, they are required of all Israel and of all humanity. The frustrations of the postexilic period, when several attempts to bring the holy community into being were largely thwarted by the

Apocalyptic Literature

Apocalyptic literature is a literary genre that foretells supernaturally inspired cataclysmic events that will transpire at the end of the world. Characteristically pseudonymous, it takes narrative form, employs esoteric language, expresses a pessimistic view of the present, and treats the final events as imminent.

The earliest apocalypses are Jewish works that date from about 200 BCE to about 165 BCE. Whereas earlier Jewish writers, the Prophets, had foretold the coming of disasters, often in esoteric language, they neither placed these disasters in a narrative framework nor conceived of them in eschatological terms. During the time of the Hellenistic domination of Palestine and the revolt of the Maccabees, however, a pessimistic view of the present became coupled with an expectation of an apocalyptic scenario, which is characterized by an imminent crisis, a universal judgment, and a supernatural resolution.

The most famous and influential of the early Jewish apocalypses is the last part of the biblical Book of Daniel (chapters 7–12), written about 167 BCE and attributed to a revered wise man who supposedly lived some four centuries earlier at the time of the Babylonian captivity. "Daniel" recounts a series of visions, the first of which (chapter 7) is the most succinct. He sees a succession of four terrible beasts, evidently representing a succession of earthly persecutors culminating in the contemporary Hellenistic tyrant Antiochus IV Epiphanes (the "eleventh horn" of the fourth beast). Daniel then sees the destruction of the last beast by the "Ancient of Days" and the coming of "one like the Son of Man," to whom is given "everlasting dominion that shall not pass away" and whose kingdom will be inhabited by "the people of the saints," who will forever serve and obey him.

The other Jewish apocalypses—the first Book of Enoch (c. 200 BCE), the fourth Book of Ezra (c. 100 CE), and the second and third Books of Baruch (c. 100 CE)—are "apocryphal" insofar as they do not belong to the canonical Hebrew Bible. They are extant in Ethiopic, Syriac, Greek, and Latin translations made by Christians rather than in their original Hebrew or Aramaic forms. The reason that the apocalypses survived in this manner seems to be that, after the failure of a series of Jewish revolts against the Roman Empire (i.e., after about 135 CE), the rabbis who began the process of codifying the Jewish tradition turned away from apocalypticism to an emphasis on upholding and interpreting the law of the Torah. Fatefully, however, while Jewish apocalypticism was still flourishing, it was taken up by Christians.

imperial designs of the great powers—as they had been in the preexilic period—led to an emphasis on the futuristic quality of messianic hope. This was abetted undoubtedly by external influences, such as Iranian thought, in which the cosmic rather than the historic aspect of a future era dominated. Because ancient cosmic myths had been part of the Israelite intellectual inheritance, as seen in literary usages throughout Scriptures, the impact of such ideas was to reinvigorate the mythic elements in Judaism. Thus, hopes for the future at the end of the Persian period and through the Hellenistic period comprised both historical expectations focused upon an earthly community and cosmic-mythic visions that moved on a broader stage. The latter were, of course, never entirely absent from historical expectations, for a renewal of nature was viewed as integral to the functioning of true society. The obedient community required, and was to be granted, a natural world in which true human relations could exist. In its most vivid form, the apocalypse (i.e., a visionary disclosure of the future), the literature of the period affords a remarkable insight into the agonies and urgencies of the people. After the disappointments of the past are recounted, the present, in transparent disguise, is portrayed, and the imminent and desired intervention of God is described in awesome detail as a means of affirming and confirming the faith of those who saw themselves as the remnant, or perhaps the promise, of the holy community.

THE KING-MESSIAH AND HIS REIGN

Israel's hope was for the restoration of divine sovereignty over all of creation. Among the variety of expressions of such hope, that which centred around the idealized king assumed an ever more important (but never exclusive) role. Many of the writings that report the ideas and attitudes of the Jewish community in the period immediately preceding and following the rise of Christianity are either ignorant of or more probably indifferent to the personal element. God is envisioned as the protagonist of the end, actively intervening or sending his messengers (i.e., angels) to perform specific acts in ending the old era and inaugurating the new one. Conversely, in some writings of the period the anointed king-messiah (Hebrew: *mashiah*, "anointed")—the title reflects the episode in 1 Samuel 16 in which David is thus singled out as the divinely chosen ruler—becomes more sharply defined as the central figure in the culminating events and, given the cosmic-mythic components, assumes suprahuman and sometimes even quasi-divine aspects. Although the doctrine of last things in Judaism is not necessarily messianic, if that term is properly limited to an inauguration of a future era through the action of a human, suprahuman, or quasi-divine person, the messianic version of eschatology played a more compelling role in Rabbinic Judaism than other modes. The same is true with regard to the locus of the "world (or age) to come." Given the ingredients noted earlier, it was possible to construct various eschatological landscapes, ranging from the mundane to the celestial, from Jerusalem in the hills of Judah to a heavenly city. Indeed, medieval theologians, confronted with an embarrassment of riches, sought to combine them into an inclusive system that involved as many of the possibilities as could be brought together. In such patterns the messianic this-worldly emphasis was understood as a preliminary movement toward an ultimate resolution. The ideal ruler, the new David, would reestablish the kingdom in its own land (in Zion, or Palestine) and would reign in righteousness, equity, justice, and truth, thus bringing into being the holy nation and summoning all humankind to dwell under divine sovereignty. As a component of this reestablished kingdom, the righteous dead of Israel would be resurrected to enjoy a life in the true community that did not exist in their days. This kingdom, however long it was destined to endure, was not permanent. It would come to an end either at a predetermined time or as a victim of unrepentant nations and cosmic foes, at which point the ultimate intervention by God would take place. All the wicked throughout history would be recalled to life, judged, and doomed, and all the righteous would be transformed and transported into a new world (i.e., creation would be totally restored).

The particular emphases that one or the other of these ideas received and the ways in which they were interpreted—philosophically, mystically, and ethically—were determined most frequently by the situations and conditions in which the Jewish community found itself. With a considerable body of ideas at its disposal and with the details of none of them ever receiving the kind of affirmation given to statements about God, Torah, and Israel, freedom of speculation in the realm of eschatology was little restricted. Thus, Joseph Albo, in his work on Jewish "dogmas"—the *Sefer ha-'iqqarim* (1485; "Book of Principles")—was not inhibited from denying that belief in the messiah was fundamental. The mystical movements of the Middle Ages found in eschatological hopes a crucial centre. The early Kabbala was little interested in messianism, for it reoriented such expectations in the direction of personal redemption. However, following the disasters of the late 15th–17th centuries (e.g., the expulsion of the Jews from Spain and the Cossack massacre of the Jews in Poland), messianic speculation in all its varieties underwent a luxuriant growth, finally running wild in the movements surrounding Shabbetai Tzevi of Smyrna and later Jacob Frank of Offenbach. These tragedies for the Jewish communities once again resulted in deferring eschatological hopes or at least limiting their application.

SECULARIZATION OF MESSIANISM

In the 19th century, with the political emancipation of the Jews in western Europe

ZIONISM

Zionism is a Jewish nationalist movement that has had as its goal the creation and support of a Jewish national state in Palestine, the ancient homeland of the Jews (Hebrew: Eretz Yisra'el, "the Land of Israel"). Alhough Zionism originated in eastern and central Europe in the latter part of the 19th century, it is in many ways a continuation of the ancient nationalist attachment of the Jews and of the Jewish religion to the historical region of Palestine, where one of the hills of ancient Jerusalem was called Zion.

In the 16th and 17th centuries a number of "messiahs" came forward trying to persuade Jews to "return" to Palestine. In reaction to tsarist pogroms from the 16th through the 19th centuries, eastern European Jews formed the Ḥovevei Ẓiyyon ("Lovers of Zion") to promote the settlement of Jewish farmers and artisans in Palestine. A political turn was given to Zionism by Theodor Herzl, an Austrian journalist who regarded assimilation by Jews into secular European culture as most desirable but, in view of anti-Semitism, impossible to realize. Thus, he argued, if Jews were forced by external pressure to form a nation, they could lead a normal existence only through concentration in one territory.

At Herzl's death in 1904, the leadership of the Zionist movement relocated from Vienna to Cologne, then to Berlin. Prior to World War I, Zionism represented only a minority of Jews, mostly from Russia but led by Austrians and Germans. Through orators and pamphlets and with its own newspapers, Zionists gave an impetus to what was called a "Jewish renaissance" in letters and arts. Yet with the failure of the Russian Revolution of 1905 and the wave of pogroms and repressions that followed caused growing numbers of Russian Jewish youth to emigrate to Palestine as pioneer settlers. By 1914 there were about 90,000 Jews in Palestine; 13,000 settlers lived in 43 Jewish agricultural settlements.

Upon the outbreak of World War I, political Zionism reasserted itself, led by Russian Jews living in England. Two such Zionists, Chaim Weizmann and Nahum Sokolow, were instrumental in obtaining from Great Britain the Balfour Declaration (Nov. 2, 1917), which promised British support for the creation of a Jewish national home in Palestine. In the following years the Zionists built up the Jewish urban and rural settlements there, perfecting autonomous organizations and solidifying Jewish cultural life and Hebrew education. In March 1925 the Jewish population in Palestine was officially estimated at 108,000, and it had risen to about 238,000 (20 percent of the population) by 1933. Jewish immigration remained relatively slow, however, until the rise of Nazism in Europe. The large-scale extermination of European Jews led many Jews to seek refuge in Palestine and many others, especially in the United States, to embrace Zionism. The creation by the United Nations of the State of Israel on May 14, 1948, brought about the Arab–Israeli war of 1948–49, in the course of which Israel obtained more land than had been provided by the UN resolution, and drove out 800,000 Arabs who became displaced persons known as Palestinians. During the next two decades Zionist organizations in many countries continued to raise financial support for Israel and to encourage Jews to immigrate there.

and the development of an optimistic evolutionism, messianism was transformed by many liberal thinkers into a version of the idea of progress, a goal that was often thought of as immediately attainable through enlightened social and political action. When disillusionment with emancipation set in, messianism was even more completely secularized by segments of the community who saw its meaning and fulfillment in some form of socialism. In others it was absorbed into the emerging political nationalism—Zionism. Similar developments took place in eastern Europe, with parallel transformations. In the 20th century, particularly after the events symbolized by Auschwitz (a Nazi death camp in Poland, where approximately one million Jews were killed), the earlier modern interpretations, particularly of messianism, but also of eschatology as a whole, were considered inadequate. Although no compelling statement was forthcoming, Jewish thinkers beginning in the second half of the 20th century attempted once again to come to grips with eschatological concepts in all their varieties and forms.

CHAPTER 7

BASIC PRACTICES AND INSTITUTIONS

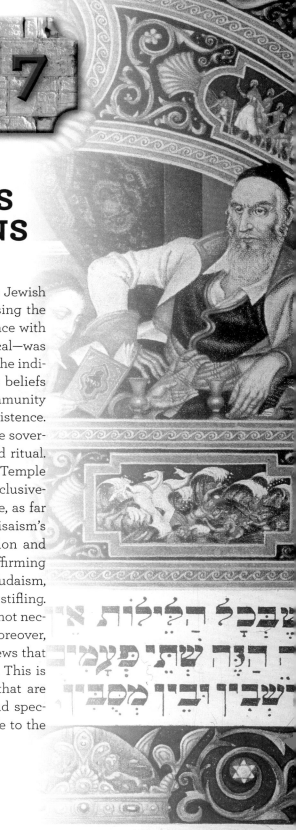

Systematic presentations of the affirmations of the Jewish community were never the sole mode of expressing the beliefs of the people. Maintaining an equal importance with speculation—Haggadic, philosophic, mystical, or ethical—was Halakhah (Oral Law), the paradigmatic statement of the individual and communal behaviour that embodied the beliefs conceptualized in speculation. Life in the holy community was understood to embrace every level of human existence. The prophets vigorously resisted attempts to limit the sovereignty of the God of Israel to organized worship and ritual. The Pharisees, even while the cult of the Jerusalem Temple was still in existence, sought to reduce priestly exclusiveness by enlarging the scope of sacral rules to include, as far as possible, all the people. Rabbinic Judaism, Pharisaism's descendant, continued the process of democratization and sought to find in every occasion of life a means of affirming the presence of the divine. Some critics of Rabbinic Judaism, however, have seen the legal aspect of Jewish life as stifling. Although legalism is always a danger, spontaneity is not necessarily lacking in a world governed by Halakhah. Moreover, the intention of the Halakhic attitude is to remind Jews that every occasion of life is a locus of divine disclosure. This is most clearly seen in the *berakhot*, the "blessings," that are prescribed to accompany the performance of a broad spectrum of human actions, from the routines of daily life to the restricted gestures of the cultic-liturgical year. In these God is addressed directly in the second person singular, his sovereignty is affirmed, and his activity as creator, giver of Torah, or redeemer—expressed in a wide variety of eulogies—is proclaimed. There are no areas of human behaviour in which God cannot be met, and the Halakhic pattern is intended to make such possibilities realities. The situation of the Jewish community, however, determines how this intention is realized. On more than one occasion, the Halakhic pattern has served as a defense against a hostile environment, thus becoming a kind of scrupulousness (an obsessive concern with minute details), but, just as often, the dynamic of the intention has broken through to reestablish its integrity and to hallow life in its wholeness.

THE TRADITIONAL PATTERN OF INDIVIDUAL AND FAMILIAL PRACTICES

The traditional pattern of an individual's life can be discerned by examining a passage from the Babylonian Talmud (tractate *Berakhot* 60b) that was reworked into a liturgical structure but which in its original form exhibits the intention previously discussed. In this passage, the blessings accompanying one's waking and returning to the routines of life are prescribed. There is a brief thanksgiving on awakening for being restored to conscious life. Next, a benediction is offered over the cock's crowing. Following this,

each ordinary act—opening one's eyes, stretching and sitting up, dressing, standing up, walking, tying one's shoes, fastening one's belt, covering one's head, washing one's hands and face—has its accompanying blessing, reminding one that the world and the life to which he has returned exist in the presence of God. These are followed by a supplication in which the petitioner asks that his life during the day may be worthy in all of its relationships. Then, as the first order of daily business, Torah, both written (Bible) and oral (Mishna), is briefly studied, introduced by doxologies to God as Giver of Torah. Finally, there is a prayer for the establishment of the kingdom of God, for each day contains within itself the possibility of ultimate fulfillment. As indicated, this was originally not a part of public worship but rather was personal preparation for a life to be lived in the presence of God (even today it is not, strictly speaking, part of the synagogue service, though it is frequently recited there).

Such individual responsibility marks much of Jewish observance, so that the synagogue—far from being the focus of observance—shares with the home and the workaday world the opportunities for divine-human encounter. The table blessings, Kiddush (the "sanctification" of the Sabbath and festivals), the erection of the booth (*sukka*) for Sukkoth (the Feast of Tabernacles), the seder (the festive Passover meal) with its symbols and narration of the Exodus, and the lighting

Jewish men walk inside a Sukkah during Sukkot, which celebrates both the 40 years the Hebrews spent wandering in the desert and the fall harvest. Menahem Kahana/AFP/Getty Images

of the lamps during the eight days of Hanukkah (the Feast of Dedication) are all the obligation of the individual and the family and have their place in the home.

It is here too where the woman's role is defined and where, as contrasted with the synagogue, she functions centrally. Given the traditional dietary regimen of the Jewish community—the exclusion of swine, carrion eaters, shellfish, and certain other creatures, the separation of meat and dairy products, the ritual slaughtering of animals, the required separation and burning of a small portion of dough (*ḥalla*) when baking, the supervision

of the Passover food requirements, and many other stipulations—there exists a large and meticulously governed area in the home that is the sphere of woman's religion. There seems not to have been a hierarchy of values in which the home-centred—as contrasted with synagogue-oriented—practices were given an inferior status. In modern times, however—particularly in Western societies, where the pervasiveness of religious obligation has been replaced by ecclesiastical institutionalism on the prevailing Christian model—this whole crucial area has lost much of its meaning as a place of divine-human meeting. Thus, for many it is only the synagogue that provides such an opportunity, and the individual act has been reduced on the scale of values. With this downgrading, woman's religion has lost its significance, so that her status—when parallels are drawn to her role in the larger society—has become inferior to that of men. However attenuated personal religious responsibility may have become, the intention of the Halakhic structure, the hallowing of the individual's total existence, remains a potent force within the Jewish community.

KOSHER

The Yiddish term kosher, *which is derived from the Hebrew term* kāshēr, *literally means "fit," or "proper," and signifies the fitness of an object for ritual purposes. Though generally applied to foods that meet the requirements of the dietary laws* (kashruth), kosher *is also used to describe, for instance, such objects as a Torah scroll, water for ritual bathing* (mikvah), *and the ritual ram's horn* (shofar). *When applied to food,* kosher *is the opposite of* terefah *("forbidden"). When applied to other things, it is the opposite of* pasul *("unfit").*

In connection with the dietary laws, kosher *implies: (1) that the food is not derived from the animals, birds, or fish prohibited in Leviticus 11 or Deuteronomy 14; (2) that the animals or birds have been slaughtered by ritual method of* shehitah; *(3) that the meat has been salted to remove the blood (Deuteronomy 12:16, 23–25, and elsewhere) after the carcass has been critically examined for physical blemishes and that the ischiatic nerve has been removed from hindquarters (Genesis 32:32); and (4) that meat and milk have not been cooked together (Exodus 23:19) and that separate utensils have been employed. In consequence of (2), the term* terefah *(that which has been torn by beasts; Genesis 31:39) is extended to all food violating the law, even, incorrectly, to admixtures of leaven on Passover, though* Kāshēr la-Pesach, *"fit for Passover," is fairly correct. So-called kosher wine is prepared under observation, to prevent libations to idols and, by Talmudic extension, to avoid handling by non-Jews. This last regulation is presently observed only by the ultra-Orthodox. A relic of Roman days, it once was common to both Judaism and early Christianity.*

The special method of slaughtering animals, called shehitah, *consists of an incision made across the neck of the animal or fowl by a qualified person especially trained for ritual slaughter, with a special knife that is razor-sharp and has a smooth edge with absolutely no nicks. The cutting must be made by moving the knife in a single swift and uninterrupted sweep, and not by pressure or by stabbing. The cut severs the main arteries, rendering the animal unconscious and permitting the blood to drain from the body. The slaughterer* (shohet) *recites a prayer before the act of* shehitah.

In Orthodox Judaism the dietary laws are considered implications of the divine command to "be holy" (Leviticus 19:2). In Reform Judaism their observance has been declared to be unnecessary to the life of piety.

THE TRADITIONAL PATTERN OF SYNAGOGUE PRACTICES

The other focus of observance is the synagogue. The origins of this institution are obscure, and a number of hypotheses have been proposed to account for the appearance of this lay-oriented form of worship. According to various ancient sources, during the period of the Second Temple—following the return from Babylon and continuing until the Temple's destruction in 70 CE—various nonsacrificial modes of worship emerged that were independent of the priesthood and the official cult. The reports by the philosopher Philo and the historian Josephus in the 1st century, buttressed by the Dead Sea Scrolls, provide some knowledge of the practices of the contemporary Essenes. Rabbinic sources, including the earliest layers of the traditional order of worship, provide insights into an apparently Pharisaic mode, and passages from the Acts of the Apostles concerning James and other Jewish Christians suggest still other varieties. In any case, the practitioners of what eventually became Rabbinic Judaism observed a form of worship that, with the destruction of the Temple cult, provided a new centre and even absorbed enough from the defunct priestly institution to suggest continuity and legitimacy with the Judaic past. This was probably the basic pattern for synagogal liturgy in the millennia that followed.

At the heart of synagogal worship is the public reading of Scriptures. This takes place at the morning service on Sabbaths, holy days, and festivals; Monday and Thursday mornings; and Sabbath afternoons. The readings from the Pentateuch are currently arranged in an annual cycle so that, beginning with Genesis 1:1 on the Sabbath following the autumnal festivals, the entire five books are read through the rest of the year. The texts for festivals, holy days, and fasts reflect the particular significance of those occasions. In addition, a second portion from the prophetic writings (Joshua, Judges, Samuel, and Kings, as well as the three major and 12 minor Prophets, but not Daniel) is read on many of these occasions. The readings take place within the structure of public worship and are incorporated into ceremonies in which the Sefer Torah ("Book of the Torah"), the Pentateuchal scroll, is removed from the ark (cabinet) at the front of the synagogue and carried in procession to the reading desk. From the desk, a reader chants the pertinent text. The text for the service is divided into subsections varying from seven on the Sabbath to three at the weekday morning service, and individuals are called forward to recite the blessings eulogizing God as Giver of Torah before and after each of these. The order of worship is composed of the preparatory blessings and prayers, to which are added passages recalling the Temple sacrificial cult (thus relating the present form of worship to the past); the recitation of a number of Psalms and biblical prayers; the Shema and its accompanying benedictions, introduced by a call to worship that marks the beginning of formal public worship; the prayer (*tefilla*) in the strict sense of petition; confession and supplication (*taḥanun*) on weekdays; the reading of Scripture; and concluding acts of worship. This general structure of the morning service varies somewhat, with additions and subtractions for the afternoon and evening services and for Sabbath, holy days, and festivals.

The prayer (*tefilla*) is often called the *shemone ʿesre*, the "Eighteen Benedictions"—though it actually has 19—or the *ʿamida*, "standing," because it is recited in that position. It is made up of three introductory benedictions (praise of the God of the Fathers, God the Redeemer who resurrects the dead, and God the Holy One who fills the earth with his glory) and three concluding acts (a prayer for the acceptance of the service, a thanksgiving, and a prayer for peace). Between the introductory and concluding sections there is a series of intermediate petitions for knowledge, well-being, acceptance of repentance, forgiveness of sin, and others. On the Sabbath and on festivals the petitions are replaced by benedictions that mention the specific occasion but are not petitionary. It is considered inappropriate to attend to workaday concerns at these times.

The general outline of this order of service is found throughout the entire Jewish world, but the details have varied in different periods and geographic and cultural areas. The public service, requiring the presence of at least 10 males, the *minyan* ("quorum"), is generally led by a synagogal official, the *ḥazzan*, or cantor, but any Jewish male with the requisite knowledge may act in this capacity, because there is no clerical class in the community to whom such leadership is limited.

The synagogue room has a simple basic form, though it may be embellished considerably. The only requirements are a container for the Torah scroll(s), called the *aron ha-qodesh* ("the holy ark"), a chest against the east wall or a recessed closet with doors and a curtain; a prayer desk (*ʿamud*) facing the ark, at which the reader stands when reciting the service; and the pulpit (bima)—in or close to the centre of the room, according to some requirements—from which the Torah is read. In the Spanish-Portuguese tradition, only one desk (called *teva*) is used. The ark contains one or more scrolls, on which are written the Five Books of Moses. These are variously ornamented, depending upon the cultural region: European communities deck them in coverings of cloth, whereas Oriental communities (North African and Near Eastern) place them in wooden or metal containers. In addition, silver ornaments (*rimonim*) in the form of towers or crowns are often set on the tops of two rods on which the scroll is wound, and a breastplate (*hoshen*) and a pointer (*yad*) are suspended from them.

Accommodations for the worshippers vary according to the cultural milieu, from rugs and cushions in Oriental synagogues to pews and standing desks in

Torah crown, Poland, late 18th century; in the Jewish Museum, New York City. Graphic House/EB Inc.

European ones. Given this essential simplicity, the synagogue room itself may be used for purposes other than worship (e.g., study and community assembly). Again, this varies with the cultural pattern.

CEREMONIES MARKING THE INDIVIDUAL LIFE CYCLES

The life of the individual is punctuated by observances that mark the notable events of personal existence. A male child is circumcised on the eighth day following birth, as a covenantal sign (Genesis 17). The rite of circumcision (*berit mila*) is accompanied by appropriate

BAR MITZVAH

The Bar Mitzvah celebrates the attainment for religious purposes of adulthood on a boy's 13th birthday. The boy, now deemed personally responsible for fulfilling all the commandments, may henceforth don phylacteries (religious symbols worn on the forehead and left arm) during the weekday-morning prayers and be counted an adult whenever 10 male adults are needed to form a quorum (minyan) for public prayers.

In a public act of acknowledging religious majority, the boy is called up during the religious service to read from the Torah. This event may take place on any occasion following the 13th birthday at which the Torah is read but generally occurs on the Sabbath. The liturgy of the day thus permits the boy to read the weekly text from the prophets, called Haftarah. This is sometimes followed by a hortatory discourse. After the religious ceremony, there is often a festive Kiddush, or prayer over a cup of wine, with a family social dinner or banquet on the same or the following day.

Though records of the 2nd century mention 13 as the age of religious manhood, most elements of the Bar Mitzvah celebration did not appear until the European Middle Ages. Reform Judaism replaced Bar Mitzvah, after 1810, with the confirmation of boys and girls together, generally on the feast of Shavuot. In the 20th century, however, many Reform congregations restored Bar Mitzvah, delaying confirmation until the age of 15 or 16. Numerous Conservative and Reform congregations have instituted a separate ceremony to mark the adulthood of girls, called Bat Mitzvah.

benedictions and ceremonies, including naming. Females are named in the synagogue, generally on the Sabbath following birth, when the father is called to recite the benedictions over the reading of Torah. A firstborn son, if he does not belong to a priestly or a levitical family, is redeemed at one month (in accordance with Exodus 13:12–13 and Numbers 18:14–16) by the payment of a stipulated sum to a *cohen* (a putative member of the priestly family). At age 13 a boy is called to recite the Torah benedictions publicly, thus signifying his religious coming-of-age. He is thenceforth obligated to observe the commandments as his own responsibility—he is now a bar mitzvah ("son of the commandment"). Many Conservative and Reform congregations have instituted a similar ceremony, called the bat mitzvah, to celebrate the coming-of-age of girls.

Marriage (*ḥatuna*, also *qiddushin*, "sanctifications") involves a double ceremony, performed together in modern times but separated in ancient times by one year. First is the betrothal (*erusin*), which includes the reading of the marriage contract (*ketubba*) and the giving of the ring with a declaration, "Behold you are consecrated to me by this ring according to the law of Moses and Israel," accompanied by certain benedictions. This is followed by the marriage proper (*nissu'in*), consisting of the reciting of the seven marriage benedictions. The ceremony is performed under a *ḥuppa*, a canopy that symbolizes the bridal bower.

The burial service is marked by simplicity. The body, prepared for the grave by the *ḥevra' qaddisha'* ("holy society"), is clad only in a simple shroud and interred as soon after death as possible. In Israel no coffin is used. There are observances connected with death, many of which belong to the realm of folklore rather than Halakhic tradition. A mourning period of 30 days is observed, of which the first seven (shivah) are the most rigorous. During the 11 months following a death, the bereaved recite a particular form of a synagogal doxology (Kaddish) during the public service as an act of memorial. The doxology, devoid of any mention of death, is a praise of God and a prayer for the establishment of the coming kingdom. It is also recited annually on the anniversary of the death (*yahrzeit*).

ḤUPPA

A ḥuppa (also spelled ḥuppah or chuppah) is the portable canopy beneath which the bride and groom stand while a Jewish wedding ceremony is performed. Depending on the local custom and the preference of the bride and groom, the ḥuppa may be a simple Jewish prayer shawl (ṭallit) suspended from four poles, a richly embroidered cloth of silk or velvet, or a flower-covered trellis. In ancient times ḥuppa signified the bridal chamber, but the canopy now symbolizes the home to be established by the newlyweds. In popular usage the term ḥuppa may also refer to the wedding ceremony itself.

HOLY PLACES: THE LAND OF ISRAEL AND JERUSALEM

The land of Israel, as is evident from the biblical narratives, played a significant role in the life and thought of the Israelites. It was the promised home, for the sake of which Abraham left his birthplace; the haven toward which those escaping from Egyptian servitude moved; and the hope of the exiles in Babylon. In the long centuries following the destruction of the Judaean state by the Romans, it was a central part of messianic and eschatological expectations.

During the early period of settlement, there apparently were many sacred localities, with one or another functioning for a time as a central shrine for all the tribes. Even the establishment of Jerusalem as the political capital by David and the building of a royal chapel there by Solomon did not bring an end to local cult centres. It was not until the reign of Josiah of Judah (640–609 BCE) that a reform centralized the cult in Jerusalem and attempted to end worship at local shrines. Although Josiah's reform was not entirely successful, during the Babylonian Exile and the subsequent return, Jerusalem and its Temple defeated its rivals and became—in law, in fact, and in sentiment—the centre of Jewish cultic life. This did not inhibit, however, the rise and development of other forms of worship and occasionally even other cult centres. Nonetheless, no matter how unpopular the priesthood of the Jerusalem Temple became with some segments of the population (the Qumrān community seems to have denied its legality; and the Pharisees complained bitterly about its arrogance and exactions, attempting, when feasible, to impose and enforce Pharisaic regulations upon it) reverence for the Temple seems to have remained a widespread sentiment. With the destruction of the Temple by the Romans in 70 CE, such reverence was transformed both by messianic expectations and by eschatological hopes into fervent devotion, which, over the following centuries, became idealized and even supernaturalized. The most ardently articulated statement of the crucial role of the land of Israel and the Jerusalem Temple is found in the *Sefer ha-Kuzari* of Judah ha-Levi, in which the two are seen as absolutely indispensable for the proper relationship between God and his people.

Symbolizing the significance of the land and the city is the practice of facing in their direction during worship. The earliest architectural evidence derived from synagogue remains in Galilee indicates that the attempt was made to arrange the building in such a way that the worshippers faced directly toward Jerusalem. This practice may have continued even in the Diaspora. But at a later date, the present practice of setting the holy ark in or before the east wall was established, making "facing Jerusalem" is now more symbolic than actual.

THE SACRED LANGUAGE: HEBREW AND THE VERNACULAR TONGUES

The transformation of Hebrew into a sacred language is closely tied to the political fate of the people. In the period following the return from the Babylonian Exile, Aramaic, a cognate of Hebrew, functioned as the international or imperial language in official life and gained a foothold as a vernacular. It did not, despite claims made by some scholars, displace the everyday Hebrew of the people. The language of the Mishna, far from being a scholar's dialect, seems to reflect popular speech, as did the Koine (common) Greek of the New Testament. Displacement of Hebrew (both in its literary form in Scriptures and in its popular usage) occurred in the Diaspora, however, as illustrated by the translation of Scriptures into Greek in some communities and into Aramaic in others. There seems also to have been an inclination on the part of some authorities to permit even the recitation of the Shema complex in the vernacular during the worship service. Struggles over these issues continued for a number of centuries in various places, but the development of formal literary Hebrew—a sacred tongue, to be used side by side with the Hebrew Scriptures in worship—brought them to an end. Although the communities of the Diaspora used the vernaculars of their environment in day-to-day living and even—as in the case of the communities of the Islamic world—for philosophical, theological, and other scholarly writings, Hebrew remained the standard in worship until modern times, when some western European reform movements sought partially (and a small fraction even totally) to displace it.

THE RABBINATE

The rabbinate, with its peculiar nature and functions, is the result of a series of developments that began after the disastrous second revolt against Rome (132–135 CE).

LEGAL, JUDICIAL, AND CONGREGATIONAL ROLES

The term *rabbi* ("my teacher") was originally an honorific title for the graduates of the academy directed by the *nasi*, or patriarch, who was the head of the Jewish community in Palestine as well as a Roman imperial official. The curriculum of the school was Torah, written and oral, according to the Pharisaic tradition and formulation. The *nasi* appointed rabbis to the law court (the *bet din*) and as legal officers of local communities; acting with the local elders, they supervised and controlled the life of the community and its members in all aspects. A similar situation obtained in Babylon under the Parthian and Sāsānian empires, where the *resh galuta*, or exilarch ("head of the exile"), appointed rabbinical officials to legal and administrative posts. In time the patriarchate and exilarchate disappeared, but the rabbinate, nourished by

RABBI

The term rabbi is derived from a Hebrew word meaning "my teacher," or "my master," and designates a person qualified by academic studies of the Hebrew Bible and the Talmud to act as spiritual leader and religious teacher of a Jewish community or congregation. Ordination (certification as a rabbi) can be conferred by any rabbi, but one's teacher customarily performs this function by issuing a written statement. Ordination carries with it no special religious status. For many generations the education of a rabbi consisted almost exclusively of Talmudic studies, but since the 19th century the necessity and value of a well-rounded, general education has been recognized.

Rabbis officiate at most Jewish weddings but not most other ceremonies, though others can do so as well. © Cindy Reiman

Differences among Orthodox, Conservative, and Reform Jewish groups are reflected, to some degree, in the functions of their respective rabbis. A rabbi associated with a Reform group, for example, will not be involved in overseeing the production of kosher foods, since his group does not observe Jewish dietary laws. Further, whereas rabbis assist at all religious marriages, their presence at most other ceremonies is not required. Nonetheless, they generally conduct religious services, assist at Bar Mitzvah, and are present at funerals and sometimes circumcisions. In questions of divorce, a rabbi's role depends on an appointment to a special court of Jewish law.

A rabbi also preaches on occasion and counsels and consoles as needs arise. A rabbi has responsibility for the total religious education of the young, but the extent of his participation, beyond the realm of general supervision, is dictated by local circumstances. Modern rabbis are likewise involved in social and philanthropic works and are expected to lend support to any project sponsored by their congregations. In some cases, rabbis function on a part-time basis, devoting the major portion of their energies to a secular profession. Because a rabbi does not have sacerdotal status, many functions that he normally performs may be assumed by others who, although not ordained, are qualified to conduct the religious ceremonies with devotion and exactitude.

By 100 CE the term rabbi was in general use to denote a sage (i.e., an interpreter of Jewish law). Gradually, salaried rabbi-judges and unsalaried rabbi-teachers (interpreters of Jewish law) came to perform routine services for their communities. From the 14th century, rabbi-teachers were receiving salaries (as rabbis generally do today) to free them from other obligations. Also in this period there began the tradition of submission of local scholars to their community's rabbi.

independent rabbinical academies, survived. An authorized scholar, when called to become the judicial officer of a community, would at the same time become the head of the local academy and, after adequate preparation and examination, would grant authorization to his pupils, who were then eligible to be called to rabbinical posts. There was thus a diffusion of authority, the communities calling, rather than a superior official appointing, their rabbis. The rabbis were not ecclesiastical personages but communal officials, responsible for the governance of the entire range of life of what was understood to be the *qehilla qedosha*, the "holy community."

In modern times, particularly in the Western world, the change in Jewish communal existence required a transformation of this ancient structure. The rabbinate became, for the most part, an ecclesiastical rather than a communal agency, reflecting the requirements of civic life in modern nation states. The education of rabbis is now carried on in seminaries whose structure and curriculum have been influenced by European and American academic institutions. The majority of their graduates serve as congregational rabbis, in roles similar to those of ministers and priests in Christian denominations but with some other functions deriving from the particular situation and nature of the Jewish community.

In the State of Israel certain larger areas, such as that of family law, are still reserved for the rabbinate. Even here, however, the rabbinate functions more as a counterpart to other ecclesiastical organizations, such as Christian and Muslim, than as an overarching and all-inclusive communal agency.

CHIEF RABBINATES

The prototype of the chief rabbinate was the Great Sanhedrin of Jerusalem, which, until the destruction of the Second Temple, issued legislation and interpreted Torah for all the Jewish people. The existence of the offices of chief rabbi in the State of Israel derives from the situation in the Ottoman Empire, where the various religious communities functioned as quasi-political entities in a multiethnic conglomerate. Israel has two chief rabbis, one for the Ashkenazic (European) and one for the Sephardic (Oriental) community, who no longer function as the heads of whole communities but only of ecclesiastical organizations. The same is true in countries outside Israel that have the office of chief rabbi (e.g., Great Britain and France). In these countries the chief rabbi's relationship with the government is like that of his ecclesiastical counterparts in the Christian churches. While the chief rabbis have certain kinds of limited authority because of their official position, they have jurisdiction only over those members of the Jewish community who are ready to accept it. Others form their own ecclesiastical units and act without reference to the chief rabbinate.

In some situations—particularly in the United States, where there is no similar structure—the title *chief rabbi* or *grand rabbi* has been assumed occasionally by individuals as a means of asserting superior dignity or even (fruitlessly) authority.

GENERAL COUNCILS OR CONFERENCES

The nature of the Sanhedrin in the last years of the Jewish commonwealth is a much disputed matter. The several councils mentioned in Talmudic literature are equally difficult to define with any precision. References scattered throughout medieval literature suggest the existence of councils and synods, but their composition and authority are uncertain. About the year 1000 a synod was held in the Rhineland in which French and German communities participated under the guidance of Rabbenu Gershom, the leading rabbinic authority of the region. In the late Middle Ages, representatives from the communities of Great Poland, Little Poland, Russian Poland (Volhynia), and Lithuania came together to form the Wa'ad Arba' Aratzot (Council of the Four Lands). At the beginning of the modern era, Napoleon in 1806 summoned the Assembly of Notables—representatives of communities under French dominion— to deal with questions arising from the dissolution of the older status of the Jews and their naturalization as individuals into the new nation-states. Decisions of the assembly that involved questions of Jewish law were subsequently submitted to a Grand Sanhedrin called by Napoleon to provide Halakhic justification for acts that the French imperial government had required of the Jewish communities.

During the 19th century the demand for the reform of Jewish life—principally the liturgy of the synagogue but many other aspects as well—prompted a series of rabbinical conferences and synods. A similar course of events took place in the United States. In both instances, after an initial period in which radicals, moderates, and conservatives argued their respective cases in the same forum, polarization set in and intellectual differences were transformed into competing organizations. In the 1970s the several tendencies within the Jewish communities in North America were institutionalized in rabbinical conferences and congregational unions—Orthodox, Conservative, and Reform—whose influence was in large measure limited to their adherents. There is also a worldwide body of Reform or Liberal Judaism—the World Union for Progressive Judaism. One result of these developments was the hardening of denominational differences, particularly in North America, especially between Orthodox and non-Orthodox (Reform, Reconstructionist, Conservative) Judaisms.

MODERN VARIATIONS

The preceding sketch of basic practices and institutions has attempted to describe the so-called traditional situation, though it has been indicated that even here there are variations—actually more than have been noted. Reference has also been made to changes that represent the abandonment of traditional practices on the basis of intellectual decisions about the nature of Judaism, its beliefs, practices, and institutions. Such changes are far too numerous to describe in detail, but it is important to indicate their motivation. The Halakhic system, both as a whole and in all of its parts, is viewed not as divinely revealed but rather as a human process that seeks to expose in mutable forms the meaning of the divine-human encounter. The practices and institutions, therefore, are understood as historically determined, reflecting the multifaceted experience of the people of Israel as they have sought to live in the presence of God. Historical scholarship has disclosed the origins, rise, development, and decline of these structures in the past, and thus suggests the propriety of changes in the present and future that appear to fulfill the needs of the community and its members. However, this kind of historicism (the explanation of values and forms in terms of their historical conditions) has been applied in widely different ways since it was first used in the 19th century. Some have seen it as justifying a disengagement from much if not all of the traditional pattern and a recognition that only the spiritual essence is of consequence for Judaism. Others have argued that the burden of proof is always upon those who would introduce changes. Since the end of World War II, the question has been whether a reconstituted Halakhic system might not be a requirement of the day.

CHAPTER 8

THE RELIGIOUS YEAR AND HOLIDAYS

The calendar of Judaism includes the cycle of Sabbaths and holidays that are commonly observed by the Jewish religious community—and officially in Israel by the Jewish secular community as well. The Sabbath and festivals are bound to the Jewish calendar, reoccur at fixed intervals, and are celebrated at home and in the synagogue according to ritual set forth in Jewish law and hallowed by Jewish custom.

THE CYCLE OF THE RELIGIOUS YEAR

According to Jewish teaching, the Sabbath and festivals are, in the first instance, commemorative. The Sabbath, for example, commemorates the Creation, and Passover commemorates the Exodus from Egypt more than 3,000 years ago. The past is not merely recalled; it is also relived through the Sabbath and festival observances. Creative physical activity ceases on the Sabbath—as it did, according to Genesis, when Creation was completed. Jews leave their homes and reside in booths during the Sukkoth festival, as did their biblical ancestors. Moreover, Sabbath and festival themes are considered to be perpetually significant, recurring and renewed in every generation. Thus, the revelation of the Torah (the divine teaching, or law) at Sinai, commemorated on Shavuot, is considered an ongoing process that recurs whenever a commitment is made to Torah study.

An important aspect of Sabbath and festival observance is sanctification. The Sabbath and festivals sanctified the Jews more than the Jews sanctified the Sabbath and festivals. Mundane meals became sacred meals. Joy and relaxation became sacred obligations (*mitzwot*). No less significant is the contribution of the Sabbath and festivals to communal awareness. Thus, neither Sabbath nor festival can be properly observed in the synagogue, according to the ancient tradition, if fewer than 10 Jewish males are present. Again, a Jew prays on Rosh Hashana and mourns on Tisha be-Av not only for his own fate but for the fate of all Jews. The sense of social cohesiveness fostered by the Sabbath and festival observances has stood the Jews well throughout their long, often tortuous history.

The seven-day week, the notion of a weekly day of rest, and many Christian and Islamic holiday observances owe their origins to the Jewish calendar, Sabbath, and festivals.

THE JEWISH CALENDAR

The Jewish calendar is lunisolar (i.e., regulated by the positions of both the Moon and the Sun). It consists usually of 12 alternating lunar months of 29 and 30 days each (except for Ḥeshvan and Kislev, which sometimes have either 29 or 30 days) and totals 353, 354, or 355 days per year. The average lunar year (354 days) is adjusted to the solar year (365 ¼ days) by the periodic introduction of leap years to assure that the major festivals fall in their proper seasons. The leap year consists of an additional 30-day month called First Adar, which always precedes the month of (Second) Adar. A leap year consists of either 383, 384, or 385 days and occurs seven times during every 19-year period (the Metonic cycle). Among the consequences of the lunisolar structure are these: the number of days in a year may vary considerably, from 353 to 385 days; and the first day of a month can fall on any day of the week, that day varying from year to year. Consequently, the days of the week upon which an annual Jewish festival falls vary from year to year despite the festival's fixed position in the Jewish month.

MONTHS AND NOTABLE DAYS

The months of the Jewish religious year, their approximate equivalent in the Western Gregorian calendar, and their notable days are as follows:

Tishri (September–October)
1–2 Rosh Hashana (New Year)
3 Tzom Gedaliahu (Fast o Gedaliah)
10 Yom Kippur (Day of Atonement)
15–21 Sukkoth (Tabernacles)
22 Shemini Atzeret (Eighth Day of the Solemn Assembly)
23 Simḥat Torah (Rejoicing of the Law)

Ḥeshvan, or Marḥeshvan (October–November)

Kislev (November–December)
> 25 Hanukkah (Feast of Dedication) begins

Ṭevet (December–January)
> 2–3 Hanukkah ends
> 10 ʿAsara be-Ṭevet (Fast of Ṭevet 10)

Shevaṭ (January–February)
> 15 Ṭu bi-Shevaṭ (15th of Shevaṭ: New Year for Trees)

Adar (February–March)
> 13 Taʿanit Esther (Fast of Esther)
> 14, 15 Purim (Feast of Lots)

Nisan (March–April)
> 15–22 Pesaḥ (Passover)

Iyyar (April–May)
> 18 Lag ba-ʿOmer (33rd Day of the ʿOmer Counting)

Sivan (May–June)
> 6, 7 Shavuot (Feast of Weeks, or Pentecost)

Tammuz (June–July)
> 17 Shiva ʿAsar be-Tammuz (Fast of Tammuz 17)

Av (July–August)
> 9 Tisha be-Av (Fast of Av 9)

Elul (August–September)

During leap year the Adar holidays are postponed to Second Adar. Since 1948 many Jewish calendars list Iyyar 5—Israel Independence Day—among the Jewish holidays.

ORIGIN AND DEVELOPMENT

The origin of the Jewish calendar can no longer be accurately traced. Some scholars suggest that a solar year prevailed in ancient Israel, but no convincing proofs have been offered, and it is more likely that a lunisolar calendar similar to that of ancient Babylonia was used. In late Second Temple times (i.e., 1st century BCE to 70 CE), calendrical matters were regulated by the Sanhedrin, or council of elders, at Jerusalem. The testimony of two witnesses who had observed the new moon was ordinarily required to proclaim a new month. Leap years were proclaimed by a council of three or more rabbis with the approval of the *nasi*, or patriarch, of the Sanhedrin. With the decline of the Sanhedrin, calendrical matters were decided by the Palestinian patriarchate (the official heads of the Jewish community under Roman rule). Jewish persecution under the Roman emperor Constantius II (reigned 337–361) and advances in astronomical science led to the gradual replacement of observation by calculation. According to Hai ben Sherira (died 1038), the head of a leading Talmudic academy in Babylonia, the Palestinian patriarch Hillel II introduced a fixed and continuous calendar in 359 CE. A summary of the regulations governing the present calendar is provided by

Maimonides, the great medieval philosopher and legist, in his *Code: Sanctification of the New Moon,* chapters 6–10.

Fragments of writings discovered in a *genizah* (a depository for sacred writings withdrawn from circulation) have brought to light a calendrical dispute between Aaron ben Meir, a 10th-century Palestinian descendant of the patriarchal (Hillel) family, and the Babylonian Jewish authorities, including Saʿadia ben Joseph, an eminent 9th–10th-century philosopher and gaon (head of a Talmudic academy). Ben Meir's calculations provided that Passover in 922 be celebrated two days earlier than the date fixed by the normative calendar. After a bitter exchange of letters, the controversy subsided in favour of the Babylonian authorities, whose hegemony in calendrical matters was never again challenged.

Calendars of various sectarian Jewish communities deviated considerably from the normative calendar described above. The Dead Sea, or Qumrān, community (made famous by the discovery of the Dead Sea Scrolls) adopted the calendrical system of the noncanonical books of Jubilees and Enoch, which was essentially a solar calendar. Elements of the same calendar reappear among the Mishawites, a sect founded in the 9th century.

The Karaites, a sect founded in the 8th century, refused, with some exceptions, to recognize the normative fixed calendar and reintroduced observation of the new moon. Leap years were determined by observing the maturation of the barley crop in Palestine. Consequently, Karaites often celebrated the festivals on dates different from those fixed by the rabbis. Later, in medieval times, the Karaites adopted some of the normative calendrical practices while rejecting others.

THE SABBATH

The Jewish Sabbath (from Hebrew *shavat,* "to rest") is observed throughout the year on the seventh day of the week—Saturday. According to biblical tradition, it commemorates the original seventh day on which God rested after completing the creation.

Scholars have not succeeded in tracing the origin of the seven-day week, nor can they account for the origin of the Sabbath. A seven-day week does not accord well with either a solar or a lunar calendar. Some scholars, pointing to the Akkadian term *shapattu,* suggest a Babylonian origin for the seven-day week and the Sabbath. But *shapattu,* which refers to the day of the full moon and is nowhere described as a day of rest, has little in common with the Jewish Sabbath. It appears that the notion of the Sabbath as a holy day of rest, linking God to his people and recurring every seventh day, was unique to ancient Israel.

IMPORTANCE

The central significance of the Sabbath for Judaism is reflected in the traditional commentative and interpretative literature called Talmud and Midrash (e.g., "if you wish to destroy the Jewish people, abolish their Sabbath first") and in numerous legends and adages from more-recent literature (e.g., "more than Israel kept the Sabbath, the Sabbath kept Israel"). Some of the basic teachings of Judaism affirmed by the Sabbath are God's acts of creation, God's role in history, and God's covenant with Israel. Moreover, the Sabbath is the only Jewish holiday the observance of which is enjoined by the Ten Commandments. Jews are obligated to sanctify the Sabbath at home and in the synagogue by observing the Sabbath laws and engaging in worship and study. The leisure hours afforded by the ban against work on the Sabbath were put to good use by the rabbis, who used them to promote intellectual activity and spiritual regeneration among Jews. Other days of rest, such as the Christian Sunday and the Islamic Friday, owe their origins to the Jewish Sabbath.

OBSERVANCES

The biblical ban against work on the Sabbath, while never clearly defined, includes activities such as baking and cooking, travelling, kindling fire, gathering wood, buying and selling, and bearing burdens from one domain into another. The Talmudic rabbis listed 39 major categories of prohibited work, including agricultural activity (e.g., plowing and reaping), work entailed in the manufacture of cloth (e.g., spinning and weaving), work entailed in preparing documents (e.g., writing), and other forms of constructive work.

At home the Sabbath begins Friday evening some 20 minutes before sunset, with the lighting of the Sabbath candles by the wife or, in her absence, by the husband. In the synagogue the Sabbath is ushered in at sunset with the recital of selected psalms and the *Lekha Dodi*, a 16th-century Kabbalistic (mystical) poem. The refrain of the latter is "Come, my beloved, to meet the bride," the "bride" being the Sabbath. After the evening service, each Jewish household begins the first of three festive Sabbath meals by reciting the Kiddush ("sanctification" of the Sabbath) over a cup of wine. This is followed by a ritual washing of the hands and the breaking of bread, two loaves of bread (commemorating the double portions of manna described in Exodus) being placed before the breaker of bread at each Sabbath meal. After the festive meal the remainder of the evening is devoted to study or relaxation. The distinctive features of the Sabbath morning synagogue service include the public reading of the Torah, or Five Books of Moses (the portion read varies from week to week), and, generally, the sermon, both of which serve to educate the listeners. Following the service, the second Sabbath meal begins, again preceded by Kiddush (of lesser significance), conforming for the most part to the first Sabbath meal. The afternoon synagogue service is followed by the third festive meal (without Kiddush). After the evening service the Sabbath comes to a close with the *havdala* ("distinction") ceremony, which consists of a benediction noting the distinction

Havdala *ceremony marking the end of the Sabbath with wine and candle; wood-cut from a* minhagim *("customs") book, Amsterdam, 1662. Jewish Museum, New York City/Art Resource, New York*

between Sabbath and weekday, usually recited over a cup of wine accompanied by a spice box and candle.

JEWISH HOLIDAYS

The major Jewish holidays are the Pilgrim Festivals—Pesaḥ (Passover), Shavuot (Feast of Weeks, or Pentecost), and Sukkoth (Tabernacles)—and the High Holidays—Rosh Hashana (New Year) and Yom Kippur (Day of Atonement). The observance of all the major holidays is required by the Torah and work is prohibited for the duration of the holiday (except on the intermediary days of the Pesaḥ and Sukkoth festivals, when work is permitted to avoid financial loss). Purim (Feast of Lots) and Hanukkah (Feast of Dedication), while not mentioned in the

Torah (and therefore of lesser solemnity), were instituted by Jewish authorities in the Persian and Greco-Roman periods. They are sometimes regarded as minor festivals because they lack the work restrictions of the major festivals. In addition, there are the five fasts—'Asara be-Ṭevet (Fast of Ṭevet 10), Shiva' 'Asar be-Tammuz (Fast of Tammuz 17), Tisha be-Av (Fast of Av 9), Tzom Gedaliahu (Fast of Gedaliah), and Ta'anit Esther (Fast of Esther)—and the lesser holidays (i.e., holidays the observances of which are few and not always clearly defined)—such as Rosh Ḥodesh (First Day of the Month), Ṭu bi-Shevat (15th of Shevaṭ: New Year for Trees), and Lag ba-'Omer (33rd Day of the 'Omer Counting). The fasts and the lesser holidays, like the minor festivals, lack the work restrictions characteristic of the major festivals. Although some of the fasts and Rosh Ḥodesh are mentioned in Scripture, most of the details concerning their proper observance, as well as those concerning the other lesser holidays, were provided by the Talmudic and medieval rabbis.

PILGRIM FESTIVALS

In Temple times, all males were required to appear at the Temple three times annually and actively participate in the festal offerings and celebrations. These were the joyous Pilgrim Festivals of Pesaḥ, Shavuot, and Sukkoth. They originally marked the major agricultural seasons in ancient Israel and commemorated Israel's early history. But after the destruction of the Second Temple in 70 CE, emphasis was placed almost exclusively on the commemorative aspect.

In modern Israel, Pesaḥ, Shavuot, and Sukkoth are celebrated for seven days, one day, and eight days, respectively (with Shemini Atzeret added to Sukkoth), as prescribed by Scripture. Because of calendrical uncertainties that arose in Second Temple times (6th century BCE to 1st century CE), each festival is celebrated for an additional day in the Diaspora.

Pesaḥ commemorates the Exodus from Egypt and the servitude that preceded it. As such, it is the most significant of the commemorative holidays, for it celebrates the very inception of the Jewish people (i.e., the event which provided the basis for the covenant between God and Israel). The term *pesah* refers originally to the paschal (Passover) lamb sacrificed on the eve of the Exodus, the blood of which marked the Jewish homes to be spared from God's plague. Its etymological significance, however, remains uncertain. The Hebrew root is usually rendered "passed over" (i.e., God passed over the homes of the Israelites when inflicting the last plague on the Egyptians), hence the term *Passover*. The festival is also called Ḥag or Matzot ("Festival of Unleavened Bread"), for unleavened bread is the only kind of bread consumed during Passover.

Passover plate from Pesaro, Italy, 1614; in the Jewish Museum, New York City. Graphic House/EB Inc.

Leaven (se'or) and foods containing leaven (ḥametz) are neither to be owned nor consumed during Pesaḥ. Aside from meats, fresh fruits, and vegetables, it is customary to consume only food prepared under rabbinic supervision and labelled "kosher for Passover," warranting that they are completely free of contact with leaven. In many homes, special sets of crockery, cutlery, and cooking utensils are acquired for Passover use. On the evening preceding the 14th day of Nisan, the home is thoroughly searched for any trace of leaven (bediqat ḥametz). The following morning the remaining particles of leaven are destroyed by fire (bi'ur ḥametz). From then until after Pesaḥ, no leaven is consumed. Many Jews sell their more valuable leaven products to non-Jews before Passover (mekhirat ḥametz), repurchasing the foodstuffs immediately after the holiday.

The unleavened bread (matzo) consists entirely of flour and water, and great care is taken to prevent any fermentation before baking. Hand-baked matzo is flat, rounded, and perforated. Since the 19th century, many Jews have preferred the square-shaped, machine-made matzo.

Passover eve is ushered in at the synagogue service on the evening before Passover, after which each family partakes of the seder ("order of service"), an elaborate festival meal in which every ritual is regulated by the rabbis. (In the Diaspora the seder is also celebrated on the second evening of Passover.) The table is bedecked with an assortment of foods symbolizing the passage from slavery (e.g., bitter herbs) into freedom (e.g., wine). The Haggada ("Storytelling"), a printed manual comprising appropriate passages culled from Scripture, Talmud, and Midrash accompanied by medieval hymns, serves as a guide for the ensuing ceremonies and is recited as the evening proceeds. The seder opens with the cup of sanctification (Kiddush), the first of four cups of wine drunk by the celebrants. An invitation is extended to the needy to join the seder ceremonies, after which the youngest son asks four prescribed questions expressing his surprise at the many departures from usual mealtime procedure. ("How different this night is from all other nights!") The father then explains that the Jews were once slaves in Egypt, were then liberated by God, and now commemorate the servitude and freedom by means of the seder ceremonies. Special blessings are recited over the unleavened bread and the bitter herbs (maror), after which the main courses are served. The meal closes with a serving of matzo recalling the paschal lamb, consumption of which concluded the meal in Temple times. The seder concludes with the joyous recital of hymns praising God's glorious acts in history and anticipating a messianic redemption to come.

The Passover liturgy is considerably expanded and includes the daily recitation of Psalms 113–118 (Hallel, "Praise"), public readings from the Torah, and an additional service (musaf). On the first day of Pesaḥ, a prayer for dew in the

SEDER

The seder is the religious meal served in Jewish homes on the 15th and 16th of the month of Nisan to commence the festival of Passover (Pesaḥ). Though Passover commemorates the Exodus, the historical deliverance of the Jewish people from Egyptian bondage, Jews are ever mindful that this event was a prelude to God's revelation on Mount Sinai. For each participant, therefore, the seder is an occasion to relive the Exodus as a personal spiritual event. The religious nature of the seder with its carefully prescribed ritual makes the dinner quite unlike family dinners held on civil holidays. Reform Jews and Jews in Israel omit the second seder because they limit Passover to seven days.

The head of the family, having usually donned a white ritual gown (kittel), begins the ceremony by sanctifying the holiday with a benediction (Qiddush) over a cup of wine. In all, four cups of wine (arba' kosot) will be drunk at certain intervals.

After all have washed their hands, the master of the seder presents celery or another raw vegetable (karpas) dipped in vinegar or salt water to all participants. Then a shank bone, symbolic of the Paschal lamb eaten in ancient times, and (commonly) a hard-boiled egg, symbolic of God's loving kindness (or, according to some, a mournful reminder of the destruction of the Temple of Jerusalem), are removed from the seder plate, while all recite a prayer.

After a second cup of wine is poured, the youngest child asks four standard questions about the unusual ceremonies: "Why does this night differ from all other nights? For on all other nights we eat either leavened or unleavened bread; why on this night only unleavened bread? On all other nights we eat all kinds of herbs; why on this night only bitter herbs? On all other nights we need not dip our herbs even once; why on this night must we dip them twice? On all other nights we eat either sitting up or reclining; why on this night do we all recline?"

The prepared answers, recited by all in unison, give a spiritual interpretation to the customs, even though some aspects of the feast were doubtless copied from Greco-Roman banquets. In essence, the narration (Haggadah) is the story of the Exodus. This unique element of the seder celebration keeps alive sacred Jewish traditions that are repeated by succeeding generations at every seder meal.

All again wash their hands, then consume unleavened bread (matza) and bitter herbs (maror) dipped into a mixture of crushed fruits and wine, signifying that freedom and spiritual progress are the reward of suffering and sacrifice. At this point the meal is eaten.

When all have eaten and recited grace, a third cup of wine is poured to express thanksgiving to God. As the ritual moves toward its conclusion, psalms of praise are recited in unison and a fourth cup of wine is poured to acknowledge God's loving Providence. Some add a fifth cup of wine (which is not drunk) in honour of Elijah, whose appearance at some future seder will signify the advent of the Messiah. Often folk songs are sung after the meal.

Holy Land is recited. On the last day, the memorial service for the departed (*yizkor*) is added.

Originally an agricultural festival marking the wheat harvest, Shavuot commemorates the revelation of the Torah on Mount Sinai. Shavuot ("Weeks") takes its name from the seven weeks of grain harvest separating Passover and Shavuot. The festival is also called Ḥag ha-Qazir (Harvest Festival) and Yom ha-Bikkurim (Day of First Fruits). Greek-speaking Jews called it *pentēkostē*, meaning "the fiftieth" day after the sheaf offering. In rabbinic literature, Shavuot is called *atzeret* ("cessation" or "conclusion"), perhaps because the cessation of work is one of its distinctive features, or possibly because it was viewed as concluding the Passover season. In liturgical texts it is described as the "season of the giving of our Torah." The association of Shavuot with the revelation at Sinai, while not attested in Scripture, is alluded to in the Pseudepigrapha (a collection of noncanonical writings). In rabbinic literature it first appears in 2nd-century materials. The association, probably an ancient one, was derived in part from the book of Exodus, which dates the revelation at Sinai to the third month (counting from Nisan), that is, Sivan.

Scripture does not provide an absolute date for Shavuot. Instead, 50 days (or seven weeks) are reckoned from the day the sheaf offering ('Omer) of the harvest was brought to the Temple, the 50th day being Shavuot. According to the Talmudic rabbis, the sheaf offering was brought on the 16th of Nisan. Hence Shavuot always fell on or about the 6th of Sivan. Some Jewish sectarians, such as the Sadducees, rejected the rabbinic tradition concerning the date of the sheaf ceremony, preferring a later date, and celebrated Shavuot accordingly.

In Temple times, aside from the daily offerings, festival offerings, and first-fruit gifts, a special cereal consisting of two breads prepared from the new wheat crop was offered at the Temple. Since the destruction of the Second Temple, Shavuot observances have been dominated by its commemorative aspect. Many Jews spend the entire Shavuot night studying Torah, a custom first mentioned in the *Zohar* ("Book of Splendour"), a Kabbalistic work edited and published in the 13th–14th centuries. Some prefer to recite the *tiqqun lel Shavu'ot* ("Shavuot night service"), an anthology of passages from Scripture and the Mishna (the authoritative compilation of the Oral Law). An expanded liturgy includes Hallel, public readings from the Torah, *yizkor* (in many congregations), and *musaf*. The Book of Ruth is read at the synagogue service, possibly because of its harvest-season setting.

Sukkoth ("Booths"), an ancient harvest festival that commemorates the booths the Israelites resided in after the Exodus, was the most prominent of the three Pilgrim Festivals in ancient Israel. Also called Ḥag ha-Asif (Festival of Ingathering), it has retained its joyous, festive character through the ages. It begins on Tishri 15 and is celebrated for seven days. The concluding eighth day (plus a ninth day in the Diaspora), Shemini Atzeret, is a separate holiday. In Temple times, each day of Sukkoth had its own prescribed number of sacrificial offerings. Other observances, recorded in the Mishna tractate *Sukka*, include the daily recitation of Hallel, daily circumambulation of the Temple altar, a daily water libation ceremony, and the nightly *bet ha-sho'eva* or *bet ha-she'uvah* ("place of water drawing") festivities starting on the evening preceding the second day. The last-mentioned observance features torch dancing, flute playing, and other forms of musical and choral entertainment.

Ideally, Jews are to reside in booths— walled structures covered with thatched roofs—for the duration of the festival. In practice, most observant Jews take their meals in the *sukka* ("booth") but reside at home. A palm tree branch (*lulav*) bound up together with myrtle (*hadas*) and willow (*'arava*) branches is held together with a citron (*etrog*) and waved. Medieval exegetes provided ample (if not always persuasive) justification for the Bible's choice of these particular branches and fruit as symbols of rejoicing. The numerous regulations governing the *sukka*, *lulav*, and *etrog* constitute the major portion of the treatment of Sukkoth in the codes of Jewish law. The daily Sukkoth liturgy includes the recitation of Hallel (Psalms, 113–118), public readings from the Torah, the *musaf* service, and the circumambulation of the synagogue dais. On the last day of Sukkoth, called Hoshana Rabba (Great Hoshana) after the first words of a prayer (*hoshana*, "save us") recited then, seven such circumambulations take place. Kabbalistic (mystical) teaching has virtually transformed Hoshana Rabba into a solemn day of judgment.

Hoshana Rabba is followed by Shemini Atzeret (Eighth Day of Solemn Assembly), which is celebrated on Tishri 22 (in the Diaspora also Tishri 23). None of the more distinctive Sukkoth observances apply to Shemini Atzeret. But Hallel, public reading from the Torah, *yizkor* (in many congregations), *musaf*, and a prayer for rain in the Holy Land are included in its liturgy. Simḥat Torah (Rejoicing of the Law) marks the annual completion of the cycle of public readings from the Torah. The festival originated shortly before the gaonic period (c. 600–1050 CE) in Babylon, where it was customary to conclude the public readings annually. In Palestine, where the public readings were concluded approximately every three years, Simḥat Torah was not celebrated annually until after the gaonic period. Israeli Jews celebrate Simḥat Torah and Shemini Atzeret on the same day. In the Diaspora, Simḥat Torah is celebrated on the second day of Shemini Atzeret. Its joyous celebrations bring the Sukkoth season to an appropriate close.

TEN DAYS OF PENITENCE

The Ten Days of Penitence begin on Rosh Hashana and close with Yom

Kippur. Already in Talmudic times they were viewed as forming an especially appropriate period of introspection and repentance. Penitential prayers (*seliḥot*) are recited prior to the daily morning service, and, in general, scrupulous observance of the Law is expected during the period.

According to Mishnaic teaching, the New Year festival ushers in the Days of Judgment for all of humankind. Despite its solemnity, the festive character of Rosh Hashana is in no way diminished. In Scripture it is called "a day when the horn is sounded" and in the liturgy "a day of remembrance." In the land of Israel and in the Diaspora, Rosh Hashana is celebrated on the first two days of Tishri. Originally celebrated by all Jews on Tishri 1, calendrical uncertainty led to its being celebrated for an additional day in the Diaspora and, depending upon the circumstances, one or two days in Palestine. After the calendar was fixed in 359, it was regularly celebrated in Palestine on Tishri 1 until the 12th century, when Provençal scholars introduced the two-day observance.

The most distinctive Rosh Hashana observance is the sounding of the ram's horn (shofar) at the synagogue service. Medieval commentators suggest that the blasts acclaim God as ruler of the universe, recall the divine revelation at Sinai, and call for spiritual reawakening and repentance. An expanded New Year liturgy stresses God's sovereignty, his concern for humankind, and his readiness to forgive those who repent. On the first day of Rosh Hashana (except when it falls on the Sabbath) it is customary for Jews to recite penitential prayers at a

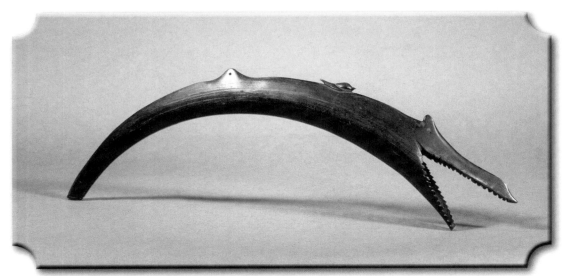

Shofar made of ram's horn in the form of a fish, Ethiopia, 19th century; in the Jewish Museum, New York City. Graphic House/EB Inc.

river, symbolically casting their sins into it in a ceremony called *tashlikh* ("thou wilt cast"). Other symbolic ceremonies, such as eating bread and apples dipped in honey, accompanied with prayers for a "sweet" and propitious year, are performed at the festive meals.

The most solemn of the Jewish festivals, Yom Kippur is a day when sins are confessed and expiated, and human beings and God are believed to be reconciled. It is also the last of the Days of Judgment and the holiest day of the Jewish year. Celebrated on Tishri 10, it is marked by fasting, penitence, and prayer. Work, eating, drinking, washing, anointing one's body, sexual intercourse, and wearing leather shoes are all forbidden.

In Temple times, Yom Kippur provided the only occasion for the entry of the high priest into the Holy of Holies (the innermost and most sacred area of the Temple). Details of the expiatory rites performed by the high priest and others are recorded in the Mishna and recounted in the liturgy. Present-day observances begin with a festive meal shortly before Yom Kippur eve. The Kol Nidre prayer (recited before the evening service) is a legal formula that absolves Jews from fulfilling solemn vows, thus safeguarding them from accidentally violating a vow's stipulations. The formula first appears in gaonic sources (derived from the Babylonian Talmudic academies, 6th–11th centuries) but may be older. The haunting melody that accompanies it is of medieval origin. Virtually the entire day is spent in prayer at the synagogue, with the closing service (*ne'ila*) concluding with the sounding of the ram's horn.

SHOFAR

On important Jewish public and religious occasions, the shofar, *a ritual musical instrument, made from the horn of a ram or other animal, is used. In biblical times the* shofar *sounded the Sabbath, announced the New Moon, and proclaimed the anointing of a new king. This latter custom has been preserved in modern Israel at the swearing in of the president of the state.*

The most important modern use of the shofar *in religious ceremonies takes place on Rosh Hashana, when it is sounded in the synagogue to call the Jewish people to a spiritual reawakening as the religious New Year begins on Tishri 1. The shofar can be made to produce sobbing, wailing, and sustained sounds in sequences that are varied strictly according to ritual. The shofar is also sounded on Yom Kippur, the Day of Atonement, as a call for repentance and sacrifice and for love of the Torah.*

MINOR FESTIVALS: HANUKKAH AND PURIM

Hanukkah and Purim are joyous festivals. Unlike the major festivals, work restrictions are not enforced during these holidays.

Hanukkah commemorates the Maccabean (Hasmonean) victories over

Hanukkah lamp from Hermann Stadt, Hungary, 1775; in the Jewish Museum, New York City. Graphic House/EB Inc.

the forces of the Seleucid king Antiochus IV Epiphanes (reigned 175–164 BCE) and the rededication of the Temple on Kislev 25, 164 BCE. Led by Mattathias and his son Judas Maccabeus (died *c.* 161 BCE), the Maccabees were the first Jews who fought to defend their religious beliefs rather than their lives. Hanukkah is celebrated for eight days beginning on Kislev 25. The Hanukkah lamp, or candelabra (menorah), which recalls the Temple lampstand, is kindled each evening. One candle is lit on the first evening, and an additional candle is lit on each subsequent evening until eight candles are burning on the last evening. According to the Talmud (*Shabbat* 21b), the ritually pure oil available at the rededication of the Temple was sufficient for only one day's light but miraculously lasted for eight days; hence the eight-day celebration. Evidence from the Apocrypha (writings excluded from the Jewish canon but included in the Roman Catholic and

MENORAH

An important symbol in both ancient and modern Israel, a menorah is a multibranched candelabra, used in Jewish religious rituals. The seven-branched menorah was originally found in the wilderness sanctuary and then later in the Temple in Jerusalem. It was a popular motif of religious art in antiquity. An eight-branched menorah modeled after the Temple menorah is used by Jews in rites during the eight-day festival of Hanukkah.

The menorah is first mentioned in the biblical book of Exodus (25:31–40), according to which the design of the lamp was revealed to Moses by God on Mount Sinai. The candlestick was to be forged out of a single piece of gold and was to have six branches, "three out of one side, and three out of the other" (Exodus 25:31). The cup atop the central shaft, which is somewhat elevated to signify the Sabbath, was flanked by three lights on each side. The Temple of Solomon, according to the book of Kings, had 10 golden candelabras, five on each side of the entrance to the inner sanctuary. The Second Temple, built after the Jews returned from exile in Babylon, contained one menorah that was seized in 169 BCE by Antiochus IV Epiphanes when he desecrated the Temple. Judas Maccabeus ordered construction of a new seven-branched candelabra, which he placed in the Temple after the desecration by Antiochus. The menorah disappeared after the destruction of the Second Temple in 70 CE. Although the Talmud forbade its reconstruction, it became a popular symbol signifying Judaism. Representations of the menorah decorated tombs and the walls and floors of the synagogues. During the early modern period the menorah as symbol gave way to the Star of David, but in the 19th century it was adopted as the symbol of the Zionists. The seven-branched candelabra depicted on the Arch of Titus became the official emblem of the state of Israel in the 20th century.

The Hanukkah lamp is an eight-branched imitation of the original Tabernacle menorah that is used to celebrate the rededication of the Second Temple. The lamp has taken many forms through the ages, but its essential feature has been eight receptacles for oil or candles and a holder for the shammash ("servant") light, which is used for kindling the other lights. During each night of Hanukkah, candles are inserted into the menorah from right to left but are lighted from left to right. The lamp is displayed in a highly visible location, and depictions of it are often found on public buildings, synagogues, and private homes.

Roman soldiers carrying a menorah, detail of a relief on the Arch of Titus, Rome, 81 CE. © Photos.com/Thinkstock

Eastern Orthodox canons) and from rabbinic literature shows an association between Hanukkah and Sukkoth, possibly accounting for the former's eight-day duration. The celebration of Hanukkah includes festive meals, songs, games, and gifts to children. The liturgy includes Hallel, public readings from the Torah, and the *'al ha-nissim* ("for the miracles") prayer. The Scroll of Antiochus, an early medieval account of Hanukkah, is read in some synagogues and homes.

As recorded in the biblical Book of Esther, Purim commemorates the

Scroll of Esther from Lwów (Lemberg), Galicia (now part of Poland), 1880; in the Jewish Museum, New York City. Graphic House/EB Inc.

delivery of the Persian Jewish community from the plottings of Haman, prime minister to King Ahasuerus (Xerxes I, king of Persia, 486–465 BCE). Mordecai and his cousin Esther, the king's Jewish wife, interceded on behalf of the Jewish community, rescinded the royal edict authorizing a massacre of the Jews, and instituted the Purim festival. The historicity of the biblical account is questioned by many modern scholars. It is now generally conceded that the Book of Esther was written in the Persian period (it contains Persian but not Greek words) and reflects Persian custom. Except for the Book of Esther, the earliest mention of the Purim festival is from the 2nd–1st centuries BCE. The name of the festival was derived from the Akkadian *pûru*, meaning "lot."

In most Jewish communities, Purim is celebrated on Adar 14 (some also celebrate it on the 15th, others only on the 15th). On the evening preceding Purim, men, women, and children gather in the synagogue to hear the Book of Esther read from a scroll (*megilla*). The reading is repeated on Purim morning. A festive meal during the day is accompanied by much song, wine, and merriment. Masquerades, Purim plays, and other forms of parody are common. Friends exchange gifts of foodstuffs and also present gifts to the poor. Aside from the Esther readings, the liturgy includes public reading from the Torah and recital of the Purim version of the *'al ha-nissim* prayer.

BOOK OF ESTHER

The Book of Esther is read on the festival of Purim, which commemorates the rescue of the Jews from Haman's plottings. The book purports to explain how the feast of Purim came to be celebrated by the Jews. Esther, the beautiful Jewish wife of the Persian king Ahasuerus (Xerxes I), and her cousin Mordecai persuade the king to retract an order for the general annihilation of Jews throughout the empire. The massacre had been plotted by the king's chief minister, Haman, and the date decided by casting lots (purim). Instead, Haman was hanged on the gallows he built for Mordecai. And on the day planned for their annihilation, the Jews destroyed their enemies.

The book may have been composed as late as the first half of the 2nd century BCE, though the origin of the Purim festival could date to the Babylonian exile (6th century BCE). The secular character of the Book of Esther (the divine name is never mentioned) and its strong nationalistic overtones made its admission into the biblical canon highly questionable for both Jews and Christians. Apparently in response to the conspicuous absence of any reference to God in the book, the redactors (editors) of its Greek translation in the Septuagint interspersed many additional verses throughout the text that demonstrate Esther's and Mordecai's religious devotion.

THE FIVE FASTS

Each of the fasts of the Jewish religious year recognizes an important event in the history of the Jewish people and Judaism. 'Asara be-Tevet (Fast of Tevet 10) commemorates the beginning of the siege of Jerusalem by Nebuchadrezzar II, king of Babylonia, in 588 BCE. Shiva' 'Asar be-Tammuz (Fast of Tammuz 17) commemorates the first breach in the wall of Jerusalem by the Romans in 70 CE. It initiates three weeks of semi-mourning that culminate with Tisha be-Av. Tisha be-Av (Fast of Av 9) commemorates the destruction of the First and Second Temples in 586 BCE and 70 CE. The most solemn of the five fasts, its self-denials are more rigorous than those prescribed for the others, and, like Yom Kippur, the fast begins at sunset. The book of Lamentations is read at the evening service, followed by poetic laments that are also recited on Tisha be-Av morning. Tzom Gedaliahu (Fast of Gedaliah) commemorates the slaying of Gedaliah, governor of Judah, after the destruction of the First Temple. Ta'anit Esther (Fast of Esther), which commemorates Esther's fast (compare Esther 4:16), is first mentioned in gaonic literature. The commemorative apsects of the fasts are closely associated with their penitential aspects, all of which find expression in the liturgy. Thus, Jews not only relive the tragic history of their people with each fast but are also afforded an opportunity to search within themselves and focus on their own (and their people's) present and future. Penitential prayers (selihot) are recited on all fasts, and the Torah is read at the morning and afternoon services.

The Minor Holidays

A major festival in the biblical period, Rosh Ḥodesh (First Day of the Month) gradually lost most of its festive character. Since Talmudic times, it has been customary to recite Hallel on Rosh Ḥodesh. In the medieval period, aside from the liturgical practices carried over from the Talmudic period, it was celebrated with a festive meal. Always more diligently observed in Palestine than in the Diaspora, attempts to revive its full festive character have been made in modern Israel.

First mentioned in the Mishna, where it marks the New Year for tithing purposes, Ṭu bi-Shevaṭ (15th of Shevaṭ: New Year for Trees) assumed a festive character in the gaonic period. In the medieval period it became customary to eat assorted fruits on the holiday. In modern times it has been associated with the planting of trees in Israel.

Lag ba-'Omer (33rd Day of the 'Omer Counting) is a joyous interlude in the otherwise-somber period of the 'Omer Counting (i.e., of the 49 days to Shavuot), which is traditionally observed as a time of semi-mourning. Usually celebrated as a school holiday with outings, it is first mentioned in medieval sources, which

attribute its origin to the cessation of a plague that was decimating the students of Akiba, an influential rabbinic sage of the 2nd century, and to the anniversary of the death of another great rabbi, Simeon ben Yoḥai (died c. 170 CE).

The Situation Today

Modern attitudes toward the Sabbath and festivals vary considerably. Western secular Jews often are ignorant of, or choose to neglect, traditional observances. Attitudes of committed Jews in the Western world mostly reflect accepted Orthodox, Conservative, and Reform practice. For example, driving to synagogue services on the Sabbath is unthinkable in Orthodox circles, a matter of dispute among Conservative rabbis, and common practice for Reform Jews. Among Orthodox Jews, who best preserve the traditional observances, contemporary discussion centres mostly on technological advances and their effect on Halakhic practice. Whether or not hearing aids may be worn on the Sabbath and how crossing the international dateline affects the observance of Sabbaths and festivals typify the sort of problem addressed in Orthodox responsa ("replies" to questions on law and observance). Discussion in modern Conservative literature has raised the possibility of abolishing the obligatory character of the additional festival days in the Diaspora (except for the second day of Rosh Hashana), thus unifying Jewish practice throughout the world. Reform

Jews, the most innovative of the three groups, observe neither the additional festival days (including the second day of Rosh Hashana) nor the fasts and have modified the liturgy and the observances of the holidays. More radical Reform congregations have experimented freely with sound and light effects and other novel forms of synagogue service.

In Israel the Sabbath is the national day of rest, and Jewish holidays are vacation periods. Municipal ordinances govern public observance of the Sabbath and festivals. Their enactment and enforcement vary with the political influence of the local Orthodox Jewish community. Attempts to interpret festivals along nationalistic lines are common, and some kibbutzim (communal farms) stress the agricultural significance of the festivals. Independence Day is a national holiday. The preceding day, Remembrance Day, commemorates Israel's war dead.

Yom Hashoah (Holocaust Remembrance and Heroism Day)—marking the systematic destruction of European Jewry between 1933 and 1945 and recalling the short-lived ghetto uprisings—is observed officially on Nisan 27, but many religious Israelis prefer to observe it on Tebet 10 (a fast day), now called Yom HaKaddish Haklali (the day on which the mourner's prayer is recited). Since the Six-Day War of June 1967, Iyyar 28—Liberation of Jerusalem Day—is celebrated unofficially by many Israelis. Appropriate services are conducted on all the aforementioned holidays by most segments of Israel's religious community.

In Israel and the Diaspora, Jewish theologians often stress the timelessness and contemporaneity of holiday observances. Nevertheless, "revised" Passover Haggadot (plural of Haggada), in which contemporary issues are accorded a central position, appear regularly.

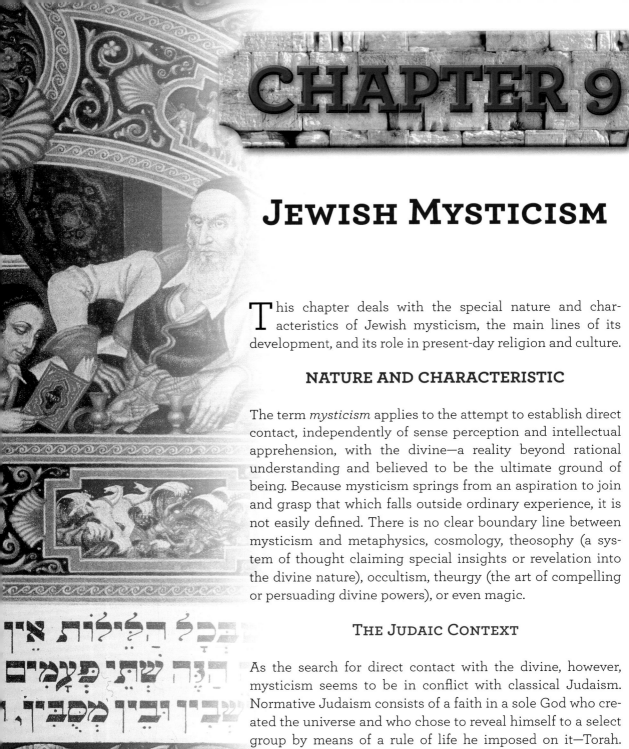

CHAPTER 9

JEWISH MYSTICISM

This chapter deals with the special nature and characteristics of Jewish mysticism, the main lines of its development, and its role in present-day religion and culture.

NATURE AND CHARACTERISTIC

The term *mysticism* applies to the attempt to establish direct contact, independently of sense perception and intellectual apprehension, with the divine—a reality beyond rational understanding and believed to be the ultimate ground of being. Because mysticism springs from an aspiration to join and grasp that which falls outside ordinary experience, it is not easily defined. There is no clear boundary line between mysticism and metaphysics, cosmology, theosophy (a system of thought claiming special insights or revelation into the divine nature), occultism, theurgy (the art of compelling or persuading divine powers), or even magic.

THE JUDAIC CONTEXT

As the search for direct contact with the divine, however, mysticism seems to be in conflict with classical Judaism. Normative Judaism consists of a faith in a sole God who created the universe and who chose to reveal himself to a select group by means of a rule of life he imposed on it—Torah.

According to traditional Judaic beliefs, the earthly destiny of the chosen nation, as well as the eternal salvation of the individual, depends on the observance of this rule of life, through which any relationship to God must take place. The fact is, however, that in the religious history of Judaism the quest for God goes beyond the relationship mediated by Torah without ever dispensing with it (because that would take the seeker outside Judaism), without pretending to reach the depths of the mystery of the divine, and without ending in an ontological identification with God (i.e., in the belief that God and human beings are the same in nature and being).

It must also be noted that the quest for God implies the search for solutions to problems that go beyond those of religion in the narrow sense and that arise even when there is no interest in the relationship between humankind and supernatural powers. Humans ponder the problems of their origins, their destiny, their happiness, their suffering. The presence or absence of religious institutions or dogmas is of little importance when it comes to these questions. They were all formulated within nonmystical Judaism and served as the basis and framework for the setting and solution of problems in the various forms of Jewish mysticism. This mysticism brought about profound transformations in the concepts of the world, God, and "last things" (resurrection, last judgment, messianic kingdom, etc.) set forth in biblical and rabbinical Judaism.

Nevertheless, Jewish mysticism's own set of problems—about the origins of the universe, humankind, evil, and sin; the meaning of history; and the afterlife and the end of time—is rooted in the very ground of Judaism and cannot be conceived outside an exegesis of revealed Scripture and rabbinical tradition.

THREE TYPES OF JEWISH MYSTICISM

There are three types of mysticism in the history of Judaism: the ecstatic, the contemplative, and the esoteric. Although they are distinct, they frequently overlap in practice.

The first type is characterized by the quest for God—or, more precisely, for access to a supernatural realm, which is itself infinitely remote from the inaccessible Deity—by means of ecstatic experiences. The second type is rooted in metaphysical meditation, which always bears the imprint of the cultural surroundings of the respective thinkers, who are exposed to influences from outside Judaism. Philo Judaeus of Alexandria and a few of the Jewish thinkers of the Middle Ages, who drew their inspiration from Greco-Arabic Neoplatonism and sometimes also from Muslim mysticism, are examples of those who felt external influences.

The third type of mysticism claims an esoteric knowledge (hereafter called esoterism) that explores the divine life itself and its relationship to the extra-divine

In nighttime religious studies, men pour over the Kabbalah. Menahem Kahana/AFP/Getty Images

level of being (i.e., the natural, finite realm), a relationship that is subject to the "law of correspondences." From this perspective, the extra-divine is a symbol of the divine; it is a reality that reveals a reality superior to itself. This form of mysticism, akin to gnosis (the secret knowledge claimed by gnosticism, a Hellenistic religious and philosophical movement) but purged—or almost purged—of the dualism that characterizes the latter, is what is commonly known as Kabbala (Hebrew: "Tradition"). By extension, this term is also used to designate technical methods, used for highly diverse ends, ranging from the conditioning of the aspirant to ecstatic experiences to magical manipulations of a superstitious character.

MAIN LINES OF DEVELOPMENT

From the beginning of Jewish mysticism in the 1st century CE to the middle of the 12th century, only the ecstatic and contemplative types existed. It was not until the second half of the 12th century that esoterism became clearly discernible; from then on, Jewish mysticism developed in various forms up to very recent times.

EARLY STAGES TO THE 6TH CENTURY CE

The centuries following the return from the Babylonian Exile were marked by increasingly widespread and intense reflection on various themes: the intermediary beings between humans and God; the divine appearances, whose special place of occurrence had formerly been the most sacred part of the Jerusalem Temple; the creation of human beings; and the creation and organization of the universe. None of these themes was absent from the Bible, which was held to be divinely revealed, but each had become the object of constant theological readjustment that also involved the adoption of concepts from outside and reactions against them. The speculative taste of Jewish thinkers between the 2nd century BCE and the 1st century CE took them in many different directions: angelology (doctrine about angels) and demonology (doctrine about devils); mythical geography and uranography (description of the heavens); contemplation of the divine manifestations, whose background was the Jerusalem Temple worship and the visions of the moving "throne" (*merkava*, "chariot") in the prophecy of Ezekiel; reflection on the double origin of human beings, who are formed of the earth but are also the "image of God"; and speculation on the end of time (eschatology), on resurrection (a concept that appeared only toward the end of the biblical period), and on rewards and punishments in the afterlife.

This ferment was crystallized in writings such as the First Book of Enoch. Almost none of it was retained in Pharisaic (rabbinical) Judaism, which became the normative Jewish tradition after the Roman conquest of Jerusalem and the destruction of the Second Temple. The Talmud and the Midrash (rabbinical legal and interpretative literature) touched these themes only with great reserve, often unwillingly, and more often in a spirit of negative polemic.

As early as the 1st century CE and probably even before the destruction of the Second Temple, there were sages or teachers recognized by the religious community for whom meditation on the Scriptures—especially the creation narrative, the public revelation of the Torah on Mount Sinai, the Merkava vision of Ezekiel, and the Song of Solomon—and reflection on the end of time, resurrection, and the afterlife were not only a matter of the exegesis of texts recognized to be of divine origin but also a matter of inner experience. However, speculation on the invisible world and the search for the means to penetrate it were probably carried on in other circles. It is undeniable that there was a certain continuity between the apocalyptic visions (i.e., of the cataclysmic advent of God's kingdom) and documents of certain sects (Dead Sea Scrolls) and the writings, preserved in Hebrew, of the "explorers of the supernatural world" (*yorde merkava*). The latter comprise ecstatic hymns, descriptions of the "dwellings" (*hekhalot*) located between the visible world and the ever-inaccessible Divinity, whose transcendence is paradoxically expressed by anthropomorphic descriptions consisting of inordinate hyperboles (*Shi'ur qoma,* "Divine Dimensions"). A few documents have been preserved that attest to the initiation of carefully chosen persons who were made to undergo tests and ordeals in accordance with psychosomatic criteria borrowed from physiognomy (the art of determining character from physical, especially facial, traits). Some theurgic efficacy was attributed to these practices, and there was some contamination from Egyptian, Hellenistic, or Mesopotamian magic. (A curious document in this respect, rich in pagan material, is the *Sefer ha-razim,* the "Treatise on Mysteries," which was discovered in 1963.)

The similarities between concepts reflected in unquestionably Jewish texts and those expressed in documents of contemporary non-Jewish esoterism are so numerous that it becomes difficult, sometimes impossible, to distinguish the giver from the receiver. Two facts are certain, however. On the one hand, gnosticism never ceases to exploit biblical themes that have passed through Judaism (such as the tale of creation and the speculation on angels and demons), whatever their original source may have been. On the other hand, though Jewish esoterism may borrow this or that motif from ancient gnosis or syncretism and may even raise a supernatural entity such as the angel Metatron—also known as "little Adonai" (i.e., little Lord or God)—to

a particularly high rank in the hierarchy of being, it still remains inflexibly monotheistic and rejects the gnostic concept of a bad or simply inferior demiurge who is responsible for the creation and governing of the visible world. Finally, during the centuries that separate the Talmudic period (2nd–5th centuries CE) from the full resurgence of Jewish esoterism in the middle of the 12th century, the texts that were preserved progressively lose their density and affective authenticity and become reduced to the level of literary exercises that are more grandiloquent than substantial.

SEFER YETZIRA

In the ancient esoteric literature of Judaism, a special place must be given to the *Sefer yetzira* ("Book of Creation"), which deals with cosmogony and cosmology. Creation, it affirms with a clearly anti-gnostic insistence, is the work of the God of Israel and took place on the ideal, immaterial level and on the concrete level. This was done according to a complex process that brings in the 10 numbers (*sefirot,* singular *sefira*) of decimal notation and the 22 letters of the Hebrew alphabet. The 10 numbers are not understood merely as arithmetical symbols: they are cosmological factors. The first, signified by the multiply ambiguous term *ruah,* is the spirit of God, while the nine others seem to be the archetypes of the three elements (air, water, fire) and the spatial dimensions (up, down, and the four cardinal points). After having been manipulated either in their graphic representation or in combination, the letters of the alphabet, which are considered transcriptions of the sounds of the language, are in turn instruments of creation. The basic idea of all this speculation is that speech (that is, language composed of words, which are in turn composed of letters or sounds) is not only a means of communication but an operational agent destined to produce being. It has an ontological value. This value, however, does not extend to every language—it belongs to the Hebrew language alone.

The *Sefer yetzira* does not proceed entirely from biblical data and rabbinical reflection upon them. Greek influences are discernible, even in the vocabulary. What is important, however, is its influence on later Jewish thought, down to the present time: philosophers and esoterists have vied with one another over its meaning, pulling it in their own direction and adjusting it to their respective ideologies. Even more important is the fact that Kabbala borrowed a great deal of its terminology from the *Sefer yetzira* (e.g., *sefira*), making semantic adaptations as required.

The speculation traced above developed during the first six centuries of the Common Era, both in Palestine and in Babylonia. Babylonian Judaism had its own social and ideological characteristics, which put it in opposition to Palestinian Judaism with regard to esoterism and other manifestations of the life of the spirit. The joint doctrinal influence of the two centres spread from the mid-8th to the 11th century among the Jews of North Africa and Europe. Mystical doctrines also filtered in, but little is known about the circumstances and means of their penetration.

SEFER YETZIRA

The Sefer yetzira ("Book of Creation") is the oldest known Hebrew text on white magic and cosmology. It contends that the cosmos derived from the 22 letters of the Hebrew alphabet and from the 10 divine numbers (sefirot). Taken together, they were said to comprise the "32 paths of secret wisdom" by which God created the universe. The book, falsely attributed to Abraham and thus sometimes called Otiyyot de Avraham Avinu ("Alphabet of Our Father Abraham"), appeared anonymously between the 3rd and 6th century CE, but interpolations were later added.

The Yetzira developed the pivotal concept of the 10 sefirot, which profoundly influenced subsequent Judaism. The first group of four represented universal elements (the spirit of God, air, water, and fire), whereas the last group represented the six spatial directions. The sefirot and the letters of the alphabet were likewise correlated to parts of the human body, thereby making man a microcosm of creation.

Medieval German pietistic Hasidism associated formulas of the Yetzira with the golem, a creature created by magic. Among the more important commentaries on the Yetzira were those of Sa'adia ben Joseph (882–942) and Isaac ben Solomon Luria (1534–72).

The Arabic-Islamic Influence (7th–13th Century)

Arabic Islamic culture was another important influence on Jewish mystical development. A considerable part of Jewry, which had fallen under Muslim domination in the 7th and 8th centuries, participated in the new Arabic-Islamic civilization. The Jews of Asia, Africa, and Spain soon adopted Arabic, the language of culture and communication. Arabic-language culture introduced elements of Greek philosophy and Islamic mysticism into Judaism and contributed to the deepening of certain theological concepts that were of Jewish origin but had become the common property of the three religions of the Book: affirming the divine unity, purging anthropomorphism from the idea of God, and following a spiritual path to the divine that leads through an ascetic discipline (both physical and intellectual) to a detachment from this world and a freeing of the soul from all that distracts it from God. Greek philosophy and Islamic mysticism moreover raised serious questions that threatened traditional beliefs about the creation of the world, the providential action of God, miracles, and eschatology. Even in the Christian West, where cultural contacts between the majority society and the Jewish minority were far from reaching the breadth and intensity of Judeo-Arab relations, Jewish intellectuals were unable to remain impervious to the incursions of the surrounding civilization. (Jewish biblical scholars were at times sought out by Christian theologians for help in understanding the Hebrew Scriptures.) Moreover, at the beginning of the 12th century if not earlier, European Judaism received part of the intellectual Arabic and Judeo-Arab heritage through translations or adaptations into Hebrew, its only cultural language.

The Making of Kabbala

Under these circumstances, starting around 1150, manifestations of markedly theosophic ideologies appeared in southern France (in the regions of Provence and Languedoc). The two types that can be distinguished at the outset are very different in appearance, form, and content.

Sefer ha-Bahir

The first type is represented in fragmentary, poorly written, and badly assembled texts that began to circulate in Provence and Languedoc during the third quarter of the 12th century. Their inspiration, however, leaves no doubt as to the community of their origin. They were in the form of a Midrash—that is, an interpretation of Scripture with the help of a particular interpretative method, full of sayings attributed to ancient rabbinical authorities. This body of texts, probably imported from the Middle East (Syria, Palestine, Iraq), is known as the "Midrash of Rabbi Nehunya ben Haqana" (from the name of a 1st-century rabbi) or *Sefer ha-bahir* ("Book of Brightness," from a characteristic word of the first verse of Scripture to be elucidated in the work). The authorities cited are all inauthentic (as was often the case in late works). The content of this Midrash may be characterized as a form of gnosticism that successfully tries to escape any ontological dualism.

The object of the *Sefer ha-bahir* is to present the origin of things and the course of history centred on the chosen people, with vicissitudes caused in turn by obedience to God and by sin, as conditioned by the manifestation of divine powers. These "powers" are not "attributes" derived and defined by philosophical abstraction, though that is one of the terms used to designate them: they are hypostases (essences or substances). They are inseparable from God, but each one is clothed in its own personality, each operates in its own manner, leaning toward severity or mercy, in dynamic correspondence with the behaviour of human beings, especially of Jews, in the visible world. They are ranked in a hierarchy, which is not as fixed as it would become starting with the second generation of Kabbalists in Languedoc and Catalonia. The rich nomenclature used to designate the "powers" exploits the resources of both the Bible and the rabbinical tradition, of the *Sefer yetzira*, of some ritual observances, and also of the letters of the Hebrew alphabet and the signs that can be added to them to indicate the vowels.

Thus, according to the *Sefer ha-bahir*, the universe is the manifestation of hierarchically organized divine powers, and the power that is at the bottom of the hierarchy has special charge of the visible world. This entity is highly complex. Undoubtedly there are survivals of gnostic speculation on Sophia ("Wisdom"), who is involved, sometimes to her misfortune, in the material world. This power is also the divine "Presence" (Shekhina) of rabbinical theology, though it is profoundly transformed: it has become a hypostasis. By a bold innovation, it is characterized as a feminine being and thus finds itself, while remaining an aspect of the Divinity, in the position of a daughter or a wife, who owns nothing herself and receives all from the father or the husband. It is also identified with the "Community of Israel," another radical innovation that was facilitated by ancient speculation based on the allegorical interpretation of the Song of Solomon, which represents the relationship of God to the chosen nation in terms of the marriage bond. Thus, a theosophical equality is established between the whole of the people chosen by God, constituted into a kind of mystical body, and an aspect of the Divinity—whence the solidarity and linked destiny of the two. A comparable relationship between the "Presence" and Israel was not totally foreign to ancient rabbinical theology. In this light, the obedience or disobedience of Israel to its particular vocation is a determining factor of cosmic harmony or disruption and extends to the inner life of the Divinity. This is the essential and definitive contribution of the *Sefer ha-bahir* to Jewish theosophy. The same document evinces the resurgence of a notion that older theologians had attempted to combat—that of *metensōmatōsis*, the reincarnation into several successive bodies of a soul that has not attained the required perfection in a previous existence.

SCHOOL OF ISAAC THE BLIND

Another theosophic tendency in Languedoc developed concurrently with—but independently of—the *Sefer ha-bahir*. The two movements would take only about 30 years to converge, constituting what may conveniently (though not quite precisely) be called classical Kabbala. The second school flourished in Languedoc during the last quarter of the 12th century and crossed the Pyrenees into Spain in the first years of the 13th century.

The most eminent spokesman of this school was Isaac ben Abraham, known as Isaac the Blind, whose extant works include an obscure commentary on the *Sefer yetzira*. In the view of the eminent Kabbala scholar Gershom G. Scholem (1897–1982), Isaac's general vision of the universe proceeds from the link he discovers between the hierarchical orders of the created world and the roots of all beings implanted in the world of the *sefirot*. A Neoplatonic influence is evident in the reflections of Isaac (e.g., the procession of things from the one and the corresponding return to the heart of the primordial undifferentiatedness, which is the fullness of being and at the same time every conceivable being). This return is not merely eschatological and cosmic but is realized in the life of prayer of the contemplative mystic—though it is not, indeed, a transforming union by which the human personality blends completely into the Deity or becomes one with it.

The synthesis of the themes of the *Bahir* and the cosmology of the *Sefer yetzira*, accomplished by Isaac or by others in the doctrinal environment inspired by his teachings, was and remains the foundation of Kabbala, whatever adjustments, changes of orientation, or radical modifications the composite may subsequently have undergone.

THE 10 *SEFIROT*

It is also in this environment that the nomenclature of the 10 *sefirot* became more or less fixed, though variant terminologies and even divergent conceptions of the nature of these entities may exist elsewhere—for example, as internal powers of the divine organism (which is similar to gnosticism), hierarchically ordered intermediaries between the infinite and the finite (which is more in-line with Neoplatonism), or simply instruments of the divine activity, neither partaking of the divine substance nor being outside it. In the development of Kabbalistic literature, the idea was expanded and elaborated to denote

KABBALA

Kabbala (Hebrew: "Tradition") is esoteric Jewish mysticism as it appeared in the 12th and following centuries. Kabbala has always been essentially an oral tradition in that initiation into its doctrines and practices is conducted by a personal guide to avoid the dangers inherent in mystical experiences. Though observance of the Torah remained the basic tenet of Judaism, Kabbala provided a means of approaching God directly. It thus gave Judaism a religious dimension whose mystical approaches to God were viewed by some as dangerously pantheistic and heretical.

The earliest roots of Kabbala are traced to Merkava mysticism, which began to flourish in Palestine in the 1st century CE and had as its main concern ecstatic and mystical contemplation of the divine throne, or "chariot" (merkava), seen in a vision by the prophet Ezekiel (Ezekiel 1). The Sefer yetzira ("Book of Creation") appeared sometime between the 3rd and the 6th century. It explained creation as a process involving the 10 divine numbers (sefirot) of God the Creator and the 22 letters of the Hebrew alphabet. Taken together, they were said to constitute the "32 paths of secret wisdom."

A major text of early Kabbala was the 12th-century Sefer ha-bahir ("Book of Brightness"), whose influence on the development of Jewish esoteric mysticism and on Judaism in general was profound and lasting. The Bahir not only interpreted the sefirot as instrumental in creating and sustaining the universe but also introduced into Judaism such notions as the transmigration of souls (gilgul) and strengthened the foundations of Kabbala by providing it with an extensive mystical symbolism. In the following century, the Sefer ha-temuna ("Book of the Image") appeared in Spain and advanced the notion of cosmic cycles, each of which provides an interpretation of the Torah according to a divine attribute. Spain also produced the famous Sefer ha-zohar ("Book of Splendour"), a book that in some circles was invested with a sanctity rivaling that of the Torah itself. It dealt with the mystery of creation and the functions of the sefirot, and it offered mystical speculations about evil, salvation, and the soul. Following their expulsion from Spain in 1492, the Jews were more than ever taken up with messianic hopes and eschatology, and Kabbala found wide favour. By the mid-16th century the unchallenged centre of Kabbala was Safed, Galilee, where one of the greatest of all Kabbalists, Isaac ben Solomon Luria, spent the last years of his life. Lurianic Kabbala developed several basic doctrines: the "withdrawal" (tzimtzum) of the divine light, thereby creating primordial space; the sinking of luminous particles into matter (qellipot: "shells"); and a "cosmic restoration" (tiqqun) that is achieved by the Jew through an intense mystical life and unceasing struggle against evil. Lurianic Kabbalism was used to justify Shabbetaianism, a Jewish messianic movement of the 17th century. It also profoundly influenced the doctrines of modern Ḥasidism, a social and religious movement that began in the 18th century and still flourishes today in small but significant Jewish communities.

the 10 stages of emanation from *En Sof* (the Infinite; the unknowable God), by which God the Creator can be discerned. Each *sefira* refers to an aspect of God as Creator. The rhythm by which one *sefira* unfolds to another was believed to represent the rhythm of creation. The mystical nature of the *sefirot* and the precise way in which they function were often disputed. Kabbalists used them as one of their principal subjects of mystical contemplation. The classical list of the *sefirot* is as follows:

1. *keter 'elyon*, the supreme crown (its identity or nonidentity with the Infinite, Ein Sof, the unknowable Deity, remains problematic)
2. *hokhma*, wisdom, the location of primordial ideas in God
3. *bina*, intelligence, the organizing principle of the universe
4. *hesed*, love, the attribute of goodness
5. *gevura*, might, the attribute of severity
6. *tif'eret*, beauty, the mediating principle between the preceding two
7. *netzah*, eternity
8. *hod*, majesty
9. *yesod*, foundation of all the powers active in God
10. *malkhut*, kingship, identified with the Shekhina ("Presence")

SCHOOL OF GERONA (CATALONIA)

The gnosticizing theosophy of the *Sefer ha-bahir* and the contemplative mysticism of the masters of Languedoc became one in the hands of the Kabbalists in Catalonia, where the Jewish community of Gerona was a veritable seat of esoterism during the first half of the 13th century. To the school of Gerona belong, among others, masters such as Ezra ben Solomon, Azriel of Gerona, Jacob ben Sheshet, and Moses ben Naḥman (or Naḥmanides), the famous Talmudist, biblical commentator, and theologian. Their influence on the subsequent course of Jewish mysticism is of fundamental importance, though none of them left a complete synthesis of his theosophy. They expressed themselves, with more or less reserve, by means of commentaries, sermons, polemic or apologetic treatises, and brief summaries (at most) for the noninitiated. It is not impossible, however, to discover through these texts their vision of the world and to compare it with the views of the Jewish thinkers who attempted to harmonize the biblical-rabbinical tradition with Greco-Arab philosophy, whether of Neoplatonic or Aristotelian inspiration.

At the base of the Kabbalistic view of the world there is an option of faith: it is by a voluntary decision that the unknowable Deity—who is "nothing" or "nothingness" (nonfinite) because he is a fullness of being totally inaccessible to any human cognition—sets into motion the process that leads to the visible world. This concept radically separates Kabbala from the determinism from which the philosophy of the period could not, without contradiction, free the principle of being. In addition, it offers a solution consistent with faith to the problem of creation ex nihilo (out of nothing). The paradoxical reinterpretation of the concept of the "nothing" eliminates the original matter coeternal with God and solves the opposition between divine transcendence (remoteness from the world) and immanence (presence in the world). Issuing from the unfathomable depth of the Deity and called to return to it, the world, visible as well as invisible, is radically separated from God, who is at the same time constantly present. The correspondence between the *sefirot* and all the degrees of being gives meaning to the structure of the world and to the history of humanity centred on the revelation given to the chosen people, a revelation that is a rule of life for this people and the criterion of merit and sin, or good and evil. Thus, from the top to the bottom of the ladder, there are corresponding realities that control one another. Contrary to the opinion of the philosophers, evil is also a reality because it is the rupture of the universal harmony. It is also the consequence of this rupture, in the form of punishment. From this perspective, scrupulous observance of the Torah, both in the written text and the oral tradition, is the essential factor for the maintenance of the universe. The "rational" motivation of the commandments, which raises insurmountable difficulties for the theologians of philosophical orientation, is in the eyes of the Kabbalists a false problem. The real problem is the fundamental nature of the Torah. Kabbala brings more than one solution to it, whereas philosophy has trouble providing a single coherent and comprehensive solution.

It follows from this general concept that the Jewish faith, with its implications—the conviction of holding the undiluted truth, the faithful preservation of ritual practices, and the eschatological expectation—is safeguarded from all the doubts that either philosophical speculation or the rival religious doctrines of Christianity and Islam could evoke in the minds of Jewish believers. Kabbala, already at the stage it had reached at Gerona, may be said to be a significant factor in the survival of Judaism, which was exposed everywhere in medieval society to a wide range of perils.

Besides the Gerona school and the doctrinal descendants of Isaac the Blind in Languedoc, there was another school of Jewish esoterism in southern Europe during the first half of the 13th century. Members of this school preferred to remain anonymous and therefore published their writings, such as the *Sefer ha-'iyyun* ("Book of Speculation"), either without an author's name or with an attribution to a fictitious authority. Their speculation was directed to the highest levels of the divine world, where it discerned aspects beyond the 10 *sefirot* and attempted to give an idea of them by resorting to the symbolism of light, as well as to the primordial causes and the archetypes contained in the Deity or directly issuing from it. The sometimes-striking similarity between these speculations and those of the Christian theologian John Scotus Erigena (810–c. 877), whose work was revived in the 12th and 13th centuries, suggests not only a kinship of themes between this Kabbalistic current and Latin-language Christian Neoplatonism but also a concrete influence of the latter upon the former. The same may be true of Isaac the Blind and the school of Gerona, but certain knowledge is lacking.

SEFER HA-TEMUNA

The anonymous writer of the *Sefer ha-temuna* ("Book of the Image") provided literary expression for another manifestation of Jewish mysticism in this period. This obscure document claims to explain the figures of the letters of the Hebrew alphabet. The speculation of this treatise bears on two themes that were not foreign to the school of Gerona, but it develops them in a personal manner that decisively influenced the future of Jewish theosophy. On the one hand, it deals with a theory of the different cycles through which the world must travel from the time of its emergence to its reabsorption into the primordial unity. On the other hand, it addresses various readings that correspond to these cycles in the divine manifestation that is constituted by the Scriptures. In other words, the interpretation and consequently the message of the Torah vary according to the cycles of existence. The passage to a cycle other than that under whose governance humanity is presently living could thus entail the modification, even the abrogation, of the rule of life to which the chosen people are presently subject, an explosive notion that threatened to overthrow the Jewish tradition.

MEDIEVAL GERMAN (ASHKENAZIC) HASIDISM

The period during which Kabbala was established in the south of France and in Spain is no less important for the shaping of Jewish mysticism in the other branch of European Judaism, which was situated in northern France (and England) and in the Rhine and Danube regions of Germany. Unlike medieval Kabbala, which experienced a broad and varied development starting in the second half of the 13th century, the movement designated as German, or Ashkenazic (from a biblical place-name conventionally used to designate Germany), Hasidism hardly survived as a living and independent current beyond the second quarter of the 13th century (it has no connection with modern Hasidism). Franco-German Judaism experienced a certain continuity of mystical tradition, based on the *Sefer yetzira* and the *hekhalot*; certain elements of theurgy and magic of Babylonian origin may also have reached it through Italy; and apparently the gnosticizing current that was crystallized in the *Sefer ha-bahir* did not pass without leaving traces in Germany. The intellectual atmosphere of Franco-German Judaism, however, differed greatly from that reigning in Spain or even Provence and Languedoc. It was characterized by an almost exclusively Talmudic culture, less intellectual contact with the non-Jewish environment than in the countries of Muslim civilization, and a rather limited knowledge of Jewish theology in Arabic from the Middle East, North Africa, and Spain. This situation did not change until the last third of the 12th century. Until then, the "philosophical" equipment of the Franco-German Jewish scholar consisted essentially of a Hebrew paraphrase, dating perhaps from the 11th century; the treatise *Beliefs and Opinions* by Sa'adia ben Joseph (the great 9th–10th-century Babylonian Jewish scholar and philosopher); and the commentary on the *Sefer yetzira* written in Hebrew in 946 by the Italian physician Shabbetai Donnolo (born 913). Even when the cultural influence of Spanish Judaism came to be felt more strongly in France, England, and Germany, speculative Kabbala hardly penetrated there. Franco-German Jewish thinkers who inclined toward theological speculation had their own problems— notably the persecutions that began during the First Crusade—which resulted in a mysticism strongly imbued with asceticism.

The main speculative problem for medieval Hasidic thinkers was that of the relationship between God and his manifestations in creation, including his revelation and communication with inspired men and women. Reflection on this problem led to the elaboration of various supernatural hierarchies between the inaccessible God and the created universe or the recipient of divine communication. Data on angels taken from the Bible and rabbinical and mystical traditions, as well as speculation on the Shekhina, were used as material for these hierarchies and also gave a peculiar coloration to liturgical practice. The latter was marked, moreover, by a concern for spiritual concentration by means of fixing attention on the words and even the letters of the synagogue prayers. These speculations, however, had no great repercussions on the subsequent course of Jewish esoterism. The only exception is the mysticism of prayer and demonology, which was sometimes influenced by the beliefs of the Christian environment and was fully developed in Hasidic circles. Conversely, the ascetic morality of the movement, which was expressed in the literary works of Eleazar ben Judah of Worms (c. 1160–1238) and in the two recensions of the "Book of the Pious" (*Sefer ḥasidim*), was to mark Jewish spirituality, esoteric or not, from then on.

The Making of the *Zohar* (c. 1260–1492)

Once the marginal episode of German Hasidism was finished, almost all creative activity in Jewish mysticism occurred in Spain, up to the expulsion of the Jews in 1492.

After the flowering of the schools described above came to an end about the year 1260, two other currents appeared. The first assumed a gnostic bent through its emphasis on the problem of evil. The texts that illustrate this tendency do not place evil in a state of dependence on the "attribute of judgment" within the structure of the *sefirot* set up by the previous Kabbalists but locate it outside the Divinity, constructing a parallel system of "left-hand *sefirot*" and a corresponding exuberant demonology. The second movement, mainly represented by the visionary and adventurer Abraham ben Samuel Abulafia (born 1240), justified itself by appeal to inner "prophetic" experiences encouraged by training methods akin to those of Yoga, Byzantine Hesychasm (mystical, quietist monasticism), and Sufism. Moreover, an important place was given to speculations on the letters and vocalic signs of the Hebrew script. Unlike the protagonists of other mystical schools of Spain, Abulafia actively promoted his ideas, worrying Jewish leaders and prompting even non-Jewish authorities to pursue him. His numerous writings later stimulated a few minds among the Kabbalists.

The work of Moses de León (1250–1305) marked one of the most important turning points in the development of Jewish mysticism. He was the author of several esoteric works, which he signed with his own name. To better spread his ideas and to more effectively combat philosophy, which he considered a mortal danger to the Jewish faith, he composed pseudepigrapha (writings ascribed to other authors, usually in past ages) in the form of Midrashim on the Pentateuch, the Song of Solomon, the Book of Ruth, and Lamentations. Only the names of the Talmudic authorities were even partially authentic, a procedure already used by the *Sefer ha-bahir*. In its most finished version (for there were several of them), the plot of the tales centred around Rabbi Simeon ben Yoḥai, a sage of the 2nd century, about whom the Talmud already related some curious anecdotes, most of them semilegendary. Over a period of about 30 years, Moses de León thus produced the *Midrash ha-ne'elam* ("The Mystical Midrash"), an allegorical work written mainly in Hebrew, and then the *Sefer ha-zohar* ("Book of Splendour")—or, more briefly, the *Zohar*—a larger work written in artificial Aramaic, whose content is theosophic. The *Zohar* culminates in a long speech in which Simeon ben Yoḥai, on the day of his death, supposedly exposes the quintessence of his mystical doctrine. The book inspired nearly contemporary imitations that were incorporated into or appended to it but were sometimes of a markedly different theological orientation: the *Ra'ya mehemana* ("Faithful Shepherd"—i.e., Moses the prophet), the particular subject of which is the interpretation and theosophic justification of the precepts of the Torah; and the *Tiqqune zohar*, consisting of elaborations in the same vein bearing upon the first word of the book of Genesis (*bereshit*, "in the beginning").

The works of Moses de León were not immediately accepted as authentic by all the esoterists and still less by scholars outside the theosophic movement. It took half a century or more for the *Zohar* and imitations of it to be recognized as authoritative ancient works, and even then it was not without some reluctance. Although critics were never fully silenced and the authenticity of the *Zohar* was already questioned in the 15th century, the myth created by Moses de León and his imitators became a spiritual reality for the majority of believing Jews. It still retains this character among many "traditional" Jews. The *Zohar*, believed to be based on supernatural revelations and reinterpreted in diverse ways, served as a support and reference for all Jewish theosophies in later centuries.

In matters of doctrine, the *Zohar* and its appendices develop, amplify, and exaggerate speculation and tendencies that already existed rather than offer any radical innovation. The main lines of the *Zohar* were ideas that had been accepted for a long time in Jewish theosophy: the springing forth of being from the depth of the divine "nothing," the solidarity between the visible world and the world of the *sefirot* (complicated by the introduction of four ontological levels, at each of which the schema of the 10 *sefirot* is reproduced), and the indispensable contribution to universal harmony by the people (i.e., the Jews) who observe the biblical and rabbinical precepts in their slightest details. But all these themes were largely organized and enhanced by the use—or rather the unscrupulous appropriation—of materials taken from rabbinical tradition and ancient esoterism as well as from more recent currents of theological and philosophical thought (the speculations of the *Sefer ha-temuna* on the cosmic cycles and the "Prophetic Kabbala" of Abulafia were tacitly set aside).

Despite the lack of esteem that the writers of the Zoharic corpus felt—and sought to make others feel—toward works created by Gentiles, the method of symbolic representation used in the Zoharic writings was supported by a system of interpretation based on the originally Christian concept of the fourfold meaning of Scripture: literal, moral, allegorical (philosophical), and mystical. The symbolism that was thus established boldly made use of an exuberant anthropomorphic and even erotic imagery whose function was to convey the manifestation of the levels of the *sefirot* to each other and to the extra-divine world. The myth of the primordial man (Adam Qadmon), a virtually divine being, reappeared here under a new form, and it remained in the subsequent development of Kabbala.

The *Zohar* thus claims to provide a complete explanation of the world, humankind, history, and the situation of the Jews. On a higher level, it purports to justify the biblical revelation and rabbinical tradition down to the slightest detail, including the messianic expectation, and thereby to neutralize philosophy. But, while portraying itself as the defender of the traditional religion regulated by the Talmud and its commentaries, the *Zohar* places itself above tradition by boisterously proclaiming the incomparable value of the theosophic teaching of Rabbi Simeon ben Yoḥai and the superiority of the esoteric doctrine over Talmudic studies. There was in this attitude—which was more accentuated in the *Ra'ya mehemana* than in the *Zohar* proper—a revolutionary potential and a threat to the primacy of Torah practice and study. The future would show that this danger was not completely unreal.

THE LURIANIC KABBALA

After the establishment of the Zoharic corpus, no major changes took place in Jewish esoterism until the middle of the 16th century, when a religious centre of extreme importance for Judaism, mainly inspired by teachers coming from families expelled from Spain, was established in Safed (in Upper Galilee, Palestine; present-day Ẓefat, Israel). Kabbalistic literary output had been abundant in Spain until the expulsion in 1492 and in Italy and the Middle East during the following two generations, but it was primarily a matter of systematizing or even popularizing the *Zohar* or of extending the speculation already developed in the 13th century. There were also some attempts at reconciling philosophy and Kabbala.

The expulsion from Spain and the forced conversions to Christianity in both Spain and Portugal were profound tragedies. These events accentuated the existing pessimism caused by the dispersal of the Jews among the nations and intensified messianic expectation. This expectation most likely contributed to the beginnings of the printed transmission of Kabbala; the first two printed editions of the *Zohar* date from 1558. All these factors, joined with certain internal developments of speculative Kabbala in the 15th century, prepared the ground for the new theosophy inaugurated by the teaching of Isaac ben Solomon Luria (1534–72), who was born in Jerusalem, educated in Egypt, and died in Safed. Although his teaching is traditionally associated with Safed, he spent only the last three years of his life there. Luria wrote very little. His doctrine was transmitted, amplified, and probably somewhat distorted through the works of his disciples, especially Ḥayyim Vital (1543–1620), who wrote *'Etz ḥayyim* ("Tree of Life"), the standard presentation of Lurianic Kabbala.

The theosophy of Luria, whose novelty was proclaimed by its creator, was perfectly realized by the esoterists who held to the Zoharistic Kabbala, which was organized and codified precisely in Safed during the lifetime of Luria by Moses ben Jacob Cordovero (1522–70). Although its details are extremely complex, it is basically an attempt to reconcile divine transcendence with immanence and to solve the problem of evil, which the believer in the divine unity can recognize neither as a power existing independently of God nor as an integral part of him.

The vision of Luria is expressed in a vast mythical construct, which is typologically akin to certain gnostic and Manichaean (3rd-century dualistic) systems but which strives at all costs to avoid dualism. The essential elements of this myth include the withdrawal (*tzimtzum*) of the divine light, which originally filled all things, to make room for the extra-divine; the sinking, as a result of a catastrophic event that occurred during this process, of luminous particles into matter (*qelippot*, "shells," a term already used in Kabbala to designate the evil powers); and the consequent need to save these particles and return them to their origin, by means of "repair" or "restoration" (*tiqqun*). This must be the work of the Jews who not only live in complete conformity to the religious duties imposed on them by tradition but who dedicate themselves, in the framework of a strict asceticism, to a contemplative life founded on mystical prayer and directed meditation (*kawwana*) on the liturgy, which is supposed to further the harmony (*yiḥud*, "unification") of the innumerable attributes within the divine life. The successive reincarnations of the soul, a constant theme of Kabbala that Lurianism developed, are also invested with an important function in the work of "repair." In short, Lurianism proclaims the absolute requirement of an intense mystical life with an unceasing struggle against the powers of evil.

Thus, it presents a myth that symbolizes the world's origin, fall, and redemption. It also gives meaning to the existence and hopes of the Jews, not merely exhorting them to a patient surrender to God but moving them to a redeeming activism, which is the measure of their sanctity. Such requirements make the ideal of Lurianism possible only for a small elite. Ultimately, it is realizable only through the exceptional personage of the "just"—the ideal holy Jew.

SHABBETAIANISM

For 60 years after the death of Luria, his version of the Kabbala, together with accretions from the other mysticisms of Safed, spread through the Jewish Diaspora and deeply permeated its spiritual life, liturgy, and devotional practices. It emphasized the need for "repair" of a world in which Jewish uneasiness continued to grow. Despite certain favourable factors—the relative tolerance of the Ottoman Empire and the peaceful establishment of an important Marrano (Iberian Jewish, or Sephardic) community in Amsterdam—there was no overall solution to the problem of the conversos who had remained in the Iberian Peninsula. The Ashkenazim also experienced a serious crisis: its most prosperous and dynamic section, the Jewish population of Poland, was sorely tried, almost totally ruined, and in large part forced to move back toward the west because of the massacres and the destruction that took place during the Cossack uprising of 1648.

These ideological and historical data may provide the necessary context for understanding the astonishing though short-lived success of Rabbi Shabbetai Tzevi of Smyrna (1626–76), who proclaimed himself messiah in 1665. Although the "messiah" was forcibly converted to Islam in 1666 and ended his life in exile 10 years later, he continued to have faithful followers. A sect was thus born and survived, largely thanks to the activity of Nathan of Gaza (c. 1644–90), an unwearying propagandist who justified the actions of Shabbetai Tzevi, including his final apostasy, with theories based on the Lurian doctrine of "repair." Tzevi's actions, according to Nathan, should be understood as the descent of the just into the abyss of the "shells" to liberate the captive particles of divine light.

The Shabbetaian crisis lasted nearly a century, and some of its aftereffects lasted even longer. It led to the formation of sects whose members were externally converted to Islam—such as the Dönme (Turkish: "Apostates") of Salonika, whose descendants still live in Turkey—or to Roman Catholicism—for example, the Polish supporters of Jacob Frank (1726–91), the self-proclaimed messiah and Catholic convert (in Bohemia-Moravia, however, the Frankists outwardly remained Jews). This crisis did not discredit Kabbala, but it did lead Jewish spiritual authorities to monitor and severely curtail its spread and to use censorship and other acts of repression against anyone—even a person of tested piety and recognized knowledge—who was suspected of Shabbetaian sympathies or messianic pretensions.

MODERN HASIDISM

Although the messianic movement centred around Shabbetai Tzevi produced only disillusionment and could have led to the destruction of Judaism, it answered both the theosophic aspirations of a small number of visionary scholars and the affective need of the Jewish masses that was left unsatisfied by the dry intellectualism of the Talmudists and the economic and social oppression of the ruling classes (both Jewish and non-Jewish). This was the case especially in Poland, which before the partition of the Polish kingdom (1772–95) included Lithuanian, Belarusian, and Ukrainian territories. It was there that the Hasidic movement originated around the middle of the 18th century (it was in no way connected with medieval German Hasidism). While maintaining the Lurian Kabbala as a theoretical basis of speculation, the movement also made adjustments and transformations that continue to the present day.

Modern Hasidism may be regarded as a mass movement having a minimum of organization and relying on itinerant teachers and preachers. According to legend, it was founded by Israel ben Eliezer (c. 1700–60), known as Ba'al

Shem Ṭov ("Master of the Good Name"; that is, a possessor—he was not the only one of his kind—of the secret of the ineffable name of God, which bestows an infallible power to heal and perform other miracles). Although relatively untrained according to the norms of the rabbinical Judaism of his time, he was a spiritual person of exceptional quality and was able to win to his ideas not only the common people but also many representatives of the intellectual elite. The mist of legend that surrounds him makes it impossible to reconstruct his entire doctrine, which he probably never systematized. Inspired by the methods of the itinerant preachers whose activity was becoming more intense among eastern European Jews in the 18th century, his teaching took the form of homiletic interpretations of sacred texts based on fables and parables borrowed from daily life and from folklore. Although this method remained constant in Hasidism, it is a mistake to conclude, as did Martin Buber, that the tale and the anecdote are the most authentic expression of the doctrine and spirituality of Hasidism. Indeed, the thought of the Hasidic "rabbis" is best expressed in doctrinal works, most of which took the form of sermons on the weekly sections of the Pentateuch and other liturgical lessons. It is a very diversified thought, for there are as many bodies of doctrine in Hasidism as there were creative spirits during the first three generations of the movement. It is possible nevertheless to point to a few traits that are fundamental and common to Hasidism as a whole.

In theory, Hasidism remains rooted in the Lurianic Kabbala, and nothing essential separates it at this point from the traditional Judaism of eastern Europe. It is unique, however, because it made *devequt*, "being-with-God," an object of aspiration and even a constant duty for all Jews and in all circumstances of life, even those seemingly most profane. In other words, it demands a total spiritualization of Jewish existence. This requirement entails a reevaluation, less new in its principle than in its concrete application, of the speculative concepts of Kabbala. Emphasis is placed on the inner life of the believer, and it is on this level that the supercosmic drama (whose stage is in the universe of the *sefirot*, according to bookish theosophy) is played out. According to several teachers, the same emphasis on inwardness holds for messianic redemption. Hasidism also transforms into social reality a requirement that was part of the Lurian doctrine of "repair," though it was unfortunately distorted by Shabbetaianism: it puts the inspired leader—an indispensable guide and unquestioned authority endowed with supernatural powers, the "just" (*tzaddiq*), the "miracle-working rabbi" (*Wunderrebbe*)—at the centre of the group's organization and religious life. Hasidism thus produced, wherever it triumphed, an undeniable spiritual renewal. Conversely, it was plagued by the cult of personality, by competition between "dynasties" of "rabbis," and by the social and economic

TZADDIQ

A tzaddiq *(also spelled* zaddik*) is literally a "righteous man" who embodies the religious ideals of Judaism. In the Bible, a* tzaddiq *is a just or righteous man (Genesis 6:9), who, if a ruler, rules justly or righteously (2 Samuel 23:3) and who takes joy in justice (Proverbs 21:15). The Talmud (compendium of Jewish law, lore, and commentary) asserts that the continued existence of the world is the result of the merits of 36 individuals, each of whom is* gamur *tzaddiq ("completely righteous"). While recognizing that* tzaddiqim *have special privileges, the Talmud also notes their special obligations. They are at least partially responsible for the sins of their generation.*

*In Hasidism, the Jewish religious leader (*tzaddiq*) was viewed as a mediator between man and God. Because the* tzaddiq's *life was expected to be a living expression of the Torah, his behaviour was even more important than his doctrine. Rabbi Leib, a disciple of Dov Baer of Mezhirich, thus was said to have visited his master not to hear explanations of the Torah but to see how Dov Baer laced and unlaced his shoes.*

In early Hasidism, the tzaddiq *traveled widely and often seemed to engage in such secular matters as idle talk and the consumption of wine. The Hasidic formula for such conduct was "descent on behalf of ascent" (*'aliyya tzrikha yerida*)—a calculated risk to strengthen the spiritual life of the Jewish community. Whereas some* tzaddiqim *lived simple and humble lives, others sought wealth and luxury. Toward the end of the 18th century the* tzaddiqim *ceased to travel. Thereafter, they were available at home for those who sought advice and instructions. This change gave rise to "practical tzaddiqism," a development that included, among other things, the writing of a* quittel *("prayer note") to guarantee the success of petitions made by visitors who offered money for the service. Such developments contributed to the gradual deterioration of an institution that had earlier been a vital spiritual force within Jewish communities.*

consequences of its obstinate insistence on isolating the Hasidic community from the surrounding society.

From its inception, Hasidism encountered strong resistance from official Judaism, which had been sensitized to the anarchism of the Shabbetaians and which at the same time was solicitous toward the prerogatives of the community leaders and rabbis. The behaviour of the followers of Hasidism, though irreproachable in its rigorous observance of ritual rules, displayed several traits that were distasteful to its adversaries (besides the unconditional submission to the *tzaddiq*, who often doubled as the rabbi of the official congregation): desertion of the general communal synagogues, meetings in small conventicles, modifications of the liturgy, excessively formal dress during prayer, and preference given to mystical meditation rather than to the

Well-known, U.S.-based Hasidic groups such as the Lubavitchers successfully relocated owing to strong organization. Mario Tama/Getty Images

dialectical study of the Talmud, which required serious intellectual concentration. Nevertheless, the conflict between the Hasidim and the "Opponents" (Mitnaggedim) did not finally degenerate into schism. After three generations, a tacit compromise was established between the two tendencies—Hasidic and Mitnaggedic—though awareness of their differences was never erased. The compromise was somewhat to the advantage of Hasidism, but not without a few concessions on its part, notably on the question of education.

The strong organization of the Hasidic groups allowed them to survive the dislocation of eastern European Judaism as a result of the events of World War II, but today its vital centres are in the United States rather than in Palestine. This relocation is partly for economic reasons and partly because of the more or less reserved, and sometimes hostile, attitude of the Hasidic "rabbis" toward political Zionism and the State of Israel. The best-known of the U.S.-based groups is the extremely active Lubavitchers (named after Lyubavichi, Russia, seat of a famous school of Hasidism), whose headquarters are in the Crown Heights district of Brooklyn, New York.

MODERN JEWISH MYSTICISM

The role played by Kabbala and Hasidism in the thought and spirituality of contemporary Judaism is far from insignificant, though its importance is not as great as in former times. Although there is hardly any living Kabbalistic and Hasidic literature, the personal thought of religious writers such as Abraham Isaac Kook (c. 1865–1935)—spiritual leader, mystic, and chief rabbi of Palestine—remains influential. Furthermore, religious thought in Westernized Jewish circles between the two World Wars received a powerful stimulus from the philosopher Martin Buber, whose work is in part devoted to the propagation of Hasidic ideology as he understood it. "Neo-Orthodoxy," the theological system founded in Germany by Samson Raphael Hirsch (1808–88), was indifferent to mysticism at the outset, but it too came to be influenced by it, especially after the rediscovery of living Judaism in Poland during World War I by Western Jewish thinkers. Also significant is the work of Abraham Joshua Heschel (1907–72), a Polish Jewish theologian of distinguished Hasidic background and dual culture—traditional and Western.

Jewish mysticism has exerted influence outside the Jewish community. Kabbala, distorted and deflected from its own intentions, has helped to nourish and stimulate certain currents of thought in Christian society since the Renaissance. "Christian Kabbala," born in the 15th century under the impetus of Jewish converts from Spain and Italy, claimed to find in the Kabbalistic documents—touched up or even forged if necessary—arguments for the truths of the Christian faith. A certain number of Christian humanist scholars became interested in Jewish mysticism, and several of them acquired a fairly extensive knowledge of it on the basis of authentic texts. Among them were Giovanni Pico della Mirandola (1463–94) and Gilles of Viterbo (Egidio da Viterbo; *c.* 1465–1532) in Italy; Johannes Reuchlin (1455–1522) in Germany, who wrote one of the principal expositions of Kabbala in a language accessible to the learned non-Jewish public (*De arte Cabbalistica*, 1517); and the visionary Guillaume Postel (1510–81) in France. The occult philosophy of the 16th century, the "natural philosophy" of the 17th and 18th centuries, and the occult and theosophic theories that are cultivated even today and that have coloured the ideology of Freemasonry—all of these continue to borrow from Kabbala, though they rarely grasp its spirit and meaning. The same is true of most of the books on Kabbala put out by publishers of occult and theosophic literature today.

The scholarly study of Jewish mysticism is quite a recent phenomenon. The state of mind and the tendencies of the founders of the "science of Judaism" (the scholarly study of Jewish religion, literature, and history) in Germany during the first half of the 19th century were too permeated with rationalism to be favourable to scholarly investigation of a movement judged to be obscurantist and retrograde. Although there were some valuable early studies, research on a large scale and application of the proved methods of philology and history of religions began only with the work of Gershom G. Scholem (1897–1982) and his disciples. This research addressed all the many areas of Jewish mysticism, but in every area the gaps in knowledge remain serious. Critical editions of mystical texts are few in number; unpublished documents are cataloged incompletely; and only a few monographs on writers and particular themes exist, though these are indispensable preliminaries to a detailed and thorough synthesis. It is to be hoped that the synthesis outlined by Scholem in his *Major Trends in Jewish Mysticism* (1941), though exceptionally valuable in its time, will be taken up again and completed.

CHAPTER 10

JEWISH MYTH AND LEGEND

Jewish myth and legend comprises a vast body of stories transmitted over the past 3,000 years in Hebrew and in the vernacular dialects spoken by Jews, such as Yiddish (Judeo-German) and Ladino (Judeo-Spanish). These stories have played an important role in the history of Jewish religion and culture. Virtually all the standard types of folktales are represented. Conspicuously absent, however, are pure fairy tales, because fairies, elves, and the like are foreign to the Jewish imagination, which prefers to populate the other-world with angels and demons subservient to God.

SIGNIFICANCE AND CHARACTERISTICS

Apart from their intrinsic appeal, Jewish myths and legends claim attention for three special reasons: (1) Those incorporated in the Hebrew Bible are now part and parcel of the cultural heritage of the Western world and have exerted a profound influence on its literature and art. (2) During the Middle Ages, Jews were among the principal transmitters of Middle Eastern and North African tales to the West, so many familiar Eastern stories can be traced to Jewish compilations. (3) Because these stories have been accumulated through centuries of constant migration, they provide an unrivalled body of "clinical" material for studying the processes by which popular tales in fact travel and are transformed.

Not all of the stories are of Jewish origin. Many have parallels elsewhere and are derived from tales the Jews picked up from their non-Jewish neighbours in the lands of their dispersion. Even what is borrowed, however, is usually impressed with a distinctive Jewish stamp. The tales were often adapted to point up some precept of the Jewish religion, illustrate some facet of Jewish life, or exemplify some trait of Jewish character and temperament. The dominant feature of the stories is their religious and moral tone. Most are told specifically as part of the homiletic exposition of Scripture. Such stories are taught to Jews from early childhood as a regular part of their religious education. To the tradition-minded Jew, therefore, they are more than mere literary fancies. Biblical characters and events are presented more in the lineaments of later legend than in their original biblical form, and popular notions about heaven and hell, reward and punishment, the coming of the messiah, and the resurrection of the dead derive mainly from these sources rather than from Scripture itself.

A distinction must be made between myth and legend. In common parlance, a myth is a story about gods or otherworldly beings. In this sense, therefore, there can be no original Jewish myths, because Judaism is a rigorously monotheistic religion. Nevertheless, from the earliest times, Jews have not disdained to borrow the myths of their pagan neighbours and adapt them to their own religious outlook. If, however, the term is interpreted in a larger sense to mean the portrayal of perennial concerns in the context of particular historical events, myth is indeed one of the essential vehicles by which Judaism conveys its message. It is only when historical happenings are translated into this wider dimension that they cease to be mere antiquarian data and acquire continuing relevance. In Judaism, for example, the Exodus from Egypt is projected mythically from something that happened at a particular time into something that is continually happening, and it comes to exemplify the situation and experience of all humans everywhere—their emergence from the bondage of obscurantism, their individual revelations at their individual Sinais, their trek through a figurative wilderness, even their death in it so that their children or children's children may eventually reach the figurative "Promised Land." By the same token, the historical destruction of the Temple of Jerusalem is transformed by myth into a paradigm of the continuing mutual estrangement of God and humans, their exile from one another. Legend, however, implies no more than a fanciful embroidering of purportedly historical fact. Unlike myth, it does not transcend the historical and the local.

MYTH AND LEGEND IN THE BIBLE

The vast repertoire of Jewish myths and legends begins with the Hebrew Bible. Their overall purpose in Scripture is to illustrate the ways of God with humans, as exemplified both in historical events and in personal experience. The stories themselves are often derived from current popular lore and possess abundant parallels in other cultures, both ancient and modern. In each case, however, they are given a peculiar and distinctive twist.

MYTHS

Biblical myths are found mainly in the first 11 chapters of Genesis, the first book of the Bible. They are concerned with the creation of the world and the first man and woman, the origin of the current human condition, the primeval Deluge, the distribution of peoples, and the variation of languages.

The basic stories are derived from the popular lore of the ancient Middle East, and parallels are found in the extant literature of the peoples of the area. The Mesopotamians, for instance, also knew of an earthly paradise such as Eden, and the figure of the cherubim—properly griffins rather than angels—was known to the Canaanites. In the Bible, however, this mythical garden of the gods becomes the scene of man's fall and the background of a story designed to account for the natural limitations of human life. Similarly, the Babylonians told of the formation of humankind from clay. But, whereas in the pagan tale the first man's function is to serve as an earthly menial of the gods, in the scriptural version his role is to rule over all other creatures. The story of the Deluge, including the elements of the ark and the dispatch of the raven and dove, appears already in the Babylonian myths of Gilgamesh and Atrahasis. There, however, the hero is eventually made immortal, whereas in the Bible this detail is omitted because, to the Israelite mind, no child of woman could achieve that status. Lastly, while the story of the Tower of Babel was told originally to account for the stepped temples (ziggurats) of Babylonia, to the Hebrew writer its purpose is simply to inculcate the moral lesson that humans should not aspire beyond their assigned station.

Scattered through the Prophets and Holy Writings (the two latter portions of the Hebrew Bible) are allusions to other ancient myths—for example, to that of a primordial combat between YHWH and a monster variously named Leviathan (Wriggly), Rahab (Braggart), or simply Sir Sea or Dragon. The Babylonians told likewise of a fight between their god Marduk and the monster Tiamat; the Hittites told of a battle between the weather god and the dragon Illuyankas; while a Canaanite poem from Ras Shamra (ancient Ugarit) in northern Syria relates the discomfiture of Sir Sea by the deity Baal and the rout of an opponent named Leviathan. Originally, this myth probably referred to the annual subjugation of the floods.

Ancient myths are used also in the form of passing allusions or poetic "conceits," much as modern Westerners may speak of Cupid or the Muses. In the prophetic books, for example, there are references to a celestial upstart hurled to earth on account of his brashness and to the imprisonment of certain rebellious constellations.

The prophets used myths paradigmatically to illustrate the hand of God in contemporary events or to reinforce their prophecies. Thus, to Isaiah the primeval dragon was the symbol of the continuing force of chaos and evil that will again have to be vanquished before the kingdom of God can be established on earth. Similarly, for Ezekiel the celestial upstart serves as the prototype of the prince of Tyre, destined for an imminent fall; and Habakkuk sees in the impending rout of certain invaders a repetition on the stage of history of YHWH's mythical sortie against the monster of the sea.

LEGENDS AND OTHER TALES

Legends in the Hebrew Scriptures often embellish the accounts of national heroes with standard motifs drawn from popular lore. Thus, the Genesis story of Joseph and Potiphar's wife recurs substantially (but with other characters) in an Egyptian papyrus of the 13th century BCE. The account of the infant Moses being placed in the bulrushes (in Exodus) has an earlier counterpart in a Babylonian tale about Sargon, king of Akkad (c. 2334–c. 2279 BCE), and is paralleled later in legends associated with the Persian Cyrus and with Tu-Küeh, the fabled founder of the Turkish nation. Jephthah's rash vow (in Judges), whereby

he is committed to sacrifice his daughter, recalls the Classical legend of Idomeneus of Crete, who was similarly compelled to slay his own son. The motif of the letter whereby David engineers the death in battle of Bathsheba's husband recurs in Homer's story of Bellerophon. The celebrated judgment of Solomon concerning the child claimed by two contending women is told, albeit with variations of detail, about Buddha, Confucius, and other sages. The story of how Jonah was swallowed by a "great fish" but was subsequently disgorged intact finds a parallel in the Indian tale of the hero Shaktideva, who endured the same experience during his quest for the Golden City. Conversely, it should be observed that many parallels commonly cited from the folklore of indigenous peoples may be mere repetitions of biblical material picked up from Christian missionaries.

Folktales in the Hebrew Bible sometimes serve to account for the names of places in Palestine or for the origins of traditional customs and institutions. Thus, the familiar story of the man who must struggle with the personified current of a river before he can cross it is localized (in Genesis) at the ford of Jabbok simply because that name suggests the Hebrew word *abk* ("struggle"), and Samson's felling of 1,000 Philistines with the jawbone of an ass is placed at Ramath-lehi because *leḥi* is Hebrew for "jawbone." Similarly, a taboo against eating the thigh muscle of an animal is validated in Genesis by the legend that Jacob was struck in the

The story of Jonah and the whale has a parallel in the Indian tale of the hero Shaktideva, who endured the same experience as he sought the Golden City. Hulton Archive/Getty Images

hip when he fought with an otherworldly being at Penuel ("Face of God"). The custom of annually bewailing the vanished spirit of fertility is rationalized in Judges as a lamentation for the hapless daughter of Jephthah.

The Hebrew Bible also contains a few examples of fables (didactic tales in which animals or plants play human roles). Thus, the serpent in Eden talks to Eve, and Balaam's ass not only speaks but also seeks to avoid an angel, unseen by Balaam, that is blocking the road, while trees compete for kingship in the celebrated parable of Jotham in Judges. Finally, in the book of Job (38:31) there are allusions to star myths concerning the binding of Orion (called "the Fool") and the "chaining" of the Pleiades.

CONTEMPORARY INTERPRETATIONS

The tendency to interpret biblical tales and legends as authentic historical records or as allegories or as the relics of solar, lunar, and astral myths is now a thing of the past. The modern folklorist is interested in the legends because they push back to remote antiquity several tales and motifs long known from later literature. For the theologian, however,

THE BOOK OF JOB

The Book of Job, often counted among the masterpieces of world literature, is found in the third section of the biblical canon known as the Ketuvim ("Writings"). The book's theme is the eternal problem of unmerited suffering, and it is named after its central character, Job, who attempts to understand the sufferings that engulf him.

The Book of Job's artful construction accounts for much of its effect. The poetic disputations are set within the prose framework of an ancient legend that originated outside Israel. This legend concerns Job, a prosperous man of outstanding piety. Satan acts as an agent provocateur to test whether or not Job's piety is rooted merely in his prosperity. But faced with the appalling loss of his possessions, his children, and finally his own health, Job still refuses to curse God. Three of his friends then arrive to comfort him, and at this point the poetic dialogue begins. The poetic discourses—which probe the meaning of Job's sufferings and the manner in which he should respond—consist of three cycles of speeches that contain Job's disputes with his three friends and his conversations with God. Job proclaims his innocence and the injustice of his suffering, while his "comforters" argue that Job is being punished for his sins. Job, convinced of his faithfulness and uprighteousness, is not satisfied with this explanation. The conversation between Job and God resolves the dramatic tension—but without solving the problem of undeserved suffering. The speeches evoke Job's trust in the purposeful activity of God in the affairs of the world, even though God's ways with man remain mysterious and inscrutable.

they pose the deeper problem of distinguishing clearly between the permanent message of Scripture and the form in which it is conveyed. The process of "demythologization" is one of the central concerns of modern religious thought. It recognizes that the natural language of religious truth is myth. Thus, the continuing relevance of ancient scriptures depends not on the total rejection of that vehicle but rather on the expansion and remodeling of it (i.e., on "remythologization" rather than demythologization). In the final analysis, the traditional portrayal of God himself is simply a mythical representation of ultimate reality, but that reality transcends the particular images in which it happens to be expressed. At the same time, it is important to note that, whereas in the modern world scriptural

BOOK OF JONAH

Unlike the other books of the Nevi'im, Jonah is not a collection of the prophet's oracles but primarily a narrative about the prophet himself. Jonah is portrayed as a recalcitrant prophet who flees from God's summons to prophesy against the excessive wickedness of the city of Nineveh. Jonah believes that its destruction is warranted and part of God's justice. Further, he seems to react against delivering a prophecy to the city's inhabitants, who are Assyrian rather than Israelites. Thus, instead of offering the prophecy that could spur its citizens to repent and possibly be spared divine wrath, Jonah rushes down to Joppa and takes passage in a ship that will carry him in the opposite direction and to "the ends of the earth." However, Jonah cannot escape God. A storm of unprecedented severity strikes the ship, and in spite of all that the master and crew can do, it shows signs of breaking up and foundering. Lots are cast, and Jonah confesses that it is his presence on board that is causing the storm. At his request, he is thrown overboard, and the storm subsides. A "great fish," appointed by God, swallows Jonah, and he stays within the fish's maw for three days and nights, after which he is "vomited out" on dry land (chapter 2). Again God commands him: "Arise, go to Nineveh." Jonah goes to Nineveh and prophesies against the city, causing the King and all the inhabitants—including the nonhuman residents, such as the livestock—to repent.

Jonah then becomes angry. Hoping for disaster, he sits outside the city to await its destruction and becomes even angrier when it does not come. He complains to God about this and also about the heat of the sun. A plant springs up overnight, providing him welcome shelter, but it is soon destroyed by a great worm. Jonah is bitter at the destruction of the plant, but God speaks and thrusts home the final point of the story: "You pity the plant, for which you did not labor, nor did you make it grow, which came into being in a night, and perished in a night. And should not I pity Nineveh, that great city, in which there are more than a hundred and twenty thousand persons who do not know their right hand from their left, and also much cattle?" (chapter 4). The book is, therefore, a satire on those who will not extend God's mercy as well as his justice even to non-Israelites.

myths are generally understood as metaphors, in the ancient world they were accepted as literal statements of fact. Gods, for example, were not merely "personifications" of natural phenomena but rather the effective potencies of the phenomena themselves conceived from the start as personal beings.

MYTH AND LEGEND IN THE PERSIAN PERIOD

In 539 BCE the Jews came under Persian domination and consequently absorbed a good deal of Iranian folklore about spirits and demons, the eventual dissolution of the world in a fiery ordeal, and its subsequent renewal. This introduced new elements into Jewish popular mythology: hierarchies of angels; archangels such as Michael, Gabriel, and Uriel (modeled loosely upon the six Iranian spiritual entities, the *amesha spentas*); and the demonic figures of Satan, Belial, and Asmodeus (corresponding to the Iranian Angra Mainyu [Ahriman], Druj, and Aēshma Daeva). There was also a preoccupation with apocalyptic visions of heaven and hell and of the Last Days. Unfortunately, no Jewish texts of this genre from the Persian period are extant, so these new elements can be recognized only inferentially from their survival in later times—notably in products of the ensuing Hellenistic Age, such as the Dead Sea Scrolls.

The principal monument of Jewish story in the Persian period is the biblical Book of Esther, which is basically a Judaized version of a Persian novella about the shrewdness of harem queens. The story was adapted to account for Purim, a popular festival, which itself is probably a transformation of the Persian New Year. Leading elements of the tale—such as the parade of Mordecai, dressed in royal robes, through the streets, the fight between the Jews and their adversaries, and the hanging of Haman and his sons—seem to reflect customs associated with Purim, such as the ceremonial ride of a common citizen through the capital, the mock combat between two teams representing the Old Year and the New Year, and the execution of the Old Year in effigy.

MYTH AND LEGEND IN THE HELLENISTIC PERIOD

Judaism entered a new phase in 330 BCE, when Alexander the Great completed his conquest of the Middle East. The dominant features of the Hellenistic Age, which began with Alexander's death in 323, were an increasing cosmopolitanism and a fusion of ancient Middle Eastern and Greek cultures.

HISTORIATED BIBLES AND LEGENDARY HISTORIES

These Hellenistic features found expression in Jewish myth and legend in the composition (in Greek) of stories designed to link the Bible with general

history, to correlate biblical and Greek legends, and to claim for the Hebrew patriarchs a major role in the development of the arts and sciences. It was asserted, for instance, that Abraham had taught astrology to the king of Egypt; his sons and those of Keturah had aided Heracles against the giant Antaeus; and Moses, blithely identified both with the semi-mythical Greek poet Musaeus and with the Egyptian Thoth, had been the teacher of Orpheus (the putative founder of one of the current mystery cults) and the inventor of navigation, architecture, and the hieroglyphic script. Leading writers in this vein included Artapanus, Eupolemus, and Cleodemus (all c. 100 BCE), but their works are known to us only from stray quotations by the early Church Fathers Eusebius and Clement of Alexandria.

The Jews also adapted the current Greek literary fashion of retelling Homeric and other ancient legends in "modernized," novelistic versions, well seasoned with romantic elaborations of their own traditions. A paraphrase of Genesis found among the Dead Sea Scrolls ornaments the biblical narrative with several familiar folklore motifs. Thus, when Noah is born, the house is filled with light, just as it is said elsewhere to have been at the birth of the Roman king Servius Tullius, of Buddha,

and (later) of several Christian saints. When Abraham's life is threatened, he dreams of a cedar about to be felled, an omen that is said to have presaged the deaths of the Roman emperors Domitian and Severus Alexander. (Although the parallels are of later date, they illustrate the persistence of age-old traditions.) The same trend toward fanciful elaboration of scriptural tales is manifested also in the *Testaments of the Twelve Patriarchs* ("testaments" meaning last wills), in which the virtues and weaknesses of the sons of Jacob are illustrated by moralistic legends. There is also a lengthy paraphrase of early biblical narratives, mistakenly attributed to Philo, the famous Alexandrian Jewish philosopher of the 1st century CE.

APOCRYPHA AND PSEUDEPIGRAPHA

The principal monuments of Jewish literature during the Hellenistic period are the works known collectively as the Apocrypha and Pseudepigrapha. The former are certain later writings excluded by Jews from the canon of the Hebrew Bible but found in the Greek Septuagint version. The latter are other late writings not included in any authorized version of the Scriptures and spuriously attributed to biblical personalities.

When his own life is in danger, Abraham dreams of a cedar tree falling, which is said to forewarn of the deaths of the Roman emperors Domitian and Severus Alexander. Shutterstock.com

The Apocrypha include several Judaized versions of tales well represented in other cultures. The book of Tobit, for instance, turns largely on the widespread motifs of the "grateful dead" and the demon in the bridal chamber. The former relates how a traveller who gives burial to a dishonoured corpse is subsequently aided by a chance companion who turns out to be the spirit of the deceased. The latter tells how a succession of bridegrooms die on the nuptial night through the presence of a demon beside the bridal bed. Similarly, in Bel and the Dragon (2nd century BCE) there is the equally familiar motif of fraud that is detected by the imprint of the culprit's foot on strewn ashes. The story reappears later in the French and Celtic romance of Tristan and Iseult. In the story of Susanna and the Elders (also 2nd century BCE), a charge of unchastity levelled against a beautiful woman is refuted when a clever youngster ("Daniel come to judgment") points out discrepancies in the testimony of her accusers. This well-worn story has a close parallel in a Samaritan tale about the daughter of a high priest in the 1st century CE. The motif of the clever youngster who surpasses seasoned judges recurs later in the Infancy Gospels and in the tale of 'Alī Khamājah in The Thousand and One Nights.

The Pseudepigrapha also contain a number of folktales that have parallels in other traditions. The Martyrdom of Isaiah (1st century CE?) tells how the prophet, fleeing from King Manasseh, hid in a tree that opened miraculously, though he eventually perished when it was sawn asunder. Similar tales are related in the Talmud and in the later Persian epic Shāh-nāmeh (c. 1000 CE).

GRATEFUL DEAD

A grateful dead is a genre of folktale found in many cultures that portrays the spirit of a deceased person who bestows benefits on the one responsible for his burial. In the prototypical story, the protagonist is a traveler who encounters the corpse of a debtor, to whom the honour of proper burial has been denied. After the traveler satisfies the debt, or, in some versions, pays for the burial, he goes on his way. In another version of the story, burial is prescribed for religious reasons but prohibited by civil authorities. It is this version that forms the theme of the apocryphal Book of Tobit in the Hebrew Bible.

The hero is soon joined by another traveler (sometimes in the form of an animal, or, in the story of Tobit, an angel), who helps him in a dramatic way. In some stories the companion saves the hero's life, and in others he helps him gain a prize. In many versions, the companion offers to aid the hero, but only on condition that they divide the prize. Then, as the hero is about to comply, the companion reveals himself as the grateful spirit of the deceased whom the hero helped to bury.

MYTH AND LEGEND IN THE TALMUD AND MIDRASH

Toward the end of the 1st century CE, the canon of the Hebrew Bible was formed when certain Hebrew writings were recognized as the authoritative corpus of divine revelation. The study of the Bible became an essential element of the Jewish religion, which meant that the sacred text had to be subjected to a form of interpretation that would bring out its universal significance and permanent relevance.

MIDRASH AND HAGGADA

This process of interpreting scripture became known as Midrash (a word meaning either "interpretation" or "investigation"). It involved the spicing of homiletic discourses with elaborative legends—a pedagogic device called Haggada ("Storytelling"). Originally transmitted orally, the legends were eventually committed to writing as part of the Talmud (the authoritative compendium of Oral Torah and commentary on it), as well as in later compilations geared to particular books or sections of the Hebrew Bible, to scriptural lessons read in the services of the synagogue, or to specific biblical characters or moral themes.

The range of Haggada is virtually inexhaustible, so a few representative examples must suffice. With regard to biblical characters, both Moses and David were born circumcised; Cain had a twin sister; Abraham will sit at the gate of hell to reproach the damned on Judgment Day; Aaron once locked the angel of death in the tabernacle; Solomon understood the language of animals; King Hiram, who supplied materials for the Temple, entered paradise alive; and the flesh of Leviathan will feed the righteous in the world to come.

In such fanciful elaborations of Scriptures, Haggada does not disdain to draw on Classical tales from ancient Greece and Rome. The men of Sodom, it is said, subjected itinerant strangers to the ordeal of Procrustes' bed. The earth opened to rescue newborn Hebrew males from the pharaoh, as it did for Amphiaraus, the prophet of Argos, when he fled from Periclymenus after the attack on Thebes. Moses spoke at birth, as did Apollo. Solomon's ring, cast into the river, was retrieved from a fish that had swallowed it, as was that of Polycrates, the tyrant of Samos, in the story told by Herodotus. The Queen of Sheba had the feet of an ass, like the child-stealing witch (Onoskelis) of Greek folklore. And no rain ever fell on the altar at Jerusalem, just as none was said to have fallen on Mt. Olympus.

There are other familiar motifs. Moses qualifies as a husband for Zipporah by alone being able to pluck a rod from Jethro's garden. David's harp is played at night by the wind, like that of Aeolus. And Isaiah, like Achilles and Siegfried, has only one vulnerable spot in his body—in his case, his mouth.

Legends are developed also from fanciful interpretations of scriptural verses.

Thus, Adam is said to have fallen only a few hours after his creation, because the Hebrew text of Psalms 49:12 can be literally rendered "Adam does not last the night in glory." Lamech slays the wandering Cain—a fanciful interpretation of his boast in Genesis 4:23–24. Melchizedek is immortal, in view of Psalms 110:4: "You are a priest for ever after the order of Melchizedek." And the first man is a hermaphrodite (this notion has analogues elsewhere), because Genesis 1:27 says of God's creation, "Male and female he created them."

FABLES AND ANIMAL STORIES

Midrash also uses fables paralleled in non-Jewish sources. Aesop's fable of *The Lion and the Crane* is quoted by a rabbi of the 1st century CE, and the tales of *The Fox in the Vineyard* and *The Camel Who Got Slit Ears for Wanting Horns* likewise make their appearance. Material is also drawn from medieval bestiaries (manuals on animals, real or imaginary, with symbolic or moralistic interpretations). Bears, according to the bestiaries, lack mother's milk; hares and hyenas can change sex; only one pair of unicorns exists at a time; and there is a gigantic bird (*ziz*) that reaches from earth to sky.

CONTRIBUTION OF HAGGADA TO CHRISTIAN AND ISLAMIC LEGENDS

Several stories related in Haggadic literature were later adapted by Christian writers. The legend that Adam was created out of virgin soil was taken to prefigure the virgin birth of the second Adam (i.e., Jesus), while the story that the soil in question was taken from the site of the future Temple was transformed into the claim that Adam had been molded out of the dust of Calvary. Similarly, the legend that, at the dedication of the Temple, the doors swung open automatically to admit the Ark of the Covenant was transferred to the consecration of a church by St. Basil (329–379). And the Talmudic tale that the bronze Nicanor gates of the Temple had floated to Jerusalem when cast overboard during their shipment from Alexandria was applied to the doors of a sacred edifice erected in honour of St. Giles (flourished 7th century).

Nor was it only the Christians who absorbed Haggadic legends. The Qur'ān, the sacred book of Islam, likewise incorporates a good deal of such material in its treatment of biblical characters such as Joseph, Moses, David, and Solomon.

MYTH AND LEGEND IN THE MEDIEVAL PERIOD

The Middle Ages was a singularly productive period in the history of Jewish myth and legend. Medieval Jews played a prominent role in the transmission of Middle Eastern and Asian tales to the West and enhanced their own repertoire with a goodly amount of secular material.

JEWISH CONTRIBUTIONS TO DIFFUSION OF FOLKTALES

Especially in Spain and Italy, Arabic versions of standard collections of folktales were translated into Hebrew and then into Latin, thus enabling the stories to spread to the Christian world. The Indian collection of animal tales known as *The Fables of Bidpai* (Sanskrit: *Panca-tantra*), for example, was rendered into Hebrew from the 8th-century Arabic version of 'Abd Allāh ibn al-Muqaffa'. In the 12th century, John of Capua's *Directorium humanae vitae* ("Guide for Human Life"), one of the most celebrated repositories of moralistic tales (*exempla*) used by Christian preachers, was developed from this Hebrew translation. So too the famous *Senbād-nāmeh* ("Fables of Sinbad")—one of the sources, incidentally, of Boccaccio's *Decameron*—was rendered from Arabic into Hebrew and then into Latin. The renowned romance of *Barlaam and Josaphat*—a Christian adaptation of tales about the Buddha—found its Jewish counterpart in a compilation titled *The Prince and the Dervish*, adapted from an Arabic text by Abraham ben Samuel ibn Ḥisdai, a leader of Spanish Jewry in the 13th century.

Hebrew Versions of Medieval Romances

Hebrew translations were also made from Latin and other European languages. There are several Hebrew adaptations of the *Alexander Romance*, based mainly (though not exclusively) on a Latin rendering of the Greek original by Callisthenes (c. 360–327 BCE). The central theme is the exploits of Alexander the Great, and the narrative includes fanciful accounts of his adventures in foreign lands and of the outlandish peoples he encounters. There is a Hebrew reworking of the Arthurian legend, in the form of a secular sermon in which Arthurian and biblical scenes are blithely mixed together. Finally, there is a Hebrew *Ysopet* (the common title for a medieval version of Aesop) that shares several of its fables with the famous collection made by Marie de France in the late 12th century.

Jewish Contributions to Christian and Islamic Tales

Apart from these Hebrew translations of Arabic and European works, a good deal of earlier Haggadic material is embodied in the *Disciplina clericalis* of Peter Alfonsi (1062–1110), a baptized Jew of Aragon originally known as Moses Sephardi. This book is the oldest European collection of novellas. It served as a primary source for the celebrated *Gesta Romanorum* ("Deeds of the Romans") of the same period—itself a major source for European storytellers, poets, and dramatists for many centuries.

Haggadic material was also absorbed by Arabic writers during this period. Not only does the Qur'ān incorporate such material, but the Egyptian recension of *The Thousand and One Nights* seems to have drawn extensively on Jewish sources. Its tales of *The Sultan and His Three Sons, The Angel of Death, Alexander and the Pious Man,* and the legend of Baliqiyah most likely come from a Jewish source.

MAJOR MEDIEVAL HEBREW COLLECTIONS

From the 11th to the 13th century, comprehensive collections of tales and fables were compiled in Europe, both for entertainment and edification. Standard examples are the Spanish *El novellino* and the aforementioned *Disciplina clericalis* and *Gesta Romanorum*. Jews, especially in Morocco and in Islamic Spain, produced similar collections. Two of the most important were *The Book of Comfort* by Nissim ben Jacob ben Nissim of Al-Qayrawān (11th century) and *The Book of Delight* by Joseph ben Meir ibn Zabara of Spain (end of the 12th century). The former, composed in Judeo-Arabic, is a collection of some 60 moralizing tales designed to comfort the author's father-in-law on the loss of a son. Belonging to a well-known genre of Arabic literature and derived mainly from Arabic sources, it is permeated by a preoccupation with divine justice, which was typical of the Mu'tazilite school of Islamic theology. It was later translated into Hebrew. *The Book of Delight* consists of 15 tales, largely about the wiles of women, exchanged between two travelling companions—a form of cadre, or "enclosing tale," later adopted on a more extensive scale in the 14th century in the *Canterbury Tales* by Chaucer (c. 1342–1400). Typical is the tale of *The Silversmith and His Wife*, which relates how a craftsman, persuaded by his greedy wife to make a statue of a princess, gets his hands cut off by the king for violating the Islamic law against making images,

while his wife reaps rich rewards from the flattered princess. Although most of the stories are taken from Arabic sources, some have parallels in rabbinic literature—including the famous tale of the matron of Ephesus, who, while keeping vigil over her husband's tomb, makes love with a guard posted nearby to watch over the corpses of certain crucified robbers. When, during one of their trysts, one of the corpses is stolen and her lover therefore faces punishment, the shrewd woman exhumes the body of her husband and substitutes it. This tale is found already in the *Satyricon* of Petronius (died 66 CE) and was later used by Voltaire (1694–1778) in his *Zadig* and by the 20th-century English playwright Christopher Fry in his *A Phoenix Too Frequent*.

Of the same genre but deriving mainly from west European rather than Arabic sources are the *Mishle shu'alim* ("Fox Fables") of Berechiah ha-Nakdan ("the Punctuator"), who may have lived in England near the end of the 12th century. About half of these tales recur in Marie de France's *Ysopet*, and only one of them is of specifically Jewish origin. Berechiah's work was translated into Latin and thereafter became a favourite of European storytellers.

Among anonymous compendiums of this type is *The Alphabet of Ben Sira*, extant in two recensions, probably of the 11th century. This is basically a collection of proverbs attributed to the famous sage of the apocryphal book Ecclesiasticus (Wisdom of Jesus the Son of Sirach). In one of the recensions the proverbs are illustrated by appropriate tales. The author is represented as an infant prodigy who performs much the same feats of sapience as are attributed to Jesus in some of the Infancy Gospels.

Medieval Legendary Histories and Haggadic Compendiums

Two other developments mark the history of Jewish myth and legend during the Middle Ages. The first was a revival of the Hellenistic predilection for large-scale compendiums in which the history of the Jews was "integrated," in legendary fashion, with that of the world in general and especially with Classical traditions. Two major works of this kind, both composed (apparently) in Italy during the 9th century, are *Josippon*, by a certain Ben Gorion, which presents a fanciful record from the Creation onward and contains numerous references to foreign nations; and the *Book of Jashar*, a colourful account from Adam to Joshua, named for the ancient book of heroic songs and sagas mentioned in the Bible (Joshua 10:13; 2 Samuel 1:18). There is also the voluminous *Chronicles of Jerahmeel*, written in the Rhineland in the 14th century, which draws largely on Pseudo-Philo's earlier compilation and includes Hebrew and Aramaic versions of certain books of the Apocrypha.

The other development was the gathering of Haggadic legends and tales into comprehensive, systematic compendiums. Works of this kind are *Yalquṭ Shim'oni* ("The Collection of Simeon"), attributed to Rabbi Simeon of Frankfurt am Main; *Midrash ha-gadol* ("The Great Midrash"), composed after the death in 1204 of Moses Maimonides, whom it quotes; and the *Midrash of David ha-Nagid*, named after the grandson of Maimonides. About 100 years later a similar work on the Prophets and holy writings, *Yalquṭ ha-Makiri* ("The Collection of Makhir"), was compiled by Makhir ben Abba Mari in Spain. It has been suggested that the production of such works was spurred by the necessity of providing "ammunition" for the public disputations with Christian ecclesiastics that the church forced upon Jewish scholars during this period.

MYTH AND LEGEND IN THE MODERN PERIOD

The modern period of Judaism began in the 16th century. During this time, Jewish myth and legend took several new directions.

Kabbalistic Tales

The disappointment of messianic expectations through the dismal eclipse of the pretender Shabbetai Tzevi increased interest in occult speculation and in the mystical lore of the Kabbala. Important schools of Kabbala arose in Italy and at Safed, in Palestine, and tales of the miraculous Faust-like powers of masters such as Isaac Luria (1534–72) and Ḥayyim ben Joseph Vital (also known as Ḥayyim Vital Calabrese) circulated freely after their deaths.

Another reaction to the dashing of messianic hopes is represented by the beautiful story of the Kabbalist Joseph della Reyna and his five disciples, who travel through the world to oust Satan and prepare the way for the Deliverer. Warned by the spirits of such worthies as Rabbi Simeon ben Yoḥai and the prophet Elijah, they nevertheless procure their blessing and are sent on to the angel Metatron. The latter furnishes them with protective spells and spices and advises Joseph to inscribe the ineffable name of God on a metal plate. However, when they reach the end of their journey, Satan and his wife, Lilith, attack them in the form of huge dogs. When the dogs are subdued, they beg for food, and Joseph gives them spices to revive them. At once they summon a host of devils, which causes two disciples to die of terror and two to go mad, leaving only Joseph and a disciple. The messiah weeps in heaven, and Elijah hides the great horn of salvation. A voice rings out telling Joseph that it is vain to attempt to hasten the footsteps of the Redeemer.

The repertoire of Jewish tales and legends was seasoned by other elements. During the 16th century—the age of the great European navigators—stories began to circulate about the discovery of the Ten Lost Tribes in remote parts of the world.

Yiddish Tales

In the 16th century, Judeo-German (Yiddish) came to replace Hebrew as the language of Jewish tales and legends in Europe, primarily because of the desire to render them accessible to women unschooled in the sacred tongue. The synagogal lessons from Scripture were embellished in Yiddish in the so-called *Taitsh Humesh* ("Yiddish Pentateuch"), the more fancifully titled *Tze'ena u-re'ena* ("Go Forth and See"; *compare* Song of Solomon 3:11), and adaptations of the story of Esther designed for dramatic presentation on the feast of Purim. The Hebrew *Chronicles of Josippon* also assumed Yiddish dress. More secular productions include a verse rendition of the Arthurian legend, titled *Artus Hof* ("The Court of King Arthur") and based largely on Gravenberg's medieval *Wigalois*, and the *Bove Buch* by Elijah Levita (1469–1549), which retold the romance of Sir Bevis of Southampton.

These "frivolous" productions were offset by collections of moral and ethical tales. The main examples of these are the *Brantspiegel* (1572; "Brant Mirro"), attributed to Moses Henoch, and the *Ma'aseh Buch* (1672; "Story Book"), a compendium of 254 tales compiled by Jacob ben Abraham of Meseritz and first published at Basel. The latter, drawn mainly from the Talmud, was supplemented by later legends about medieval rabbis. Jewish legends also circulated in the form of chapbooks, a large selection of which is preserved in the library of the Yiddish Scientific Institute in New York City.

Judeo-Persian and Judeo-Spanish (Ladino) Tales

A similar development, though on a lesser scale, took place among Jews who spoke other vernacular dialects. Major monuments of Judeo-Persian literature are poetic embellishments of biblical narratives composed by Shāhīn of Shīrāz in the 14th century and by Joseph ben Isaac Yahudi (i.e., "the Jew") some 300 years later. These, however, are exercises in virtuosity rather than in creative storytelling. Versified elaborations of the story of Joseph appear in Judeo-Spanish (Ladino) in *Coplas de Yoçef* ("Song of Joseph"), composed in 1732 by Abraham de Toledo and embodying a certain amount of traditional Haggadic material. From a revival of literary activity in the 18th century comes a comprehensive "legendary Bible" called *Me'am Lo'ez* ("From a People of Strange Tongue") (compare Psalms 114:1), begun by Jacob Culi (died 1732) and continued by later writers, as well as several renderings of standard Hebrew collections and a number of Purim plays. Judeo-Spanish folktales were still current in Macedonia and Yugoslavia until the Nazi occupation of the early 1940s, but these stories drew more from Balkan than from Jewish sources.

HASIDIC TALES

The rise of the Hasidic sect in eastern Europe at the end of the 18th century engendered a host of legends (circulated mainly through chapbooks) concerning the lives, wise sayings, and miracles of *tzaddiqim*, or masters, such as Israel ben Eliezer, "the Beshṭ" (1700–60), and Dov Baer of Meseritz (died 1772). These tales, however, are anecdotes rather than formally structured stories and often borrow from non-Jewish sources.

DROLL STORIES

To the popular creativity of the ghetto belong also the droll tales of the Wise Men of Chełm (in Poland)—Jewish counterparts of the German noodles ("stupid people"; hence "noodle stories") of Schildburg and of the more familiar Wise Men of Gotham (in England). These too were circulated mainly in Yiddish popular prints. A typical story is that of the two "sages" who went for a walk, one with an umbrella and the other without one. Suddenly it began to rain. "Open your umbrella," said the one without one. "It won't help," answered the other, "it's full of holes." "Then why did you bring it?" rejoined his friend. "I didn't think it would rain," was the reply.

MODERN ISRAELI FOLKTALES

The gathering of Jews from many lands into the State of Israel has made that country a treasure trove for the student of Jewish folktales. Assiduous work has been undertaken by Dov Noy of Hebrew University in Jerusalem, aided by enthusiastic amateurs throughout the country. Mainly, however, the stories are retellings of traditional material.

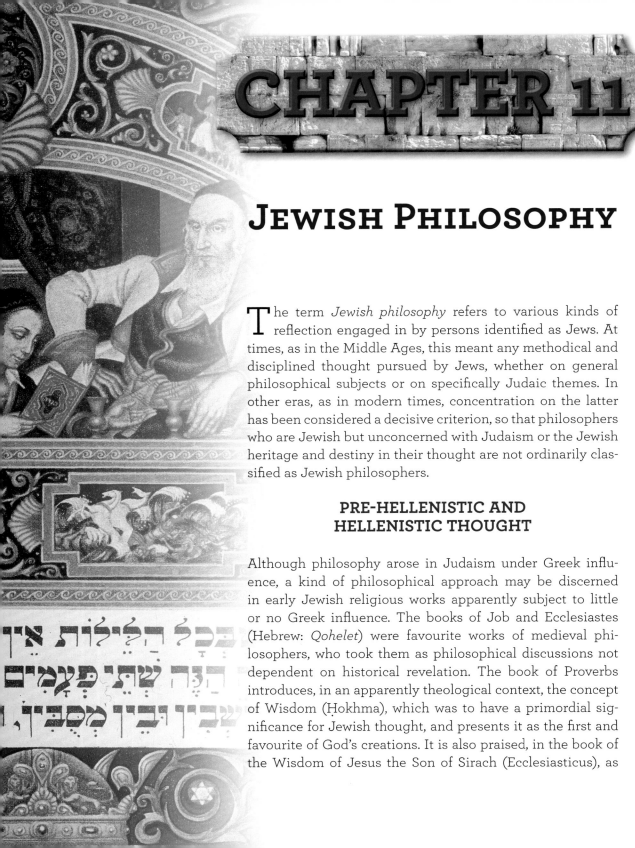

CHAPTER 11

JEWISH PHILOSOPHY

The term *Jewish philosophy* refers to various kinds of reflection engaged in by persons identified as Jews. At times, as in the Middle Ages, this meant any methodical and disciplined thought pursued by Jews, whether on general philosophical subjects or on specifically Judaic themes. In other eras, as in modern times, concentration on the latter has been considered a decisive criterion, so that philosophers who are Jewish but unconcerned with Judaism or the Jewish heritage and destiny in their thought are not ordinarily classified as Jewish philosophers.

PRE-HELLENISTIC AND HELLENISTIC THOUGHT

Although philosophy arose in Judaism under Greek influence, a kind of philosophical approach may be discerned in early Jewish religious works apparently subject to little or no Greek influence. The books of Job and Ecclesiastes (Hebrew: *Qohelet*) were favourite works of medieval philosophers, who took them as philosophical discussions not dependent on historical revelation. The book of Proverbs introduces, in an apparently theological context, the concept of Wisdom (Ḥokhma), which was to have a primordial significance for Jewish thought, and presents it as the first and favourite of God's creations. It is also praised, in the book of the Wisdom of Jesus the Son of Sirach (Ecclesiasticus), as instilled by God into all his works and granted in abundance to those he loves. It is sometimes equated with fearing God and keeping the Law. In other passages, however, piety seems to be regarded as superior to Wisdom. The Wisdom of Solomon, probably originally written in Greek, praises Wisdom, which is held to be an image of God's goodness and a reflection of the eternal light. God is said to have given the author knowledge of the composition of the world, the powers, the elements, the nature of animals, the divisions of time, and the positions of the stars. In its vocabulary and perhaps in some of its doctrines, the work shows the influence of Greek philosophy. It also has had considerable influence on Christian theology.

PHILO JUDAEUS

The first systematic attempt to apply Greek philosophical concepts to Jewish doctrines was made by Philo Judaeus (Philo of Alexandria) in the 1st century CE. Philo was influenced by Platonic and Stoic writings and probably also by certain postbiblical Jewish beliefs and speculations. He apparently had some knowledge of the Oral Law, which was developing in his time, and he also knew of the Essenes, whom he praised highly.

Philo provided Jewish religious doctrines with intellectual and cultural respectability by stating them in Greek philosophical terms. He also showed that much of Greek philosophy was consonant with Judaism as he conceived it

and with the allegorical sense of biblical texts as he read them. The fact that he stressed the primacy of Jewish religious tradition over Greek philosophy may have been more than mere lip service. It may be argued that—in central points of his thought, such as his conception of Logos (the Divine Reason or Word)—Philo used philosophical notions as expressions of religious beliefs. For him, Logos is primarily an intermediary between a transcendent, unknowable God and the world. On basic philosophical and theological problems, such as the creation of the world or the existence of free will, Philo's writings provide vague or contradictory answers. He placed mystic ecstasy, of which he may have had personal experience, above philosophical and theological speculations.

Philo's approach, his method of interpretation, his way of thinking, as well as some of his ideas—especially that of Logos—exerted considerable influence on early Christian thought but not, to any comparable extent, on Jewish thought in the same period. In the Middle Ages, knowledge of Philo among Jews was either very slight or nonexistent. Not until modern times was his importance in the history of Jewish religious thought recognized.

OTHER ANCIENT SOURCES

Some traces of ancient philosophy, mainly Stoic, may be found in the Mishna and in the subsequent Talmudic literature compiled in Palestine and Babylonia.

Jewish theological and cosmological speculations occur in the Midrashim (plural of Midrash), which propound allegories, legends, and myths under the guise of interpreting biblical verses, and in the *Sefer yetzira* ("Book of Creation"), a combination of cosmogony and grammar that was once attributed to Abraham. There is no clear evidence of the period in which the *Sefer yetzira* was written, and both the 3rd century and the 6th or 7th century have been suggested. The book became a key work in later Jewish mysticism.

MEDIEVAL THOUGHT

In the 9th and 10th centuries, after a long hiatus, systematic philosophy and ideology reappeared among the Jews, a phenomenon indicative of their contacts with Islamic civilization. The evolution of Islam in the 9th and 10th centuries showed that Greek scientific and philosophical lore could be separated, at least to some extent, from its pagan associations and could be adapted to another language and another culture. It also showed that a monotheistic, prophetic religion that in all relevant essentials, including adherence to a basic religious law, was closely akin to Judaism could be the basis of a culture in which science, philosophy, and theology were an indispensable part. The question of whether philosophy is compatible with religious law (the answer sometimes being negative) constituted the main theme of the foremost medieval Jewish thinkers. From

approximately the 9th to the 13th century, Jewish thought participated in the evolution of Islamic philosophy and theology and manifested only in a limited sense a specifically Jewish character. Jewish philosophers showed no particular preference for philosophical texts written by Jewish authors over those composed by Muslims, and in many cases the significant works of Jewish thinkers constituted a reply or a reaction to the ideas of Islamic philosophical and scientific writings.

JEWISH *KALĀM*

Although several Jewish intellectuals in 9th- and 10th-century Babylonia were steeped in Greek philosophy, the most productive and influential Jewish thinkers of this period represented a very different tendency, that of the Muʿtazilite *kalām*. *Kalām* (literally "speech") is an Arabic term used in both Islamic and Jewish vocabulary to designate several theological schools that were ostensibly opposed to Greek, and particularly Aristotelian, philosophy. Islamic and Jewish Aristotelians regarded *kalām* theologians (called the *mutakallimūn*) with a certain contempt, holding them to be mere apologists and indifferent to the philosophical question of truth. Herein they did not do justice to their adversaries, for many representatives of *kalām* displayed a genuine speculative impulse. The school's theology, forged in disputes with Zoroastrians, Manichaeans, and Christians, claimed to be based on reason.

SA'ADIA BEN JOSEPH

The belief in reason, as well as some of the tenets of Mu'tazilite theology, were taken over by Sa'adia ben Joseph (882–942), who was also influenced (either directly or through the intermediary of an Arabic philosopher) by John Philoponus (6th century), a Christian philosopher who argued against certain Aristotelian and Neoplatonic positions. Sa'adia's main theological work, *Kitāb al-amānāt wa al-i'tiqādāt* (*Beliefs and Opinions*), is modeled on similar Mu'tazilite treatises and on the Mu'tazilite classification of theological subject matter known as the Five Principles.

Like many Mu'tazilite authors, Sa'adia set forth in his introduction a list and theory of the various sources of knowledge. He distinguished four sources: (1) the five senses; (2) the intellect, or reason; (3) necessary inferences; and (4) reliable information given by trustworthy persons. In Sa'adia's sense of the word, intellect, or reason (*al-'aql*), is an immediate, a priori cognition, independent of sense experience. In *Beliefs and Opinions* the intellect is characterized as having immediate ethical cognitions—that is, as discerning what is good and what is evil—in opposition to the medieval Aristotelians, who did not regard even the most general ethical rules as knowable a priori. The third source of knowledge comprises inferences of the type "if there is smoke, there is fire," which are based on data furnished by the first two sources of knowledge. The fourth source of

KALĀM

In Islam, kalām *is speculative theology. The term is derived from the phrase* kalām Allāh *(Arabic: "word of God"), which refers to the Qur'ān, the sacred scripture of Islam. Those who practice* kalām *are known as* mutakallimūn.

In its early stage, kalām *was merely a defense of Islam against Christians, Manichaeans, and believers in other religions. As interest in philosophy grew among Muslim thinkers,* kalām *adopted the dialectic (methodology) of the Greek skeptics and the stoics, and directed these against the Islamic philosophers who attempted to fit Aristotle and Plato into a Muslim context. It eventually exerted great influence over Jewish and Christian philosophers and theologians as well.*

Several schools of kalām *developed. The most significant was the* Mu'tazilah, *often described as the rationalists of Islam, who appeared in the 8th century. They believed in the autonomy of reason with regard to revelation and in the supremacy of reasoned ('aqlī) faith against traditional (naqlī) faith. The* Mu'tazilah *championed the freedom of the human will, holding that it was against divine justice either to punish a good man or to pardon an unrighteous one. The* Ash'arīyah, *a 10th-century school of* kalām, *was a mediation between the rationalization of the* Mu'tazilah *and the anthropomorphism of the traditionalists and represented the successful adaptation of Hellenistic philosophical reasoning to Muslim orthodox theology. They too affirmed the freedom of the human will but denied its efficacy. Closely resembling but more liberal than the* Ash'arīyah *was the* al-Māturīdīyah *(also 10th century).*

knowledge is meant to validate the teachings of Scripture and of the religious tradition, which must be regarded as true because of the trustworthiness of the men who propounded them. One of the work's main purposes was to show that the knowledge deriving from the fourth source concords with that discovered by means of the other three (i.e., that religion and human reason agree).

Sa'adia opposed Aristotle's view that the natural order was eternal. He held, with other partisans of the Mu'tazilite *kalām*, that the demonstration of the temporal creation of the world must precede and pave the way for the proof of the existence of God the Creator. Given the demonstrated truth that the world has a beginning in time, it can be proved that it could have been produced only through the action of a creator. It can further be proved that there must have been only one creator.

The theology of Sa'adia, like that of the Mu'tazilites, hinges on two principles: the unity of God and the principle of justice. The latter takes issue with the view (widespread in Islam and present also in Judaism) that the definition of what is just and what is good depends solely on God's will, to which none of the moral criteria found among human beings are applicable. According to this view, a revelation from God can convert an action generally recognized as evil into a good action. Against this way of thinking, Sa'adia and the Mu'tazilites believed that being good and just or being evil

and unjust are intrinsic characteristics of human actions and cannot be changed by divine decree. The notions of justice and of good, as conceived by humans, are binding even on God himself. Indeed, the ethical cognitions of humans are the same as those of the Deity.

Sa'adia also addressed the issue of the function of religious law. Of central importance in traditional Judaism and Islam, the law was thought to have been established to compel humans to perform good actions and avoid bad ones. Because Sa'adia believed that humans have a priori knowledge of good and evil and that this knowledge coincides with the principles underlying the most important portions of the revealed law, he was forced to ask whether this law is not superfluous. He could, however, point out that, whereas the human intellect recognizes that certain actions—for instance, murder or theft—are evil, it cannot by itself discover the best definition of what constitutes a particular transgression; nor can it, on its own, determine an appropriate punishment. On both points, Sa'adia asserted, the commandments of religious law give the best possible answers.

Sa'adia called the commandments that accord with the behests of the human intellect the intellectual, or rational, commandments. According to him, they include the duty of manifesting gratitude to the Creator for the benefits he has bestowed upon humans. Sa'adia recognized that a considerable number of commandments—for instance, those dealing with the prohibition of work on the Sabbath—do not belong to this category. He held, however, that the obligation to obey them can be derived from the rational commandment that humans must be grateful to God, for such gratitude entails obedience to his orders.

THE KARAITES

Sa'adia's adoption of the rational Mu'tazilite theology was a part of his overall effort to consolidate rabbinical Judaism (based on the Mishna and Talmud), which was being attacked by the Karaites. This Jewish sect, founded by Anan ben David in the 8th century, rejected the authority of the Oral Law and the commentaries on it—that is, of the Mishna and the Talmud. In the 10th century and afterward, the Karaites accepted as their guides the Hebrew Bible and human reason, in the Mu'tazilite sense of the word. Their repudiation of postbiblical Jewish religious tradition facilitated a rational approach to theological doctrine. This approach led Karaite authors to criticize the adherents of rabbinical Judaism for holding anthropomorphic beliefs based in part on texts of the Talmudic period. Karaite authors propounded, in conceptual terms, a theology of Jewish history in exile (*galut*). Life in exile is a diminished existence. Nevertheless, the good or bad actions of the Jewish people (rather than their material strength or weakness) affect the course of history.

Redemption may come when all Jews are converted to Karaism.

The Karaites adopted Mu'tazilite *kalām* wholesale, including its atomism. The Mu'tazilite atomists held that everything that exists consists of minute, discrete parts. This applies not only to bodies but also to space, time, motion, and the "accidents"—that is, qualities, such as colour—which the Islamic and Jewish atomists regarded as being joined to the corporeal atoms but not determined by them, as had been believed by the Greek atomists. An instant of time or a unit of motion does not continue the preceding instant or unit. All apparent processes are discontinuous, and there are causal connections between their successive units of change. The fact that cotton put into fire generally burns does not mean that fire is a cause of burning. Rather, it may be explained as a "habit" that has no character of necessity. God's free will is the only agent of everything that occurs, with the exception of one category—human actions. These are causes that produce effects. For instance, one who throws a stone at someone else, who is then killed, directly brings about the latter's death. This inconsistency on the part of the theologians was required by the principle of justice, for it would be unjust to punish someone for a murder that was a result not of this person's action but of God's. This grudging admission that causality exists in certain strictly defined and circumscribed cases was occasioned by moral, not physical, considerations.

JEWISH NEOPLATONISM

Outside Babylonia, philosophical studies were pursued by Jews in the 9th and 10th centuries in Egypt and in the Maghrib (northwest Africa). The work of the 9th-century Muslim popularizer of Greek philosophy, Abū Yūsuf Ya'qūb al-Kindī (and also, in all probability, upon a lost pseudo-Aristotelian text) propounded a peculiar form of Neoplatonism, a philosophical and quasi-religious movement from the 3rd and 4th centuries CE whose systematization of the thought of Plato exerted a tremendous influence not only on Judaism but on Christianity and Islam. The Neoplatonic doctrine that seems to have been set forth in this text had, directly and indirectly, a considerable influence on medieval Jewish philosophy.

ISAAC ISRAELI

The most notable Jewish Neoplatonist was Isaac ben Solomon Israeli (832/855–932/955), an Egyptian-born North African who authored such works as the *Kitāb al-ustuqusat* ("Book of Elements") and the *Kitāb al-hudud* ("Book of Definitions"). Indeed, he has often been called "the first Jewish Neoplatonist."

According to Israeli, God creates through his will and power. The two things that were created first were form, identified with wisdom, and matter, which is designated as the genus of genera (the classes of things) and which is the substratum of everything, not only of

NEOPLATONISM

Neoplatonism is a form of Platonism developed by Plotinus in the 3rd century CE and modified by his successors. It came to dominate the Greek philosophical schools and remained predominant until the teaching of philosophy by pagans ended in the late 6th century. It postulated an all-sufficient unity, the One (also called the Good), from which emanated the Intellect (nous), the mental activity of the One and the abode of the transcendent Forms. Below that was the Soul (psyche), which facilitated the emergence of all things in the material world by contemplating the Forms. Those three hypostases (entities) were thought to support the visible world, which emerged from the One through emanation. Individual souls could rise to a mystical vision of the One through contemplation, which would enable the soul to rise to the level of the Intellect. The thought of Plotinus and those who subsequently developed and expanded his thought exerted profound influence on medieval philosophy and on the three great Western religious traditions: Judaism, Christianity, and Islam.

bodies but also of incorporeal substances. This conception of matter apparently was derived from the Greek Neoplatonists Plotinus (205–270) and Proclus (c. 410–485), particularly from the latter. In Proclus's opinion, generality was one of the main criteria for determining the ontological priority of an entity (its place in the hierarchy of being). Matter, because of its indeterminacy, obviously has a high degree of generality. Consequently, it figures among the entities having ontological priority. According to the Neoplatonic view, which Israeli seems to have adopted, the conjunction of matter and form gives rise to the intellect. A light sent forth from the intellect produces the rational soul, which in turn gives rise to the vegetative soul.

Israeli was perhaps the first Jewish philosopher to attribute prophecy to the influence of the intellect on the faculty of imagination. According to Israeli, this faculty receives from the intellect spiritual forms that are intermediate between corporeality and spirituality. This explanation implies that these forms, "with which the prophets armed themselves," are inferior to purely intellectual cognitions.

SOLOMON IBN GABIROL

In its essentials, the schema of creation and emanation propounded by Isaac Israeli and his Neoplatonic source (or sources) was taken over by Solomon ibn Gabirol, a celebrated 11th-century Hebrew liturgical poet who was also the earliest Jewish philosopher of Spain. His chief philosophical work, written in Arabic but preserved in full only in a 12th-century Latin translation titled *Fons vitae* ("Fountain of Life"), makes no reference to Judaism or to specifically Jewish doctrines and is a dialogue between a disciple and a master who teaches him true philosophical knowledge. Despite its prolixity and many contradictions, it is an impressive work. Few medieval texts so effectively communicate the Neoplatonic conception of the existence of a number of planes of being that differ according to their ontological priority, the derivative and inferior ones constituting a reflection in a grosser mode of existence of those that are prior and superior.

One of Ibn Gabirol's central concerns was the divine will, which appears to be both part of and separate from the divine essence. Infinite according to its essence, the will is finite in its action. It is described as pervading everything that exists and as being the intermediary between the divine essence and matter and form. Will was one of the traditional terms used by medieval theologians to identify the entity intermediate between the transcendent Deity and the world or the aspect of the Deity involved in creation. According to a statement in *Fons vitae*, matter derives from the divine essence, whereas form derives from the divine will. This suggests that the difference between matter and form has some counterpart in the Godhead and also that universal matter is superior to universal form. Some of Ibn Gabirol's statements seem to support the superiority of universal matter; other passages, however, appear to imply the superiority of universal form.

Form and matter, whether universal or particular, exist only in conjunction. All things, with the sole exception of God, are constituted through the union of the two, the intellect no less than corporeal substance. In fact, the intellect is the first being in which universal matter and form are conjoined. The intellect contains and encompasses all things. It is through the grasp of the various planes of being, through ascending in knowledge to the world of the intellect and apprehending what is above it—the divine will and the world of the Deity—that humans may "escape death" and reach "the source of life."

JUDAH HA-LEVI

Judah ben Samuel ha-Levi (c. 1075–1141), another celebrated Hebrew poet from Spain, was the first medieval Jewish thinker to base his thought consciously and consistently on arguments drawn from Jewish history. His views are set forth in an Arabic dialogue, *al-Hazari* (Hebrew *Sefer ha-Kuzari*), the full title of which is translated as "The Book of Proof and Argument in Defense of the Despised Faith." This work is usually called *Kuzari* (i.e., "the Khazar").

Basing his narrative on the historical conversion to Judaism of the Khazars (c. 740), a Turkic-speaking people in central Eurasia, ha-Levi relates that their king, a pious man who did not belong to any of the great monotheistic religions, dreamed of an angel who said to him, "Your intentions are pleasing to the Creator, but your works are not." To find the correct way to please God, the king sought guidance from a philosopher, a Christian, a Muslim, and finally—after hesitating to invite a representative of a people degraded by historical misfortune—a Jewish scholar,

who then converted him to Judaism. The angel's words in the king's dream may be regarded as a kind of revelation. Ha-Levi used this element of the story to suggest that it is not the spontaneous activity of reason that impels human beings to undertake the quest for the true religion but the gift of prophecy—or at least a touch of the prophetic faculty (or a knowledge of the revelations of the past).

The argument of the philosopher whose advice is sought by the king confirms this point. This disquisition is a brilliant piece of writing that lays bare the essential differences between the Aristotelian God, who is wholly indifferent to human individuals, and the God of the Jewish religion. The God of the philosophers, who is pure intellect, is not concerned with the works of human beings. Moreover, the cultural activities to which the angel clearly refers—activities that involve both mind and body—cannot, from a philosophical point of view, either help or hinder humans in the pursuit of the philosophers' supreme goal, the attainment of union with the active intellect, a "light" of the divine nature. This union was supposed to confer knowledge of all intelligible things on the individual. The supreme goal, therefore, was purely intellectual in nature.

In opposition to the philosopher's faith, the religion of the Jewish scholar in the *Kuzari* is based on the fact that God may have a close, direct relationship with humans, who are not conceived primarily as beings endowed with intellect. The postulate that God can have intercourse with a creature made of the disgusting materials that compose the human body is scandalous to the king and prevents his acceptance of the doctrine concerning prophecy, expounded by the Muslim sage (just as the extraordinary nature of the Christological dogmas deters him from adopting Christianity).

The Jewish scholar argues that it is contemplation not of the cosmos but of Jewish history that procures knowledge of God. Ha-Levi was aware of the odium attached to the doctrine of the superiority of one particular nation. He held, however, that this teaching alone explains God's dealings with humanity, which, like many other things, reason is unable to grasp. The controversies of the philosophers serve as proof of the failure of human intelligence to find valid solutions to the most important problems.

Ha-Levi's dialogue was also directed against the Karaites. He shows the necessity and celebrates the efficacy of a blind, unquestioning adhesion to tradition, which the Karaites rejected. Yet he expounds a theology of Jewish exile that seems to have been influenced by Karaite doctrine. According to ha-Levi, even in exile the course of Jewish history is not determined like that of other nations by natural causes, such as material strength or weakness. The decisive factor is whether the Jews are religiously observant or disobedient. The advent of Christianity and Islam, in his view, prepares other nations for conversion to Judaism, an event that will occur in the eschatological period at the end of history.

OTHER JEWISH THINKERS, C. 1050–C. 1150

Many other Jewish thinkers appeared in Spain during the period from the second half of the 11th century to the first half of the 12th. Bahya ben Joseph ibn Pakuda wrote one of the most popular books of Jewish spiritual literature, *Kitāb al-hidāyah ilā farā'iḍ alqulūb* ("Guidance to the Duties of the Heart"), which combines a theology influenced by Sa'adia with a moderate mysticism inspired by the teachings of the Muslim Sufis. The commandments of the heart—that is, those relating to thoughts and sentiments—are contrasted with the commandments of the limbs—that is, the Mosaic commandments enjoining or prohibiting certain actions. Bahya maintained that both sets of commandments should be observed (thus rejecting the antinomian position) but made clear that he was chiefly interested in the commandments of the heart.

Abraham bar Hiyya Savasorda, a mathematician, astrologer, and philosopher, outlined in *Megillat ha-megalle* ("Scroll of the Revealer") a view of Jewish history reminiscent of ha-Levi, but it does not emphasize its uniqueness to the same degree and is set forth in much less impressive fashion. Living in Barcelona under Christian rule, Bar Hiyya wrote scientific and philosophical treatises not in Arabic but in Hebrew. Hebrew was also used by Abraham ibn Ezra (died 1167), a native of Spain who travelled extensively in Christian Europe. His commentaries on the Bible contributed to the diffusion among the Jews of Greek philosophical thought, to which Ibn Ezra made many disjointed references. His astrological doctrine had a great influence on some philosophers.

The last outstanding Jewish philosopher of the Islamic East, Abū al-Barakāt al-Baghdādī (who died as a very old man sometime after 1164), also belongs to this period. An inhabitant of Iraq, he was converted to Islam in his old age (for reasons of expediency, according to his biographers). His philosophy appears to have had a strong effect on Islamic thought, though its influence on Jewish philosophy and theology is difficult to pin down and may be practically nonexistent. His chief philosophical work, *Kitāb al-mu'tabar* ("The Book of That Which Has Been Established by Personal Reflection"), contains few references to Jewish texts or topics. Abū al-Barakāt rejected Aristotelian physics completely. According to him, time is the measure of being and not, as Aristotle taught, the measure of motion. He also replaced Aristotle's two-dimensional concept of place with the three-dimensional notion of space, the existence of which is independent of the existence of bodies.

JEWISH ARISTOTELIANISM

Jewish thinkers in Muslim Spain and the Maghrib adopted Aristotelianism (as well as systems that stemmed from but also profoundly modified pure Aristotelian doctrine) considerably later than did their counterparts in the Islamic East.

ABRAHAM IBN DAUD

Abraham ibn Daud (12th century), who is regarded as the first Jewish Aristotelian of Spain, was primarily a disciple of Avicenna, the great 11th-century Islamic philosopher. He may have translated or helped to translate some of Avicenna's works into Latin, according to one plausible hypothesis, for he lived under Christian rule in Toledo, a town that in the 12th century was a centre for translators. His historical treatises, written in Hebrew, manifest his desire to familiarize his fellow Jews with the historical tradition of the Latin world, which at that time was alien to most of them. But his philosophical work, *Sefer ha-emuna ha-rama* ("Book of Sublime Faith"), written in 1161 in Arabic, shows few if any signs of Christian influence.

The doctrine of emanation set forth in this work describes in the manner of Avicenna the procession of the 10 incorporeal intellects, the first of which derives from God. This intellect produces the second intellect, and so on. Ibn Daud was fairly explicit in his questioning of Avicenna's views on the way the second intellect is produced. His discipleship did not mean total adherence. Ibn Daud's psychology was also, and more distinctively, derived from Avicenna. The argumentation leading to a proof that the rational faculty is not corporeal attempts to derive the nature of the soul from the fact of immediate self-awareness. Like Avicenna, Ibn Daud founded psychology on a theory of consciousness.

Ibn Daud often referred to the accord that, in his view, existed between philosophy and religious tradition. As he remarked, the *Sefer ha-emuna ha-rama* was not for readers who, in their simplicity, are satisfied with what they know of religious tradition or for those who have a thorough knowledge of philosophy. It was intended for readers of one type only: those who, being acquainted with the religious tradition on the one hand and having some rudiments of philosophy on the other, are "perplexed." It was for the same audience that Maimonides wrote *The Guide for the Perplexed.*

MAIMONIDES

Moses Maimonides (Moses ben Maimon; 1135–1204), a native of Spain, is incontestably the greatest name in Jewish medieval philosophy, but his reputation is not derived from any outstanding originality in philosophical thought. Rather, the distinction of Maimonides, who is also the most eminent codifier of Jewish religious law, is to be found in the vast scope of his attempt, in the *Dalālat al-hā'irin* (*The Guide for the Perplexed*), to safeguard both religious law and philosophy (the public communication of

Maimonides is said to be the preeminent Jewish medieval philosopher. Manuel Cohen/Getty Images

which would be destructive of the law) without suppressing the issues between them and without trying to impose, on a theoretical plane, a final, universally binding solution to the conflict.

As Maimonides states in his introduction to the *Guide*, he regarded his self-imposed task as perilous, and he therefore had recourse to a whole system of precautions designed to conceal his true meaning from people who, lacking the necessary qualifications, might misread the book and abandon observance of the law. Maimonides himself notes that these precautions include deliberately contradictory statements meant to mislead the undiscerning reader. The apparent or real contradictions encountered in the *Guide* are perhaps most flagrant in Maimonides' doctrine concerning God. There seems to be no plausible hypothesis capable of explaining away the inconsistencies between the following three views:

1. God has an eternal will that is not bound by natural laws. Through an act of his will, he created the world in time and imposed on it the order of nature. This creation is the greatest of miracles. Only if it is admitted can other miracles, which interfere with the causally determined concatenations of events, be regarded as possible. The philosophers' God, who is not free to cut the wings of a fly, is to be rejected. This

conception is in keeping with the traditional religious view of God and is avowedly adopted by Maimonides because failure to do so would undermine religion.

2. Humans are incapable of having any positive knowledge concerning God. No positive attributes (e.g., wisdom or life) can be ascribed to God. Contrary to the attributes predicated of created beings, the divine attributes are strictly negative. They state what God is not. For instance, he is not not-wise, and such a statement is not a positive assertion. Hence, only a negative theology is possible—saying what God is not. The way God acts can, however, be known. This knowledge is to be found in natural science.

3. God is an intellect. The formula used by medieval philosophers—which maintains that in God the knowing subject, the object known, and the act of intellectual knowledge are identical—derives from Aristotle's thesis that God knows only himself. In adopting the formula, however, Maimonides interpreted it in the light of human psychology and epistemology, pointing out that, according to Aristotle, the act of human (as well as divine) cognition brings about an identity of the cognizing subject and the cognized object. The parallel drawn by

Maimonides between the human and the divine intellect quite evidently implies a certain similarity between the two. In other words, it is incompatible with the negative theology of other passages of the *Guide*. Nor can it be reconciled with his theological doctrine that the structure of the world—created in time—came into being through the action of God's will.

There would be no enigma in the *Guide* if Maimonides had believed that truth can be discovered in a suprarational way, through revelations vouchsafed to the Prophets. This, however, is not the case. Maimonides held that the Prophets (with the exception of Moses) combine great intellectual ability, which qualifies them to be philosophers, with a powerful imagination. The intellectual faculty of the philosophers and the prophets receives an overflow from the active intellect. In the case of the Prophets, this overflow not only brings about intellectual activity but also passes over into the imaginative faculty, giving rise to visions and dreams. The fact that prophets have a strong imagination gives them no superiority in knowledge over philosophers, who do not have it. Moses, who belonged to a higher category than did the other Prophets, did not have recourse to imagination.

The laws and religion as instituted by Moses are intended not only to ensure the bodily welfare and safety of the members of the community but also to facilitate the attainment of intellectual truths by individuals gifted enough to uncover the various hints embodied in religious laws and practices. This does not mean that all the beliefs inculcated by Judaism are true. Some indeed express philosophical truths—though in an inaccurate way, in a language suited to the intellectual capacity of the common people, who generally cannot grasp the import of the dogmas they are required to profess. Other beliefs, however, are false but necessary for the preservation of public order and justice (e.g., the belief that God is angry with wrongdoers).

There are two noteworthy aspects of Maimonides' position on the Law (i.e., the religious commandments). First, he maintained that it is unique in its excellence and valid for all time. This profession of faith, at least with regard to its assumptions about the future, lacked philosophical justification. However, it could be regarded as necessary for the survival of Judaism. Second, he asserted that certain precepts of the Mosaic Law were related to specific historical situations and to the need to avoid too sharp a break with popular customs and practices—for instance, the commandments concerning sacrifice.

For at least four or five centuries, *The Guide for the Perplexed* exercised an extremely strong influence in the European centres of Jewish thought. In the 13th century, when the *Guide* was twice translated into Hebrew, these centres were Spain, the south of France, and Italy. Rather paradoxically, in view of the unsystematic character of Maimonides' exposition, it was used as a standard textbook of philosophy and condemned as such when the teaching of philosophy came under attack. The *Guide* could be used in this way because from the 13th century onward the history of Jewish philosophy in European countries acquired a continuity it had never had before. This development seems to have resulted from the substitution of Hebrew for Arabic as the language of philosophical exposition. Because of the existence of a common and relatively homogeneous philosophical background—Hebrew texts were much less numerous and less diverse than Arabic philosophical works—and the fact that Jewish philosophers reading and writing in Hebrew read the works of their contemporaries and immediate predecessors, something like a dialogue can be discerned. In striking contrast to the immediately preceding period, European Jewish philosophers in the 13th century and later frequently devoted a very considerable part of their treatises to discussions of the opinions of other Jewish philosophers. That many of the Jewish philosophers in question wrote commentaries on the *Guide* undoubtedly furthered this tendency.

AVERROISTS

The influence of Maimonides' great Islamic contemporary Averroës, many of whose commentaries and treatises were translated into Hebrew, was second only to that of Maimonides on Jewish intellectual development. Indeed, it may be argued that for philosophers (as distinct from the general reading public) it often came first. In certain cases, commentators on the *Guide* quote Averroës' opinions to clarify those of Maimonides, despite the frequent divergences between the two.

The apparently significant influence of Christian Scholastic thought on Jewish philosophy was often not openly acknowledged by Jewish thinkers in the period beginning with the 13th century. Samuel ibn Tibbon (*c.* 1150–*c.* 1230), one of the translators of the *Guide* into Hebrew and a philosopher in his own right, remarked that the philosophical sciences were more widely known among Christians than among Muslims. Somewhat later, at the end of the 13th century and after, Jewish scholars in Italy translated into Hebrew various texts of St. Thomas Aquinas and other Christian representatives of Scholasticism. Some of them frequently acknowledged the debt they owed their Christian masters. In Spain and in the south of France, a different convention seems to have prevailed up to the second half of the 15th century. Whereas Jewish philosophers of these countries felt no reluctance about referring to Greek, Arabic, and other Jewish philosophers, they refrained from citing Christian thinkers whose views had, in all probability, influenced them. In the case of certain Jewish thinkers, this absence of reference to the Christian Scholastics served to disguise the fact that in many essentials they were representative of the philosophical trends, such as Latin Averroism, that were current among the Christian Scholastics of their time.

There is a striking resemblance between certain views of the Latin Averroists and the parallel opinions of Isaac Albalag, a Jewish philosopher who lived in the second half of the 13th century, probably in Catalonia, Spain, and who wrote a commentary in Hebrew on the *Tahāfut al-falāsifah* ("The Inconsistencies of the Philosophers"), an exposition of Avicenna's doctrine written by the Muslim philosopher al-Ghazālī (1058–1111). Albalag's assertion that both the teachings of the Bible and the truths demonstrated by reason must be believed even if they are contradictory raises the possibility that some historical connections exist between this view and the Latin Averroist doctrine that there are two sets of truths—the religious and the philosophical—which are not necessarily in accord. On most other points Albalag was a follower of the system of Averroës himself. This position is exemplified by Albalag's rejection of the view that the world was created in time. Although he professed to believe in what he called "absolute creation in time," this expression merely signifies that at any given moment the continued existence of the world depends on God's existence, an opinion that is essentially in harmony with Averroës.

Joseph Caspi (1297–1340), a prolific philosopher and exegetical commentator, maintained a somewhat unsystematic philosophical position that seems to have been influenced by Averroës. He expressed the opinion that knowledge of the future, including that possessed by God himself, is probabilistic in nature. The prescience of the Prophets is the same. Caspi's interest in this problem may well have had some connection with the debate about future contingencies in which Christian Scholastics were engaged at that time.

Moses of Narbonne, or Moses Narboni, like many other Jewish scholars of the 14th century, wrote mainly commentaries, including those on biblical books, on treatises of Averroës, and on Maimonides' *Guide*. In his commentary on the *Guide*, Narboni often interprets the earlier philosopher's opinions by recourse to Averroës' views. Narboni also expounded and gave radical interpretations to certain conceptions that he understood as implied in the *Guide*. According to Narboni, God participates in all things, because he is the measure of all substances. God's existence appears to be bound up with that of the world, to which he has a relation analogous to that between a soul and its body (a comparison already made in the *Guide*).

GERSONIDES

Gersonides, also known as Levi ben Gershom (1288–1344), wrote the systematic philosophical work *Sefer milḥamot Adonai* ("The Book of the Wars of the Lord"), as well as many philosophical commentaries. Gersonides cited Greek, Arabic, and Jewish thinkers, and in many ways his system appears to have stemmed from the doctrines of Maimonides or Averroës, regardless of whether he agreed with them. For example, he explicitly rejected Maimonides' doctrine of negative theology. Although he never explicitly mentioned Christian Scholastic philosophers, a comparison of his opinions and of the particular problems that engaged his attention with the Scholastic writings of his period suggests that he was influenced by the Latins on certain points.

Gersonides disagreed both with the Aristotelian philosophers who maintained the eternity of the world and with the religious partisans who believed in the creation of the world in time out of nothing. He argued instead that God created the world in time out of a preexistent body that lacked all form. As Gersonides conceived it, this body seems to be similar to primal matter.

The problem of human freedom of action and a particular version of the problem of God's knowledge of future contingencies form an important part of Gersonides' doctrine. Unlike the great Jewish and Muslim Aristotelians, Gersonides believed in astrology and held that all happenings in the world except human actions are governed by a strict determinism. God's knowledge does not extend to individual human acts but embraces the general order of things. It grasps the laws of universal determinism but is incapable of apprehending events resulting from human freedom. Thus, the object of God's knowledge is a totally determined world order, which differs from the real world insofar as the latter is in some measure formed according to human freedom.

Gersonides does not appear to have assigned to the prophets any political function. According to him, their role consists of predicting future events. The providence exercised by the heavenly bodies ensures the existence in a given political society of people with an aptitude for the handicrafts and professions necessary for the survival of the community. He remarked that in this way the various human activities are distributed in a manner superior to that outlined in the *Republic* of Plato. Thus, he explicitly rejected Plato's political philosophy, which, because it was suitable to a society ruled through laws promulgated by a prophet (Muhammad), had been an important element of Jewish philosophy in the Arabic period.

HASDAI CRESCAS

The Spanish Jewish thinker Ḥasdai ben Abraham Crescas (1340–1410), like Gersonides, had thorough knowledge of Jewish philosophy and partial knowledge of Islamic philosophy. In both areas he seems to have been influenced by Christian Scholastic thought. Moreover, in certain important respects Crescas was influenced by Gersonides himself. One of Crescas's main works, *Or Adonai* ("The Light of the Lord"), was quite contrary to Gersonides in its attempt to expose the weaknesses of Aristotelian philosophy. This attitude may be placed in the wider context of the return to religion itself, as opposed to the Aristotelian rationalization of religion, and the vogue of Kabbala (esoteric Jewish mysticism), both of which were characteristic features of Spanish Jewry in Crescas's time. This change in attitude may have been a reaction to the increasing precariousness of the position of the Jewish community in Spain.

The criticism of the extreme rationalism of some medieval Aristotelians coincided historically with a certain disintegration of and disaffection toward classical Aristotelian Scholasticism. This trend was associated with the so-called voluntarism of John Duns Scotus (*c.* 1266–1308), the nominalism of William of Ockham (*c.* 1285–1347/49) and other 13th–14th-century Christian Scholastics, and the development of anti-Aristotelian physics at the University of Paris and elsewhere beginning in the 14th century. Significantly, there is a pronounced resemblance between Crescas's views and two of these trends, Scotism (the teachings of Duns Scotus and his followers) and the "new" physics.

Crescas accepted Gersonides' view that divine attributes cannot be negative, but unlike his predecessor his explanation of the difference between the attributes of God and those of created beings centred on the contrast between an infinite being and finite beings. It is through infinitude that God's essential attributes—wisdom, for instance—differ from the corresponding and otherwise similar attributes found in created beings. In Crescas's doctrine, as in that of Spinoza, God's attributes are infinite in number. The central place assigned to the doctrine of God's infinity in Crescas's system suggests the influence of Duns Scotus's theology, which is similarly founded upon the concept of divine infinity.

The problem of the infinite was approached from an altogether different perspective in Crescas's critique of Maimonides' 25 propositions, which Maimonides had set forth in the *Guide* as the basis of his proof of the existence of God. Crescas's purpose in criticizing and rejecting several of these propositions was to show that the traditional Aristotelian proofs (founded in the first place on physical doctrines) were not valid. In his critique, Crescas attempted to disprove the Aristotelian thesis that the existence of an actual infinite is impossible. He held that space is not a limit but a three-dimensional extension, that it is infinite, and that, contrary to Aristotle, the existence of a vacuum and of more worlds than one is possible. He also argued that the thesis of the Aristotelian philosophers that there exists an infinite number of causes and effects, which have order and gradation, was impossible. This thesis refers not to a temporal succession of causes and effects that have a similar ontological status but to a vertical series, descending from God to the lowest rung in creation. His attacks were likewise directed against the Aristotelians' conceptions of time and matter.

Crescas's fundamental opposition to Aristotelianism is perhaps most evident in his rejection of the conception of intellectual activity as the supreme state of being for humans and for God. Crescas's God is not first and foremost an intellect, and humanity's supreme goal is not to think but to love God with a love corresponding, as far as possible, to his infinite greatness and to rejoice in the observance of his commandments. God too loves human beings, and his love, in spite of the lowliness of its object, is proportionate to his infinity.

Crescas attacked the Aristotelian teaching of the separation of the intellect from the soul and attempted, perhaps in part under the influence of Judah ha-Levi, to refute the Aristotelian doctrine that the actualized intellect, as distinct from the soul, survives the death of the body. According to Crescas, the soul is a substance in its own right. It can be separated from the body and subsists after the body's death.

Joseph Albo

Whereas Crescas regarded the Aristotelian philosophers as adversaries, Joseph Albo (c. 1380–c. 1444), who considered Crescas his teacher, expressed a much more ambivalent attitude toward them. Albo did not eschew self-contradiction, apparently considering it a legitimate precaution on the part of a philosophical or theological author. Indeed, he indulged in it in a much more obvious way than did Maimonides. But, whereas the latter's fundamental philosophical position is fairly clear, it is much less apparent who Albo's true masters were—Crescas and the Jewish religious tradition, or Maimonides and Averroës. Because of this perhaps deliberate failure to explain to the reader where he really stood, Albo has often been dismissed as an eclectic. Indeed, along with the authors just mentioned, Albo was strongly influenced by Sa'adia and seems to have had considerable knowledge of Christian theology, even adopting for his own purposes certain Scholastic doctrines. He differs from Crescas and to some extent resembles Maimonides in having a marked interest in political theory.

The theme of Albo's magnum opus, *Sefer ha-'iqqarim* ("Book of Principles"), is the investigation of the theory of Jewish religious dogmas. Maimonides, in a nonphilosophical work, set the number of dogmas at 13, whereas Albo, following a doctrine that seems to go back to Averroës, limited the number to three: the existence of God, divine providence in reward and punishment, and the Torah as divine revelation. One section, usually including the philosophical and the traditional religious interpretations side by side, is devoted to each of these dogmas. Albo's principal and relatively novel contribution to the evolution of Jewish doctrine is the classification, in his introduction, of natural, conventional, and divine law.

Natural law (the universal moral law inherent in human nature) is necessary because human beings, who are political by nature, must belong to a community, which may be restricted in size to one town or may extend over the whole earth. Natural law preserves society by promoting right and repressing injustice. Thus, it restrains humans from stealing, robbing, and murdering. The positive laws instituted by the wise take into account the particular nature of the people for whose benefit they are instituted, as well as other circumstances. This means that they differ from the natural law in not being universally applicable. Neither natural law nor the more elaborate conventional laws, however, lead humans toward true spiritual happiness. This is the function of divine laws instituted by a prophet, which teach humans true theoretical opinions. Whereas Maimonides maintained that Judaism was the only divine law promulgated by a true prophet, Albo considered that the commandments given to Noah for all humankind—the Noahide Laws that Noah received after the Flood—also constitute divine law, which ensures, though to a lesser degree than does Judaism, the happiness of its adherents. This position justifies a certain universalism. In accordance with a Talmudic saying, Albo believed that the pious among the non-Jews (i.e., those who observe Noah's laws) have a share

NATURAL LAW

In jurisprudence and political philosophy, natural law is a system of right or justice common to all humankind and derived from nature rather than from the rules of society, or positive law. The concept can be traced to Aristotle, who held that what was "just by nature" was not always the same as what was "just by law." In the modern period, Hugo Grotius insisted on the validity of natural law even on the assumption that God does not exist, and Thomas Hobbes defined a law of nature as "a precept of general rule found out by reason, by which a man is forbidden to do that which is destructive of his life." Hobbes attempted to construct an edifice of law by rational deduction from a hypothetical "state of nature" and a social contract of consent between rulers and subjects. John Locke departed from Hobbes in describing the state of nature as an early society in which free and equal men observe the natural law. Jean-Jacques Rousseau postulated a savage who was virtuous in isolation and actuated by two principles "prior to reason": self-preservation and compassion. The authors of the U.S. Declaration of Independence refer only briefly to "the Laws of Nature" before citing equality and other "unalienable" rights as "self-evident." The French Declaration of the Rights of Man and of the Citizen asserts liberty, property, security, and resistance to oppression as "imprescriptible natural rights."

in the world to come. But he rejected the pretensions of Christianity and Islam to encompass divine laws comparable—or even superior—to Judaism.

MODERN PHILOSOPHY

The expulsion of the Jews from Spain and Portugal in 1492 and 1497, respectively, produced a new centre of Jewish thought: Holland, where many exiled Jews found a new and safer domicile. The tolerance of the regime seemed to provide guarantees against external persecution. This did not prevent, and indeed may have furthered, the establishment of an oppressive internal orthodoxy that was prepared to chastise rebellious members of the community. This was evident in the cases of Uriel Acosta (Gabriel da Costa) and Benedict de Spinoza, two 17th-century philosophers who rebelled against Jewish orthodoxy and were excommunicated for their views (Acosta twice).

URIEL ACOSTA

Belonging to a family of Marranos in Portugal, Acosta arrived in Amsterdam after having been brought up in the Catholic faith. His philosophical position was to a great extent determined by his antagonism to the dogmatism of the traditional Judaism that he encountered in Amsterdam. His growing estrangement from generally accepted Jewish doctrine is attested by his Portuguese treatise *Sobre a mortalidade da alma* ("On the Mortality of the Soul"). He held that the belief in the immortality of the soul has many evil effects, and that it impels people to choose an ascetic way of life and even to seek death. According to him,

nothing has tormented human beings more than the belief in an inner, spiritual good and evil. At this stage, Acosta affirmed the authority of the Bible, from which, according to him, the mortality of the soul can be proved.

In his autobiography, *Exemplar Humanae Vitae* ("Example of a Human Life"), Acosta took a more radical position. He proclaimed the supreme excellence of the natural moral law. When arguing before Jews, he seemed to identify this law with the Noahide Laws (the commandments given to Noah), thus suggesting a correspondence with the view of Albo. Accordingly, Acosta denied the validity of the argument that natural law is inferior to Judaism and Christianity, because he believed that both religions teach the love of one's enemies, a precept that is not a part of natural law and is a manifest impossibility.

BENEDICT DE SPINOZA

Born in Amsterdam but of Portuguese Marrano descent, Spinoza is unique in the history of modern Jewish thought. Although his work does not deal with specifically Judaic themes, he is traditionally included in this history for several reasons. First, it was through the study of Jewish philosophical texts that Spinoza was first initiated into philosophy. Second, Spinoza's system is in part a radicalization of, or perhaps a logical corollary to, medieval Jewish doctrines, and the impact of Maimonides and of Crescas is evident.

Third, a considerable portion of Spinoza's *Tractatus Theologico-Politicus* deals with problems related to Judaism. He drew from Jewish religion and history, even using the Israelite commonwealth in the *Tractatus* as the template for his ideal state, though he was not centrally concerned with matters of Jewish theology and ritual.

The first chapters of the *Tractatus* show that the doctrine of prophecy is of central importance to Spinoza's explanation of Judaism and that, in dealing with this subject, he used Maimonides' categories, though he applied them to different people or groups of people. Maimonides held that the prophets combined intellectual perfection, which made them philosophers, with perfection of the imaginative faculty. He also referred to a category of persons, including lawyers and statesmen, endowed with a strong imagination but possessing no extraordinary intellectual gifts. Spinoza applied this category to the prophets, whom he described as possessing vivid imaginations but as not necessarily having outstanding intellectual capacities. He denied that the biblical Prophets were philosophers and used a philosophical and historical approach to the Scriptures to show that the contrary assertion is not borne out by the texts.

Spinoza also denied Maimonides' assertion that the prophecy of Moses was essentially different from that of the other Prophets and that this was because Moses, in prophesying, had no recourse to the imaginative faculty. According to Spinoza, Moses' prophecy was unique because he heard the voice of God in a prophetic vision—that is, in a state in which his imagination was active. In this assertion, Spinoza employed one of Maimonides' categories of prophecy. Maimonides thought it improbable, however, that the voice of God was ever heard in prophetic vision, and he held that this category is purely hypothetical. In his classification of Moses, Spinoza was not concerned with what really happened in history. Rather, he was attempting to fashion the biblical evidence according to Maimonides' theoretical framework so that it would further his own theological and political purpose: to show that there could be a religion superior to Judaism.

This purpose made it imperative to propound in the *Tractatus Theologico-Politicus* a theory concerning Jesus, whom Spinoza designates as Christus. The category and the status assigned to Jesus are similar to those that Maimonides attributed to Moses. Jesus is referred to in the *Tractatus* as a religious teacher who makes recourse not to the imaginative faculty but to the intellect. His authority may be used to institute and strengthen the religion Spinoza called *religio catholica* ("universal religion"), which has little or nothing in common with any of the major manifestations of historic Christianity.

The difference between Judaism and Spinoza's *religio catholica* corresponds to the difference between Moses and Jesus. After leaving Egypt, the Jews found themselves, in Spinoza's view, in the position of people who had no allegiance to any positive law. They had, as it were, reverted to a state of nature and were faced with the need to enter into a social pact. They were also an ignorant people and quite prone to superstition. Moses, a man of outstanding ability, made use of the situation and the characteristics of the people to make them accept a social pact and a state founded upon it that, contrary to Spinoza's scheme for his ideal communities, were not based first and foremost upon utilitarian—that is, reasonable—consideration of the advantages of life in society over the state of nature.

According to Spinoza, the social pact concluded by the children of Israel in the desert was based upon a superstitious view of God as "King" and "Judge," to whom the children of Israel owed their political and military successes. The children of Israel transferred political sovereignty to God rather than to the representatives of the popular will. In due course, political sovereignty was vested in Moses, God's representative, and in his successors. In spite of Spinoza's insistence on the superstitious foundations of the ancient Israelite state, however, his account of its regime was not wholly unsympathetic, especially regarding its ability to curb human tyranny by its doctrine of divine sovereignty. Spinoza believed that the state contained the seeds of its own destruction and that, with its extinction, the social pact devised by Moses had lapsed and all the political and religious obligations incumbent upon the Jews had become null and void.

It could be argued that, because the state conceived by Spinoza is based not on superstitious faith but on a social contract originating in rational, utilitarian considerations, it does not need to have its authority safeguarded and stabilized by means of religion. Nevertheless, Spinoza apparently believed that religion is necessary. To fulfill this need and to obviate the danger of harmful religions, he devised the *religio catholica*, the universal religion, which is characterized by two distinctive traits. First, its main purpose, a practical one (which is furthered by recourse to the authority of Jesus), is to impel people to act in accordance with justice and charity. Such conduct is tantamount to obedience to the laws of the state and to the orders of the magistrates, in whom sovereignty is vested. Disobedience, however, even if it springs from compassionate motives, weakens the social pact, which safeguards the welfare of all the members of the community. In consequence, its evil effects outweigh whatever good it may produce. Second, although religion, according to Spinoza, is not concerned with theoretical truth, in order to be effective the *religio catholica* requires dogmas, which he set forth in the *Tractatus*. These dogmas are formulated in terms that can be interpreted in accordance both with the philosophical conception of God that Spinoza regarded as true and with widespread superstitious ideas. It follows that if they are accepted as constituting the only creed that everybody is obliged to profess, people cannot be persecuted on account of their beliefs.

The philosophies of Benedict de Spinoza do not deal with Jewish themes in particular, although his work does draw from Jewish religion and history. Imagno/Hulton Archive/Getty Images

Spinoza held that such persecution may lead to civil war and may thus destroy the state. Philosophers are free to engage in the pursuit of truth and to attain, if they can, the supreme goal of humanity—freedom grounded in knowledge. There can be little doubt that the furtherance of the cause of tolerance for philosophical opinions was one of Spinoza's main objects in writing the *Tractatus*.

As compared with the *Tractatus Theologico-Philosophicus*, the *Ethics*, Spinoza's major philosophical work, bears a much more ambiguous relation to Jewish medieval philosophy. In a way, Spinoza's metaphysical system, contained in the *Ethics*, can be regarded as drawing aspects of medieval Aristotelianism to their logical conclusions, a step that most Jewish (and Christian and Muslim) thinkers were unwilling to take, owing to their theological conservatism.

MOSES MENDELSSOHN

The era opened by Moses Mendelssohn (1729–86)—that is, *c.* 1750 to *c.* 1830—is sometimes called the German period of Jewish philosophy because of the large number of works on Jewish philosophy that were written in German. The German period is also marked by the emancipation of the Jews (i.e., by the abrogation of discriminatory laws directed against them) and by their partial or complete assimilation. In this time in particular, the term *Jewish philosophy* applied especially to works that were primarily concerned with

defining Judaism and offering a justification of its existence. The second of these tasks was often conceived of as involving a confrontation with Christianity rather than with philosophy. This change from what would have been the practice in the Middle Ages seems to have resulted from the demarcation of the sphere of religion in such a way that, at least in the opinion of the philosophers, possible points of collision with philosophy no longer existed. This development was stimulated by the doctrine of Spinoza, from whom Mendelssohn and others took certain fundamental ideas concerning Judaism.

Like Spinoza, Mendelssohn held that it is not the task of Judaism to teach rational truths, though such truths may be referred to in the Bible. Contrary to what he called Athanasian Christianity—that is, the doctrine set forth in the Athanasian Creed—Judaism has no binding dogmas. It is centred on inculcating belief in certain historical events and on the observance of religious law, which includes the ceremonial commandments. Such observance is supposed to lead to happiness in this world and in the afterlife. Mendelssohn did not reject this view out of hand, as Spinoza would have done. Indeed, he seems to have been prepared to accept it, God's mysteries being inscrutable, and the radicalism and what may be called the consistency of Spinoza being the complete antithesis of Mendelssohn's apologetics. Non-Jews were supposed by Mendelssohn to owe allegiance to the natural moral law.

HASKALA

The Haskala, also known as the Jewish Enlightenment, was a late 18th- and 19th-century intellectual movement among the Jews of central and eastern Europe that attempted to acquaint Jews with the European and Hebrew languages and with secular education and culture as supplements to traditional Talmudic studies. Though the Haskala owed much of its inspiration and values to the European Enlightenment, its roots, character, and development were distinctly Jewish. When the movement began, Jews lived mostly in pales of settlement and ghettoes and followed a form of life that had evolved after centuries of segregation and discriminatory legislation. A move toward change was initiated by a relatively few "mobile Jews" (mainly merchants) and "court Jews" (agents of various rulers and princes), whose contact with European civilization had heightened their desire to become a part of society as a whole.

Early proponents of Haskala were convinced that Jews could be brought into the mainstream of European culture through a reform of traditional Jewish education and a breakdown of ghetto life. This meant adding secular subjects to the school curriculum, adopting the language of the larger society in place of Yiddish, abandoning traditional garb, reforming synagogue services, and taking up new occupations.

The revival of Hebrew writing was given impetus with the publication in 1784 of the first modern Hebrew periodical, a significant attempt to recover a sense of "classical" Jewish civilization. Though basically rationalistic, Haskala also exhibited such romantic tendencies as a desire to return to nature, a high regard for manual work, and an aspiration to revive a glorious and better past. Haskala advocated the study of Jewish history and the ancient Hebrew language as a means of reviving a Jewish national consciousness. These values and attitudes later merged with those of the Jewish nationalist movement known as Zionism. More immediately, Haskala's call to modernize the Jewish religion provided the impetus for the emergence of Reform Judaism in Germany in the early 19th century.

The movement's development varied with the political, social, and cultural conditions of individual countries. In Germany, Yiddish was rapidly abandoned and assimilation was widespread, but interest in Jewish history revived and gave birth to Wissenschaft des Judentums (i.e., modern critical historico-philological Jewish studies). In the Austrian Empire, a Hebrew Haskala developed that promoted Jewish scholarship and literature. The adherents of Haskala fought rabbinic orthodoxy and especially Ḥasidism, the mystical and pietistic tendencies of which were attacked bitterly. In Russia, some followers of Haskala hoped to achieve "improvement of the Jews" by collaborating with the government plan for educational reform, but the increasingly reactionary and anti-Semitic policies of the tsarist regime drove some Jews to support the revolutionary movement, others to support nascent Zionism. By the end of the 19th century, some ideals of Haskala had become permanent features of Jewish life. Modern Judaism is thus unthinkable without reference to Haskala, for it created a middle class that was loyal to historical Jewish traditions and yet part of modern Western civilization.

Solomon Formstecher

Whereas Mendelssohn continued the medieval tradition (at least to some extent) or adapted Spinoza's doctrine for his own purposes, the Jewish philosophers of the first half of the 19th century generally followed the teachings of the non-Jewish philosophers of their own time. In *Die Religion des Geistes* ("The Religion of the Spirit"), Solomon Formstecher (1808–89) may have been influenced by F.W.J. von Schelling (1775–1854) in his conception of nature and spirit as manifestations of the divine. In Formstecher's view, there are two types of religions that correspond to these manifestations: the religion of nature, in which God is conceived as the principle of nature or as the world soul, and the religion of the spirit, in which God is understood as an ethical being. According to the religion of the spirit, God has produced the world as his manifestation in full freedom and not, as the religion of nature tends to profess, because the world was necessary for his existence.

The religion of the spirit, which corresponds to absolute religious truth, was first manifested in the Jewish people. The religious history of the world may be understood as a process of universalization of the Jewish religion, according to Formstecher. Thus, although Christianity propagated Jewish conceptions among the nations, it combined them with pagan ideas. The pagan element is gradually being eliminated—Protestantism, in this respect, marks considerable progress.

When at long last the Jewish element in Christianity is victorious, the Jews will be right to give up their isolation. The progress that will bring about this final religious union is already under way.

Samuel Hirsch

The main philosophical work of Samuel Hirsch (1815–89), titled *Die Religionsphilosophie der Juden* ("The Philosophy of Religion of the Jews"), was decisively influenced by G.W.F. Hegel (1770–1831). Hegel's impact is most evident in Hirsch's method and in the task that he assigned to the philosophy of religion—the transformation of religious consciousness into conceptual truth. Contrary to Hegel, however, he did not consider religious truth to be inadequate compared with philosophical truth.

In Hirsch's view, God revealed himself in the first stages of Jewish history by means of miracles and prophecy. At present, he manifests himself in the miracle of the existence of the Jewish people. Hirsch further maintained that Christianity and Judaism were identical at the time of Jesus and that a decisive break between them was caused by Paul. When the Pauline elements are eliminated from Christianity, it will be essentially in agreement with Judaism, though Judaism will preserve its separate existence.

Nachman Krochmal

Nachman Krochmal (1785–1840), a native of Galicia (at that time part of Austria), wrote the highly influential Hebrew treatise *More nevukhe ha-zman* ("Guide for the Perplexed for Our Time"), on the philosophy of history and on Jewish history. Krochmal's philosophical thought was based on the notion of spirit. He was mainly concerned with the "national spirit" that is proper to each people and that accounts for the characteristics differentiating one people from another in every domain of human activity. The national spirits of all peoples except the Jewish are, according to Krochmal, essentially particular. Hence, when the nation becomes extinct, the national spirit either disappears or, if it is powerful, is assimilated by some other nation. The perpetuity of the Jewish people, according to Krochmal, is the result of their special relation to the Universal Spirit, who is the God of Israel.

SOLOMON STEINHEIM

Solomon Ludwig Steinheim (1789–1866), the author of *Die Offenbarung nach dem Lehrbegriff der Synagoge* ("The Revelation According to the Doctrine of the Synagogue"), was apparently influenced by the antirationalism of the German philosopher Friedrich Heinrich Jacobi (1743–1819). His criticism of science is based on Jacobi's work, though he did not agree with Jacobi in opposing discursive reason to the intuitive knowledge of God. Steinheim contrasted human reason with divine revelation. The main point of opposition between revelation, vouchsafed to the prophets of Israel, and

reason is that the God posited by reason is subject to necessity—he can act only in accordance with laws. Moreover, reason affirms that nothing can come from nothing. Accordingly, God is free to create not a good world but only the best possible world. Revealed religion, on the other hand, affirms the freedom of God and the creation of the world out of nothing.

HERMANN COHEN

There seems to be little connection between the Jewish philosophers of the first half or two-thirds of the 19th century and Hermann Cohen (1842–1918), the head of the Neo-Kantian school centred at the University of Marburg. Cohen may be regarded as a rather unusual case among the Jewish philosophers of his and the preceding generations because of the dual nature of his philosophical thought—the general and the Jewish—and the uneasy equilibrium between them. Judaism was by no means the only important theme of his philosophical system; indeed, it was not even his point of departure. For most of his life, Cohen was wholly committed to his brand of Kantianism, and he displayed considerable originality in its elaboration. It has been maintained with some justification that his doctrine manifests a certain (unintentional) kinship with Hegel's, though Cohen's idea of God is based on an analysis and development of certain conceptions of Immanuel Kant. In Cohen's view, reason requires that nature be conceived of as conforming to a single rational plan and that there be harmony

NEO-KANTIANISM

A revival of Kantianism in German universities that began c. 1860, Neo-Kantianism slowly extended over the whole domain of philosophy. The first decisive impetus toward reviving Immanuel Kant's ideas came from natural scientists. Hermann von Helmholtz applied physiological studies of the senses to the question of the epistemological significance of spatial perception raised by The Critique of Pure Reason *(1781). Neo-Kantianism reached its apex in the early 20th-century Marburg school, which included Hermann Cohen (1842–1918) and Paul Natorp (1854–1924). They repudiated Helmholtz's naturalism and reaffirmed the importance of the transcendental method. Ernst Cassirer, another Marburg-school figure, brought Kantian principles to bear on the whole realm of cultural phenomena. Wilhelm Windelband (1848–1915) and Heinrich Rickert (1863–1936) introduced Kantianism into the philosophy of history. Neo-Kantianism also influenced the phenomenology of Edmund Husserl and of the early works of Martin Heidegger.*

between the domains of natural and moral teleology (ultimate purposes or ends). These two requirements in turn require the adoption of the idea of God—the word *idea* being used in the Kantian sense, which means that no assertion is made about the metaphysical reality of God.

Cohen's later works increasingly emphasized generally religious and specifically Judaic elements. Some scholars, most notably his student Franz Rosenzweig, interpreted this as a major turn in Cohen's thought. In the late 20th century, however, most scholars held that the more-pronounced Judaism in Cohen's later works was the culmination of his overall philosophical system, not a radical departure from it.

FRANZ ROSENZWEIG

Franz Rosenzweig (1886–1929) published his main philosophical work, *Der Stern der Erlösung* (*The Star of Redemption*), in 1921. It begins by rejecting the traditional philosophical denial of the fear of death, maintaining instead that this fear is the beginning of the cognition of the All. Humans should fear death, despite the indifference of philosophy and its predilection for accepting death. Traditional philosophy is interested exclusively in the universal, and it is monistic—its aim is to discover one principle from which everything can be derived. This tendency of philosophy, however, denatures human experience, which knows not one but three separate domains (which Kant had referred to in a different context), namely, God, the world, and humanity.

According to Rosenzweig, God (like the world and like humankind) is known through experience (the experience of revelation). In Greek religion, the most perfect manifestation of paganism, every one of these domains subsists by itself:

the gods, the cosmos, and the human as the tragic, solitary, silent hero. Biblical religion is concerned with the relation between the three: the relation between God and the world, which is creation; the relation between God and human beings, which is revelation; and the relation between humans and the world, which leads to salvation. Under the influence of Schelling, whose term and concept he adopted, Rosenzweig pursued a "narrative philosophy" that renounces the ambition to find one principle for everything that exists and that follows biblical religion in focusing on the connections between the three domains and between the words and acts that bring about and develop these connections.

Biblical faith brought forth two valid religions—Christianity and Judaism. The first is described by Rosenzweig as the eternal way; the Christian peoples seek in the vicissitudes of time and history the way to salvation. In contrast to them, the existence of the stateless Jewish people is not concerned with time and history; it is—notwithstanding the hope for final salvation—already an eternal life, renewed again and again according to the rhythm of the Jewish liturgical year.

MARTIN BUBER

Among the leading thinkers of the 20th century was Martin Buber (1878–1965), whose impact was felt by both Jews and non-Jews. In his early period, Buber was led, partly through empathy with Jewish and non-Jewish mysticism, to stress unitive experience and knowledge, in which the difference between one person and another and between the individual and God tend to disappear. But in his final period he taught—following, as he claimed, a suggestion of Ludwig Feuerbach (1804–72)—that a human being can realize himself or herself only in a relation with another, who may be another person or God. This conception of the "I and Thou" relationship led to the formulation of Buber's view of the dialogical life—the mutual, responsive relation between one person and another—and accounts for the importance that he attached to the category of "encounter."

EMMANUEL LÉVINAS

During the late 20th century the thought of the French Jewish philosopher Emmanuel Lévinas (1905–95) exercised worldwide influence. In his main work, *Totality and Infinity* (1961), Lévinas emphasized ethics, as opposed to epistemology, as the primary means for achieving one's relation to the "Other." This relationship is based on the existential and material need of the other person rather than on one's abstract knowledge of him. In this philosophical program, Lévinas drew upon rabbinic tradition as well as the philosophical anthropology of Cohen, Rosenzweig, and Buber.

CHAPTER 12

FOUNDATIONAL FIGURES OF JEWISH TRADITION

The history of the Jewish people begins with Abraham, the first of the patriarchs. To him was made the divine promise, in a covenant with God, that his descendants would constitute a great nation. Abraham's son Isaac, according to tradition, would produce the heir whose own progeny would fulfill the divine promise. This nation calls itself Israel after Abraham's grandson, the third patriarch, originally named Jacob but granted the byname Israel ("He who struggles with God") after wrestling an angel of the Lord. Moses, the great prophet whom God called to lead the people of Israel out of servitude in Egypt, renewed the covenant after receiving the divine Law from God atop Mount Sinai. Although the historical existence of these figures is disputed by some, none doubts the centrality to Jewish tradition of these figures or of the narrative of the rise of Israel as a nation from Abraham's call to Moses's revelation of the divine injunctions that provided order and meaning to the lives of the Israelites during this foundational time.

ABRAHAM

According to tradition, Abraham (flourished, according to tradition, early 2nd millennium BCE) was the first of the Hebrew patriarchs. He subsequently became revered not only by Judaism but also by Christianity and Islam, all of which trace their origins back to him. According to the biblical book of Genesis, Abraham left Ur, in Mesopotamia, because God called him to found a new nation in an undesignated land that he later learned was Canaan. He obeyed unquestioningly the commands of God, from whom he received repeated promises and a covenant that his "seed" would inherit the land.

THE CRITICAL PROBLEM OF A "BIOGRAPHY" OF ABRAHAM

There can be no biography of Abraham in the ordinary sense. The most that can be done is to apply the interpretation of modern historical finds to biblical materials so as to arrive at a probable judgment as to the background and patterns of events in his life. This involves a reconstruction of the patriarchal age (of Abraham, Isaac, Jacob, and Joseph; early 2nd millennium BCE), which until the end of the 19th century was unknown and considered virtually unknowable. It was assumed, based on a presumed dating of hypothetical biblical sources, that the patriarchal narratives in the Bible were only a projection of the situation and concerns of a much later period (9th–5th century BCE) and of dubious historical value.

Several theses were advanced to explain the narratives—for example, that the patriarchs were mythical beings or the personifications of tribes or folkloric or etiological (explanatory) figures created to account for various social, juridical, or cultic patterns. However, after World War I, archaeological research made enormous strides with the discovery of monuments and documents, many of which date back to the period assigned to the patriarchs in the traditional account. The excavation of a royal palace at Mari, an ancient city on the Euphrates, for example, brought to light thousands of cuneiform tablets (official archives and correspondence and religious and juridical texts) and thereby offered exegesis a new basis, which specialists utilized to show that, in the biblical book of Genesis, narratives fit perfectly with what, from other sources, is known today of the early 2nd millennium BCE but imperfectly with a later period.

Thus, there are two main sources for reconstructing the figure of father Abraham: the book of Genesis, from the genealogy of Terah, Abraham's father, and his departure from Ur to Harran in chapter 11 to the death of Abraham in chapter 25; and recent archaeological discoveries and interpretations concerning the area and era in which the biblical narrative takes place.

THE BIBLICAL ACCOUNT

According to the biblical account, Abram ("The Father [or God] Is Exalted"), who is later named Abraham ("The Father of Many Nations"), a native of Ur in Mesopotamia, is called by God to leave his own country and people and journey to an undesignated land, where he will become the founder of a new nation. He obeys the call unquestioningly and (at 75 years of age) proceeds with his barren wife, Sarai, later named Sarah ("Princess"), his nephew Lot, and other companions to the land of Canaan (between Syria and Egypt).

There the childless septuagenarian receives repeated promises and a covenant from God that his "seed" will inherit the land and become a numerous nation. He not only has a son, Ishmael, by his wife's maidservant Hagar but has, at 100 years of age, by Sarah, a legitimate son, Isaac, who is to be the heir of the promise. Yet Abraham is ready to obey God's command to sacrifice Isaac, a test of his faith, which he is not required to consummate in the end because God substitutes a ram. At Sarah's death, he purchases the cave of Machpelah near Hebron, together with the adjoining ground, as a family burying place. It is the first clear ownership of a piece of the promised land by Abraham and his posterity. Toward the end of his life, he sees to it that his son Isaac marries a girl from his own people back in Mesopotamia rather than a Canaanite woman. Abraham dies at the age of 175 and is buried next to Sarah in the cave of Machpelah.

Abraham Driving Out Hagar and Ishmael, *oil on canvas by Il Guercino, 1657–58; in the Brera Picture Gallery, Milan.* SCALA/Art Resource, New York

Abraham is pictured with various characteristics: a righteous man, with wholehearted commitment to God; a man of peace (in settling a boundary dispute with his nephew Lot), compassionate (he argues and bargains with God to spare the people of Sodom and Gomorrah), and hospitable (he welcomes three visiting angels); a quick-acting warrior (he rescues Lot and his family from a raiding party); and an unscrupulous liar to save his own skin (he passes off Sarah as his sister and lets her be picked by the Egyptian pharaoh for his harem). He appears as both a man of great spiritual depth and strength and a person with common human weaknesses and needs.

THE GENESIS NARRATIVE IN THE LIGHT OF RECENT SCHOLARSHIP

The saga of Abraham unfolds between two landmarks: the exodus from "Ur of the Chaldeans" (Ur Kasdim) of the family, or clan, of Terah; and "the purchase of" (or "the burials in") the cave of Machpelah. Tradition seems particularly firm on this point. The Hebrew text, in fact, locates the departure specifically at Ur Kasdim, the Kasdim being none other than the Kaldu of the cuneiform texts at Mari. It is manifestly a migration of which one tribe is the centre. The leader of the movement is designated by name: Terah, who "takes them out" from Ur, Abram his son, Lot the son of Haran, another son of Terah, and their wives, the best known being Sarai, the wife of Abram. The existence of another son of Terah, Nahor, who appears later, is noted.

Most scholars agree that Ur Kasdim was the Sumerian city of Ur, today Tall al-Muqayyar (or Mughair), about 200 miles (300 km) southeast of Baghdad in lower Mesopotamia, which was excavated from 1922 to 1934. It is certain that the cradle of the ancestors was the seat of a vigorous polytheism whose memory had not been lost and whose uncontested master in Ur was Nanna (or Sin), the Sumero-Akkadian moon god. "They served other gods," Joshua, Moses' successor, recalled, speaking to their descendants at Shechem.

After the migration from Ur (c. 2000 BCE), the reasons for which are unknown, the first important stopping place was Harran, where the caravan remained for some time. The city has been definitely located in upper Mesopotamia, between the Tigris and the Euphrates rivers, in the Balikh valley, and can be found on the site of the modern Harran in Turkey. It has been shown that Harran was a pilgrimage city, for it was a centre of the Sin cult and consequently closely related to the moon-god cult of Ur. The Mari tablets have shed new light on the patriarchal period, specifically in terms of the city of Harran.

There have been many surprising items in the thousands of tablets found in the palace at Mari. Not only are the Ḥapiru ("Hebrews") mentioned but so also remarkably are the Banu Yamina ("Benjaminites"). It is not that the latter are identical with the family of Benjamin, a son of Jacob, but rather that a name with such a biblical ring appears in these extrabiblical sources in the 18th century BCE. What seems beyond doubt is that these Benjaminites (or Yaminites, meaning "Sons of the Right," or "Sons of the South," according to their habits of orientation) are always indicated as being north of Mari and in Harran, in the Temple of Sin.

The Bible provides no information on the itinerary followed between Ur and Harran. Scholars think that the caravan went up the Euphrates, then up the Balikh. After indicating a stay of indeterminate length in Harran, the Bible says only that Terah died there, at the age of 205, and that Abraham was 75 when he took up the journey again with his family and his goods. This time the migration went from east to west, first as far as the Euphrates River, which they may have crossed at Carchemish, because it can be forded during low-water periods.

Here again, the Mari texts supply a reference, for they indicate that there were Benjaminites on the right bank of the river, in the lands of Yamhad (Aleppo), Qatanum (Qatna), and Amurru. Because the ancient trails seem to have been marked with sanctuaries, it is noteworthy that Nayrab, near Aleppo, was, like Harran and Ur, a centre of the Sin cult and that south of Aleppo, on the road to Ḥamāh, there is still a village that bears the name of Benjamin. The route is in the direction of the "land of Canaan," the goal of the journey.

If a stop in Damascus is assumed, the caravan must next have crossed the land of Bashan (the Ḥawrān of today), first crossing the Jabboq, then the Jordan River at the ford of Dāmiyā, and arriving in the heart of the Samaritan country, to reach at last the plain of Shechem, today Balāṭah, at the foot of the Gerizim and Ebal mountains. Shechem was at the time a political and religious centre, the importance of which has been perceived more clearly as a result of recent archaeological excavations. From the mid-13th to the mid-11th century BCE, Shechem was the site of the cult of the Canaanite god Ba'al-Berit (Lord of the Covenant). The architecture uncovered on the site by archaeologists would date to the 18th century BCE, in which the presence of the patriarchs in Shechem is placed.

The next stopping place was in Bethel, identified with present-day Baytīn, north of Jerusalem. Bethel was also a holy city, whose cult was centred on El, the Canaanite god par excellence. Its name does not lend itself to confusion, for it proclaims that the city is the *bet*, "house," or temple, of El (God). The Canaanite sanctuary was taken over without hesitation by Abraham, who built an altar there and consecrated it to YHWH, at least if the Yahwistic tradition in Genesis is to be believed.

Abraham had not yet come to the end of his journey. Between Shechem and Bethel he had gone about 31 miles. It was about as far again from Bethel to Hebron, or more precisely to the oaks of Mamre, "which are at Hebron" (according to the Genesis account). The location of Mamre has been the subject of some indecision. At the present time, there is general agreement in setting it 1.5 miles (3 km) northwest of Hebron at Rāmat al-Khalīl, an Arabic name which means the "Heights of the Friend," the friend (of God) being Abraham.

Mamre marked the site of Abraham's encampment, but this did not at all exclude episodic travels in the direction of the Negeb, to Gerar and Beersheba. Life was a function of the economic conditions of the moment, of pastures to follow and to find, and thus the patriarchs moved back and forth between the land of Canaan and the Nile River delta. They remained shepherds and never became cultivators.

It was in Mamre that Abraham received the revelation that his race would be perpetuated, and it was there that he learned that his nephew Lot had been taken captive. The latter is an enigmatic episode, an "erratic block" in a story in which nothing prepared the way for it. Suddenly, the life of the patriarch was inserted into a slice of history in which several important persons ("kings") intervene: Amraphel of Shinar, Arioch of Ellasar, Ched-or-laomer of Elam, and Tidal of Goiim. Scholars of previous generations tried to identify these names with important historical figures (e.g., Amraphel with Hammurabi of Babylon), but little remains today of these suppositions. The whole of chapter 14 of Genesis, in which this event is narrated, differs completely from what has preceded and

what follows. It may be an extract from some historical annals, belonging to an unknown secular source, for the meeting of Melchizedek, king of Salem and priest of God Most High (El ʿElyon), and Abraham is impressive. The king-priest greets him with bread and wine on his victorious return and blesses him in the name of God Most High.

In this scene, the figure of the patriarch takes on a singular aspect. How is his religious behaviour to be characterized? He swears by "the Lord God Most High" (i.e., by both YHWH and El ʿElyon). It is known that, on the matter of the revelation of YHWH to man, the biblical traditions differ. According to what

ISAAC

In the Book of Genesis, Isaac is the second of the patriarchs of Israel, the only son of Abraham and Sarah, and father of Esau and Jacob. Although Sarah was past the age of childbearing, God promised Abraham and Sarah that they would have a son, and Isaac was born. Later, to test Abraham's obedience, God commanded Abraham to sacrifice the boy. Abraham made all the preparations for the ritual sacrifice, but God spared Isaac at the last moment.

In the Hebrew Bible, God is called the God of Abraham, Isaac, and Jacob, because with them God's relationship of promise and purpose was fixed for all those who descended from them. The story of Abraham's acquiescence to God's command to sacrifice Isaac was cited in appeals for the mercy of God.

scholars call the Yahwistic source (J) in the first five books of the Bible, YHWH had been known and worshiped since Adam's time. According to the so-called Priestly source (P), the name of YHWH was revealed only to Moses. It may be concluded that it was probably El whom the patriarchs, including Abraham, knew.

As noted previously, in Mesopotamia the patriarchs worshiped "other gods." On Canaanite soil, they met the Canaanite supreme god, El, and adopted him, but only partially and nominally, bestowing upon him qualities destined to distinguish him and to assure his preeminence over all other gods. He was thus to become El 'Olam (God the Everlasting One), El 'Elyon (God Most High), El Shaddai (God, the One of the Mountains), and El Ro'i (God of Vision). In short, the god of Abraham possessed duration, transcendence, power, and knowledge. This was not monotheism but monolatry (the worship of one among many gods), with the bases laid for a true universalism. He was a personal god, too, with direct relations with the individual, but also a family god and certainly still a tribal god. Here truly was the "God of our fathers," who in the course of time was to become the "God of Abraham, Isaac, and Jacob."

It is not surprising that this bond of the flesh should still manifest itself when it came to gathering together the great ancestors into the family burial chamber, the cave of Machpelah. This place is venerated today in Hebron, at the Ḥaram al-Khalīl (Holy Place of the Friend), under the mosque. Abraham, "the friend of God," was forevermore the depositary of the promise, the beneficiary of the Covenant, sealed not by the death of Isaac but by the sacrifice of the ram that was offered up in place of the child on Mount Moriah.

JACOB

According to the Genesis account, Jacob was the son of Abraham's son Isaac and the younger twin brother of Esau. The two brothers are representatives of two different grades of social order, Jacob being a pastoralist and Esau a nomadic hunter. During her pregnancy, Rebekah was told by God that she would give birth to twins. Each of them would found a great nation, and Esau, the elder, would serve his younger brother. As it turned out, Jacob, by means of an elaborate double deception, managed to obtain his older brother's birthright from their father. Jacob then fled his brother's wrath and went to take refuge with the Aramaean tribe of his ancestors at Haran in Mesopotamia.

Along his journey Jacob received a special revelation from God, who promised Jacob lands and numerous offspring that would prove to be the blessing of the entire Earth. Jacob named the place where he received his vision Bethel ("House of God"). Arriving at his uncle Laban's home in Haran, Jacob fell in love with his cousin Rachel. He worked for her father, Laban, for seven years to obtain Rachel's hand in marriage, but then Laban substituted his older daughter, Leah, for Rachel at the wedding ceremony. Unwittingly married to Leah, Jacob was thus compelled to serve Laban for another seven years so that he could take his beloved Rachel as his wife as well. Jacob then served Laban for another six years, during which he amassed a large amount of property. He then set out with his wives and children to return to Palestine. On the way Jacob wrestled with a mysterious stranger, an angel of God, who changed Jacob's name to Israel (literally "He has struggled with God"). Jacob then met and was reconciled with Esau and settled in Canaan.

Jacob had 13 children, 10 of whom were founders of tribes of Israel. Leah bore him his only daughter, Dinah, and six sons—Reuben, Simeon, Levi (who did not found a tribe, but was the ancestor of the Levites), Judah (from whom a tribe and the Davidic monarchy were descended), Issachar, and Zebulun. Leah's maidservant, Zilpah, bore him Gad and Asher, and Rachel's maidservant, Bilhah, bore him Dan and Naphtali. Rachel's sons were Benjamin and Joseph (who did not found a tribe, but whose sons founded the tribes of Manasseh and Ephraim).

The story of Jacob's later years more properly belongs to the story of Joseph. Late in his life, a famine prompted Jacob and his sons to migrate to Egypt, where he was reunited with his son Joseph, who had disappeared some years before. Israel died in Egypt at the age of 147 years and was buried in Canaan at Hebron.

MOSES

Moses was a Hebrew prophet, teacher, and leader who, in the 13th century BCE, delivered his people from Egyptian slavery. In the Covenant ceremony at Mt. Sinai, where the Ten Commandments were promulgated, he founded the religious community known as Israel. As the interpreter of these Covenant stipulations, he was the organizer of the community's religious and civil traditions. In the Jewish tradition, he is revered as the greatest prophet and teacher, and Judaism has sometimes loosely been called Mosaism, or the Mosaic faith, in Western Christendom. His influence continues to be felt in the religious life, moral concerns, and social ethics of Western civilization, and therein lies his undying significance.

THE HISTORICAL PROBLEM

Few historical figures have engendered such disparate interpretations as has Moses. Early Jewish and Christian traditions considered him the author of the Torah ("Law," or "Teaching"), also called the Pentateuch ("Five Books"), comprising the first five books of the Bible, and some conservative groups still believe in Mosaic authorship.

Opposing this is the theory of the contemporary German scholar Martin Noth, who, while granting that Moses may have had something to do with the preparations for the conquest of Canaan, was very skeptical of the roles attributed to him by tradition. Although recognizing a historical core beneath the Exodus and Sinai traditions, Noth believed that two different groups experienced these events and transmitted the stories independently of each other. He contended that the biblical story tracing the Hebrews from Egypt to Canaan resulted from an editor's weaving separate themes and traditions around a main character Moses, actually an obscure person from Moab.

Historical Views of Moses

The biblical archaeologist and historian W.F. Albright presents a point of view that falls somewhere between these two extremes. While the essence of the biblical story (narrated between Exodus 1:8

Moses Showing the Tables of the Law to the People, *oil painting by Rembrandt, 1659; in the Staatliche Museen Preussischer Kulturbesitz, Berlin.* Courtesy of Staatliche Museen Preussischer Kulturbesitz Gemaldegalerie, Berlin

and Deuteronomy 34:12) is accepted, it is recognized that, during the centuries of oral and written transmission, the account acquired layers of accretions. The reconstruction of the documentary sources of the Pentateuch by literary critics is considered valid, but the sources are viewed as varying versions of one series of events. Other critical methods (studying the biblical text from the standpoint of literary form, oral tradition, style, redaction, and archaeology) are equally valid. The most accurate answer to a critical problem is therefore likely to come from the convergence of various lines of evidence. The aid of critical scholarship notwithstanding, the sources are so sketchy that the man Moses can be portrayed only in broad outline.

The Date of Moses

According to the biblical account, Moses' parents were from the tribe of Levi, one of the groups in Egypt called Hebrews. Originally the term *Hebrew* had nothing to do with race or ethnic origin. It derived from Habiru, a variant spelling of Ḥapiru (Apiru), a designation of a class of people who made their living by hiring themselves out for various services. The biblical Hebrews had been in Egypt for generations, but apparently they became a threat, so one of the pharaohs enslaved them. Unfortunately, the personal name of the king is not given, and scholars have disagreed as to his identity and, hence, as to the date of the events of the narrative of Moses. One theory takes literally the statement in 1 Kings 6:1 that the Exodus from Egypt occurred 480 years before Solomon began building the Temple in Jerusalem. Because this occurred in the fourth year of his reign, about 960 BCE, the Exodus would date about 1440 BCE.

This conclusion, however, is at variance with most of the biblical and archaeological evidence. The storage cities Pithom and Rameses, built for the pharaoh by the Hebrews, were located in the northeastern part of the Egyptian delta, not far from Goshen, the district in which the Hebrews lived. It is implicit in the whole story that the pharaoh's palace and capital were in the area, but Thutmose III (the pharaoh in 1440) had his capital at Thebes, far to the south, and never conducted major building operations in the delta region. Moreover, Edom and Moab, petty kingdoms in Transjordan that forced Moses to circle east of them, were not yet settled and organized. Finally, as excavations have shown, the destruction of the cities the Hebrews claimed to have captured occurred about 1250, not 1400.

Inasmuch as tradition figured about 12 generations from Moses to Solomon, the reference to 480 years is most likely an editorial comment allowing 40 years for each generation. Because an actual generation was nearer 25 years, the most probable date for the Exodus is about 1290 BCE. If this is true, then the oppressive pharaoh noted in Exodus (1:2–2:23) was Seti I (reigned 1318–04), and the pharaoh during the Exodus was Ramses II (c. 1304–c. 1237). In short, Moses was probably born in the late 14th century BCE.

YEARS AND DEEDS

One of the measures taken by the Egyptians to restrict the growth of the Hebrews was to order the death of all newborn Hebrew males. According to tradition, Moses' parents, Amram and Jochebed (whose other children were Aaron and Miriam), hid him for three months and then set him afloat on the Nile in a reed basket daubed with pitch. The child, found by the pharaoh's daughter while bathing, was reared in the Egyptian court. While some doubt the authenticity of this tradition, the name Moses (Hebrew: Moshe) is derived from Egyptian *mose* ("is born") and is found in such names as Thutmose ([The God] Thoth Is Born). Originally, it is inferred, Moses' name was longer, but the deity's name was dropped. This could have happened when Moses returned to his people or possibly even earlier, because the shortened form Mose was very popular at that time.

THE FORMATIVE YEARS

Moses' years in the court are passed over in silence, but it is evident from his accomplishments later that he had instruction in religious, civil, and military matters. Because Egypt controlled Canaan (Palestine) and part of Syria and had contacts with other nations of the Fertile Crescent, Moses undoubtedly had general knowledge of life in the ancient Near East. During his education he learned somehow that he was a Hebrew, and his sense of concern and curiosity impelled him to visit his people. According to the biblical narrative, Moses lived 120 years and was 80 when he confronted Pharaoh, but there is no indication how old he was when he went to see the Hebrews. Later Jewish and Christian tradition assumed 40-year periods for his stay in the Egyptian court, his sojourn in Midian, and his wilderness wanderings.

Most likely Moses was about age 25 when he took the inspection tour among his people. There he saw the oppressive measures under which they laboured. When he found an Egyptian taskmaster beating a Hebrew, probably to death, he could control his sense of justice no longer. After checking to make sure that no one was in sight, he killed the tough Egyptian overlord. As a prince in the court, Moses was probably in excellent physical condition, and apparently he knew the latest methods of combat.

The flush of victory pulled Moses back the next day. He had removed one threat to his people and was determined to assist them again. This time, however, he found two Hebrews fighting. After parting them, he questioned the offender in an attempt to mediate the disagreement. Two questions jolted him: "Who made you a prince and a judge over us? Do you intend to kill me as you killed the Egyptian?" The confidence of the self-appointed deliverer turned into fear. One of his own knew his "secret" and soon Pharaoh would, too. Realizing that

he would have to flee, he went to Midian (mainly in northwest Arabia).

Moses in Midian

In noting the flight to Midian the narrative says nothing of the difficulties involved. Like Sinuhe, the Egyptian court official whose flight in about 1960 BCE was narrated in a famous story, Moses undoubtedly had to filter through the "Wall of the Ruler," a series of forts at the eastern border, approximately where the Suez Canal is now located. From there he made his way southeast through extremely desolate country. Unfortunately, the Bible does not specify the part of Midian in which Moses resided. Midian proper was east of the Gulf of Aqaba, in the northern section of Hejaz in Arabia, but there is evidence that some of the Midianite clans crossed over the Arabah (the great valley south of the Dead Sea) and settled in the eastern and southern sections of the Sinai Peninsula.

While Moses was resting at a well, according to the biblical account, seven daughters of the Midianite priest Jethro came to water their father's flocks. Other shepherds arrived and drove the girls away so they could to water their own flocks. Again Moses showed his courage and prowess as a warrior, because he took on the shepherds (perhaps with the girls' help) and routed them. Moses stayed on with Jethro and eventually married Zipporah, one of the daughters. In assuming the responsibility for Jethro's flocks,

Moses roamed the wilderness looking for pasture.

One day at the base of a mountain, his attention was attracted by a flaming bush, but, oddly, it was not consumed. He had seen bushes brilliant with flamelike blossoms, but this phenomenon was different. So he turned aside to investigate it. Before he could do so, he was warned to come no closer. Then he was ordered to remove his sandals because he was standing on holy ground.

Regardless of how one interprets the burning bush, the important fact is that Moses was conscious of an encounter with the deity. This God, who claimed to be the God of Abraham, Isaac, and Jacob, was calling him to deliver the Hebrews from Egypt. Although on his own he had been zealous to help his own people, now that he was commissioned to deliver them, he expressed doubt concerning his qualifications. The underlying reason was probably fear—he had fled from Seti I, and he did not relish confrontation with Ramses II. God reassured Moses that in the future he and the Hebrews would worship at this mountain. Then Moses asked to know the name of the Deity commissioning him. The God of the fathers had been known mostly as El 'Elyon (God Most High) or El Shaddai (God of the Mountain or Almighty God), and also as the Lord, but he identified himself to Moses as YHWH (derived from the Hebrew verb "to be") and gave instructions that he was to be called by his new name from then on. This revelation enabled Moses to understand the God of the Hebrews as the sovereign Lord over nature and the nations of the world.

Even after further assurances, Moses was still reluctant to accept YHWH's call and pleaded for release because he was a stammerer. YHWH acknowledged the defect but promised to help him express himself. Awed by his assignment, Moses made a final desperate plea, "Oh, my Lord, send, I pray, some other person." Although angry at Moses, YHWH refused to yield. Moses would still be God's representative, but his golden-tongued brother Aaron would be the spokesman. Apparently, Moses was ready to play the role of God to Pharaoh providing Aaron would serve as his prophet. He returned to Jethro and requested permission to visit his people in Egypt, but he did not disclose that he had been commissioned by YHWH.

MOSES AND PHARAOH

Ramses II became king as a teenager and reigned for 67 years. He aspired to defeat the Hittites and control all of Syria, but in the fifth year of his reign Ramses walked into a Hittite trap laid for him at Kadesh, on the Orontes River in Syria. By sheer determination he fought his way out, but in the light of his purpose the battle was an utter failure. Yet Ramses, like all the pharaohs, claimed to be divine. Therefore, the defeat had to be interpreted as a marvellous victory in which he alone subdued the Hittites. His wounded ego expressed itself in massive building operations throughout Egypt, and before his reign ended the boast of his success literally filled acres of wall space.

It was probably only a few years after the Kadesh incident that Moses and Aaron confronted Ramses with their demand, "Thus says the Lord, the God of Israel, 'Let my people go.' " As a god in human form, Ramses was unaccustomed to taking orders from lesser gods, let alone an unknown like YHWH. "Who is the Lord," he inquired, "that I should heed his voice and let Israel go? I do not know the Lord, and moreover I will not let Israel go." Thus the stage was set for a long struggle between a distrustful ruler with an outsized ego and a prophet with a new understanding of YHWH and his power.

Ramses increased the oppression of the Hebrews by the fiendish plan of requiring them to gather the straw binder for the bricks and still produce the same quota each day. Some Hebrews rebuffed Moses, and in frustration he asked the Lord, "Why didst thou ever send me?" Moses' doubt was allayed by God's promise to take action against Pharaoh. Scholars differ widely concerning the narrative about the plagues. Some claim that three sources have been combined, but more recent scholarship finds only the two traditions. While granting that some of the plagues had a core of historicity, older critics tended to discount the present accounts as fantastic stories with pious decorations. A recent school of research suggests that, notwithstanding some later additions, all the plagues probably had a historical core.

The basic cause, according to one interpretation, was an unusually high flooding of the Nile. The White Nile originates in the lake region of east central Africa, known today as Uganda. The flow is fairly even throughout the year because of consistent equatorial rains. The Blue Nile, however, originates in the headwaters of the Ethiopian highlands, and it varies from a small stream to a raging torrent. At the time Moses was bargaining with Ramses, excessively heavy summer rains in Ethiopia washed powdery, carmine-red soil from the slopes of the hills. Around the Lake Tana region the blood-red torrent picked up bright red algae (known as flagellates) and their bacteria. Because there were no dams at that time, the Nile flowed blood-red all the way to the Mediterranean. It probably reached the delta region in August. Thus, this rare natural event, it is held, set in motion a series of conditions that continued until the following March.

During these months Moses used the plagues of the frogs, gnats, mosquitoes, cattle murrain, boils, hail, locusts, and thick darkness to increase the pressure on Ramses. At first the King was adamant. The Hebrews were not the only disgruntled slaves, and, if he agreed to let them go, then other groups would want the same privilege. To protect his building program, he had to suppress the slave rebellion at its outset. Yet he could not discount the effect of the plagues, and grudgingly he began to acknowledge YHWH's power. As an expedient attempt to restore order, he offered to let the Hebrews sacrifice in Goshen. When this failed, he suggested that they make offerings to YHWH at the edge of the Egyptian border. Moses, however, insisted on a three-day journey into the wilderness. Pharaoh countered by allowing the Hebrew men to make the journey, but this, too, was rejected. As his final offer Pharaoh agreed to let the people go. He would keep the livestock, however, as the guarantee of their return. Moses spurned the condition, and in anger Pharaoh drove him out. After nine rounds with Pharaoh it appeared that the deliverance of the Hebrews was no nearer, but, in contrast to his earlier periods of doubt and frustration, Moses showed no despair. Apparently, he had an inner assurance that Pharaoh would not have the last word.

FROM GOSHEN TO SINAI

Chapters 11–14 of Exodus comprise an exceedingly complex section, and at times the traditions have contradictory statements. The drama is more blurred than usual, and scholars vary tremendously in their interpretation of the material. One tradition notes that Pharaoh was shaken when death took his son, and he ordered the Hebrews to leave. Another source indicates that Moses used the period of mourning for the first-born son as the occasion for fleeing secretly from the country. In either case, it is clear that Pharaoh finally had his forces pursue the Hebrews. Although tradition interpreted the Hebrew text to claim that about 2,000,000 people left Egypt, interpretation by critical methods reduces the number to 15,000 or so.

The Egyptian army cornered them at the Sea of Reeds (papyrus), which barred their exit to the east. Later Jewish tradition understood the body of water to be the Red Sea, and this erroneous interpretation persists today, even in some of the most recent English translations of the Bible. Scholars disagree as to the precise location of the Reed Sea, but, because papyrus grows only in freshwater, it was probably a shallow lake in the far northeastern corner of Egypt.

Hemmed in by the Egyptians, the people vented their complaints on Moses. According to one tradition, Moses shared their uneasiness, and he called to the Lord for help. Another account claims that Moses confidently challenged them to be calm and watch for deliverance. A strong east wind blew all night, creating a dry corridor through the lake and permitting the Hebrews to cross. The pursuing Egyptians were destroyed when the waters returned. The timing of this natural event gave the final answer to Pharaoh's arrogant question, "Who is YHWH?" Safely on the other side, Moses and his sister Miriam led the people in a victory song of praise to YHWH (Ex. 15:1–21). The style of the poetry is similar to

Moses commanded the waters of the Red Sea to return, drowning the Egyptian army. Hulton Archive/Getty Images

that of 14th-century Canaanite literature, and there is every reason to believe that the poem virtually preserves the original form of the song, with its refrain, "Sing to the Lord, for he has triumphed gloriously; the horse and his rider he has thrown into the sea."

The route of the Hebrews is contested by scholars, but the most likely possibility is the southern route to Jabal Mūsā, the traditional location of Mt. Sinai (Horeb), in the granite range at the southern tip of the Sinai Peninsula. The journey there traversed some extremely desolate country, and Moses had to contend with bitter complaints about the lack of water and food. Finally, however, he brought the people to "the mountain of God," where YHWH had appeared to him in the burning bush.

The Covenant at Sinai

During the 14th century BCE the Hittites of Asia Minor made a number of treaties with neighbouring rulers who came under their control. The agreement was not between equals, but between the

Hittite king (the suzerain) and a subordinate ruler (the vassal). In the prologue the Hittite ruler described himself as "the great king," the one granting the treaty. Then followed a historical survey of relationships between the Hittite suzerain and his vassal. Special attention to the kindnesses shown the underling by the overlord was intended to remind the vassal of his obligation to abide by the treaty stipulations. The basic requirement was an oath of loyalty. Because Egypt was involved with the Hittites in the international politics of the time, Moses probably learned about the Hittite treaty form during his years in the Egyptian court.

The appearance of YHWH in a terrific storm at Mt. Sinai, narrated in chapters 19 and 20 of Exodus, was a revelatory experience for Moses, just as the burning bush had been. Somehow he realized that the Hittite treaty was an accurate analogy of the relationship between YHWH and the Hebrews. The Lord had a claim upon them because he had delivered them. The only proper response to his love and care would be a pledge of obedience to his will. Scholars have tended to date the Ten Commandments, or Decalogue (contained in the revelation at Sinai), after the conquest of Canaan, but there is absolutely nothing in these guidelines to indicate their origin in an agricultural context. More likely they were the stipulations in the covenant ceremony at Mt. Sinai.

Because YHWH was proclaimed the only true God, one of the first commands was appropriately a ban against all other gods. Authorities have debated whether or not this understanding was interpreted as monotheism. Most certainly it was not the philosophical monotheism of later periods, but it was a practical monotheism in that any gods recognized by other nations were under YHWH's control. Inasmuch as he had brought them into being and authorized their presence in his council, he was Lord over all gods and nations.

Another early command has been taken to mean a ban on making images of other gods, but originally the prohibition applied to representations of YHWH himself. Worship in the ancient world was unthinkable without some idol or image, making the uniqueness of Moses' restriction all the more evident. YHWH is the unimageable Deity who cannot be represented in material forms. Because YHWH had revealed the meaning of his name to Moses, it was fitting that the Decalogue should also prohibit any magical or unethical use of his name. Undoubtedly the ideas underlying the other commands came from the religious culture of his day, but they were raised to a significantly higher level because of the holy, righteous character of YHWH. Moses realized that, if the Covenant people were to have a stable, just society, they would have to emulate their God. Concern for his creatures would mean respect for them as persons. Murder, adultery, theft, lying, and covetousness would never be legitimate because they lead to chaos and breakdown of the community. Moreover, inasmuch as YHWH had been concerned to protect the powerless Hebrews in Egypt, they in turn would have to guarantee justice for the orphans, widows, resident aliens, and any other disadvantaged persons under their jurisdiction.

On confirmation of the Covenant, Moses and the people faced the task of living by the stipulations. This called for interpretations of the commands, so Moses began issuing ordinances for specific situations. Many of these he drew from the case law of his day, but insight as to their selection and application probably came in the "tent of meeting" (a simple sanctuary tent pitched outside the camp), where YHWH spoke to Moses "face to face, as a man speaks to his friend." Breaches of the Covenant necessitated means of atonement, which in turn meant provision of a priesthood to function at sacrifices and in worship. In short, the rudiments of the whole Hebrew cult, according to tradition, originated at Sinai. At Jethro's suggestion Moses instituted a system of judges and hearings to regulate the civil aspects of the community. It was at Sinai, perhaps, where the people were organized into 12 tribes.

One of Moses' most remarkable characteristics was his concern for the Hebrews, in spite of their stubborn, rebellious ways. When they reverted to worshipping a golden calf, YHWH was ready to disown them and begin anew with Moses and his descendants. Moses rejected the offer, however, and later, when pleading for the forgiveness of the people, he even asked to have his own name blotted out of the Lord's book of remembrance if the Lord would not forgive them.

MOUNT SINAI

Mount Sinai (Hebrew: Har Sinai; Arabic: Jabal Mūsā) is a granitic peak of the south-central Sinai Peninsula, Janūb Sīnā' (South Sinai) muḥāfaẓah (governorate), Egypt. It is renowned as the principal site of divine revelation in Jewish history, where God is purported to have appeared to Moses and given him the Ten Commandments (Exodus 20; Deuteronomy 5). According to Jewish tradition, not only the Decalogue but also the entire corpus of biblical text and interpretation was revealed to Moses on Sinai. The mountain is also sacred in both the Christian and Islamic traditions. Because scholars differ as to the route of the Israelite exodus from Egypt and the place-names in the scriptural account cannot be identified in terms of present sites, a positive identification of the biblical Mount Sinai cannot be made. Mount Sinai itself, however, has long been accepted as the site in the traditions of Judaism, Christianity, and Islam.

The mountain, which rises to 2,285 metres (7,497 feet) above sea level, was under Israeli administration from the Six-Day War of 1967 until 1979, when it was returned to Egypt. It has become an important pilgrim and tourist site.

FROM SINAI TO TRANSJORDAN

After leaving Mt. Sinai, Moses faced increasing resistance and frustration, according to the narrative in the book of Numbers. Apparently his virility did not diminish during these years because he took a Cushite woman as his second wife. But Miriam, with the support of Aaron, opposed the marriage. At Kadesh-barnea the pessimistic majority report of the spies who had been sent out to reconnoitre thwarted Moses' desire to march north and conquer the land of Canaan. When he urged the people to reconsider their action they almost stoned him. But here again, according to tradition, Moses interceded for the people with YHWH, who threatened to destroy them and raise up another and greater nation. In one instance, however, tradition recalled that Moses' anger overrode his compassion. At Meribah, probably in the area of Kadesh-barnea, Moses addressed the complaining people as rebels and struck a rock twice in anger, whereupon water flowed forth for the thirsty people. He had been angry before in defense of God's name, honour, and cause, but this time his anger stemmed from utter frustration with his contentious people. Although tradition interpreted this lapse as the reason why God would not permit Moses to enter Canaan, the remarkable fact is that Moses was able to bear up under such continuous pressure.

In Transjordan the new states of Edom and Moab, vassals of the Midianites, rejected Moses' request for passage. He wisely circled east of them and moved north to conquer Sihon, king of the Amorites, and Og, king of Bashan. Moses permitted some of the tribes to settle in Transjordan, a decision that evoked opposition from the Moabites and their Midianite overlords. They hired the Syrian diviner Balaam to put a curse on the Hebrews, but instead he pronounced a blessing. Some scholars interpret this as proof that Balaam was a convert to worship of the Israelites' god. If this was indeed the case, he must have reverted later on, because the biblical tradition implies that Balaam incited his former employers to weaken the Hebrews by religious seduction. Moses responded to the enmity of the Midianites with a successful holy war against them not long before his death.

As his last official act Moses renewed the Sinai Covenant with those who had survived the wilderness wanderings. From his camp in the Jordan Valley, Moses climbed to a vantage point on Mt. Pisgah. There he viewed the land of promise. The Hebrews never saw him again, and the circumstances of his death and burial remain shrouded in mystery.

MOSES THE MAN

Although time undoubtedly enhanced the portrait of Moses, a basic picture emerges from the sources. Five times the narratives claim that Moses kept written records (Exodus 17:14; 24:4; 34:27–28; Numbers 33:2; and Deuteronomy 31:9,

24–26). Even with a generous interpretation of the extent of these writings, they do not amount to more than a fifth of the total Pentateuch. Therefore, the traditional claim of Mosaic authorship of the whole Pentateuch is untenable. Moses formulated the Decalogue, mediated the Covenant, and began the process of rendering and codifying supplemental interpretations of the Covenant stipulations. Undoubtedly he kept some records, and they served as the core of the growing corpus of law and tradition. In a general sense, therefore, the first five books of the Hebrew Bible can be described as Mosaic. Without him there would have been no Israel and no collection known as Torah.

Moses was a gifted, well-trained person, but his true greatness probably resulted from his personal experience of and relationship with the Lord. This former stammering murderer understood his preservation and destiny as coming from the grace of a merciful Lord who had given him another chance. Moses had an understanding spirit and a forgiving heart because he knew how much YHWH had forgiven him. He was truly humble because he recognized that his gifts and strength came from YHWH.

Because of the uniqueness of his situation, Moses had to function in a number of roles. As God's agent in the deliverance of the Hebrews, he was their prophet and leader. As mediator of the Covenant, he was the founder of the community. As interpreter of the Covenant, he was an organizer and legislator. As intercessor for the people, he was their priest. Moses had a special combination of gifts and graces that made it impossible to replace him. Although his successor, Joshua, and the priest Eleazar, the son of Aaron, tried to do so, together they did not measure up to him. Later prophets were great men who spoke out of the spirit that Moses had, but they were not called to function in so many roles. As tradition claimed, he was indeed the greatest of the prophets, and, as history shows, few of humankind's great personalities outrank him in influence.

CHAPTER 13

RULERS

The people of Israel were intended to form a peaceful, harmonious, and flourishing society within the land of Canaan under the terms of the divine covenant. Yet from the beginning the tensions and discord that Moses had attempted to dispel during the sojourn in the Sinai wilderness threatened this vision. The Israelites, divided into tribes claiming descent from one of the 12 sons of Jacob, fell into cyclical patterns of apostasy. Thus began the period of the judges, tribal leaders whom God called into service to bring the people back to holiness. These cycles of apostasy and redemption, as portrayed in the deuteronomistic history presented by the Tanakh, ultimately spurred the establishment of the kingship for Israel. Saul, the first king, was appointed by the judge Samuel. David, Saul's successor, united the Israelite tribes into a holy kingdom. According to tradition, David was a warrior and poet who was deeply loved by God and established Jerusalem as his capital. His son Solomon was renowned for his wisdom and as the builder not only of great cities but of the first Temple. The current archaeological record does not unambiguously support the biblical account of the so-called House of David. Nevertheless, the figures of David and Solomon and the stories about them remain influential.

DAVID

The first great Israelite king and the founder of the united kingdom over all Israel was David (reigned, according to tradition, *c.* 1000–*c.* 962 BCE) who established a united kingdom over all Israel, with Jerusalem as its capital. In Jewish tradition he became the ideal king, the founder of an enduring dynasty, around whose figure and reign clustered messianic expectations of the people of Israel.

EARLY LIFE

The youngest son of Jesse, the grandson of Boaz and Ruth, David began his career as an aide at the court of Saul, Israel's first king, and became a close friend of Saul's son and heir, Jonathan, and the husband

JUDAEA

Judaea was the southernmost of the three traditional divisions of ancient Palestine. The other two were Galilee in the north and Samaria in the centre. No clearly marked boundary divided Judaea from Samaria, but the town of Beersheba was traditionally the southernmost limit. The region presents a variety of geographic features, but the real core of Judaea was the upper hill country, known as Har Yehuda ("Hills of Judaea"), extending south from the region of Bethel (at present-day Ramallah) to Beersheba and including the area of Jerusalem, Bethlehem, and Hebron.

Before the Israelites entered Palestine, the Canaanites dominated the region, and the town of Hebron was an important centre. When the tribes of Israel entered the country, the tribe of Judah claimed the entire area from just south of the site of Jerusalem into the Negev region (the area south of Beersheba). The tribes of Simeon, Benjamin, and Dan also at one time or another settled some small areas of the region. When David became king of Judah, he captured the old Canaanite (Jebusite) stronghold, Jerusalem, and made it the capital of the united kingdom of the tribes of Israel. After the death of David's son, King Solomon (10th century), the 10 northern tribes separated from Judah, and Jerusalem remained the capital of the kingdom of Judah, which continued until 587/586, when the Babylonians conquered it and destroyed Jerusalem. Later, however, Persian kings permitted captive Jews to return from Babylonia to their native land and to rebuild their temple and the walls of Jerusalem.

After Alexander the Great's conquest of the Middle East, Judah came first under the rule of the Ptolemies and later under that of the Seleucids. Opposition to the Seleucid attempt to suppress the Jewish ancestral faith led to the rise of the family of Jewish leaders known as the Maccabees, who gradually drove the Seleucids from the country and set up a revived kingdom of Judaea. Family disputes, however, led to Roman intervention in 63 BCE. Under Roman control, Herod the Great was made king of Judaea in 37 BCE and later of all Palestine (20–4 BCE). After Herod's death the country was ruled alternately by Herod's direct descendants and by Roman procurators. As a result of the Jewish revolt that broke out in 66 CE, the city of Jerusalem was destroyed (70 CE). The name Judaea is still used to describe approximately the same area in modern Israel.

of Saul's daughter Michal. He so distinguished himself as a warrior against the Philistines that his resultant popularity aroused Saul's jealousy, and a plot was made to kill him. He fled into southern Judah (later called Judaea) and Philistia, on the coastal plain of Palestine, where, with great sagacity and foresight, he began to lay the foundations of his career.

Beginning as an outlaw, with a price on his head, David lived on the desert frontier of Judah. He became the leader and organizer of other outlaws and refugees; and, according to the Bible, ". . . everyone who was in distress, and everyone who was in debt, and everyone who was discontented, gathered to him; and he became captain over them." This group progressively ingratiated itself with the local population by protecting them from other bandits or, in case they had been raided, by pursuing the raiders and restoring the possessions that had been taken. Though sometimes dependent upon the Philistine kings of Gath for protection from the pursuit of King Saul, David managed to retain his status as a patriot in the eyes of his own people in Judah and, even as one who had, indeed, been an innocent and loyal servant of the demented Saul. He also won the favour of many Judaean elders by various politic gestures. Thus, by biding his time, he eventually had himself "invited" to become king, first by Judah in Hebron and later by all Israel, not as a rebel against Saul but as his true successor. This opportunity emerged when Saul and Jonathan were slain while engaged in battle against the Philistines on Mount Gilboa.

KINGSHIP

David entered Hebron, where he was proclaimed king. He had to struggle for a few years against the contending claim and forces of Ishbaal, Saul's surviving son, who had also been crowned king, but the civil war ended with the murder of Ishbaal by his own courtiers and the anointing of David as king over all Israel, including tribes beyond Judah. He proceeded to conquer the walled city of Jerusalem, held by the alien Jebusites, which he made the capital of the new united kingdom, and to which he moved the sacred ark of the Covenant, the supreme symbol of Israelite religion. He defeated the Philistines so thoroughly that they were never again a serious threat to the Israelites' security, and he annexed the coastal region. He went on to establish an empire by becoming the overlord of many small kingdoms bordering on Israel, including Edom, Moab, and Ammon.

David's great success as a warrior and empire builder was marred by family dissensions and political revolts, which were interrelated. To tie together the various groups that constituted his kingdom, David took wives from them and created a harem. The resultant family was an extreme departure from the family in the consanguineal context, the traditional clan structure. David's wives were mostly completely alien to one another, and his children were without the directing support of established social patterns that provided precedents for the resolution of conflict or for establishing the rights of succession. Thus, David's third son, Absalom, murdered the eldest son, Amnon, for the latter's rape of Tamar, the former's sister and the latter's half sister. After a period of exile and then of reconciliation with King David, Absalom used the favour he had gained among the people and some courtiers to launch a rebellion that sent his father fleeing across the Jordan, and that made him master of Jerusalem and the royal harem for a time. Eventually, Absalom's forces were defeated, and he was killed by Joab, David's general, and it was Solomon, born of David's union with Bathsheba, who became the King's eventual heir.

The authors of the biblical accounts, found in books I and 2 Samuel of David's political career display a deep insight into his character. David was a man who could make an indelible personal impression in a specific situation. His doubling of the bride price set by Saul for Michal illustrates this capacity for imaginative action and dramatic publicity. Coupled with this ability to exploit the immediate situation in the service of his momentary requirements, he possessed the knack of making his conduct in particular situations serve his persistent and long-range aims. For example, the two versions of his refusal to assassinate King Saul when he had it in his power to do so (in 1 Samuel 24 and 26) do not simply present

an inspiring example of gallantry in a moment of dramatic confrontation. They also contribute to the enduring reputation of David as a man who, even in his years as an outlaw, had a deep respect for established institutions, especially for the sacred office of the king (who was "the Lord's anointed"). Later, after the death of Saul and Jonathan, David again confirmed this point at a moment in which it was crucially important for him to do so for the sake of his own career. A young Amalekite who came to report Saul's death to David intimated that he had had a share in it. He thought that as the bearer of good news he would be rewarded, but his miscalculation cost him his life. David sensed that in an hour of national disaster the differences between him and Saul were of no importance. He had the Amalekite slain for having laid hands on the Lord's anointed, and with his men he performed the mourning rites for Saul and Jonathan, memorializing them in a deeply moving elegy. Somewhat later, after David had become king in Hebron, he learned that the men of Jabesh-Gilead, a town across the Jordan that had been fanatically attached to King Saul, had recovered the bodies of Saul and Jonathan to give them honourable burial. David sent the town a message commending it for its act of reverent loyalty, which had been undertaken at great risk. His action in this episode also was both political and sincere, and it was eminently suited to the situation in which the conciliation of all Israelites was of the greatest

King David, as a young boy, won the legendary showdown with Goliath and eventually became one of the great kings of Israel. Kean Collection/Archive Photos/Getty Images

importance for both the career of David and the survival of the nation.

In the case of Absalom's rebellion, a poignant conflict took place between parental love and political power. When the news of his son's slaying came to him he broke down into deep grief and lamented, "O my son Absalom, my son, my son Absalom! Would I had died instead of you!" But he was rebuked by his general Joab (who had ignored the King's direct order and had the young rebel killed) as showing more concern for his enemies than his supporters and risking the loss of public esteem and so of his rule. Thereupon he returned with his old energy and wile to the task of uniting and reconciling the various factions in Israel, including putting down another revolt, this time by Sheba, the son of Bichri, of the tribe of Benjamin.

POLITICAL ACHIEVEMENT

David was Israel's first successful king. He united all of the Israelite tribes, became the effective ruler over all, and was the founder of an enduring dynasty. Thus, he succeeded where King Saul had failed and attained a unique place in Israel's history and tradition. The primary sources for the history of David's reign and of the succession are 2 Samuel 9–20 and 1 Kings 11–22. It is generally agreed that this "history" was written quite soon after the reign of David. Known as the "Family History of David," and also as "The Succession History," it is an especially clear mirror

in which to study the problems David faced in displacing charismatic political leadership and authority with hereditary monarchy.

For centuries before David's rise to kingship, Israelites had been held together in loose tribal confederacies comprising several clans. Both the revolt of Absalom, which necessitated David's exile for a time, and the grasp of the eldest surviving son, Adonijah, for the succession, in competition with the sponsors of Solomon, very nearly succeeded because they appealed to traditions of local and tribal authority, winning the support of many who were disillusioned with the swift centralization of power that had accompanied the establishment of the Davidic empire. In 2 Samuel 15, for example, Absalom, in his bid for support, says that he would like to exercise judgment in the premonarchic manner, as an elder in the gate. Ironically, he was attempting to displace his father by the same means by which David had so successfully risen to power (i.e., appealing to local clans). Later, after Solomon's reign had ended, the united kingdom broke up when these tribalistic traditions again reasserted themselves. The relentless movement of social evolution made impossible the reestablishment of a tribal society, but the vitality of the tribal heritage was still very strong, both in David's day and later. Thus, there was a basic instability in his position. He faced the problem of winning consent for and establishing the legitimacy of his office, for it was an imported novelty in the social structures and traditions of Israel, on the model of the ancient Near Eastern kingships.

David's position in the tribal units that made up Judah was secure, for he had united them and had risen to authority over Judah through his adroit use of the indigenous social and political instruments of its clan structures. Therefore, Judah accepted his legitimacy and never disowned his dynasty. He sought to win the consent of all Israel, first by the decisively successful war against the Philistines, which made the whole land secure, and then by establishing the city of Jerusalem as the centre both of Israel's political power and of its worship. On the political level this effort was insufficient, for the kingdom was divided after the death of Solomon. But on the religious and cultic level, it did eventually succeed, for Jerusalem, the "city of David," became the Holy City for all Jews, and the messiah, "the anointed one" of the house of David, a sign of the relationship between the God of Israel and his people.

RELIGIOUS ROLE AND SIGNIFICANCE

In Israel's religious tradition the royal line, or "house," of David became a primary symbol of the bond between God and the nation. The king was the mediator between the deity and his people. As in many ancient traditions, the king was thought of as both divine and human. The English word messiah is derived from *hameshiach* ("the anointed one"), the title of the kings of the line of David. Thus, in later times of disaster, Israel began to wait for a messiah, a new mediator of the power of God that would redeem the people and its land. David lived in the memory of his people in a double way: as the great founder of their political power and as the symbol of a central facet of their religious faith.

The process by which David achieved this status for himself, his house, and his city may be traced in 2 Samuel 5–8. When David took Jerusalem, he assumed the rule over its inhabitants and their religious institutions with the cult centred on Mt. Zion. The previous Jebusite ruler had been both king and high priest, and played the role of mediator between the city and its deity. There was no precedent for such a mediative and priestly role of kings in Israelite religion, nor of walled cities as the seat of government and worship. Apparently, David simply took over the Jebusite cult on Zion and adapted it to his own use. Beginning with David and throughout the entire period of the monarchy, for about four centuries, Israel's worship on Zion gave a central place to the king, not simply as officiant but substantively, as the figure who in his office and person embodied the relationship between God and the nation. In contrast, the premonarchic worship of Israel, at Shechem and elsewhere, had featured a Covenant between God and the people, through their tribal heads, as the bond in the relationship. By taking over and adapting Jerusalem's ancient cult, David provided Israel with a new worship, one that featured his own status and its sacral significance.

Israel's God was named YHWH. David made this name the supreme name for deity in Jerusalem (previously perhaps "Salem," as the name "Jerusalem" may be derived from the phrase "City of Salem"), to indicate his conquest of the city. All former names and titles of deity became attributes or titles of the God of Israel, the conqueror—for example, El 'Elyon (God Most High). While the Israelite name for God displaced all others, the substance of the worship remained similar: YHWH had created the world and ruled the nations; he had established kingship as the sign and means of his universal rule; and Zion was the seat of his chosen king, David, his anointed. YHWH himself was enthroned on Zion, and his king sat at his right hand as his regent. David thus continued the line of king-priests that had reigned in Jerusalem from the founding of the city, and, according to a legend that may have developed in this context, the patriarch Abraham had been blessed by Melchizedek, an earlier representative of the line, when he had presented tithes to him.

Having adopted the ancient cult of Jerusalem as a means of giving sacral significance to his royal status and having devoted it to YHWH, by whose power he had conquered, David also made an important move to make the new shrine and its worship relate to the premonarchic experience of Israel. He brought the ark to Jerusalem and established it as the central object of the cult. According to tradition, it had travelled with Israel in the wilderness and led the way into the land. It was a rectangular wooden box, originally without a cover, that established and located the presence of YHWH with the people of Israel. The ark was carried into battle to demonstrate that YHWH fought for Israel, and it was carried in the wilderness, to show that he travelled with his people. In worship, it was apparently carried in procession in the pilgrimages that were features of the annual feasts. It was a sign and even the embodiment of YHWH's presence. David could have chosen no better way of making premonarchic Israelites accept the royal cult on Zion than by incorporating the ark, with all its ancient associations, into the new ceremonial.

David's adaptation of the Zion cult, with its understanding of kingship as the substance and means of the presence of God on earth, was to have momentous consequences for the religious history of humankind, notably for the experience of the entire Western world. Because of it Jerusalem became the Holy City and David became the prototype of an awaited messiah. As symbol of the Messiah, the return of David, or the coming of David's "son" stood for the reassertion of the divine rule and presence in history: to judge it, to redeem it, to renew it. David thus became the symbol of a fulfillment in the future, final peace.

SOLOMON

Solomon (flourished 10th century BCE) was the son and successor of David and traditionally regarded as the greatest king of Israel. He maintained his dominions with military strength and established Israelite colonies outside his kingdom's borders. The crowning achievement of his vast building program was the famous temple at his capital, Jerusalem.

Background

Nearly all that is known of Solomon comes from the Bible (especially 1 Kings 1–11 and 2 Chronicles 1–9). His father, David, was a self-made king, who, against great odds, founded the Judaean dynasty and carved out an empire from the border of Egypt to the Euphrates River. His first and greatest enemies were the Philistines, who controlled Palestine and kept the Tyrians and Sidonians from prospering on the sea. By training the Israelite infantry, especially the bowmen, he proved more than a match for Philistine and other foes who employed horses and chariots. In addition, David made common cause with King Hiram of Tyre, forming a land and sea alliance that endured into Solomon's reign. Solomon, accordingly, inherited a considerable empire, along with a Phoenician ally of prime importance for naval and merchant-marine operations.

Solomon's mother was Bathsheba, formerly the wife of David's Hittite general, Uriah. She proved to be adept at court intrigue. David seems to have been senile toward the close of his reign, and one of his wives, Haggith, tried to execute a plot in which her son, Adonijah, would be appointed as David's successor. Adonijah enlisted the aid of powerful allies: David's senior general, Joab, Abiathar the priest, and several other court figures. It was only through the efforts of Bathsheba, in concert with the prophet Nathan, that Solomon, who was younger than several of his brothers, was anointed king while David was still alive.

Empire Builder

As soon as he acceded to the throne, Solomon consolidated his position by liquidating his opponents ruthlessly, one by one. Once rid of his foes, he established his friends in the key posts of the military, governmental, and religious institutions. In an ancient Middle Eastern empire, this was almost the only means of establishing stable government.

Solomon also strengthened his position through marital alliances. Although the astonishing harem of Solomon—700 wives and 300 concubines—recorded in 1 Kings is no doubt an exaggeration of popular tradition, the figures do indicate his position as a grand monarch. Such a ménage brought prestige as well as pleasure, and the marriages were a form of diplomacy. He wed the sisters and daughters of kings from far and wide, cementing alliances of arms and trade to facilitate his establishment of a huge commercial empire. One of his brides was the daughter of an Egyptian pharaoh. The pharaoh captured and burned down the Canaanite city of Gezer and gave it to his son-in-law Solomon.

Like all empire builders, Solomon maintained his dominions with military strength. In addition to infantry, he had at his disposal impressive chariotry and cavalry. 2 Chronicles 8 recounts Solomon's successful military operations in Syria, where his targets included Tadmor-Palmyra, a caravan oasis city in the desert, midway between Syria and Mesopotamia. His aim was the control of a great overland trading route. To consolidate his interests in the province, he planted Israelite colonies to look after military, administrative, and commercial matters. Such colonies, often including cities in which chariots and provisions were kept, were in the long tradition of combining mercantile and military personnel to take care of their sovereign's trading interests far from home. Megiddo, a town located at the pass through the Carmel range connecting the coastal plain with the Plain of Esdraelon, is the best preserved example of one of Solomon's cities. The remains of stalls for 450 horses discovered in Megiddo show

King Solomon bartered with the Queen of Sheba for products and trade routes, but tales include a possible romance between the two leaders as well. Hulton Archive/Getty Images

that the figures of 1,400 chariots and 12,000 horses given for Solomon's forces in 1 Kings are scarcely exaggerated. (Some scholars question whether these are horse stalls or shop stalls.) The network of Solomon's far-flung trading posts eventually formed the nucleus of the first great Jewish Diaspora.

Palestine was destined to be an important centre because of its strategic location for trade by land and sea. By land, it alone connects Asia and Africa, and, along with Egypt, it is the only area with ports on the Atlantic-Mediterranean and Red Sea–Indian Ocean waterways. It was Solomon who fulfilled the commercial destiny of Palestine and brought it to its greatest heights. The nature of his empire was predominantly commercial—it served him and friendly rulers to increase trade by land and sea. The Phoenician king Hiram of Tyre, for example, needed the port of Ezion-geber, near Elath on the Gulf of Aqaba, which leads into the Red Sea and thence into the Indian Ocean. The joint merchant-marine expeditions of Hiram and Solomon sailed practically to the ends of the known world.

A celebrated episode in the reign of Solomon is the visit of the Queen of Sheba. Her southern Arabian kingdom lay along the Red Sea route into the Indian Ocean, and her terrain was rich in gold, frankincense, and myrrh. Solomon needed her products and her trade routes for maintaining his commercial network. She needed Solomon's cooperation for marketing her goods in the Mediterranean via his Palestinian ports. Legend makes much of a romance between the Queen of Sheba and Solomon, for his granting her "all that she desired, whatever she asked" (1 Kings 10:13) has been interpreted to include an offspring.

SOLOMON'S TEMPLE

The demand for fortresses and garrison cities throughout his homeland and empire made it necessary for Solomon to embark on a vast building program. The prosperity of the nation made such a program possible. He was especially lavish with his capital, Jerusalem, where he erected a city wall, a construction called the Millo, the royal palace, and the famous Temple. Around Jerusalem (but not in the Holy City itself), he built facilities, including shrines, for the main groups of foreigners on trading missions in Israel. Later generations, in less secure and less prosperous times, destroyed those shrines around Jerusalem in a parochial spirit that could not accommodate itself to Solomon's ecumenical outlook. Solomon's Temple was to assume an importance far beyond what its dimensions might suggest, for its site became the only central shrine for Judaism and early Christianity.

The vigour of Solomon's building program made it oppressive. For example, men had to put in one month out of every three in forced labour. In theory, such labour was to be performed by the Canaanites—not by the noble Hebrew tribesmen, who were supposed to be the administrators, priests, and fighters.

Temple of Jerusalem

The First Temple was constructed, according to the biblical account, during the reign of David's son, Solomon, as a place for the Ark containing the tablets on which the Law was written. Other sanctuaries retained their religious functions, however, until Josiah (reigned c. 640–609 BCE) abolished them and established the Temple of Jerusalem as the only acceptable place of sacrifice.

The Temple suffered at the hands of Nebuchadrezzar II of Babylonia, who removed the Temple treasures in 604 and 597 BCE and totally destroyed the building in 587/586. This destruction and the deportations of Jews to Babylonia in 586 and 582 were seen as fulfillments of prophecy and, therefore, strengthened Judaic religious beliefs and awakened the hope for the reestablishment of the independent Jewish state. Cyrus II, founder of the Achaemenian dynasty of Persia and conqueror of Babylonia, in 538 BCE issued an order allowing exiled Jews to return to Jerusalem and rebuild the Temple. There is no known detailed plan of the Second Temple, which was constructed as a modest version of the original building. It was surrounded by two courtyards with chambers, gates, and a public square. It did not include the ritual objects of the First Temple; of special significance was the loss of the Ark itself. Ritual was elaborate and was conducted by well-organized families of priests and Levites. During the Persian and Hellenistic (4th–3rd century BCE) periods, the Temple generally was respected, and in part subsidized, by Judaea's foreign rulers. Antiochus IV Epiphanes, however, plundered it in 169 BCE and desecrated it in 167 BCE by commanding that sacrifices be made to Zeus on an altar built for him. This final act touched off the Hasmonean revolt, during which Judas Maccabaeus cleansed and rededicated the Temple. During the Roman conquest, Pompey entered (63 BCE) the Holy of Holies but left the Temple intact. In 54 BCE, however, Crassus plundered the Temple treasury.

Of major importance was the rebuilding of the Second Temple begun by Herod the Great, king (37 BCE–4 CE) of Judaea. Construction began in 20 BCE and lasted for 46 years. The area of the Temple Mount was doubled and surrounded by a wall with gates. The Temple was raised, enlarged, and faced with white stone. The new Temple square served as a gathering place, and its porticoes sheltered merchants and money changers. A stone fence (soreg) and a rampart (ḥel) surrounded the consecrated area forbidden to Gentiles. The Herodian Temple was again the centre of Israelite life. It was not only the focus of religious ritual but also the repository of the Holy Scriptures and other national literature and the meeting place of the Sanhedrin, the highest court of Jewish law during the Roman period. The rebellion against Rome that began in 66 CE soon focused on the Temple and effectively ended with the Temple's destruction on the 9th/10th of Av, 70 CE. All that remained of the Second Temple was a portion of the Western Wall (also called the Wailing Wall), which continues to be the focus of Jewish aspirations and pilgrimage. Made part of the wall surrounding the Muslim Dome of the Rock and Al-Aqṣā Mosque in 691 CE, it returned to Jewish control in 1967.

But Solomon's demands were such that there were not enough Canaanites to go around, so that Israelites were forced to do menial labour for the crown.

Solomon was a vigorous administrator, and he realized that the old division of the nation into 12 tribes posed a threat to the unity of the realm because the tribal feeling that was retained was not for the good of the state. Accordingly, he redivided the realm into 12 administrative districts, deviating, for the most part, from the tribal boundaries. The figure of 12 was retained because each district was to "support the palace" (i.e., shoulder federal obligations) for one of the 12 months in the year. Each district had its royally appointed governor, and a chief ruled over the 12 governors. Another important but unpopular appointee of the king was the chief of taxation. Taxes were exacted most commonly in the form of forced labour and in kind.

His Legendary Wisdom

Solomon also became famous as a sage. When two harlots each claimed to be the mother of the same baby, he determined the real mother by observing each woman's reaction to the prospect of dividing the child into two halves. Solomon was deemed wiser than all the sages of Egypt and the Middle East—even wiser than some ancient paragons of wisdom. The biblical Book of Proverbs contains collections of aphorisms and other wise teachings attributed to him. Solomon was also famed as a poet who composed 1,005 songs. The biblical Song of Solomon is (spuriously) attributed to him in the opening verse. His reputation as a great lover, reflected in the size of his harem, is appropriately a major theme in the Song of Solomon. Post-biblical tradition attributed later works to him: the apocryphal Wisdom of Solomon, on the one hand, and the *Odes of Solomon* and *Psalms of Solomon,* on the other, are tributes to him as sage and poet.

Decline of the Kingdom

Solomon's personal prestige and genius were required to perpetuate the powerful nation he had acquired from his father and then further strengthened. It is suspected that the increase in Israel's wealth was matched by an increase in extravagance and that the wealth was not diffused to the people. It is also considered possible that Solomon's treatment of the northern tribes showed favouritism to his own tribe of Judah. When his son Rehoboam succeeded him, the northern tribes wanted to know his policy concerning the burdens borne by the people. Rehoboam ill-advisedly announced a harsher course, whereupon the northern tribes seceded and formed their own Kingdom of Israel, leaving the descendants of Solomon with the southern Kingdom of Judah. Thus Solomon's empire was lost beyond recall, and even the homeland was split into two, often hostile, kingdoms.

CHAPTER 14

PROPHETS

The kingdom fell into disunity after Solomon's death. The separation of God's chosen into two kingdoms—the kingdoms of Israel in the north and Judah in the south—culminated in invasion and exile first of Israel by the Assyrians in 722 and then of Judah 150 years later. The inhabitants of both were repeatedly warned of the Lord's wrath and impending punishment by several prophetic figures who, with few exceptions (e.g., Amos), exhorted the people to return to the Lord.

ELIJAH

The first prominent prophet of the divided kingdom was Elijah (flourished 9th century BCE). He ranks with Moses in saving the religion of YHWH from being corrupted by the nature worship of Baal. Elijah's name means "YHWH is my God" and is spelled Elias in some versions of the Bible. The story of his prophetic career in the northern kingdom of Israel during the reigns of Kings Ahab and Ahaziah is told in 1 Kings 17–19 and 2 Kings 1–2. Elijah claimed that there was no reality except the God of Israel, stressing monotheism to the people with possibly unprecedented emphasis. He is commemorated by Christians on July 20 and is recognized as a prophet by Islam.

HISTORICAL SETTING

The Israelite king Omri had allied himself with the Phoenician cities of the coast, and his son Ahab was married to Jezebel, daughter of Ethbaal, king of Tyre and Sidon. Jezebel, with her Tyrian courtiers and a large contingent of pagan priests and prophets, propagated her native religion in a sanctuary built for Baal in the royal city of Samaria. This meant that the Israelites accepted Baal as well as YHWH, putting YHWH on a par with a nature-god whose supreme manifestations were the elements and biological fertility, celebrated often in an orgiastic cult. Jezebel's policies intensified the gradual contamination of the religion of YHWH by the Canaanite religion of Baal, a process made easier by the sapping of the Israelites' faith in YHWH.

STORY

Elijah was from Tishbe in Gilead. The narrative in 1 Kings relates how he suddenly appears during Ahab's reign to proclaim a drought in punishment of the cult of Baal that Jezebel was promoting in Israel at YHWH's expense. Later Elijah meets 450 prophets of Baal in a contest of strength on Mount Carmel to determine which deity is the true God of Israel. Sacrifices are placed on an altar to Baal and one to YHWH. The pagan prophets' ecstatic appeals to Baal to kindle the wood on his altar are unsuccessful, but Elijah's prayers to YHWH are answered by a fire on his altar. This outcome is taken as decisive by the Israelites, who slay the priests and prophets of Baal under Elijah's direction. The drought thereupon ends with the falling of rain.

Elijah flees the wrath of the vengeful Jezebel by undertaking a pilgrimage to Mount Horeb (Sinai), where he is at first disheartened in his struggle and then miraculously renewed. In a further narrative, King Ahab has a man named

Elijah (foreground) *is recognized as a prophet in Judaism as well as Christianity and Islam.* SuperStock/Getty Images

Naboth condemned to death in order to gain possession of his vineyard. Ahab's judicial murder of Naboth and confiscation of his vineyard arouse Elijah as the upholder of the moral law, as before he had come forward as the champion of monotheism. Elijah denounces Ahab for his crimes, asserting that all men are subject to the law of God and are therefore equals. Later Ahab's son, King Azariah, appeals to Baal to heal him of an illness, and Elijah once more upholds the exclusive rights of YHWH by bringing down "fire from heaven." After bestowing his mantle on his successor, Elisha, the prophet Elijah is taken up to heaven in a whirlwind.

ELIJAH'S CUP

During the family seder dinner on Passover, a fifth ceremonial cup of wine is poured. It is left untouched in honour of Elijah, who, according to tradition, will arrive one day as an unknown guest to herald the advent of the Messiah. During the seder dinner, biblical verses are read while the door is briefly opened to welcome Elijah, who, it is further said, will resolve all controversial questions connected with the Law. In this way the seder dinner not only commemorates the historical redemption from Egyptian bondage of the Jewish people but also calls to mind their future redemption when Elijah and the Messiah shall appear.

THEOLOGICAL SIGNIFICANCE

One of the most important moments in the history of monotheism is the climax of Elijah's struggle with Baalism. His momentous words, "If YHWH is God, follow him, but if Baal, then follow him"— especially when taken with the prayer "Hear me, YHWH, that this people may know that you, YHWH, are God"—show that more is at stake than simply allotting to divinities their particular spheres of influence. The true question is whether YHWH or Baal is God, simply and universally. Elijah's words proclaim that there is no reality except the God of Israel, there are no other beings entitled to the name of divinity. The acclamation of the people, "YHWH, he is God" expresses a fully conscious monotheism,

never before perhaps brought home to them so clearly.

Elijah's deepest prophetic experience takes place on his pilgrimage to Horeb, where he learns that God is not in the storm, the earthquake, or the lightning. Nature, so far from being God's embodiment, is not even an adequate symbol. God is invisible and spiritual and is best known in the intellectual word of revelation, "the still, small voice." The transcendence of God receives here one of its earliest expressions. Elijah's story also expresses for the first time a thought that was to dominate Hebrew prophecy: in contrast to the bland hopes of the people, salvation is bestowed only on a "remnant," those purified by God's judgment. The theme of the later prophets, that morality must be at the heart of ritual worship, is also taught by Elijah, who upholds the unity of law and religion against the despotic cruelty of a king influenced by a pagan wife. Elijah's work may also be regarded as a protest against every effort to find religious experience in self-induced ecstasy and sensual frenzy rather than in a faith linked with reason and morality.

ISAIAH

The next significant Hebrew prophet was Isaiah (flourished 8th century BCE). His call to prophecy in about 742 BCE coincided with the beginnings of the westward expansion of the Assyrian empire, which threatened Israel and which Isaiah proclaimed to be a warning from God to a godless people.

Isaiah's Vision

The earliest recorded event in his life is his call to prophecy as now found in the sixth chapter of the Book of Isaiah. The vision (probably in the Jerusalem Temple) that made him a prophet is described in a first-person narrative. According to this account he "saw" God and was overwhelmed by his contact with the divine glory and holiness. He became agonizingly aware of God's need for a messenger to the people of Israel, and, despite his own sense of inadequacy, he offered himself for God's service: "Here am I! Send me." He was thus commissioned to give voice to the divine word.

It was no light undertaking. He was to condemn his own people and watch the nation crumble and perish. As he tells it, he was only too aware that, coming with such a message, he would experience bitter opposition, willful disbelief, and ridicule, to withstand which he would have to be inwardly fortified. All this came to him in the form of a vision and ended as a sudden, firm, and lifelong resolve.

Isaiah, an important figure in the Jewish prophetic tradition, watched the defeat of the of he people as he gave voice to the divine word. Hulton Archive/Getty Images

Personal History

Presumably, Isaiah was already prepared to find meaning in the vision before the arrival of that decisive moment. Information about that period of his life is inconclusive, however, and consists mainly of inferences drawn from the biblical text.

At times the prophet's private life shows through the record as an aspect of his public message. Once when he went to confront a king, he took with him, to reenforce his prophetic word, a son with the symbolic name Shear-yashuv ("A Remnant Shall Return"). Again, to memorialize a message, he sired a son on the "prophetess" (his wife) and saddled the child with his message as a name: Maher-shalal-hash-baz ("Speed-spoil-hasten-plunder"), referring to the imminent spoliations by the Assyrians. If the sons had not been wanted as walking witnesses to the prophet's forebodings, posterity would not know of this wife or these sons.

Of Isaiah's parental home it is known only that his father's name was Amoz. Because he often spoke with kings, it is sometimes suggested that Isaiah was an aristocrat, possibly even of royal stock. The same reasoning, however, might apply to any number of prophets. From Nathan in David's time onward, prophets had dealings with kings and were, like Isaiah, well informed about public affairs. Moreover, Isaiah's sympathies were emphatically with the victimized poor, not with the courtiers and well-to-do. Also, it is sometimes argued that he was of a priestly family, but his knowledge of cultic matters and the fact that his commissioning seemingly occurred in the Temple in Jerusalem are slender evidence for his priestly descent as against his unreserved condemnation of the priests and their domain: "I am fed up with roasting rams and the grease of fattened beasts," he has God proclaim in a famous passage in the first chapter.

One could argue with equal force that Isaiah is descended from a family of prophets (though his father, the otherwise unknown Amoz, is not to be confused with the prophet Amos). He is thoroughly schooled in the traditional forms and language of prophetic speech. It is an educated speech—strong, vivid, the finest of classical Hebrew. Isaiah is particularly well acquainted with the prophetic tradition known to his slightly older contemporary, Amos. Four eminent Hebrew prophets addressed themselves to the people of Israel and Judah in the latter half of the 8th century: Amos, Hosea, Micah, and Isaiah. Strangely, no evidence suggests that any of these knew in person any of the others. Seemingly, they were apart and alone, yet Isaiah and Amos follow essentially the same lines of thought and differ significantly only in that Amos had addressed the northern kingdom of Israel while Isaiah would emphatically include Judah and Jerusalem. The basic similarities in style and substance strongly suggest influence, direct or indirect, of the one on the other—and both invoke a recognizable Israelite tradition.

Isaiah's experience bridges the classes and occupations. Whatever his family circumstances, still in his youth he came to know the face of poverty—and the debauchery of the rich. He was at home with the unprotected, the widowed and orphaned; the dispossessed, homeless, landless; and the resourceless victims of the moneyed man's court. He was also acquainted with the rapacious authors of the prevailing misery: promulgators of discriminatory laws, venal judges, greedy landgrabbers, fancy women, thieving and carousing men of means, and irresponsible leaders, both civil and religious. In other words, he was intimately aware of the inequities and evils of human society—which may have been no worse in Israel in the 8th century before Christ than many critics believe they are almost everywhere in the 21st century after Christ.

Isaiah's Theology

It is in his theology that Isaiah leans most heavily on Israelite tradition and shows an acquaintance with the thoughts of Amos. Isaiah shared with him and with the people the long-standing tradition that a special bond united Israel and its God. Since patriarchal times there had been an agreement, a solemn "Covenant" between them: Israel was to be God's people and he their God. He had chosen them and cared for them. His solicitude for their welfare had been clearly established. Such was the traditional message. Isaiah knew and honoured this ancient tradition. But more significantly, he also shared the conviction of Amos that this arrangement was wholly conditional, contingent on the people's conduct. Behaviour such as Amos saw about him in Samaria and Isaiah saw about him in Jerusalem could cancel that Covenant—had in fact done so. That is the meaning of the vineyard parable in the fifth chapter of Isaiah. There God is compared to the careful and industrious cultivator of a vineyard—Israel—who, angry at the "wild grapes" of injustice and violence that is his crop, threatens to take away his care and protection.

As Isaiah knew him, Israel's God did not fit into the picture of utter injustice and consequent misery rampant in 8th-century Israel. To that people's God, as Isaiah knew him, persons mattered. God was, in fact, more concerned about people than about how his subjects performed for him their oft-rehearsed rituals. A literal interpretation of the 13th verse of chapter 29 and verses 10–15 of chapter 1 would suggest that God finds the motions of worship repugnant, and this may well have been Isaiah's meaning. He was overawed by the holiness—the otherness—of his God and must have thought that the customary gifts of meat, grain, and flattery were unseemly or, at the least, irrelevant. Although, like Amos, Isaiah appears most often to speak in absolutes, it is indeed possible to interpret these two passages less strictly (as some scholars do) and to say that he spoke in relative terms and that, in his scale of religious values, he merely ranked moral conduct above ritual conformity.

Isaiah's theology included the sometimes comforting view that God shapes history, traditionally entering the human scene to rescue his people from national peril. But, according to Isaiah's discomfiting surmise, God could intervene quite as properly to chastise his own aberrant nation, and he could employ a

BOOK OF ISAIAH

The Book of Isaiah is one of the major prophetical writings of the Hebrew Bible. The superscription identifies Isaiah as the son of Amoz and his book as "the vision of Isaiah . . . concerning Judah and Jerusalem in the days of Uzziah, Jotham, Ahaz, and Hezekiah, kings of Judah." According to 6:1, Isaiah received his call "in the year that King Uzziah died" (742 BCE), and his latest recorded activity is dated in 701 BCE. Only chapters 1–39, however, can be assigned to this period, and only some of them may actually be said to have originated with Isaiah. Chapters 40–66 are much later in origin and therefore known as Deutero-Isaiah (Second Isaiah). Sometimes a further distinction is made between Deutero-Isaiah (chapters 40–55) and Trito-Isaiah (chapters 56–66).

Chapters 1–39 consist of numerous sayings and reports of Isaiah along with several narratives about the prophet that are attributed to his disciples. The growth of the book (1–39) was a gradual process, its final form dating from perhaps as late as the 5th century BCE, a date suggested by the arrangement of the materials and the late additions. In spite of the lengthy and complicated literary history of the book, however, Isaiah's message is clearly discernible. He was much influenced by the cult in Jerusalem, and the exalted view of YHWH in the Zion traditions is reflected in his message. He was convinced that only an unshakable trust in YHWH, rather than in political or military alliances, could protect Judah and Jerusalem from the advances of their enemies—specifically, in this period, the Assyrians. He called for a recognition of the sovereignty of YHWH and passionately denounced anything that worked against or obscured YHWH's purposes—from social injustices to meaningless cultic observances. Although Isaiah pronounced YHWH's judgment upon Judah and Jerusalem for their unfaithfulness, he also announced a new future for those who relied on YHWH.

Deutero-Isaiah (40–55), consisting of a collection of oracles, songs, and discourses, dates from the Babylonian Exile (6th century BCE). The anonymous prophet is in exile and looks forward to the deliverance of his people. The destruction of Babylon is prophesied and the return of the exiles to their homeland is promised. The servant-of-YHWH songs in Deutero-Isaiah (42:1–4; 49:1–6; 50:4–9; 52:13–53:12) have generated animated discussions among scholars, but the ideas reflected in the songs suggest that they were written under the influence of the ideology of the king—the anointed one who, through his righteous rule, had the power to effect his people's deliverance.

Trito-Isaiah (56–66), coming from a still later period, reflects a Palestinian point of view, with the latter chapters in particular addressed to the cultic concerns of the restored community. The diversity of materials in these chapters suggests multiple authorship. How the three "Isaiahs" came together is unknown.

human agent (e.g., a conquering foe) to that end.

More readily than Amos, perhaps because a decade had passed, Isaiah could identify the agent: Assyria. Isaiah's call to prophecy roughly coincides with the beginning—after a period of relative inactivity—of the westward expansion of the Assyrian empire under the victorious generalship of Tiglath-pileser III (reigned 745–727 BCE). Current events did not escape the prophet's attention. Isaiah appears to have read the omens, as Amos had done. He could clearly see in Assyria the instrument of God's wrath: "Ah, Assyria, the rod of my anger, the staff of my fury! Against a godless nation I send him . . ." (10:5–6).

PROPHETIC MISSION

If, then, Isaiah was prepared by schooling in tradition and life for the vision that set him on his prophetic course, the preparation involved the mingling in his nature of such elements as those sketched previously. In the year that King Uzziah died (742 BCE), according to chapter 6, Isaiah was one of a crowd gathered for an occasion at the Jerusalem Temple when it suddenly occurred—and he became a prophet: "Go, and say to this people . . ." The experiences that had gone into the shaping of his young life—his acquaintance with the arrogant rich and the suffering poor; his seeming knowledge of Amos and his heritage of tradition, ethnic and religious; his dismay at the threat of Assyria; and above all, perhaps, a new and overwhelming sense of the majestic

holiness of God—all merged, or coalesced. He knew that his God was sending him with words for his people and that, reluctant or not, he was compelled to go. From the start or retrospectively, he was aware of a frantic need—impossible to satisfy—to call his people back from the brink of peril. His vision was his moment of insight and resolve when, with complete clarity and instantaneously, he knew what he must do and say.

In its present sophisticated form, the record of this experience is hardly contemporary with the event. He did not go home from the Temple and write down chapter 6. The record is the reflection not of a confident and eager youth but of a man buffeted by long experience, embittered and despairing. Three times in other chapters the prophet says of his people that they have "refused" to hear him. It was as though he, a messenger, had been ordered irrationally to "close their minds, plug their ears, veil their eyes," as he says in chapter 6 of his errand to those to whom he was sent. The message that he had to deliver was bad news—unwelcome tidings. And when he spoke of it, as repeatedly he did, he chose such unambiguous language and spoke with so much moral certainty that, as men normally do, his hearers tuned him out. He was foredoomed to speak unheard. A great deal of anguished living intervened between the vision itself and the writing of it. His words "How long, O Lord?" are an expression of utter weariness.

If chapter 6 marks the beginning of his career as prophet, the judgment oracle about the conquest of Jerusalem in chapter 22 probably brings his grim story to a close. It is at any rate the latest Isaianic product that can be dated with any degree of certainty. The last recorded words of Isaiah, in chapter 22, do nothing to relieve the sombre tone of his message, but they do shed further light on his mood and personality. After he had exclaimed in the vision in chapter 6, "How long, O Lord?" he learned to his dismay that even a last remaining 10th of the populace must in turn succumb. Here the oracle ends with assurance of total disaster: the nation's guilt can be purged by nothing short of death—"Surely this iniquity will not be forgiven you till you die . . ." Chapters 6 and 22 set the tone of his message and the hue of his mood, and from the first to the last the gloom has not lifted.

This 22nd chapter contains the most personally revealing of all Isaiah's words. Quite unexpectedly, the Assyrians have lifted the siege and departed, and the amazed defenders of Jerusalem, flushed and jubilant, give way to celebration. Isaiah cannot share the holiday spirit because for him there has been only a postponement. Nothing has changed, and in his "valley of vision" he sees the day of rout and confusion that God yet has in store for Zion. And so it is that he lays bare his private grief:

> Look away from me, let me weep bitter tears; do not labor to comfort me for the destruction of the daughter of my people.

Message to Israel

The historical allusions in the scattered chapters of Isaiah's work agree with the title verse, according to which he was a contemporary of the Judaean kings Uzziah, Jotham, Ahaz, and Hezekiah. His prophetic call is precisely dated by him "in the year that King Uzziah died." At least a part of chapter 7 refers to the event of the year 734 BCE when Ephraim and Syria jointly threatened King Ahaz of Judah. In 732 BCE Tiglath-pileser conquered Damascus, the fall of which Isaiah had anticipated. In 722 BCE Samaria, the capital of Ephraim, fell to King Sargon of Assyria, an event Isaiah had also foreseen. By the end of the century (701 BCE) Sennacherib had laid siege to Jerusalem—and had subsequently withdrawn. Chapters 1:4–8; 10:27–34; 28:14–22; 30:1–7; and 31:1–4 point to those difficult days when Jerusalem was beleaguered and King Hezekiah feverishly sought help from Egypt. Isaiah brought sparse comfort to his kings—even when the siege was lifted, as noted in the passage cited from chapter 22.

It would be wrong to suppose that Isaiah came to Israel simply to announce the approaching disaster. Painfully sensitive to the rottenness of his society, Isaiah foresaw its consequent collapse. But he also knew and offered an alternative to tragedy: his people's survival depended on their acceptance again of the ancient moral demands. By returning they might be saved. To obtain their return was his program. Or, differently and more properly stated, because he spoke for God and of God, his goal was to redirect his people into the ways acceptable to the God whom by their conduct they had alienated, and so to save them from catastrophe. He screamed dread warnings and pleaded for amendment. He gave way to despair only because his program had no success. His people seemed to him bent on self-destruction; that was the sickening course of their destiny as he saw it unfolding.

His impossible program comes through in the crisis of 701 BCE, during which he stands in violent opposition to the generals ready to go to Egypt for help against the Assyrians laying siege to Zion. Isaiah looked neither to allies nor to armaments for security. If it is God who decides the destiny of nations, security is for God to grant and men to deserve. Isaiah held the daring view that the best defense is no defense—none other than the reconciling response to the moral demand. No men are secure when some are denied security. "This," he said, "is rest [i.e., security]: give rest to the weary."

A case can be made for a theory that Isaiah drew back at the brink, incapable of conceiving a world wholly emptied of his people. What supports this view is a paradox: the observation that, irrationally, he entrusted his rejected message to his disciples and preserved it in a book for the instruction of the survivors of a people doomed to leave no survivors.

There is no consensus as concerns the precise limits of the words of the 8th-century Isaiah or the degree of consistency with which he sustained his tragic monotone. Certainly, in his book as it has come down, his nature is elusive—both stern and tender. Magnificently hopeful passages constantly mingle with the prevailing atmosphere of doom. Probably his son's name, Shear-yashuv, means something like "a mere fragment will survive," but possibly it has a hopeful ring: no total disaster—some shall survive. Possibly the name Immanuel (God Is with Us), prophesied for the child who shall be a sign from God that Judah will not be overcome by Israel and Syria, expresses the confidence that God will never forsake his people. And possibly other such assurances are in fact words of Isaiah himself, compelled by his love to palliate the blow.

But there is an alternative solution. Although Isaiah was far from popular in his day, he does appear to have attracted some followers: "Seal the teaching among my disciples." These may have been the circle that kept alive his name and his words—in writing or learned "by heart"—the nucleus of what was to become, through a developing tradition, the biblical Book of Isaiah. And quite possibly successive generations of such Isaiah-men, piously keeping his words alive through radically changing times, added the sustaining messages of hope, well designed to seize the fancy of suffering humanity down the centuries.

LATER INTERPRETATIONS OF ISAIAH'S MESSAGE

Ironically, perhaps, the Book of Isaiah is most widely known and loved just for those comforting words—which may not be his. A passage in the Babylonian Talmud (one of the two Talmud compilations, the other being Palestinian) can say that from beginning to end the book is consolation. The presence of Isaiah scrolls in the archives of the Qumrān (Dead Sea) community is not surprising. By that time (c. 1st century BCE) it had become the fashion to assume that prophets spoke not to their times only but of things to come, and in times of stress men studied prophetic texts intent on learning when redemption was to come.

JEREMIAH

Jeremiah (650–570 BCE) was the next major Hebrew prophet and reformer after Isaiah. He was closely involved in the political and religious events of a crucial era in the history of the ancient Near East. His spiritual leadership helped his fellow countrymen survive disasters that included the capture of Jerusalem by the Babylonians in 586 BCE and the exile of many Judaeans to Babylonia.

LIFE AND TIMES

Jeremiah was born and grew up in the village of Anathoth, a few miles northeast of Jerusalem, in a priestly family. In his childhood he must have learned some of the traditions of his people, particularly the prophecies of Hosea, whose influence can be seen in his early messages.

The era in which Jeremiah lived was one of transition for the ancient Near East. The Assyrian empire, which had been dominant for two centuries, declined and fell. Its capital, Nineveh, was captured in 612 by the Babylonians and Medes. Egypt had a brief period of resurgence under the 26th dynasty (664–525 BCE) but did not prove strong enough to establish an empire. The new world power was the Neo-Babylonian empire, ruled by a Chaldean dynasty whose best known king was Nebuchadrezzar. The small and comparatively insignificant state of Judah had been a vassal of Assyria and, when Assyria declined, asserted its independence for a short time. Subsequently, Judah vacillated in its allegiance between Babylonia and Egypt and ultimately became a province of the Neo-Babylonian empire.

According to the biblical Book of Jeremiah, he began his prophetic career in 627/626 BCE—the 13th year of King Josiah's reign. It is told there that he responded to YHWH's (God's) call to prophesy by protesting "I do not know how to speak, for I am only a youth," but he received YHWH's assurance that he would put his own words into Jeremiah's mouth and make him a "prophet to the nations." A few scholars believe that after his call Jeremiah served as an official prophet in the Temple, but most believe that this is unlikely in view of his sharp criticism of priests, prophets, and the Temple cult.

Jeremiah's early messages to the people were condemnations of them for their false worship and social injustice, with summons to repentance. He proclaimed the coming of a foe from the north, symbolized by a boiling pot facing from the north in one of his visions, that would cause great destruction. This foe has often been identified with the Scythians, nomads from southern Russia who supposedly descended into western Asia in the 7th century and attacked Palestine. Some scholars have identified the northern foe with the Medes, the Assyrians, or the Chaldeans (Babylonians). Others have interpreted his message as vague eschatological predictions, not concerning a specific people.

In 621 BCE King Josiah instituted far-reaching reforms based upon a book discovered in the Temple of Jerusalem in the course of building repairs, which was probably Deuteronomy or some part of it. Josiah's reforms included the purification of worship from pagan practices, the centralization of all sacrificial rites in the Temple of Jerusalem, and perhaps an effort to establish social justice following principles of earlier prophets (this program constituted what has been called "the Deuteronomic reforms").

Jeremiah's attitude toward these reforms is difficult to assess. Clearly, he would have found much in them with which to agree. A passage in chapter 11 of Jeremiah, in which he is called on by YHWH to urge adherence to the ancient Covenant upon "the men of Judah and the inhabitants of Jerusalem," is frequently interpreted as indicating that the prophet travelled around Jerusalem and the villages of Judah exhorting the people to follow the reforms. If this was the case, Jeremiah later became disillusioned with the reforms because they dealt too largely with the externals of religion and not the inner spirit and ethical conduct of the people. He may have relapsed into a period of silence for several years because of the indifferent success of the reforms and the failure of his prophecies concerning the foe from the north to materialize.

Some scholars doubt that Jeremiah's career actually began as early as 627/626 BCE and question the accuracy of the dates in the biblical account. This view arises from the difficulty of identifying the foe from the north, which seems likely to have been the Babylonians of a later time, as well as the difficulty of determining the prophet's attitude toward the Deuteronomic reforms and of assigning messages of Jeremiah to the reign of Josiah. In the opinion of such scholars, Jeremiah began to prophesy toward the end of the reign of Josiah or at the beginning of the reign of Jehoiakim (609–598 BCE).

Early in the reign of Jehoiakim, Jeremiah delivered his famous "Temple sermon," of which there are two versions, one in Jeremiah, chapter 7, verses 1 to 15, the other in chapter 26, verses 1 to 24. He denounced the people for their dependence on the Temple for security and called on them to effect genuine ethical reform. He predicted that God would destroy the Temple of Jerusalem, as he had earlier destroyed that of Shiloh, if they continued in their present path. Jeremiah was immediately arrested and tried on a capital charge. He was acquitted but may have been forbidden to preach again in the Temple.

The reign of Jehoiakim was an active and difficult period in Jeremiah's life. That king was very different from his father, the reforming Josiah, whom Jeremiah commended for doing justice and righteousness. Jeremiah denounced Jehoiakim harshly for his selfishness, materialism, and practice of social injustice.

In 605 BCE, near the time of the Battle of Carchemish, when the Babylonians decisively defeated the Egyptians and the remnant of the Assyrians, Jeremiah delivered an oracle against Egypt. Realizing that this battle made a great difference in the world situation, Jeremiah soon dictated to his scribe, Baruch, a scroll containing all of the messages he had delivered to this time. The scroll was read by Baruch in the Temple. Subsequently, it was read before King Jehoiakim, who cut it into pieces and burned it. Jeremiah went into hiding and dictated another scroll, with additions.

When Jehoiakim withheld tribute from the Babylonians (about 601 BCE), Jeremiah began to warn the Judaeans that they would be destroyed at the hands of those who had previously been their friends. When the King persisted in resisting Babylonia, Nebuchadrezzar sent an army to besiege Jerusalem. King Jehoiakim died before the siege began and was succeeded by his son, Jehoiachin, who surrendered the capital to the Babylonians on March 16, 597 BCE, and was taken to Babylonia with many of his subjects.

JEHOIAKIM

Jehoiakim was the son of the reformist King Josiah and king of Judah (c. 609–598 BCE). He is mentioned in the Hebrew Bible (2 Kings 23:34–24:17; Jeremiah 22:13–19; 2 Chronicles 36:4–8). When Josiah died at Megiddo, his younger son, Jehoahaz (or Shallum), was chosen king by the Judahites, but the Egyptian conqueror Necho took Jehoahaz to Egypt and made Jehoiakim king. Jehoiakim reigned under the protection of Necho for some time and paid heavy tribute. When the new Chaldean Empire under Nebuchadrezzar II defeated Egypt at the Battle of Carchemish (605 BCE), however, Jehoiakim changed his allegiance from the Egyptian king to Nebuchadrezzar. He remained loyal for three years and then revolted against Nebuchadrezzar. After several battles and invasions, Nebuchadrezzar led the decisive invasion against Judah and besieged Jerusalem (598 BCE). Jehoiakim died at this time, but the circumstances of his death remain uncertain.

The Babylonians placed on the throne of Judah a king favourable to them, Zedekiah (597–586 BCE). He was more inclined to follow Jeremiah's counsel than Jehoiakim had been but was weak and vacillating, and his court was torn by conflict between pro-Babylonian and pro-Egyptian parties. After paying Babylonia tribute for nearly 10 years, the King made an alliance with Egypt. A second time Nebuchadrezzar sent an army to Jerusalem, which he captured in August 586 BCE.

Early in Zedekiah's reign, Jeremiah wrote a letter to the exiles in Babylonia, advising them not to expect to return to their homeland immediately, as false prophets were encouraging them to believe, but to settle peaceably in their place of exile and seek the welfare of their captors. When emissaries from surrounding states came to Judah in 594 BCE to enlist Judah's support in rebellion against Babylonia, Jeremiah put a yoke upon his neck and went around proclaiming that Judah and the surrounding states should submit to the yoke of Babylonia, for it was YHWH who had given them into the hand of the King of Babylonia. Even to the time of the fall of Jerusalem, Jeremiah's message remained the same: submit to the yoke of Babylonia.

When the siege of Jerusalem was temporarily lifted at the approach of an Egyptian force, Jeremiah started to leave Jerusalem to go to the land of the tribe of Benjamin. He was arrested on a charge of desertion and placed in prison. Subsequently, he was placed in an abandoned cistern, where he would have died had it not been for the prompt action of an Ethiopian eunuch, Ebed-melech, who rescued the prophet with the King's permission and put him in a less confining place. King Zedekiah summoned him from prison twice for secret interviews, and both times Jeremiah advised him to surrender to Babylonia.

When Jerusalem finally fell, Jeremiah was released from prison by the Babylonians and offered safe conduct to Babylonia, but he preferred to remain with his own people. So he was entrusted to Gedaliah, a Judaean from a prominent family whom the Babylonians appointed as governor of the province of Judah. The prophet continued to oppose those who wanted to rebel against Babylonia and promised the people a bright and joyful future.

After Gedaliah was assassinated, Jeremiah was taken against his will to Egypt by some of the Jews who feared reprisal from the Babylonians. Even in Egypt he continued to rebuke his fellow exiles. Jeremiah probably died about 570 BCE. According to a tradition that is preserved in extrabiblical sources, he was stoned to death by his exasperated fellow countrymen in Egypt.

PROPHETIC VOCATION AND MESSAGE

This sketch of Jeremiah's life portrays him as a courageous and persistent prophet who often had to endure physical suffering for his fidelity to the prophetic call. He also suffered inner doubts and conflicts, as his own words reveal, especially those passages that are usually called his "confessions" (Jer. 11:18–12:6; 15:10–21; 17:9–10, 14–18; 18:18–23; 20:7–12, 14–18). They reveal a strong conflict between Jeremiah's natural inclinations and his deep sense of vocation to deliver YHWH's message to the people. Jeremiah was by nature sensitive, introspective, and perhaps shy. He was denied participation in the ordinary joys and sorrows of his fellowmen and did not marry. He thus could say, "I sat alone," with

God's hand upon him. Jeremiah had periods of despondency when he expressed the wish that he had never been born or that he might run away and live alone in the desert. He reached the point of calling God "a deceitful brook, ...waters that fail" and even accused God of deceiving and overpowering him. Yet there were times of exaltation when he could say to God: "Thy words became to me a joy and the delight of my heart"; and he could speak of YHWH as "a dread warrior" fighting by his side.

As a prophet Jeremiah pronounced God's judgment upon the people of his time for their wickedness. He was concerned especially with false and insincere worship and failure to trust YHWH in national affairs. He denounced social injustices but not so much as some previous prophets, such as Amos and Micah. He found the source of sin to be in the weakness and corruption of the hearts of men—in what he often called "the stubbornness of the evil heart." Considering sin to be unnatural, he emphasized that some foreign nations were more loyal to their pagan (false) deities than Judah was to YHWH (the real God) and often contrasted nature's obedience to law with man's disobedience to God.

Jeremiah had more to say about repentance than any other prophet. He called upon men to turn away from their wicked ways and dependence upon idols and false gods and return to their early covenantal loyalty to YHWH. Repentance thus had a strong ethical colouring,

because it meant living in obedience to YHWH's will for the individual and the nation.

In the latter part of his career Jeremiah had to struggle against the despair of his people and give them hope for the future. He expressed his own hope vividly by an action that he undertook when the Babylonians were besieging Jerusalem and he was in prison. He bought, from a cousin, a field in Anathoth, his native town. In the presence of witnesses he weighed out the money and made the contracts and said, "Thus says the Lord of hosts, the God of Israel: Houses and fields and vineyards shall again be bought in this land." In this and other ways he expressed his hope for a bright future for Israel in its own land.

Jeremiah's most important prophecy concerning the future is one regarding the New Covenant (Jer. 31:31–34). While the present literary form of the passage is probably not Jeremiah's, the thought is essentially his. He prophesied of a time when YHWH would make a covenant with Israel, superseding the old Mosaic Covenant. YHWH would write his law upon the hearts of men (rather than on tables of stone), and all would know God directly and receive his forgiveness.

EZEKIEL

The last of the major Hebrew prophets was Ezekiel (flourished 6th century BCE), a prophet-priest of ancient Israel and the subject and in part the author of a biblical book that bears his name. Ezekiel's early oracles in Jerusalem were pronouncements of violence and destruction. His later statements addressed the hopes of the Israelites exiled in Babylon. The faith of Ezekiel in the ultimate establishment of a new covenant between God and the people of Israel has had profound influence on the postexilic reconstruction and reorganization of Judaism.

Ezekiel's ministry was conducted in Jerusalem and Babylon in the first three decades of the 6th century BCE. For Ezekiel and his people, these years were bitter ones because the remnant of the

Ezekiel was the last of the great Hebrew prophets, whose early prophecies foretold of death and destruction. Hulton Archive/ Getty Images

Israelite domain, the little state of Judah, was eliminated by the rising Babylonian empire under Nebuchadrezzar (reigned 605–562 BCE). Jerusalem surrendered in 597 BCE. Israelite resistance was nevertheless renewed, and in 587–586 the city was destroyed after a lengthy siege. In both debacles, and indeed again in 582, large numbers from the best elements of the surviving population were forcibly deported to Babylonia.

Before the first surrender of Jerusalem, Ezekiel was a functioning priest probably attached to the Jerusalem Temple staff. He was among those deported in 597 to Babylonia, where he was located at Tel-abib on the Kebar canal (near Nippur). It is evident that he was, among his fellow exiles, a person of uncommon stature. Ezekiel's religious call came in July 592 when he had a vision of the "throne-chariot" of God. He subsequently prophesied until 585 BCE and then is not heard of again until 572 BCE. His latest datable utterance can be dated about 570 BCE, 22 years after his first.

These two periods of prophesying, separated by 13 years, represent various emphases in Ezekiel's message. His earlier oracles to the Jews in Palestine were pronouncements of God's judgment on a sinful nation for its apostasy. Ezekiel said that Judah was guiltier than Israel had been and that Jerusalem would fall to Nebuchadrezzar and its inhabitants would be killed or exiled. According to him, Judah trusted in foreign gods and foreign alliances, and Jerusalem was a city full of injustice. Pagan rites abounded in the courts of the Temple.

After the fall of Jerusalem and his period of silence, Ezekiel now addressed himself more pointedly to the exiles and sought to direct their hopes for the restoration of their nation. His theme changed from the harsh judgment of God to the promise of the future. Ezekiel prophesied that the exiles from both Judah and Israel would return to Palestine, leaving none in the Diaspora. In the imminent new age, a new covenant would be made with the restored house of Israel, to whom God would give a new spirit and a new heart. The restoration would be an act of divine grace, for the sake of God's name. Ezekiel's prophecies conclude with a vision of a restored Temple in Jerusalem. The Temple's form of worship would be reestablished in Israel, and each of the ancient tribes would receive appropriate allotments of land. In contrast to those hoping for national restoration under a Davidic king, Ezekiel envisaged a theocratic community revolving around the Temple and its cult as the nexus of the restored Jewish state.

More than any of the classical biblical prophets, Ezekiel was given to symbolic actions, strange visions, and even trances (although it is quite gratuitous to deduce from these, and from his words "I fell upon my face" [1:28], that he was a cataleptic). He eats a scroll on which words of prophecy are written, to symbolize his appropriation of the message (3:1–3). He lies down for an extended time to symbolize Israel's punishment (4:4ff). One one occasion he is apparently struck dumb for an unspecified length of time (3:26). As other prophets have done before him, he sees the God-to-People relationship as analogous to that of husband to unfaithful wife and therefore understands the collapse of the life of Judah as a judgment for essential infidelity.

CHAPTER 15

POST-EXILIC AND HELLENISTIC PERIOD FIGURES

After the Jewish leaders were allowed to return from Babylon to Jerusalem, they set about the great project of nation rebuilding. The Temple was rebuilt and the various texts, traditions, and writings were first compiled into a Hebrew scripture. Under the influence of the two great cultural powers of the time—first the Persian empire and then the Hellenistic (Greek) world—the Jewish leaders began to interpret their various traditions to meet the changing political and intellectual climate. New concepts—such as resurrection of the dead (possibly influenced by the Persians) and then elements of Greek philosophy and religion—inspired Jews and informed the ways that they thought about God and his relationship to his creation and, particularly, his people. The relationship between the Jewish people and the larger political powers that at times held political dominance over them was not always smooth. Attempts by a Greek emperor to install an image of Zeus in the Temple touched off a revolt that profoundly transformed Judaism, and the destruction of the Temple by the Romans triggered a shift away from Temple service and toward synagogues and the influence of learned scholars.

EZRA

The Jews who returned from exile in Babylon were led by a religious reformer who reconstituted the Jewish community on the basis of the Torah. This reformer, Ezra (flourished 4th century), helped make Judaism a religion in which law was central, enabling the Jews to survive as a community when they were dispersed all over the world. Because his efforts did much to give Jewish religion the form that was to characterize it for centuries after, Ezra has with some justice been called the father of Judaism (i.e., the specific form the Jewish religion took after the Babylonian Exile). So important was he in the eyes of his people that later tradition regarded him as no less than a second Moses.

Knowledge of Ezra is derived from the biblical books of Ezra and Nehemiah, supplemented by the Apocryphal book of I Esdras (Latin Vulgate form of the name Ezra), which preserves the Greek text of Ezra and a part of Nehemiah. It is said that Ezra came to Jerusalem in the seventh year of King Artaxerxes (which Artaxerxes is not stated) of the Persian dynasty then ruling the area. Because he is introduced before Nehemiah, who was governor of the province of Judah from 445 to 433 BCE and again, after an interval, for a second term of unknown length, it is sometimes supposed that this was the seventh year of Artaxerxes I (458 BCE), though serious difficulties are attached to such a view. Many scholars now believe that the biblical account is not chronological and that Ezra arrived in the seventh year of Artaxerxes II (397 BCE), after Nehemiah had passed from the scene. Still others, holding that the two men were contemporaries, regard the seventh year as a scribal error and believe that perhaps Ezra arrived during Nehemiah's second term as governor. But the matter must be left open.

When Ezra arrived the situation in Judah was discouraging. Religious laxity was prevalent, the Torah was widely disregarded, and public and private morality was at a low level. Moreover, intermarriage with foreigners posed the threat that the community would mingle with the pagan environment and lose its identity.

Ezra was a priest and "a scribe skilled in the law." He represented the position of stricter Babylonian Jews who had been upset by reports of laxity in Judah and desired to see matters corrected. Ezra set out in the spring at the head of a sizable caravan and arrived four months later. Ezra apparently had official status as a commissioner of the Persian government, and his title, "scribe of the law of the God of heaven," is best understood as "royal secretary for Jewish religious affairs," or the like. The Persians were tolerant of native cults but, to avert internal strife and to prevent religion from becoming a mask for rebellion, insisted that these be regulated under responsible authority. The delegated authority over the Jews of the satrapy (administrative area) "beyond

NEHEMIAH

Nehemiah was the Jewish leader who supervised the rebuilding of Jerusalem in the mid-5th century BCE after his release from captivity by the Persian king Artaxerxes I. He also instituted extensive moral and liturgical reforms in rededicating the Jews to the God of Israel.

Nehemiah was the cupbearer to King Artaxerxes I at a time when Judah in Palestine had been partly repopulated by Jews released from their exile in Babylonia. The Temple at Jerusalem had been rebuilt, but the Jewish community there was dispirited and defenseless against its non-Jewish neighbours. Distressed at news of the desolate condition of Jerusalem, Nehemiah obtained permission from Artaxerxes to journey to Palestine to help rebuild its ruined structures. He was provided with an escort and with documents that guaranteed the assistance of Judah's Persian officials. So about 444 BCE Nehemiah journeyed to Jerusalem and aroused the people there to the necessity of repopulating the city and rebuilding its walls. Nehemiah encountered hostility from the (non-Jewish) local officials in neighbouring districts, but in the space of 52 days the Jews under his direction succeeded in rebuilding Jerusalem's walls.

Nehemiah then apparently served as governor of the small district of Judaea for 12 years, during which he undertook various religious and economic reforms before returning to Persia. On a second visit to Jerusalem he strengthened his fellow Jews' observance of the Sabbath and ended the custom of Jewish men marrying foreign-born wives. This latter act helped to keep the Judaeans separate from their non-Jewish neighbours. Nehemiah's reconstructive work in Palestine was subsequently continued by the religious leader Ezra.

Nehemiah's story is told in the Book of Nehemiah, part of which indeed seems to be based upon the memoirs of Nehemiah. The book itself, however, was compiled by a later, anonymous writer who apparently also compiled the books of Ezra and the Chronicles.

the river" (Avar-nahara), or west of the Euphrates River, was entrusted to Ezra. For a Jew to disobey the Torah he brought was to disobey "the law of the king."

The order in which Ezra took the various measures attributed to him is uncertain. He probably presented the Torah to the people during the Feast of Tabernacles in the autumn, most likely in the year of his arrival. He also took action against mixed marriages and succeeded in persuading the people to voluntarily divorce their foreign wives. His efforts reached their climax when the people engaged in solemn covenant before God to enter into no more mixed marriages, to refrain from work on the Sabbath, to levy on themselves an annual tax for the support of the Temple, regularly to present their tithes and offerings, and otherwise to comply with the demands of the Torah.

PHILO JUDAEUS

The most representative philosopher of Hellenistic Judaism was Philo Judaeus, also called Philo of Alexandria. His writings provide the clearest view of this development of Judaism in the Diaspora. As the first to attempt to synthesize revealed faith and philosophic reason, he occupies a unique position in the history of philosophy.

Life and Background

Little is known about Philo's life. Josephus, the historian of the Jews who also lived in the 1st century, says that Philo's family surpassed all others in the nobility of its lineage. Apparently, his father had played a prominent role in Palestine before moving to Alexandria. Philo's brother Alexander Lysimachus, who was a general tax administrator in charge of customs in Alexandria, was the richest man in the city and indeed must have been one of the richest men in the Hellenistic world, because Josephus says that he gave a huge loan to the wife of the Jewish king Agrippa I and that he contributed the gold and silver with which nine huge gates of the Temple in Jerusalem were overlaid. Alexander was also extremely influential in Roman imperial circles, being an old friend of the emperor Claudius and having acted as guardian for the Emperor's mother.

Philo was born between 15 and 10 BCE. The community of Alexandria, to judge from the language of the Jewish papyri and inscriptions, had for nearly three centuries been almost exclusively Greek-speaking and indeed regarded the Septuagint (the 3rd-century BCE translation of the Hebrew Bible into Greek) as divinely inspired. During the century and a half before Philo's birth, Alexandria had been the home of a number of Jewish writers whose works exist now only in fragments. These men were often influenced by the Greek culture in which they lived and wrote apologies for Judaism.

The Alexandrian Jews were eager to enroll their children of secondary school age in Greek gymnasiums, institutions with religious associations dedicated to the liberal arts and athletics. In them, Jews were certainly called upon to make compromises with their traditions. It may be assumed that Philo was a product of such an education: he mentions a wide range of Greek writers, especially the epic and dramatic poets; was intimately acquainted with the techniques of the Greek rhetorical schools; and praises the gymnasium. Philo's education, like that which he ascribes to Moses, most probably consisted of arithmetic, geometry, astronomy, harmonics, philosophy, grammar, rhetoric, and logic.

Like the cultured Greeks of his day, Philo often attended the theatre, though it had distinctly religious connotations, and he noted the different effects of the same music on various members of the audience and the enthusiasm of the audience for a tragedy of Euripides. He was

Philo Judaeus, or Philo of Alexandria, often attended theatre, boxing contests, and chariot races in Alexandria, Egypt. De Agostini/Getty Images

a keen observer of boxing contests and attended chariot races as well. He also mentions the frequency with which he attended costly suppers with their lavish entertainment.

Philo says nothing of his own Jewish education. The only mention of Jewish education in his work indicates how relatively weak it must have been, because he speaks only of Jewish schools that met on the Sabbath for lectures on ethics. That he was far from the Palestinian Hellenizers and that he regarded himself as an observant Jew is clear, however, from his statement that one should not omit the observance of any of the Jewish customs that have been divinely ordained. Philo is critical of those who took the Bible too literally and thus encountered theological difficulties, particularly anthropomorphisms (i.e., describing God in terms of human characteristics). He also criticized those who went to excesses in their allegorical interpretation of the laws, with the resulting conclusion, anticipating Paul's antinomianism, that because the ceremonial laws were only a parable, they need no longer be obeyed. Philo says nothing of his own religious practices, except that he made a festival pilgrimage to Jerusalem, though he nowhere indicates whether he made more than one such visit.

In the eyes of the Palestinian rabbis the Alexandrian Jews were particularly known for their cleverness in posing puzzles and for their sharp replies. As the largest repository of Jewish law apart from the Talmud before the Middle Ages, Philo's work is of special importance to those who wish to discern the relationship of Palestine and the Diaspora in the realm of law (*halakah*) and ritual observance. Philo's exposition of the law may represent either an academic discussion giving an ideal description of Jewish law or the actual practice in the Jewish courts in Egypt. On the whole, Philo is in accord with the prevailing Palestinian point of view. Nonetheless he differs from it in numerous details and often depends on Greek and Roman law.

That Philo experienced some sort of identity crisis is indicated by a passage in his *On the Special Laws*. In this work, he describes his longing to escape from worldly cares to the contemplative life, his joy at having succeeded in doing so (perhaps with the Egyptian Jewish ascetic sect of the Therapeutae described in his treatise *On the Contemplative Life*), and his renewed pain at being forced once again to participate in civic turmoil. Philo appears to have been dissatisfied with his life in the bustling metropolis of Alexandria: He praises the Essenes—a Jewish sect who lived in monastic communities in the Dead Sea area—for

avoiding large cities because of the iniquities that had become inveterate among city dwellers, for living an agricultural life, and for disdaining wealth.

The one identifiable event in Philo's life occurred in the year 39 or 40, when, after a pogrom against the Jews in Alexandria, he headed an embassy to the emperor Caligula asking him to reassert Jewish rights granted by the Ptolemies (rulers of Egypt) and confirmed by the emperor Augustus. Philo was prepared to answer the charge of disloyalty levelled against the Jews by the notorious anti-Semite Apion, a Greek grammarian, when the Emperor cut him short. Thereupon Philo told his fellow delegates not to be discouraged because God would punish Caligula, who was indeed assassinated shortly thereafter.

WORKS

Philo's genuine works may be classified into three groups:

1. Scriptural essays and homilies based on specific verses or topics of the Pentateuch (the first five books of the Bible), especially Genesis. The most important of the 25 extant treatises in this group are *Allegories of the Laws*, a commentary on Genesis, and *On the Special Laws*, an exposition of the laws in the Pentateuch.
2. General philosophical and religious essays. These include

That Every Good Man Is Free, proving the Stoic paradox that only the wise man is free; *On the Eternity of the World,* perhaps not genuine, proving, particularly in opposition to the Stoics, that the world is uncreated and indestructible; *On Providence,* extant in Armenian, a dialogue between Philo, who argues that God is providential in his concern for the world, and Alexander, presumably Philo's nephew Tiberius Julius Alexander, who raises doubts; and *On Alexander,* extant in Armenian, concerning the irrational souls of animals.

3. Essays on contemporary subjects. These include *On the Contemplative Life,* a eulogy of the Therapeutae sect; the fragmentary *Hypothetica* ("Suppositions"), actually a defense of the Jews against anti-Semitic charges to which Josephus' treatise *Against Apion* bears many similarities; *Against Flaccus,* on the crimes of Aulus Avillius Flaccus, the Roman governor of Egypt, against the Alexandrian Jews and on his punishment; and *On the Embassy to Gaius,* an attack on the Emperor Caligula (i.e., Gaius) for his hostility toward the Alexandrian Jews and an account of the unsuccessful embassy to the Emperor headed by Philo.

A number of works ascribed to Philo are almost certainly spurious. Most important of these is *Biblical Antiquities,* an imaginative reconstruction of Jewish history from Adam to the death of Saul, the first king of Israel.

Philo's works are rambling, having little sense of form; repetitious; artificially rhetorical; and almost devoid of a sense of humour. His style is generally involved, allusive, strongly tinged with mysticism, and often obscure. This may be a result of a deliberate attempt on his part to discourage all but the initiated few.

ORIGINALITY OF HIS THOUGHT

The key influences on Philo's philosophy were Plato, Aristotle, the Neo-Pythagoreans, the Cynics, and the Stoics. Philo's basic philosophic outlook is Platonic, so much so that Jerome and other Church Fathers quote the apparently widespread saying: "Either Plato philonizes or Philo platonizes." Philo's reverence for Plato, particularly for the *Symposium* and the *Timaeus,* is such that he never took open issue with him, as he did with the Stoics and other philosophers. But Philo is hardly a plagiarist; he made modifications in Plato's theories. To Aristotle he was indebted primarily in matters of cosmology and ethics. To the Neo-Pythagoreans, who had grown in importance during the century before Philo, he was particularly indebted for his views on the mystic significance of numbers, especially the number seven, and the scheme of a peculiar, self-disciplined way of life as a preparation for immortality. The Cynics, with their diatribes, influenced him in the form of his sermons. Though Philo more often employed the terminology of the Stoics than that of any other school, he was critical of their thoughts.

In the past, scholars attempted to diminish Philo's importance as a theological thinker and present him merely as a preacher, but in the mid-20th century H.A. Wolfson, an American scholar, demonstrated Philo's originality as a thinker. In particular, Philo was the first to show the difference between the knowability of God's existence and the unknowability of his essence. Again, in his view of God, Philo was original in insisting on an individual Providence able to suspend the laws of nature in contrast to the prevailing Greek philosophical view of a universal Providence who is himself subject to the unchanging laws of nature. As a Creator, God made use of assistants: hence the plural "Let us make man" in Genesis, chapter 1. Philo did not reject the Platonic view of a preexistent matter but insisted that this matter too was created. Similarly, Philo reconciled his Jewish theology with Plato's theory of Ideas in an original way: he posited the Ideas as God's eternal thoughts, which God then created as real beings before he created the world.

Philo saw the cosmos as a great chain of being presided over by the Logos, a term going back to pre-Socratic philosophy, which is the mediator between God and the world, though at one point he identifies the Logos as a second God. Philo departed from Plato principally in using the term Logos for the Idea of Ideas and for the Ideas as a whole and in his statement that the Logos is the place of the intelligible world. Philo called the Logos the first-begotten Son of God, the man of God, the image of God, and second to God.

Philo was also novel in his exposition of the mystic love of God that God has implanted in human beings and through which a human becomes Godlike. According to some scholars, Philo used the terminology of the pagan religions and mystery cults, including the term *enthousiasmos* ("having God within one"), merely because it was part of the common speech of the day. But there is nothing inherently contradictory in Judaism in the combination of mysticism and legalism in the same thinker. The influence of the mystic notions of Platonism, especially of the *Symposium,* and of the popular mystery cults on Philo's attempt to present Judaism as the one true mystery is hardly superficial. Indeed, Philo is a major source of knowledge of the doctrines of these mystery cults, notably that of rebirth. Perhaps, through his mystic presentation of Judaism, Philo hoped to enable Judaism in the Diaspora to compete with the mystery religions in its proselyting efforts, as well as in its attempts to hold on to its adherents. That he was essentially in the mainstream of

LOGOS

In Greek philosophy and theology, the divine reason implicit in the cosmos, ordering it and giving it form and meaning, is called the Logos. Though the concept defined by the term Logos is found in Greek, Indian, Egyptian, and Persian philosophical and theological systems, it became particularly significant in Christian writings and doctrines to describe or define the role of Jesus Christ as the principle of God active in the creation and the continuous structuring of the cosmos and in revealing the divine plan of salvation to humanity. It thus underlies the basic Christian doctrine of the preexistence of Jesus.

The idea of the logos in Greek thought harks back at least to the 6th-century BCE philosopher Heracleitus, who discerned in the cosmic process a logos analogous to the reasoning power in human beings. Later, the Stoics, philosophers who followed the teachings of the thinker Zeno of Citium (4th–3rd century BCE), defined the Logos as an active rational and spiritual principle that permeated all reality. They called the Logos providence, nature, god, and the soul of the universe, which is composed of many seminal logoi that are contained in the universal Logos. Philo of Alexandria, a 1st-century CE Jewish philosopher, taught that the logos was the intermediary between God and the cosmos, being both the agent of creation and the agent through which the human mind can apprehend and comprehend God. According to Philo and the Middle Platonists, philosophers who interpreted in religious terms the teachings of the 4th-century BCE Greek master philosopher Plato, the logos was both immanent in the world and at the same time the transcendent divine mind.

Judaism, however, is indicated by his respect for the literal interpretation of the Bible, his denunciation of the extreme allegorists, and his failure to mention any specific rites of initiation for proselytes, as well as the lack of evidence that he was himself a devotee of a particular mystery cult.

The purpose of what Philo called mystic "sober intoxication" was to lead one out of the material into the eternal world. Like Plato, Philo regarded the body as the prison house of the soul. In his dualism of body and soul, as in his description of the flight from the self,

the contrast between God and the world, and the yearning for a direct experience of God, he anticipated much of gnosticism, a dualistic religion that became important in the 2nd century BCE. But unlike all the Greek philosophers, with the exception of the Epicureans, who believed in limited freedom of will, Philo held that a human being is completely free to act against all the laws of his own nature.

In his ethical theory Philo described two virtues, under the heading of justice, that are otherwise unknown in Greek philosophic literature—religious faith and humanity. Again, for him repentance was a virtue, whereas for other Greek philosophers it was a weakness. Perfect happiness comes, however, not through men's own efforts to achieve virtue but only through the grace of God.

In his political theory Philo often said that the best form of government is democracy. But for him democracy was far from mob rule, which he denounced as the worst of polities, perhaps because he saw the Alexandrian mob in action. For Philo democracy meant not a particular form of government but due order under any form of government in which all men are equal before the law. From this point of view, the Mosaic constitution, which embodies the best elements of all forms of government, is the ideal. Indeed, the ultimate goal of history is that the whole world be a single state under a democratic constitution.

HILLEL

The foremost master of biblical commentary and interpreter of Jewish tradition in his time was the sage Hillel (flourished 1st century BCE–c. first quarter of the 1st century CE). He was the revered head of the school known by his name, the House of Hillel, and his carefully applied exegetical discipline came to be called the Seven Rules of Hillel.

Hillel was born in Babylonia, where he received both his early and secondary education. As a young man he went to Palestine to continue advanced studies under the leading teachers of Scripture and the Oral Law who belonged to the group or party called Pharisees. Although a strictly biographical account of Hillel's life cannot be set forth, for virtually every narrative about him is encrusted with legend, the literary sources do combine coherently to summon up what may be called the first distinct personality of Talmudic Judaism, the branch of Jewish thought and tradition that created the Talmud, a commentary work on the Oral Law. Put another way, it can be said that the life of Hillel is more than a vague recollection of anecdotes or a name with a saying or two attached.

More than one story underscores Hillel's whole-hearted devotion to study. As with most of the Talmudic sages, no miracles or supernatural performances are ascribed to Hillel, but he is represented as a person of exemplary, even superlative virtues. He is, in the traditional accounts, the model of patience, and, even when repeated attempts are made by some to insult him, his equanimity and civility remain unaffected. He appears as a fervent advocate of peaceful conduct, a lover of all men, a diligent student, a persuasive and ready teacher, and a man of thorough and cheerful trust in God. In short, he appears as the model of the ideal Jewish sage.

This idealization is not entirely storyteller's praises. Critical analysis of Hillel's sayings, of his two legal enactments to relieve economic hardships in society, and even of the motifs the legends seek to emphasize leave little doubt that Hillel did indeed affect the texture of Jewish life profoundly.

While he is nowhere described as the originator of rules to guide the student in the legitimate interpretation of Holy Scriptures, Hillel is unquestionably one of the most influential Talmudic sponsors and practitioners of a conscious, carefully applied exegetical discipline necessary for the proper explanation of the contents of the Bible. The "Seven Rules" he employed—some of which are reminiscent of rules prevailing in Hellenistic schools where Homer was studied and interpreted—were to serve as the basis for more elaborate rules in the 2nd century. Homilies or parables ascribed to Hillel reveal him as a superb pedagogue.

Along with his other gifts, Hillel had an epigrammatic felicity that is apparent in his sayings and which inevitably contributed to their being long remembered. Significantly, in the unique treatise of the Mishna (the authoritative collection of Oral Law), *Pirqe Avot* ("Chapters of the Fathers"), Hillel is quoted more than any other Talmudic sage. As head of the House of Hillel, he succeeded in winning wide acceptance for his approach, which liberated texts and law from slavishly literal and strict interpretation. Indeed, without him an uncompromising rigidity and severity might have developed in the inherited traditions.

Hillel's appreciation of the socioeconomic needs of his age and of the large possibilities that are inherent in biblical statements and values, plus his preference for persuasiveness to get across his point of view, led to the adoption, with few exceptions, of the Hillelite view of Talmudic teaching and to its establishment as the legal norm.

Talmudic sources speak of Hillel's promotion to patriarchal leadership after he had proved his intellectual superiority to the incumbents then in office. In any event, the Jewish patriarchs—the Roman term for the official leaders of the Palestinian Jews—down to about the 5th century, when the patriarchate came to an end, were descendants of Hillel.

Many stories about Hillel, especially those in which he is contrasted with Shammai, are among the most popular Talmudic tales in Jewish literature and folklore.

AKIBA BEN JOSEPH

The great sage Akiba ben Joseph (40–135 CE) was a principal founder of rabbinic Judaism. He introduced a new method of interpreting Jewish oral law (Halakhah), thereby laying the foundation of what was to become the Mishna, the first postbiblical written code of Jewish law.

The subject of numerous popular legends, Akiba is said to have been an illiterate shepherd who began to study after the age of 40. His devoted wife, Rachel, supported him both morally and materially during this arduous period of late learning (12 years, according to one account). His principal teachers were the great masters of the Law, Eliezer ben Hyrcanus and Joshua ben Hananiah. Akiba established his academy in Bene Beraq (near present-day Tel Aviv–Yafo), and the leading sages of the following generation, especially Meïr and Simeon ben Yoḥai, were his disciples.

Akiba perfected the method of biblical interpretation called "Midrash," whereby legal, sacral, and ethical tenets that had been sanctioned by Jewish oral tradition were viewed as being implied in Scripture. Thus, Scripture, in addition to its overt meaning, is understood as replete with implied teaching. It is, in fact, all-encompassing. The "Written Law" of Scripture and the "Oral Law" of tradition are ultimately one. Many midrashic works of the 2nd century originated in Akiba's school. In addition, he collected the oral traditions that regulated the conduct of Jewish personal, social, and religious life and arranged them systematically. (Akiba has been called "the father of the Mishna.") His apprehension of Scripture was opposed by the contemporary exegete Rabbi Ishmael ben Elisha, who taught that "the Torah speaks in the language of men" and should not be forced to yield special meanings but instead should be interpreted exclusively by means of set, logical rules of interpretation.

Akiba's importance lies both in his achievements as a rabbinic scholar and in the impact of his personality on his time. He was strict in matters of law ("No pity in judgment!"—i.e., compassion is irrelevant in establishing what the law is

or means), but he opposed the death penalty. He respected the role of the woman in life and attributed the redemption of the Israelites from Egyptian bondage to the meritoriousness of women of that generation. He was modest in his personal life, and he was known for his concern for the poor.

As judge he addressed litigating parties: "Know before whom you are standing. You are standing before him whose word created the world, not before Akiba ben Joseph."

His lectures were on legal subjects, scriptural exegesis, and religious thought. For him the central teaching of Judaism resided in the commandment "love your neighbour as yourself." God's love for man is expressed in that he created man in his image. Man has freedom of will ("Everything is foreseen, yet freedom of choice is given"). His deeds determine his fate, yet his true reward will be granted only in the world to come. In the present life there is much suffering, but "suffering is precious" and man should praise God for it. The people of Israel, who in a special sense are "God's children," have the task to "proclaim the glory of God to all the nations of the world." Akiba interpreted the Song of Solomon as a dialogue of love between Israel and God. For the sake of this love Israel withdraws from the affairs of the world. In these teachings—partly in answer to early Christian tenets—Akiba laid the basis for an ideology of Israel in dispersion among the nations of the world.

About the year 95, Akiba and other sages journeyed to Rome. Arriving at the seaport Puteoli they beheld the power and grandeur of the empire. While his companions wept, remembering the victory of Rome over Judaea some two decades ago, Akiba remained calm. If God is so kind to the wicked Romans, he explained, he will, in the end, be even kinder to Israel. He was equally calm when he visited the ruins of the Jerusalem Temple, destroyed by the Romans in the year 70. The prophecies of doom have come true, he commented; now we may anticipate the fulfillment of the prophecies of reconstruction.

Scholarly opinion is divided on the extent of Akiba's participation in an ill-fated rebellion against Rome (132–135) led by Bar Kokhba (originally Simeon ben Koziba). Some consider Akiba to have been the spiritual force behind the uprising. Others take note of the Talmudic report that Akiba considered Bar Kokhba to be the promised messianic king but see no evidence of further action on his part. Akiba was, it is true, apprehended by the Romans, imprisoned in Caesarea, and finally martyred (c. 135), but his offense is recorded as having been his continued public teaching rather than revolutionary activity. He accepted the agony of martyrdom serenely (he was flayed alive, according to tradition), grateful for the opportunity to fulfill the commandment to "love God...with all your life," which he always interpreted to mean "even when he takes your life." His last words were, "the Lord is one," the final words of the Jewish confession of faith ("Hear, O Israel! The Lord is our God, the Lord is one.").

JOHANAN BEN ZAKKAI

As is the case with all the Talmudic teachers, little strictly biographical information about Johanan ben Zakkai (flourished 1st century CE) has been preserved: Talmudic and Midrashic sources (commentative and interpretative writings) are principally devoted to the teachings of the sages and of what they came to represent. Thus, what can be reported essentially about this thinker who had a decisive influence on the continuance and development of traditional Judaism after the destruction of the Temple in 70 CE is this: even before the Temple's destruction Johanan had acted as a leading representative of the Pharisees in debate with priestly and Sadducean authorities. The Pharisees stressed rigorous observance of the Torah, inclusion of the oral tradition as normative, and an interpretative adaptation of traditional precepts to new situations. The Sadducees, a conservative group associated with the Temple, accepted only the written Torah as authoritative and were more literalist and static in their interpretation. Johanan's school was apparently famous, and one in search of learning would go to extremes, if need be, to be admitted there. Furthermore, Johanan was opposed to the policy of those who were determined on war with Rome at all costs. By quitting beleaguered Jerusalem according to most accounts in 70 (though it is possible that he left as early as 68) and being brought to the Roman camp, he somehow succeeded in getting permission to set up an academy in Jabneh, where he was joined by a number of his favourite disciples. Two of them, Eliezer ben Hyrcanus and Joshua ben Hananiah, who are credited with having smuggled their master out of Jerusalem in a coffin, were to become, by the end of the century and the beginning of the following one, the leading teachers of their generation and had a profound influence on the greatest scholars of the next generation.

It is therefore hardly excessive to say that Johanan's teachings are to be traced not merely to the relatively few statements specifically attributed to him but to many views that become articulate during the 2nd century: for example, that acts of loving kindness atone no less effectively than the former Temple sacrificial ritual and are indeed at the core of the universe since its creation; that the study of Torah (the divine instruction or Law) is a central purpose of man and a paramount form of serving God; that a number of ceremonies and regulations once confined to the Temple were to be adopted even outside the Temple complex "to serve as memorials of the Sanctuary"; at the same time, despite the unique sanctity of Jerusalem, basic decisions regarding practice and instruction

were now to be permitted to the authorized scholars wherever circumstances compelled them to sit in session. Such views, truly radical in origin, became normative rabbinical teaching and permanent components of Judaism.

Thus, it may be said that, by establishing in Jabneh a major academy and authoritative rabbinic body, Johanan fixed the conditions for continuing Judaism's basic traditions after the destruction of the Temple. And by his lively sense of the need for reinterpreting inherited concepts in new circumstances, he laid the foundations on which Talmudic and rabbinic Judaism built their structure.

The chief preoccupation of Johanan and his students was the study and continuing development of the Law (Halakhah). He and they also engaged in the study of nonlegal subjects (Haggada), especially in connection with biblical exegesis (Midrash), explanation and interpretation of the biblical contents. In addition, he was interested in esoteric themes related to the subject of creation and the visions of the Merkava (the divine chariot of Ezekiel 1), discourses on which were even delivered by some of his disciples. And, at least before the destruction of the Temple, if not thereafter as well, he seems to have held occasional sessions when certain ethical-philosophical questions, typical of Hellenistic-Roman popular philosophical discussion, were raised and explored. His homiletic interpretations of scripture often unite the symbolic with the rationalistic in a remarkable way. Why were not hewn stones permitted in the building of the altar? Because iron is for weapons of destruction, and the altar of God is intended to bring peace, he answers. Why is the ear of one who prefers servitude to have a hole bored in it? Because we are God's servants, and man heard at Sinai with his own ears. Let the unlistening ear be bored. Such are typical comments by Johanan. Although he had discouraged what must have seemed to him unwarranted messianic proclamations, a saying attributed to him in his last illness suggests that messianic speculation was not alien to him.

Of all the Palestinian Jewish sages of the 1st century CE, none apparently proved so fundamentally influential in his own time and for subsequent generations of scholars and spiritual leaders as Johanan ben Zakkai. In the history of Talmudic literature and thought, Johanan is rightly seen as continuing the Hillelite tradition, although this should not be interpreted to mean that he inherited only Hillel's teachings.

CHAPTER 16

MEDIEVAL FIGURES

Jewish communities across Europe and the Middle East met varying degrees of toleration or persecution from the majority Christian or Islamic populations. Persecution increased particularly in Christian lands during the medieval period. Religious figures arose to offer both a defense of Judaism and also spiritual support that would sustain the faithful during tribulation. Two streams of religious response arose. One looked to Greek and Islamic learning, particularly that of the philosophers and theologians who commented on Aristotle and other Greek writers. Another turned to mysticism and expanded Kabbala.

MOSES MAIMONIDES

The foremost intellectual figure of medieval Judaism and one of the most influential Jewish thinkers was Moses Ben Maimon, more widely known among non-Jews by a Greek version of his name, Moses Maimonides, or among Jews as Rambam. A jurist and physician as well as a theologian and philosopher, Maimonides is known for numerous works, including his commentary on the Mishna (which he began at age 23) and his Arabic-language work *The Guide for the Perplexed*. His contributions in religion, philosophy, and medicine have influenced Jewish and non-Jewish scholars alike.

LIFE

Maimonides was born on March 30, 1135, into a distinguished family in Córdoba (Cordova), Spain. The young Moses studied with his learned father, Maimon, and other masters and at an early age astonished his teachers by his remarkable depth and versatility. Before Moses reached his 13th birthday, his peaceful world was suddenly disturbed by the ravages of war and persecution.

As part of Islamic Spain, Córdoba had accorded its citizens full religious freedom. But now the Islamic Mediterranean world was shaken by a revolutionary and fanatical Islamic sect, the Almohads (Arabic: *al-Muwaḥḥidūn,* "the Unitarians"), who captured Córdoba in 1148, leaving the Jewish community faced with the grim alternative of submitting to Islam or leaving the city. The Maimons temporized by practicing their Judaism in the privacy of their homes, while disguising their ways in public as far as possible to appear like Muslims. They remained in Córdoba for some 11 years, and Maimonides continued his education in Judaic studies as well as in the scientific disciplines in vogue at the time.

When the double life proved too irksome to maintain in Córdoba, the Maimon family finally left the city about 1159 to settle in Fez, Morocco. Although it

Around 1159 the family of Moses Maimonides settled in Fez, Morocco, in hopes of trying to appear like Muslims rather than submitting to Islam. Shutterstock.com

was also under Almohad rule, Fez was presumably more promising than Córdoba because there the Maimons would be strangers, and their disguise would be more likely to go undetected. Moses continued his studies in his favourite subjects, rabbinics and Greek philosophy, and added medicine to them. Fez proved to be no more than a short respite, however. In 1165 Rabbi Judah ibn Shoshan, with whom Moses had studied, was arrested as a practicing Jew, found guilty, and then executed. This was a sign to the Maimon family to move again, this time to Palestine, which was in a depressed economic state and unable to offer them the basis of a livelihood. After a few months they moved again, now to Egypt, settling in Fostat, near Cairo. There Jews were free to practice their faith openly, though any Jew who had once submitted to Islam courted death if he relapsed to Judaism. Moses himself was once accused of being a renegade Muslim, but he was able to prove that he had never really adopted the faith of Islam and so was exonerated.

Though Egypt was a haven from harassment and persecution, Moses was soon assailed by personal problems. His father died shortly after the family's arrival in Egypt. His younger brother, David, a prosperous jewelry merchant on whom Moses leaned for support, died in a shipwreck, taking the entire family fortune with him. Moses was left as the sole support of his family. He could not turn to the rabbinate because in those days the rabbinate was conceived of as a public service that did not offer its practitioners any remuneration. Pressed by economic necessity, Moses took advantage of his medical studies and became a practicing physician. His fame as a physician spread rapidly, and he soon became the court physician to the sultan Saladin, the famous Muslim military leader, and his son al-Afḍal. He also continued a private practice and lectured before his fellow physicians at the state hospital. At the same time he became the leading member of the Jewish community, teaching in public and helping his people with various personal and communal problems.

Maimonides married late in life and was the father of a son, Abraham, who was to make his mark in his own right in the world of Jewish scholarship.

WORKS

The writings of Maimonides were numerous and varied. His earliest work, composed in Arabic at the age of 16, was the *Millot ha-Higgayon* ("Treatise on Logical Terminology"), a study of various technical terms that were employed in logic and metaphysics. Another of his early works, also in Arabic, was the "Essay on the Calendar" (Hebrew title: *Ma'amar ha'ibur*).

The first of Maimonides' major works, begun at the age of 23, was his commentary on the Mishna, *Kitāb al-Sirāj*, also written in Arabic. The Mishna is a compendium of decisions in Jewish law that dates from earliest times to the 3rd century. Maimonides' commentary clarified individual words and phrases, frequently citing relevant information in archaeology, theology, or science. Possibly the work's most striking feature is a series of introductory essays dealing with general philosophic issues touched on in the Mishna. One of these essays summarizes the teachings of Judaism in a creed of Thirteen Articles of Faith.

He completed the commentary on the Mishna at the age of 33, after which he began his magnum opus, the code of Jewish law, on which he also laboured for 10 years. Bearing the name of *Mishne Torah* ("The Torah Reviewed") and written in a lucid Hebrew style, the code offers a brilliant systematization of all Jewish law and doctrine. He wrote two other works in Jewish law of lesser scope: the *Sefer ha-mitzwot* (*Book of Precepts*), a digest of law for the less sophisticated reader, written in Arabic; and the *Hilkhot ha-Yerushalmi* ("Laws of Jerusalem"), a digest of the laws in the Palestinian Talmud, written in Hebrew.

His next major work, which he began in 1176 and on which he laboured for 15 years, was his classic in religious philosophy, the *Dalālat al-ḥā'irīn* (*The Guide for the Perplexed*), later known under its Hebrew title as the *Moreh nevukhim*. A plea for what he called a more rational philosophy of Judaism, it constituted a major contribution to the accommodation between science, philosophy, and religion. It was written in Arabic and

MISHNE TORAH

Maimonides authored the Mishne Torah, an extensive commentary on the Talmud, in the 12th century. Each of its 14 volumes deals with a group of laws covering one subject. Among the subjects are ethical conduct, civil laws, torts, marriage and divorce, and gifts to the poor.

Maimonides intended the Mishne Torah to combine religious law and philosophy and to serve as a code of laws that teaches as well as prescribes conduct. He attempted to make the Mishne Torah accessible to as many readers as possible, rather than restricting it for use only by scholars. Readers are encouraged to probe into the rationale underlying the laws. Like the Talmud that is its base, the Mishne Torah contains instruction in secular subjects, such as physics, astronomy, dietetics, and psychology.

sent as a private communication to his favourite disciple, Joseph ibn Aknin. The work was translated into Hebrew in Maimonides' lifetime and later into Latin and most European languages. It has exerted a marked influence on the history of religious thought.

Maimonides also wrote a number of minor works, occasional essays dealing with current problems that faced the Jewish community, and he maintained an extensive correspondence with scholars, students, and community leaders. Among his minor works those considered to be most important are *Iggert Teman* (*Epistle to Yemen*), *Iggeret ha-shemad* or *Ma'amar Qiddush ha-Shem* ("Letter on Apostasy"), and *Iggeret le-qahal Marsilia* ("Letter on Astrology," or, literally, "Letter to the Community of Marseille"). He also wrote a number of works dealing with medicine, including a popular miscellany of health rules, which he dedicated to the sultan, al-Afḍal. A mid-20th-century historian, Waldemar Schweisheimer, has said of Maimonides' medical writings: "Maimonides' medical teachings are not antiquated at all. His writings, in fact, are in some respects astonishingly modern in tone and contents."

Maimonides complained often that the pressures of his many duties robbed him of peace and undermined his health. He died in 1204 and was buried in Tiberias, in the Holy Land, where his grave continues to be a shrine drawing a constant stream of pious pilgrims.

SIGNIFICANCE

Maimonides' advanced views aroused opposition during his lifetime and after his death. In 1233 one zealot, Rabbi Solomon of Montpellier, in southern France, instigated the church authorities to burn *The Guide for the Perplexed* as a dangerously heretical book. The controversy abated after some time, and Maimonides came to be recognized as a pillar of the traditional faith—his creed became part of the orthodox liturgy—as well as the greatest of the Jewish philosophers.

Maimonides' epoch-making influence on Judaism extended also to the larger world. His philosophic work, translated into Latin, influenced the great medieval Scholastic writers, and even later thinkers, such as Benedict de Spinoza and G.W. Leibniz, found in his work a source for some of their ideas. His medical writings constitute a significant chapter in the history of medical science.

ISAAC BEN SOLOMON LURIA

The eponymous founder of the Lurianic school of Kabbala, Isaac ben Solomon Luria, poses a striking contrast to the more rational, Aristotelian Maimonides. Luria was born in Jerusalem in 1534 and spent his youth in Egypt, where he became versed in rabbinic studies, engaged in commerce, and eventually concentrated on study of the *Sefer ha-zohar* ("Book of Splendour"), also known as the *Zohar*, the central work of Kabbala. In 1570 he went to Safed in Galilee, where he studied under Moses ben Jacob Cordovero, the greatest Kabbalist of the time, and developed his own Kabbalistic system. Although he wrote few works beyond three famous hymns, Luria's doctrines were recorded by his pupil Ḥayyim Vital, who presented them in a voluminous posthumous collection.

Luria's father was an Ashkenazi (a German or Polish Jew), while his mother was a Sephardi (of Iberian-North African Jewish stock). Legend has it that the prophet Elijah appeared to his father and foretold the birth of the son, whose name was to be Isaac. As a child, Luria was described as a young genius, "a Torah scholar who could silence all opponents by the power of his arguments," and also as possessed of divine inspiration.

The main source for his life story is an anonymous biography, *Toledot ha-Ari* ("Life of the Ari"), written or perhaps edited some 20 years after his death, in which factual and legendary elements are indiscriminately mingled. According to the *Toledot*, Luria's father died while Isaac was a child, and his mother took him to Egypt to live with her well-to-do family. While there, he became versed in rabbinic studies, including Halakhah, and even wrote glosses on a famous compendium of legal discussions, the *Sefer ha-Halakhot* of Isaac ben Jacob Alfasi. He also engaged in commerce during this period.

While still a youth, Luria began the study of Jewish mystical learning and lived for nearly seven years in seclusion at his uncle's home on an island in the Nile River. His studies concentrated on the *Zohar*, the central and revered work of the Kabbala, but he also studied the early Kabbalists. The greatest Kabbalist of Luria's time was Moses ben Jacob Cordovero of Safed (modern Ẓefat), in Palestine, whose work Luria studied while still in Egypt. During this period he wrote a commentary on the *Sifra di-tzeni'uta* ("Book of Concealment"), a section of the *Zohar*. The commentary still shows the influence of classical Kabbala and

contains nothing of what would later be called Lurianic Kabbala.

Early in 1570 Luria journeyed to Safed, the mountain town in the Galilee that had become a centre of the Kabbalistic movement, and he studied there with Cordovero. At the same time, he began to teach Kabbala according to a new system and attracted many pupils. The greatest of these was Ḥayyim Vital, who later set Luria's teachings down in writing. Luria apparently expounded his teachings only in esoteric circles, so not everyone was allowed to take part in these studies. While he devoted most of his time to the instruction of his pupils, he probably made his living in trade, which prospered at that time in Safed, situated as it was at the crossroads between Egypt and Damascus.

At the time of Luria's arrival in Safed, the group of Kabbalists gathered there around Cordovero had already developed a unique style of living and observed special rituals, going out, for instance, into the fields to welcome the Sabbath, personified as the Sabbath Queen. With Luria's arrival, new elements were added to these excursions, such as communion with the souls of the tzaddiqim (men of outstanding piety) by means of special *kawwanot* (ritual meditations) and *yiḥudim* ("unifications") that were in essence a kind of lesser redemption whereby the souls were lifted up from the *kelipot* ("shells"; i.e., the impure, evil forms) into which they were banned until the coming of the Messiah.

The strong influence of Luria's personality helped to bring about in Safed an atmosphere of spiritual intensity, messianic tension, and the fever of creation that accompanies the sense of a great revelation. Deep devoutness, asceticism, and withdrawal from the world marked the Kabbalists' way of life. Luria apparently looked upon himself as the Messiah ben Joseph, the first of the two messiahs in Jewish tradition, who is fated to be killed in the wars of Gog and Magog that will precede the final redemption. In Safed there was an expectation (based on the *Zohar*) that the Messiah would appear in Galilee in the year 1575.

Even though he did not distinguish himself as a writer, as is evident from his own remarks about the difficulty of writing, Luria composed three hymns that became widely known and part of the cultural heritage of the Jewish people. These are hymns for the three Sabbath meals, which became part of the Sephardic Sabbath ritual and were printed in many prayer books. The three meals were linked

SEFER HA-ZOHAR

The Sefer ha-zohar *(Hebrew: "Book of Splendour"), a 13th-century book composed mostly in Aramaic and commonly known as the* Zohar, *is the classic text of esoteric Jewish mysticism, or Kabbala. Though esoteric mysticism was taught by Jews as early as the 1st century* CE, *the* Zohar *gave new life and impetus to mystical speculations through the 14th and subsequent centuries. Many Kabbalists, in fact, invested the* Zohar *with a sanctity that is normally accorded only to the Torah and the Talmud.*

The Zohar *consists of several units, the largest of which—usually called the* Zohar *proper—deals with the "inner" (esoteric) meaning of biblical texts, especially those taken from the Torah, the Book of Ruth, and the Song of Solomon. The lengthy homilies of the* Zohar *are mixed with short discourses and parables, all centred on Simeon ben Yoḥai (2nd century* CE*) and his disciples. Though the text names Simeon as the author, modern scholars are convinced that the major portion of the* Zohar *should be credited to Moses de León (1250–1305) of Spain. They do not rule out the possibility, however, that earlier mystical materials were used or incorporated into the present text.*

Because the mystery of creation is a recurrent theme in the Zohar, *there are extensive discussions of the 10 sefirot, the emanations from God the Creator, to explain the creation and continued existence of the universe. Other major topics are the problem of evil and the cosmic significance of prayer and good deeds.*

After their expulsion from Spain in 1492, the Jews were much taken up with thoughts of the Messiah and eschatology and turned to the Zohar *as a guide for mystical speculations. The greatest influence of the* Zohar, *especially among the masses, did not occur, therefore, until several centuries after the book was composed.*

by means of mystical "intention" or meditation (*kawwana*) to three *partzufim* (aspects of the Godhead). The hymns are known as "Azamer be-she-vahim" ("I Will Sing on the Praises"), "Asader se'udata" ("I Will Order the Festive Meal"), and "Bene hekh-ala de-khesifin" ("Sons of the Temple of Silver"). They are mystical, erotic songs about "the adornment (or fitting) of the bride" (i.e., the Sabbath, who was identified with the community of Israel) and on the other *partzufim*: *arikh anpin* (the long-suffering: the countenance of grace) and *ze'ir anpin* (the impatient: the countenance of judgment).

During his brief sojourn in Safed—a scant two years before his death—Luria managed to construct a many-faceted and fertile Kabbalistic system from which many new elements in Jewish mysticism drew their nourishment. He set down almost none of his doctrine in writing, with the exception of a short text that seems to be only a fragment: his commentary on the first chapter of the *Zohar*—"Be-resh hormanuta de-malka"—as well as commentaries on isolated passages of the *Zohar* that were collected by Ḥayyim Vital, who attests to their being in his teacher's own hand. Luria died in an epidemic that struck Safed on Aug. 5, 1572.

What is called Lurianic Kabbala is a voluminous collection of Luria's Kabbalistic doctrines, recorded after his death by Ḥayyim Vital and appearing in two versions under different editorship. Because of this work, Lurianic Kabbala

became the new thought that influenced all Jewish mysticism after Luria, competing with the Kabbala of Cordovero. Vital laboured much to give Lurianic Kabbala its form as well as to win legitimization for it.

Lurianic Kabbala propounds a theory of the creation and subsequent degeneration of the world and a practical method of restoring the original harmony. The theory is based on three concepts: *tzimtzum* ("contraction," or "withdrawal"), *shevirat ha-kelim* ("breaking of the vessels"), and *tiqqun* ("restoration"). God

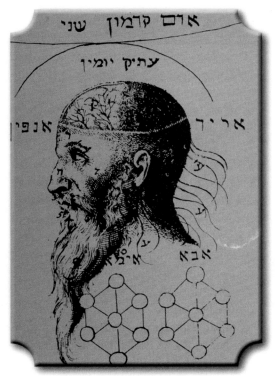

Adam Qadmon is the emblematic man of Luria's Kabbalah. Time & Life Pictures/ Getty Images

as the Infinite (En Sof) withdraws into himself to make room for the creation, which occurs by a beam of light from the Infinite into the newly provided space. Later the divine light is enclosed in finite "vessels," most of which break under the strain, and the catastrophe of the "breaking of the vessels" occurs, whereby disharmony and evil enter the world. Hence comes the struggle to rid the world of evil and accomplish the redemption of both the cosmos and history. This event occurs in the stage of *tiqqun*, in which the divine realm itself is reconstructed, the divine sparks returned to their source, and Adam Qadmon, the symbolic "primordial man," who is the highest configuration of the divine light, is rebuilt. Humanity plays an important role in this process through various *kawwanot* used during prayer and through mystical intentions involving secret combinations of words, all of which is directed toward the restoration of the primordial harmony and the reunification of the divine name.

The influence of Luria's Kabbala was far-reaching. It played an important role in the movement of the charismatic figure Shabbetai Tzevi in the 17th century and in the popular Ḥasidic (mystical-pietistic) movement a century later.

CHAPTER 17

MODERN FIGURES

Modern Jewish thinkers (from the 18th century to the early 21st century) have displayed a wide variety of approaches to Jewish religious traditions and culture. A development within Jewish mysticism developed into Hasidism, a movement whose emphasis on personal piety and on the sacredness of everyday life helped it to spread quickly from its origins in Poland throughout Eastern Europe. The Haskala, influenced by the Enlightenment writers, greatly assisted many Jews in Germany and Eastern Europe in gaining a foothold, both socially and intellectually, in mainstream middle-class society. Zionism developed into a political force. Also, several thinkers steeped themselves in mainstream continental philosophy and (often Christian) theology in order to present wholehearted Jewish responses to the conditions of modern Western secular culture.

BA'AL SHEM ṬOV

The Jewish spiritual movement known as Hasidism, which began in the mid-18th century, is characterized by mysticism and opposition to secular studies and Jewish rationalism. Its founder was Israel Ben Eliezar, a charismatic figure who won popularity and also aroused controversy through his insistence on the holiness of ordinary bodily existence. He was also responsible for divesting Kabbala of the rigid asceticism imposed on it by Isaac ben Solomon Luria in the 16th century. The honorific Ba'al Shem Ṭov means "Master of the Good Name" in Hebrew. But among followers he is more commonly called "the Besht," a byname composed of the initial letter in each word of his title.

LIFE

The Besht's life has been so adorned with fables and legends that a biography in the ordinary historical sense is impossible. He came from humble and obscure beginnings in a village known to contemporary Jews as Okop or Akuf, depending on the Hebrew vocalization, in Poland about the year 1700. As a young orphan he held various semi-menial posts connected with synagogues and Hebrew elementary religious schools. After marrying the daughter of the wealthy and learned Ephraim of Kuty, he retired to the Carpathian Mountains to engage in mystical speculation, meanwhile eking out his living as a lime digger. During this period his reputation as a healer, or *ba'al shem*, who worked wonders by means of herbs, talismans, and amulets inscribed with the divine name, began to spread. He later became an innkeeper and a ritual slaughterer and, about 1736, settled in the village of Medzhibozh, in Podolia. From this time until his death, he devoted himself almost entirely to spiritual pursuits.

Though the Besht gained no special renown as a scholar or preacher during his lifetime, he made a deep impression on his fellow Jews by going to the marketplace to converse with simple people

and by dressing like them. Such conduct by a holy man was fiercely condemned in some quarters but enthusiastically applauded in others. The Besht defended his actions as a necessary "descent for the sake of ascent," a concept that eventually evolved into a socio-theological theory that placed great value on this type of spiritual ministration.

While still a young man, the Besht had become acquainted with such figures as Rabbi Naḥman of Gorodënka and Rabbi Naḥman of Kosov, already spoken of as creators of a new life, and with them he regularly celebrated the ritual of the three Sabbath meals. In time it became customary for them to deliver pious homilies and discourses after the third meal, and the Besht took his turn along with the others. Many of these discourses were later recorded and have been preserved as the core of Hasidic literature. When the Besht's spiritual powers were put to a test by other members of the group—an indication that he probably was not yet recognized as the "first among equals"—he reportedly recognized a mezuzah (ritual object affixed to a doorpost) as ritually "unfit" by means of his clairvoyant powers.

The Besht gradually reached the point where he was prepared to renounce the strict asceticism of his companions. In words recorded by his grandson Rabbi Baruch of Medzhibozh, he announced:

I came into this world to point a new way, to prevail upon men to live by the light of these three things: love of God, love of Israel, and love of Torah. And there is no need to perform mortifications of the flesh.

By renouncing mortification in favour of new rituals, the Besht in effect had taken the first step toward initiating a new religious movement within Judaism. The teaching of the Besht centred on three main points: communion with God, the highest of all values; service in ordinary bodily existence, proclaiming that every human deed done "for the sake of heaven" (even stitching shoes and eating) was equal in value to observing formal commandments; and rescue of the "sparks" of divinity that, according to the Kabbala, were trapped in the material world. He believed that such sparks are related to the soul of every individual. It was the Besht's sensitivity to the spiritual needs of the unsophisticated and his assurance that redemption could be attained without retreat from the world that found a ready response among his listeners, the common Jewish folk. He declared that they were, one and all, "limbs of the divine presence."

The Besht and his followers were fiercely attacked by rabbinical leaders for "dancing, drinking, and making merry all their lives." They were called licentious, indifferent, and contemptuous of tradition—epithets and accusations that were wild exaggerations, to say the least.

An understanding of the Besht's view of the coming of the Messiah depends to a great extent on the interpretation of a letter attributed to, but not signed by, the Besht. It affirms that the author made "the ascent of the soul," met the Messiah in heaven, and asked him when he would come. The answer he received was: "when your well-springs shall overflow far and wide"—meaning that the Besht had first to disseminate the teaching of Hasidism. According to one view, the story indicates that the messianic advent was central in the Besht's belief; according to another, it effectively removes messianic redemption from central spiritual concern in the life that must be lived here and now.

INFLUENCE

During his lifetime, the Besht brought about a great social and religious upheaval and permanently altered many traditional values. In an atmosphere marked by joy, new rituals, and ecstasy, he created a new religious climate in small houses of prayer outside the synagogues. The changes that had occurred were further emphasized by the wearing of distinctive garb and the telling of stories. Though the Besht never did visit Israel and left no writings, by the time he died, he had given to Judaism a new religious dimension in Hasidism that continues to flourish to this day.

Among the Besht's most outstanding pupils was Rabbi Jacob Joseph of Polonnoye, whose books preserve many of the master's teachings. He speaks with holy awe of his religious teacher in tones that were echoed by other disciples, such as Dov Baer of Mezrechye, Rabbi Nahum of Chernobyl, Aryeh Leib of Polonnoye, and a second grandson, Rabbi Ephraim of Sydoluvka, who was but one of many to embellish the image of his grandfather with numerous legends.

MOSES MENDELSSOHN

The great German-Jewish philosopher, critic, and Bible translator and commentator Moses Mendelssohn (born Sept. 26, 1729), whose life's work greatly contributed to the efforts of Jews to assimilate into the German bourgeoisie, came from humble origins. The son of an impoverished scribe called Menachem Mendel Dessau, he was known as Moses Dessau but used Mendelssohn, the German equivalent of the Hebrew *ben Mendel* ("the Son of Mendel"), as his surname on his written work. His own choice of the German Mendelssohn over the Hebrew equivalent reflected the same acculturation to German life that he sought for other Jews. In 1743 he moved to Berlin, where he studied the thought of the English philosopher John Locke and the German thinkers Gottfried von Leibniz and Christian von Wolff.

In 1750 Mendelssohn became tutor to the children of the silk manufacturer Issak Bernhard, who in 1754 took Mendelssohn into his business. The same year, he met a major German playwright, Gotthold Ephraim Lessing, who had portrayed a noble Jew in his play *Die Juden* (1749; "The Jews") and came to see Mendelssohn as the realization of his ideal. Subsequently, Lessing modeled the central figure of his drama *Nathan der Weise* (1779; *Nathan the Wise*, 1781) after Mendelssohn, whose wisdom had caused him to be known as "the German Socrates." Mendelssohn's first work, praising Leibniz, was printed with Lessing's help as *Philosophische Gespräche* (1755; "Philosophical Speeches"). That year Mendelssohn also published his *Briefe über die Empfindungen* ("Letters on Feeling"), stressing the spiritual significance of feelings.

In 1763 Mendelssohn won the prize of the Prussian Academy of Arts in a literary contest, which persuaded King Frederick the Great of Prussia to exempt Mendelssohn from the disabilities to which Jews were customarily subjected. Mendelssohn's winning essay compared the demonstrability of metaphysical propositions with that of mathematical ones and was the first to be printed under his own name (1764). His most celebrated work, *Phädon, oder über die Unsterblichkeit der Seele* (1767; "Phaedo, or on the Immortality of the Soul"), defended the immortality of the soul against the materialism prevalent in his day. The title reflects his respect for Plato's *Phaedo*.

In 1771 Mendelssohn experienced a nervous breakdown as the result of an intense dispute over Christianity with the Swiss theologian J.C. Lavater, who two years earlier had sent him his own translation of a work by his compatriot Charles Bonnet. In his dedication, Lavater had challenged Mendelssohn to become a Christian unless he could refute Bonnet's arguments for Christianity. Although Mendelssohn deplored religious controversy, he felt compelled to reaffirm his Judaism. The strain was relaxed only when he began a translation of the Psalms in 1774. He next embarked on a project designed to help Jews relate their own religious tradition to German culture—a version of the Pentateuch, the first five books of the Hebrew Bible, written in German but printed in Hebrew characters (1780–83). At the same time, he became involved in a new controversy that centred on the doctrine of excommunication. The conflict arose when his friend Christian Wilhelm von Dohm agreed to compose a petition for the Jews of Alsace, who originally had sought Mendelssohn's personal intervention for their emancipation. Dohm's *Über die bürgerliche Verbesserung der Juden* (1781; "On the Civil Improvement of the Jews") pleaded for emancipation but, paradoxically, added that the state should uphold the synagogue's right to excommunicate its members. To combat the resulting hostility to Dohm's book, Mendelssohn denounced excommunication in his preface (1782) to a German translation of *Vindiciae Judaeorum* ("Vindication of the Jews") by Manasseh ben Israel. After an anonymous author accused him of subverting an essential part of Mosaic law, Mendelssohn wrote *Jerusalem, oder über religiöse Macht und Judentum* (1783; "Jerusalem, or on Religious Power and Judaism"). This work held that force may be used by the state to control actions, but thoughts are inviolable by both church and state.

A final controversy, revolving around allegations that Lessing had supported the pantheism of Benedict de Spinoza, engaged Mendelssohn in a defense of Lessing, while he wrote his last work, *Morgenstunden* (1785; "Morning Hours"), in support of the theism of Leibniz. His collected works, which fill seven volumes, were published in 1843–45. Mendelssohn died in Berlin on Jan. 4, 1786.

Through his own example Mendelssohn showed that it was possible to combine Judaism with the rationalism of the Enlightenment. He was accordingly one of the initiators and principal voices of the Haskala, also called the "Jewish Enlightenment," which helped bring Jews into the mainstream of modern European culture. Through his advocacy of religious toleration and through the prestige of his own intellectual accomplishments, Mendelssohn did much to further the emancipation of the Jews from prevailing social, cultural, political, and economic restrictions in Germany. His son Abraham was the father of the composer Felix Mendelssohn.

FRANZ ROSENZWEIG

In 1913 a conversion to Christianity had seemed imminent in Franz Rosenzweig's life. Yet a religious experience caused him to devote his life to the study, teaching, and practice of Judaism. While on active service in World War I, he began his magnum opus, *Der Stern der Erlösung* (1921; *The Star of Redemption*, 1971). From 1922 he was afflicted with progressive paralysis but continued work on numerous projects, including a new

German translation of the Hebrew Bible in collaboration with Martin Buber. The German-Jewish religious existentialist ultimately became one of the most influential modern Jewish theologians because of his fresh handling of traditional religious themes.

Franz Rosenzweig was born on Dec. 25, 1886, the only child of Georg and Adele (née Alsberg) Rosenzweig. His father was a well-to-do dye manufacturer and member of the city council; his mother, a deeply sensitive and cultured woman. Franz grew up in an environment of civic responsibility and cultivation of literature and the arts. Religious beliefs and observance were no longer evident, beyond perfunctory participation on some occasions. In his university days the gifted young man first started to study medicine (at Göttingen, Munich, and Freiburg) but after a few semesters turned to his real interest: modern history and philosophy (at Berlin and Freiburg). In 1910 he embarked on a study of Hegel's political doctrines. His doctoral dissertation (1912) was to become a section of *Hegel und der Staat* ("Hegel and the State"), a comprehensive work completed some years later. Yet, while steeped in this research, Rosenzweig developed a critical attitude toward Hegel's overemphasis on history and his treatment of the individual person's life as irrelevant to the "whole." In rejecting Hegel, Rosenzweig opposed the philosophic movement known as German Idealism, with its attempt to construct reality out of abstract concepts.

Increasingly he tended toward an "existential" philosophy that found its starting point in the experience and concerns of the concrete individual person.

Some of his friends (especially the jurist and historian Eugen Rosenstock-Huessy), who were equally critical of the academic philosophy of the day, had found the solution to the problem of man in religious faith (specifically, conversion to Christianity) and in a dialogical relationship between man and God. After an intense inner struggle Rosenzweig decided in July 1913 to relinquish his Jewish heritage (barely known to him), to accept his friends' interpretation of modern Protestantism as an existential, dialogical faith, and to undergo Baptism. At this critical point in his life, however, he attended the Day of Atonement service in a small, traditional synagogue in Berlin (Oct. 11, 1913). The liturgy of this fast day focusses on the motifs of human sinfulness and divine forgiveness, the realization of life as a standing before God, the affirmation of the oneness of God and of his love. The drama of the liturgy had a powerful effect on Rosenzweig. What he thought he could find only in the church—faith providing an orientation in the world—he found that day in the synagogue. He felt he had to remain a Jew. There followed a period of self-examination to determine whether the emotional experience of that Day of Atonement would stand up to rational criteria. After this clarification, Rosenzweig was determined to devote his life to the study, teaching, and practice of Judaism. The academic year 1913–14 was entirely devoted to an intensive reading of classical Hebrew sources and to attending lectures by Hermann Cohen, an eminent German-Jewish thinker, the founder of the Neo-Kantian school in philosophy.

With the outbreak of World War I, Rosenzweig joined the armed forces and spent most of the duration of the war at the Balkan front, in an anti-aircraft gun unit. The relatively undemanding service allowed Rosenzweig time for study and writing. In 1916–17 he engaged in an exchange of letters with Rosenstock-Huessy on core theological problems in Judaism and Christianity, published in *Judentum und Christentum* (*Judaism Despite Christianity*, 1969), wrote newspaper articles on political and strategic questions, drew up a plan for a reform of the German school system, and wrote "Zeit ist's" ("It Is Time"), a program for a reorganization of Jewish education and scholarship (included in *On Jewish Learning*, 1955). In 1918, while attending an officers' training course near Warsaw, in German-occupied Poland, he had opportunity to observe the life and the customs of eastern European Jews and was deeply impressed by the vitality and richness of their faith. Upon returning to the trenches he felt ready to embark on what was to become his magnum opus: an existentialist religious philosophy demonstrating the mutual relationships between God, man, and the world. This "new thinking" is based on human experience, common sense, and the reality of language and dialogue. The central point of the architectonically arranged work in which this thought is expressed is the act of "revelation" in which God in his love turns to man and awakens within him the consciousness of an "I." *Der Stern der Erlösung*, completed in 1919, appeared in 1921. The work was ignored by the various trends in academic philosophy but highly regarded by existentialist and, especially, younger Jewish theologians.

EXISTENTIALISM

Philosophical movement oriented toward two major themes, the analysis of human existence and the centrality of human choice. Existentialism's chief theoretical energies are thus devoted to questions about ontology and decision. It traces its roots to the writings of Søren Kierkegaard and Friedrich Nietzsche. As a philosophy of human existence, existentialism found its best 20th-century exponent in Karl Jaspers. As a philosophy of human decision, its foremost representative was Jean-Paul Sartre. Sartre finds the essence of human existence in freedom—in the duty of self-determination and the freedom of choice—and therefore spends much time describing the human tendency toward "bad faith," reflected in humanity's perverse attempts to deny its own responsibility and flee from the truth of its inescapable freedom.

In early 1920 Rosenzweig married Edith Hahn of Berlin and wrote "Bildung und kein Ende" (included in *On Jewish Learning* as "Towards a Renaissance of Jewish Learning"), outlining a plan for a Jewish adult study centre. Later in the year he was appointed head of such a centre (the Freies Jüdisches Lehrhaus) in Frankfurt am Main. There students were encouraged to examine classical Hebrew sources, searching for what is vital and relevant. The school became a model for similar institutions elsewhere in Germany. Rosenzweig's active directorship did not last long. Early in 1922 he was afflicted with amyotrophic lateral sclerosis, an often fatal form of progressive paralysis. In September 1922 his son Rafael was born. The child brought comfort to the father, whose paralysis affected his whole body, including the vocal organs. In a true heroism of the spirit, although unable to speak or write in a direct physical sense, he managed to continue living as an active scholar, writer, and friend, deeply concerned for his fellow humans and community. With the help of his wife, a system of signals between them, and a specially constructed typewriter, he produced important essays and an annotated German version of the medieval Hebrew poetry of Judah ha-Levi.

From 1925 on he embarked, together with Martin Buber, the eminent German-Jewish philosopher and biblical interpreter, on a new German translation of the Hebrew Bible. The translation occasioned a series of articles by him on aspects of biblical thought and style. As a hobby he also wrote reviews of records of classical and sacred music. Nowhere in these works of his paralytic years did the reader detect that the author was mortally ill. Everywhere in them there is evidence of a fresh, keen spirit, intellectual clarity, religious faith, and a sense of humour. He died in 1929. His influence on Jewish religious thought grew remarkably in the decades after his death.

MARTIN BUBER

Martin Buber, a German-Jewish biblical translator, was renowned as a master of German prose style. Yet Buber made his mark with a philosophy centred on the encounter, or dialogue, of man with other beings, particularly exemplified in the relation with other men but ultimately resting on and pointing to the relation with God. This thought reached its fullest dialogical expression in Buber's most famous work, *Ich und Du* (1923; *I and Thou*).

FROM VIENNA TO JERUSALEM

Buber was born in Vienna on Feb. 8, 1878, to Carl Buber, an agronomist, and his wife—both assimilated Jews. When Martin was three his mother left his father, and the boy was brought up by his grandparents in Lemberg (now Lviv, Ukraine). The search after the lost mother became a strong motive for his dialogical thinking—his I–Thou philosophy.

Solomon Buber (1827–1906), the Lemberg grandfather, a wealthy philanthropist, dedicated his life to the critical edition of Midrashim, a part of the nonlegal rabbinic lore. His works show him as a Hebrew gentleman-scholar who was also interested in Greek linguistic parallels. His wife, Adele, was even more a product of the 19th-century Enlightenment movement among eastern European Jewry that sought to modernize Jewish culture. Though strongly influenced by both his grandparents and taught Hebrew by Solomon, young Martin was drawn more to Schiller's poems than to the Talmud. His inclination toward general culture was strengthened by his grammar-school education, which provided him with an excellent grounding in the classics. During his adolescence his active participation in Jewish religious observances ceased altogether.

In his university days—he attended the universities of Vienna, Berlin, Leipzig, and Zürich—Buber studied philosophy and art. His doctoral dissertation, which he earned from Vienna in 1904, dealt with the theories of individuation in the thought of two great Christian philosophical mystics, Nicholas of Cusa and Jakob Böhme, but it was the German philosopher Friedrich Nietzsche's proclamation of heroic nihilism and his criticism of modern culture that exerted the greatest influence on Buber at that time. The Nietzschean influence was reflected in Buber's turn to Zionism and its call for a return to roots and a more wholesome culture.

On the invitation of the Zionist leader Theodor Herzl, in 1901 he became editor of the Zionist weekly *Die Welt* ("The World"). But soon a significant

Martin Buber. Consulate General of Israel in New York

difference of opinion developed between the two men. Buber favoured an overall spiritual renewal and, at its core, immediate agricultural settlements in Palestine, as against Herzl's emphasis on diplomacy to bring about the establishment of a Jewish homeland secured by public law. Consequently, Buber resigned his post the same year he assumed it. He remained a Zionist but generally stood in opposition to official party policies and later to official state policies of Israel. He was among the early protagonists of a Hebrew university in Jerusalem.

In 1916 Buber founded the influential monthly *Der Jude* ("The Jew"), which he edited until 1924 and which became the central forum for practically all German-reading Jewish intellectuals. In its pages he advocated the unpopular cause of Jewish-Arab cooperation in the formation of a binational state in Palestine.

After his marriage (1901) to a non-Jewish, pro-Zionist author, Paula Winckler, who converted to Judaism, Buber took up the study of Hasidism. His *Chassidischen Bücher* (1927) made the legacy of this popular 18th-century eastern European Jewish pietistic movement a part of Western literature. In Hasidism Buber saw a healing power for the malaise of Judaism and mankind in an age of alienation that had shaken three vital human relationships: those between man and God, man and man, and man and nature. They can be restored, he asserted, only by man's again meeting the other person or being who stands over against him, on all three levels—the divine, human, and natural. Buber maintained that early Hasidism accomplished this encounter and that Zionism should follow its example.

In *Paths in Utopia* (1949) he referred to the Israeli kibbutz—a cooperative agricultural community the members of which work in a natural environment and live together in a voluntary communion—as a "bold Jewish undertaking" that proved to be "an exemplary non-failure," one example of a "utopian" socialism that works. Yet he did not ascribe ultimate success to it. His reservation stemmed from the fact that, generally, members of the kibbutz disregarded the relation between man and God, denying or doubting the existence or presence of a divine counterpart. In the interpersonal area they fulfilled God's commandment to build a just community while yet denying the divine origin of the implicit imperative. As an educator Buber tried to refute these ideological "prejudices of youth," who, he asserted, rightly criticize outworn images of God but wrongly identify them with the imageless living God himself.

Buber's pedagogical work reached a climax under the new conditions created by the Nazi assumption of power. In November 1933 he became head of the newly reopened Freies Jüdisches Lehrhaus for Jewish adult education in Frankfurt am Main. In 1934 he became director of the whole organization of Jewish adult education and retraining of Jewish teachers in Nazi Germany, where Jewish teachers and students were being progressively excluded from the educational system. He was a courageous spokesman of spiritual resistance. As against the Nazi nationalism of "blood and soil," he stressed that, while the Jew must maintain his authentic Jewish existence, the educational aim could not be racist (*Völkisch*). His old slogan "to be human in a Jewish way" was now completed by the demand to be Jewish in a humane way.

After the Nazi secret police forbade his public lectures and then all his teaching activities, he emigrated to Palestine. He was 60 years old at the time. Buber activated his Hebrew and soon took part in the social and intellectual life of the Palestinian Jewish community. He was appointed to a professorship in social philosophy at Hebrew University in Jerusalem, a post he held until 1951. He was the first president of the Israeli Academy of Sciences and Arts. After the establishment of the State of Israel and with the beginning of mass immigration from the Islamic countries, Buber initiated the founding of the Teachers Training College for Adult Education in Jerusalem and became its head (1949). This college trained what were probably the best educators for the immigrants from the Middle East and North Africa, many of them having been chosen from among the immigrants.

As a teacher of adults, Buber enjoyed the cooperation of his political adversaries and sometimes also of his religious adversaries. Though he denied the obligatory character of Torah and emphasized a nonlegalistic prophetic type of religion, some of the Orthodox also worked with him. Buber's endeavours in adult education were based on his insight that adults again become educable when crisis threatens their spurious security.

FROM MYSTICISM TO DIALOGUE

Buber's manifold activities were inspired by his philosophy of encounter—of man's meeting with other beings. An early mystical period culminated in *Daniel* (1913), five dialogues on orientation and realization, man's two basic stances toward the world. Orientation takes the world as a static state of affairs governed by comprehensible laws. It is a receptive, analytical, or systematizing attitude. Realization, however, is a creative, participative attitude that realizes the possibilities in things, experiencing through one's own full reality the full reality of the world. It operates within an open horizon of possibilities.

The *Reden über das Judentum* (1923; "Talks on Judaism") mark another step in his development. The early "Talks" were delivered in 1909–11 before large Zionist student audiences in Prague. Each speech tries to answer its opening question: "Jews, why do we call ourselves Jews?" To half-assimilated Zionists in search of a rationale for their Jewish existence, Buber offered his theories regarding the essence of Judaism, basing his quest for it on his listeners' assumed identity as Jews. In some of the "Talks," as well as in *Daniel*, the mystic element still prevails, but Buber later abandoned the notion of a mystical union between man and God and embraced instead the notion of their encounter, which presupposes and preserves their separate existence.

This basic view underlies Buber's mature thinking; it was expressed with great philosophic and poetic power in his famous work *Ich und Du* (1923; *I and Thou*). According to this view, God, the great Thou, enables human I–Thou relations between man and other beings. Their measure of mutuality is related to the levels of being: it is almost nil on the inorganic and botanic levels, rare on the animal level, but always possible and sometimes actual between human beings. A true relationship with God, as experienced from the human side, must be an I–Thou relationship, in which God is truly met and addressed, not merely thought of and expressed.

Between man and man, the I–Thou relationship into which both parties enter in the fullness of their being—as in a great love at its highest moment or in an ideal friendship—is an exception. Generally, we enter into relationships not with the fullness of our being but only with some fraction of it. This is the I–It relationship, as in scholarly pursuits in which other beings are reduced to mere objects of thought or in social relations (e.g., boss and worker) wherein persons are treated largely as tools or conveniences. This form of relationship enables the creation of pure and applied science as well as the manipulation of man by man. Buber's ethical concept of the demarcation line—to be drawn anew every day between the maximum of good that can be done in a concrete situation and the minimum of evil that must be done in it—calls for an I–Thou relation whenever possible and settles for an I–It relation whenever necessary (e.g., for the purpose of human survival).

Toward God, any type of I–It relationship should be avoided, be it theoretical by making him an object of dogmas, juridical by turning him into a legislator of fixed rules or prayers, or organizational by confining him to churches, mosques, or synagogues. Buber's so-called religious

I-THOU

Martin Buber developed the theological doctrine of the full, direct, mutual relation between beings, which he characterized as the I–Thou relationship. The basic and purest form of this relation is that between man and God (the Eternal Thou), which is the model for and makes possible I–Thou relations between human beings. The relation between man and God, however, is always an I–Thou one, whereas that between man and man is very frequently an I–It one, in which the other being is treated as an object of thought or action. According to Buber, man's relation to other creatures may sometimes approach or even enter the I–Thou realm. Buber's book Ich und Du *(1923;* I and Thou*) is the classic work on the subject.*

anarchism—his rejection of any fixed rules of behaviour in the relation between man and God—opened to him new insights in his works on the Bible but also served as a block to an objective evaluation of biblical, let alone Talmudic, Law. He saw the Bible as originating in the ever-renewed encounter between God and his people, followed by a tradition that authentically reflected this experience and another that distorted it to serve later ideological aims. He ascribed most of the legal prescriptions of the Talmud to what he called the spurious tradition removed from the Thou relation with God. This interpretation has been criticized as one-sided and subjective. Buber mitigated it somewhat in his later years.

After the religious philosopher Franz Rosenzweig, Buber's friend and fellow translator of the Bible, read *Ich und Du*, he remarked: "Buber gives more recognition to the 'Thou' than anybody before him, but he wrongs the 'It'." To this Buber replied, many years later, that had he lived in a time when the Thou was flowering, he would have "sounded the praises of the It," but that in his time, when the Thou was withering, he had to do the reverse. This argument between Buber and his closest and greatest friend indicates his attitude toward normative Judaism. While Rosenzweig tried to live it as much as possible and became more and more a practicing Jew, Buber stood his ground as one who embodied his Judaism in no prescribed, special manner. This stance, in addition to his political views (i.e., his opposition to Zionist policy toward the Arabs), set him apart from his own people. It made him, however, their main spokesman in the Jewish–Christian dialogue. In his *Zwei Glaubensweisen* (1950) he construed two religious types according to their approach to God: one called by the Hebrew term for trust, *emuna*, spelling mutual confidence between God and man (I and Thou), and the other called by the Greek term for faith, *pistis*, spelling the belief in the factuality of crucial events in salvation history (e.g., Paul's statements about Jesus' life, death, and Resurrection). Judaism for Buber was the classical example of *emuna* and Christianity of *pistis*, although there was a good deal of *pistis* in historical Judaism and a good deal of *emuna* in historical Christianity. His Christian opponents on this and other matters still found a common ground with Buber, because he agreed to a dialogically open, if not dogmatically defined, universe of discourse in which they could talk fruitfully with one another.

THE FINAL YEARS

In his last years a group of kibbutz members turned to him with their personal and communal problems. Buber died on June 13, 1965, and his responses to their problems and concerns were published posthumously. *Siḥot loḥamin* (1967; *The Seventh Day*, 1970), published shortly after the Six-Day War, testifies to Buber's living spirit by its self-searching attitude on ethical questions of war and peace and on Arab–Jewish relations.

An unprecedented event occurred at Buber's funeral in Jerusalem, a high state function: a delegation of the Arab Students' Organization placed a wreath on the grave of one who strove mightily for peace between Israel's and Palestine's two peoples.

THEODOR HERZL

Although Theodor Herzl died more than 40 years before the establishment of the State of Israel, he was an indefatigable organizer, propagandist, and diplomat who had much to do with making Zionism into a political movement of worldwide significance. His pamphlet *The Jewish State* (1896) proposed that the question of a Jewish state was a political one to be settled by a world council of nations. He organized a world congress of Zionists that met in Basel, Switzerland, in August 1897 and became first president of the World Zionist Organization, established by the congress.

Early Years

Herzl was born in Budapest on May 2, 1860, of well-to-do middle-class parents. He first studied in a scientific secondary school, but to escape from its anti-Semitic atmosphere he transferred in 1875 to a school where most of the students were Jews. In 1878 the family moved from Budapest to Vienna, where he entered the University of Vienna to study law. He received his license to practice law in 1884 but chose to devote himself to literature. For a number of years he was a journalist and a moderately successful playwright.

In 1889 he married Julie Naschauer, daughter of a wealthy Jewish businessman in Vienna. The marriage was unhappy, although three children were born to it. Herzl had a strong attachment to his mother, who was unable to get along with his wife. These difficulties were increased by the political activities of his later years, in which his wife took little interest.

Conversion to Zionism

A profound change began in Herzl's life soon after a sketch he had published in the leading Viennese newspaper, *Neue*

Freie Presse, led to his appointment as the paper's Paris correspondent. He arrived in Paris with his wife in the fall of 1891 and was shocked to find in the homeland of the French Revolution the same anti-Semitism with which he had become so familiar in Austria. Hitherto he had regarded anti-Semitism as a social problem that the Jews could overcome only by abandoning their distinctive ways and assimilating to the people among whom they lived. At the same time, his work as a newspaperman heightened his interest in, and knowledge of, social and political affairs and led him to the conviction that the answer to anti-Semitism was not assimilation but organized counterefforts by the Jews. The Dreyfus affair in France also helped crystallize this belief. French military documents had been given to German agents, and a Jewish officer named Alfred Dreyfus had been falsely charged with the crime. The ensuing political controversy produced an outburst of anti-Semitism among the French public. Herzl said in later years that it was the Dreyfus affair that had made a Zionist out of him. So long as anti-Semitism existed, assimilation would be impossible, and the only solution for the majority of Jews would be organized emigration to a state of their own.

Herzl was not the first to conceive of a Jewish state. Orthodox Jews had traditionally invoked the return to Zion in their daily prayers. In 1799 Napoleon had thought of establishing a Jewish state in the ancient lands of Israel. The English statesman Benjamin Disraeli, a Jew, had written a Zionist novel, *Tancred*. Moses Hess, a friend and co-worker of Karl Marx, had published an important book, *Rom und Jerusalem* (1862), in which he declared the restoration of a Jewish state a necessity both for the Jews and for the rest of humanity. Among the Jews of Russia and eastern Europe, a number of groups were engaged in trying to settle emigrants in agricultural colonies in Palestine. After the Russian pogroms of 1881, Leo Pinsker had written a pamphlet, "Auto-Emanzipation," an appeal to western European Jews to assist in the establishment of colonies in Palestine. When Herzl read it some years later, he commented in his diary that, if he had known of it, he might never have written *The Jewish State*.

Herzl's first important Zionist effort was an interview with Baron Maurice de Hirsch, one of the wealthiest men of his time. De Hirsch had founded the Jewish Colonization Association with the aim of settling Jews from Russia and Romania in Argentina and other parts of the Americas. The 35-year-old journalist arrived at the Baron's mansion in Paris with 22 pages of notes, in which he argued the need for a political organization to rally the Jews under a flag of their own, rather than leaving everything to the philanthropic endeavours of individuals like the Baron. The conversation was notable for its effect on Herzl rather than on the Baron de Hirsch, who refused to hear him out. It led to Herzl's famous pamphlet *The Jewish State*, published in February 1896 in Vienna. The Jewish question, he wrote,

Theodor Herzl. Photos.com/Jupiterimages

was not a social or religious question but a national question that could be solved only by making it "a political world question to be discussed and settled by the civilized nations of the world in council." Some of Herzl's friends thought it a mad idea, but the pamphlet won favourable response from eastern European Zionist societies. In June 1896, when Herzl was en route to Constantinople (Istanbul) in the hope of talking to the Ottoman sultan about obtaining the grant of Palestine as an independent country, his train stopped in Sofia, Bulg. Hundreds of Jews greeted Herzl at the station and hailed him as a leader. Although he remained in Constantinople for 11 days, he failed to reach the Sultan. But he had begun the career as organizer and propagandist that would end only with his death eight years later.

The First Zionist Congress

Herzl went to London in an effort to organize the Jews there in support of his program. Not all the Jewish leaders in England were happy to see him because his political approach was not in tune with their ideas, but at public meetings in the East End he was loudly cheered. He was a tall, impressive figure with a long black beard and the mien of a prophet. Despite his personal magnetism, he found that his efforts to influence Jewish leaders in England were of little avail and therefore decided to organize a world congress of Zionists in the hope of winning support from the masses of Jews in all countries. He proposed to hold the congress in Munich, but as the Jews there—who were mostly assimilated—opposed it, he settled upon Basel. The congress met at the end of August 1897, attended by about 200 delegates, mostly from central and eastern Europe and Russia along with a few from western Europe and even the United States. They represented all social strata and every variety of Jewish thought— from Orthodox Jews to atheists and from businessmen to students. There were also several hundred onlookers, including some sympathetic Christians and reporters for the international press. When Herzl's imposing figure came to the podium, there was tumultuous applause.

"We want to lay the foundation stone," he declared, "for the house which will become the refuge of the Jewish nation. Zionism is the return to Judaism even before the return to the land of Israel." One of Herzl's most faithful supporters was the writer Max Nordau, who gave a brilliant address in which he described the plight of the Jews in the East and in the West. The three-day congress agreed upon a program, henceforth to be known as the Basel Program, declaring that "Zionism aspires to create a publicly guaranteed homeland for the Jewish people in the land of Israel." It also set up the Zionist Organization with Herzl as president.

Later Accomplishments

The seven remaining years of his life were devoted to the furtherance of the Zionist cause, although he remained literary editor of the *Neue Freie Presse* to earn a living. He established a Zionist newspaper, *Die Welt*, published as a German-language weekly in Vienna. He unsuccessfully negotiated with the Sultan of Turkey for the grant of a charter that would allow Jewish mass settlement in Palestine on an autonomous basis. He then turned to Great Britain, which seemed favourable to the establishment of a Jewish settlement in British territory in the Sinai Peninsula. When this project failed, the British proposed Uganda in East Africa. This offer, which he and some other Zionists were willing to accept, aroused violent opposition at the Zionist congress of 1903, particularly among the

Russians. Herzl was unable to resolve the conflict. He died of a heart ailment at Edlach, near Vienna, at the age of 44. He was buried in Vienna, but, in accordance with his wish, his remains were removed to Jerusalem in 1949 after the creation of the Jewish state and entombed on a hill west of the city now known as Mt. Herzl.

After the First Zionist Congress in Basel, Herzl had written in his diary:

> *If I had to sum up the Basel Congress in one word—which I shall not do openly—it would be this: At Basel I founded the Jewish state. If I were to say this today, I would be greeted by universal laughter. In five years, perhaps, and certainly in 50, everyone will see it.*

While the Jewish state was the product of many complex historic forces, including two world wars and the labours of Herzl's many followers, it was he who organized the political force of Jewry that was able to take advantage of the accidents of history. Through the strength of his personality, he aroused the enthusiasm of the Jewish masses and gained the respect of many statesmen of his time, in spite of the opposition of some Jewish leaders to his plans.

EMMANUEL LÉVINAS

The career of the Lithuanian-born French philosopher Emmanuel Lévinas stands in contrast to those of many other Jewish philosophers. Where Philo stood in the tradition of Plato and introduced into Judaism such concepts as the divine Logos that provides order to the universe, and Maimonides interpreted the metaphysical framework of Aristotle, for example, Lévinas was renowned for his powerful critique of the preeminence of ontology, the philosophical study of being, in the history of Western philosophy. He particularly singled out the work of the German philosopher Martin Heidegger (1889–1976).

Lévinas was born in Kaunas, Lith., on Dec. 30, 1905. He began his studies in philosophy in 1923 at the University of Strasbourg. He spent the academic year 1928–29 at the University of Freiburg, where he attended seminars by Edmund Husserl (1859–1938) and Heidegger. After completing a doctoral dissertation at the Institut de France in 1928, Lévinas taught at the École Normale Israelite Orientale (ENIO), a school for Jewish students, and the Alliance Israelite Universelle, both in Paris. Serving as an officer in the French army at the outbreak of World War II, he was captured by German troops in 1940 and spent the next five years in a prisoner of war camp. After the war he was director of the ENIO until 1961, when he received his first academic appointment at the University of Poitiers. He subsequently taught at the University of Paris X (Nanterre; 1967–73) and the Sorbonne (1973–78).

The principal theme of Lévinas's work after World War II is the traditional place of ontology as "first philosophy"—the most fundamental philosophical discipline. According to Lévinas, ontology by its very nature attempts to create a totality in which what is different and "other" is necessarily reduced to sameness and identity. This desire for totality, according to Lévinas, is a basic manifestation of "instrumental" reason—the use of reason as an instrument for determining the best or most efficient means to achieve a given end. Through its embrace of instrumental reason, Western philosophy displays a destructive and objectifying "will to domination." Moreover, because instrumental reason does not determine the ends to which it is applied, it can be—and has been—used in the pursuit of goals that are destructive or evil. In this sense, it is responsible for the major crises of European history in the 20th century, in particular the advent of totalitarianism. Viewed from this perspective, Heidegger's attempt to develop a new "fundamental ontology," one that would answer the question of the "meaning of Being," is misguided, because it continues to reflect the dominating and destructive orientation characteristic of Western philosophy in general.

Lévinas claims that ontology also displays a bias toward cognition and theoretical reason—the use of reason in the formation of judgments or beliefs. In this respect ontology is philosophically inferior to ethics, a field that Lévinas construes as encompassing all the practical dealings of human beings with each other. Lévinas holds that the primacy of ethics over ontology is justified by the "face of the Other." The "alterity," or otherness, of the Other, as signified by the "face," is something that one acknowledges before using reason to form judgments or beliefs about him. Insofar as the moral debt one owes to the Other can never be satisfied—Lévinas claims that the Other is "infinitely transcendent, infinitely foreign"—one's relation to him is that of infinity. In contrast, because ontology treats the Other as an object of judgments made by theoretical reason, it deals with him as a finite being. Its relationship to the Other is therefore one of totality.

Lévinas claims that ethics can be given a theological foundation in the biblical commandment "Thou shalt not kill" (Exodus 20:13). He explores the ethical implications of this mandate in religious studies such as *Difficult Freedom: Essays on Judaism* (1963) and *Nine Talmudic Readings* (1990). Among Lévinas's other major philosophical works are *Existence and Existents* (1947), *Discovering Existence with Husserl and Heidegger* (1949), *Difficult Freedom* (1963), and *Otherwise than Being, or Beyond Essence* (1974).

CHAPTER 18

JUDAISM
IN WORLD
PERSPECTIVE

The biblical tradition out of which Judaism emerged was predominantly exclusivist. The Ten Commandments enjoined the people of Israel to have "no other gods" other than YHWH. The gods of the nations were regarded as "no gods" and their worshippers as deluded, while the God of Israel was acclaimed as the sole lord of history and the creator of heaven and earth. The unexpected universalist implications of this exclusivism are most forcibly expressed in an oft-quoted verse from Amos (9:7):

> *"Are you not like the Ethiopians to me, O people of Israel?" says the Lord. "Did I not bring up Israel from the land of Egypt, and the Philistines from Caphtor and the Syrians from Kir?"*

Here the universal rule of the God of Israel is unmistakably proclaimed. Yet in the same book (3:1–2), after referring to the deliverance from Egypt—an act recognized as similar to that occurring in the affairs of other peoples—the prophet Amos, speaking for God, says: "You only have I known of all the families of the earth." Thus, the exclusivism has two focuses: one universal, the other particularistic. The ultimate claim of the universalistic position is found in Malachi 1:11: "For from the

Sunrise over the skyline of Jerusalem. Malachi 1:11 includes the ultimate claim of the universalistic position: "For from the rising of the sun to its setting my name is great among the nations." Jon Hicks/Photographer's Choice/Getty Images

rising of the sun to its setting my name is great among the nations." This, however, in no way negates the special covenantal relationship between God and his people, because this universalistic theme emphasizes that special bond. To interpret Judaism's stance toward other religious systems in any other way is to fail to do justice to its inner dialectic. It neither blandly admits any or all viewpoints and practices nor promotes a fanatical intolerance. Rather, it features a subtle interplay of affirmation and rejection. The latter is directed primarily against idolatry—the basic failure of the peoples who are the objects of the same divine solicitude as is Israel. If the religions of the nations are rejected because of their failure to know God fully and truly, the peoples themselves are not. Living under the covenant with Noah, their fulfillment of such responsibilities provides for their acceptance, for they are not expected to live within the realm of Torah.

RELATION TO CHRISTIANITY

Judaism's relation to Christianity is complicated because of the close historical interconnections between them. From a Judaic standpoint, Christianity is or was a Jewish "heresy," and, as such, it may be judged somewhat differently than other religions. Christianity's claim to be the true fulfillment of the covenant—and, thus, the true Israel—has given rise throughout the centuries to polemics of varying intensity. The rise to power of the church and the embodiment of its anti-Judaic sentiments and attitudes in the political structures and processes of Christian nations made sharply negative Jewish responses inevitable. Nevertheless, during the Middle Ages, Jewish thinkers attempted to avoid designating Christianity as idolatry. Some even argued that, because Christianity was derived from Judaism, it was fulfilling—at least on a moral plane—the divine purpose.

In modern times the relation between the two religions has undergone changes necessitated by the newer situations into which the Jewish community has moved. This does not mean that the polemical-apologetic stance came to an end. The rejection of Judaism as a living religion by some Christians has continued, though it was argued less on dogmatic than on scholarly grounds. The Jewish response has often been countercriticism. Beyond this, however, there has been a growing inclination within the Jewish community to respond to the development of an affirmative theology of Judaism in both the Roman Catholic and Protestant churches by providing a theology of Christianity within Jewish thought. Occasional formulations in this direction have appeared, but some within the Jewish community have seen no need for such a movement.

Beginning in the early 1960s many Christian churches, especially the Roman Catholic Church, began to rethink their relationship to Judaism. During the Second Vatican Council (1962–65), Pope Paul VI issued the declaration *Nostra aetate* ("In Our Era"), which recognized the moral and historical integrity of Judaism, a remarkable reversal of centuries of Catholic teaching. *Nostra aetate* also acknowledged Judaism as a vibrant religion with an identity independent of its role in the formation of historical Christianity. Most mainline Protestant churches responded with a declaration similar to *Nostra aetate*. During his pontificate, John Paul II (1978–2005), who had a great theological admiration for and understanding of Judaism, further improved Catholic-Jewish relations.

RELATION TO ISLAM

The emergence of Islam in Arabia in the 7th century CE brought Judaism face to face with a second religious movement that derived some of its ideas and structures from the older tradition. In this case, as in that of Christianity, the new religion claimed a special relation with Judaism. Muhammad held that the faith he proclaimed was none other than the pristine religion of Abraham, the father of Ishmael (the progenitor of the Arabs) and Isaac (from whom the people of Israel descended). That religion had been distorted by both Judaism and Christianity, and Muhammad, the "seal" of the Prophets, had been called by God to restore it to its purity. The confrontation between Judaism and Islam, like that between Judaism and Christianity, was coloured by political and social considerations both before and after Islam spread beyond Arabia to other areas of the Middle East (including Palestine) and to parts of Europe. During the subsequent period, the intellectual development of the Islamic world and the emergence of theologians and philosophers of the highest order challenged Judaism and exerted considerable influence on similar thinkers within that community. Given the strong monotheism and the anti-iconic attitude of Islam, many of the questions that arose between Judaism and

Trinitarian and iconic Christianity were not an issue between Judaism and Islam. Rather, the crucial point of dispute was the nature of prophecy, which arose because of Muhammad's claim concerning his culminating role in the prophetic tradition. Thus, during the medieval period there were polemics directed against that claim, as well as expositions of the nature of prophecy that, without dealing directly with Muhammad's claim, could be taken to undercut it—as in the case of Maimonides' *The Guide for the Perplexed*). Nonetheless, Islam too was understood to contribute to the fulfillment of the divine purpose. From the late medieval period onward, the intellectual engagement between the two religions diminished with the general decline in the Turkish empire that then embraced the Muslim world. In modern times it has not yet been renewed for many reasons, the most important of which has been the political and military conflict between the State of Israel and the Arab countries of the Middle East.

RELATIONS WITH OTHER RELIGIONS

Judaism's encounters with religions other than Christianity and Islam have been in large measure limited to the past. In the Hellenistic world, it confronted and rejected the varieties of syncretistic cults that grew up. Within the Sāsānian empire it was forced to deal with Zoroastrianism, but the outlines of its response have not yet been entirely disentangled from the literature of the period. In the modern world, particularly in the most recent period, it has come face to face with the religions of the Middle East and Asia, but beyond a few tentative explorations nothing tangible has appeared. Because of the growing interest and exchange between East and West, however, Jewish thinkers will not be able to rest with older formulations concerning the nature of other religious systems. Without compromising its own faith or falling into an uncritical relativism, Judaism may indeed seek a new way of understanding and relating to the varieties of religious systems facing it on the world scene.

THE ROLE OF JUDAISM IN WESTERN CULTURE AND CIVILIZATION

Judaism has played a significant role in the development of Western culture because of its unique relationship with Christianity, the dominant religious force in the West. Although the Christian church drew from other sources as well, its retention of the sacred Scriptures of the synagogue as an integral part of its Bible—a decision sharply debated in the 2nd century CE—was crucial. Not only was the development of its ideas and doctrines deeply influenced, but it also received an ethical dynamism that constantly overcame an inclination to withdraw into world-denying isolation.

It was, however, not only Judaism's heritage but its persistence that touched Western civilization. The continuing existence of the Jews, even as a pariah

Martin Luther, the leader of the Protestant movement, drew on Jewish biblical commentary. Archive Photos/Getty Images

people, was both a challenge and a warning. Their liberation from the shackles of discrimination, segregation, and rejection at the beginning of the modern era was understood by many to be the touchstone of all human liberty. Until the final ghettoization of the Jew—it is well to remember that the term *ghetto* belongs in the first instance to Jewish history—at the end of the Middle Ages and the beginning of the Renaissance, intellectual contact between Judaism and Christianity, and thus between Judaism and Western culture, continued. St. Jerome translated the Hebrew Bible into Latin with the aid of Jewish scholars; the exegetical work of the scholars of the monastery of St. Victor in the 12th century borrowed heavily from Jewish scholars; and the biblical commentary of Rashi (Solomon ben Isaac of Troyes) was an important source for Martin Luther (1483–1546). Jewish thinkers helped to bring the remarkable intellectual achievements of the Islamic world to Christian Europe and added their own contributions as well. Even heresies within the church, on occasion, were said to have been inspired by or modeled after Judaism.

In the modern world, while the influence of Jews has increased in almost every realm of cultural life, the effect of Judaism itself has diminished. The reason for this is not difficult to find. The Gentile leaders who extended emancipation to the Jews at the end of the 18th century and the beginning of the 19th were eager to grant political equality, but they also insisted that certain reforms of Judaism be accepted. With the transformation of Judaism into an ecclesiastical institution, largely on the model of German Protestant churches, its ideas and structures took on the cast of its environment in a way quite unlike what had ensued in its earlier confrontations with various philosophical systems. Indeed, for some, Judaism and 19th-century European thought were not merely congruent but identical. Thus, while numerous contributors to diverse aspects of Western culture and civilization are to be found among Jews of the 20th and 21st centuries—scientists, politicians, statesmen, scholars, musicians, artists—their activities cannot, except in specific instances, be considered as deriving from Judaism as it has been sketched previously.

CONCLUSION: FUTURE PROSPECTS

The two central events of 20th-century Jewish history were the Holocaust and the establishment of the State of Israel. The former was the great tragedy of the Jewish people, while the latter was the light of a rebirth, which promised political, cultural, and economic independence. The rest of the world has been forced to reconsider and reorient its relationship with Judaism and the Jewish people because of these two events. At the same time, the centres of Jewish life have moved almost exclusively to Israel and

North America. The virtual absence of official anti-Semitism in North America allowed Jews to flourish in pursuits previously the preserve of Gentiles. Along with these developments, theological considerations and practical realities, such as interfaith marriage, have made Jewish religious culture a point of interest for many non-Jews.

The Israeli coat of arms. Shutterstock.com

In the early 21st century, Jewish religious life continued to fragment along ideological lines, but that very fragmentation animated both moral imagination and ritual life. While ultra-Orthodox Judaism grew more insular, and some varieties of Liberal Judaism moved ritual practice even farther away from traditional observance, a vital centre emerged, running from Reform Judaism to modern Orthodoxy. This centre sought to understand Judaism within a broader context of interaction with other cultures while leaving unaffected the essentials of belief and practice. Predicting the future of Judaism is not an easy or enviable task, but there is reason to hope that the world will continue to draw upon the religious and cultural traditions of Judaism, both past and present.

Glossary

amora In ancient times, a Jewish scholar attached to one of several academies in Palestine or Babylonia, who collaborated in writing the Gemara and collected interpretations of and commentaries on the Mishna and its critical marginal notes.

apostasy The abandonment of loyalty or the rejection of religious commitment.

covenant A binding contractual agreement; in the Hebrew Scriptures this refers to the promises made between God and the people of Israel.

demiurge Subordinate god who shapes and arranges the physical world.

exegesis Exposition or explanation, especially critical interpretation of a text or portion of Scripture.

gaon Title accorded to the Jewish spiritual leaders and scholars who headed Talmudic academies that flourished, with lengthy interruptions, from the 7th to the 13th century in Babylonia and Palestine.

Gemara Commentary on the collection of Jewish law known as the Mishna.

ghetto The quarter of a city in which Jews were required to live.

gnosis Immediate knowledge of spiritual truth; especially such knowledge as professed by the ancient gnostics and held to be attainable through faith alone.

Halakhah In Judaism, the totality of laws and ordinances that have evolved since biblical times to regulate religious observances and the daily life and conduct of the Jewish people.

hortatory Giving or characterized by exhortation.

Mishna Oldest authoritative collection of Jewish oral law, supplementing the written laws in the Hebrew Scriptures.

monotheism Belief in the existence of one god.

pale A territory or district within certain bounds or under a particu-lar jurisdiction.

patriarch One of the Scriptural fathers of the human race or of the Hebrew people; specifically, one of a group comprising Abraham, Isaac, Jacob, and the 12 sons of Jacob.

piety Zeal in religious service or worship.

pogrom Mob attack, condoned by authorities, against persons and property of a religious, racial, or national minority.

polytheism Belief in many gods.

preordain To decree or ordain in advance; to order or assure the occurrence of beforehand.

sacrament Religious action or symbol in which spiritual power is believed to be transmitted through material elements or the performance of ritual.

salvation In religion, deliverance from fundamentally negative conditions, or the restoration or elevation of the natural world to a higher, better state.

Talmud In Judaism, the systematic amplification and analysis of passages of the Mishna, the Gemara, and other oral law, including the Tosefta.

theurgy The art or science of compelling or persuading a god or beneficent supernatural power to do or refrain from doing something.

Torah In Hebrew, "way," or "teaching." The term refers specifically to the first five books of the Bible—Genesis, Exodus, Leviticus, Numbers, and Deuteronomy—and also to the body of wisdom and law contained both in this Scripture and in other sacred literature and oral tradition.

Tosefta A collection of oral traditions related to Jewish oral law that supplement the Mishna.

yeshiva Academy of higher Talmudic learning.

BIBLIOGRAPHY

GENERAL HISTORY

Noteworthy studies are Salo W. Baron, *A Social and Religious History of the Jews*, 2nd ed., rev. and enlarged, 18 vol. (1952–83), a comprehensive presentation of the intertwined social and religious history, with copious bibliographical information critically evaluated; Louis Finkelstein (ed.), *The Jews: Their History, Culture, and Religion*, 4th ed., 3 vol. (1970–71), critical essays by outstanding authorities on the major aspects of Jewish history and culture; and Robert M. Seltzer, *Jewish People, Jewish Thought: The Jewish Experience in History* (1980), a thorough account of Jewish history and civilization in one volume.

MODERN JUDAISM

The most convenient summary for the study of modern Jewish history is Howard M. Sachar, *The Course of Modern Jewish History*, rev. and updated ed. (1990). Modern Jewish thought and belief are covered in Joseph L. Blau, *Modern Varieties of Judaism* (1966); and *The Condition of Jewish Belief: A Symposium* (1966, reissued 1995), a book published by the editors of *Commentary Magazine*. Arthur Hertzberg (ed.), *The Zionist Idea* (1959, reissued 1997), is a comprehensive reader in English on the issue of Zionism. An excellent exposition of Judaism from a Reform-Liberal point of view is Leo Baeck, *The Essence of Judaism*, trans. by Victor Grubenweiser and Leonard Pearl, rev. ed. (1948, reissued 1976; originally published in German, 1905). Conservative Judaism is well described in Jacob B. Agus, *Dialogue and Tradition: The Challenges of Contemporary Judeo-Christian Thought* (1971). Mordecai M. Kaplan, *Judaism as a Civilization*, enlarged ed. (1957, reissued 1994), is the best discussion of Reconstructionism. The standard single volume about Orthodox Judaism is Isidore Epstein, *Judaism* (1935). Joseph B. Soloveitchik, *Halakhic Man*, trans. by Lawrence Kaplan (1983, reissued 1991; originally published in Hebrew, 1979), is a statement of the centrality of Halakhah to Judaism by the most influential Orthodox theologian of the 20th century. The best discussion of Neo-Hasidism, by the movement's greatest exponent, is Martin Buber, *The Origin and Meaning of Hasidism*, ed. and trans. by Maurice Friedman (1960, reissued 1988; originally published in German, 1948).

BASIC BELIEFS, PRACTICES, AND INSTITUTIONS

Jacob Neusner, *The Way of Torah: An Introduction to Judaism*, 7th ed.

(2004), is a very useful statement with a history-of-religions approach. Michael Wyschogrod, *The Body of Faith: Judaism of Corporeal Election* (1983), is an attempt to restore election as the most important idea in Judaism. David Novak, *The Election of Israel: The Idea of the Chosen People* (1995), is a theological meditation on the retrieval of the doctrine of election for contemporary Jews. Jewish ceremonies are covered in Lewis N. Dembitz, *Jewish Services in Synagogue and Home* (1898, reprinted 1975); Hayim Shoys (Hayyim Schauss), *The Jewish Festivals: From Their Beginning to Our Own Day*, trans. by Samuel Jaffe (1938; also published as *The Jewish Festivals: A Guide to Their History and Observance*, 1996; originally published in Hebrew, 1933); and Ismar Elbogen, *Jewish Liturgy: A Comprehensive History*, trans. by Raymond P. Scheindlin (1993; originally published in German, 1913).

RELATIONS WITH NON-JUDAIC RELIGIONS

David Novak, *The Image of the Non-Jew in Judaism* (1983), is a study of the Noahide Laws as the basis of Jewish interaction with Gentiles, and *Jewish-Christian Dialogue: A Jewish Justification* (1989), is a theological rationale for a new relationship between Jews and Christians. Robert Chazan, *Medieval Antisemitism and Modern Stereotypes* (1997); and Jacob Katz, *From Prejudice to Destruction: Anti-Semitism, 1700–1933* (1980, reissued 1997), treat the history of anti-Semitism. F.E. Peters, *Children of Abraham: Judaism, Christianity, Islam* (1982), examines differences and similarities between the three monotheistic faiths.

JEWISH MYSTICISM

Gershom Scholem, *Major Trends in Jewish Mysticism*, 3rd rev. ed. (1954, reissued 1995), is the standard survey of the subject. Translations of important mystical texts include Harry Sperling (trans.) and Maurice Simon (trans.), *The Zohar*, 2nd ed., 5 vol. (1984); Moses Cordovero, *The Palm Tree of Deborah*, trans. by Louis Jacobs, 3rd ed. (1981; originally published in Hebrew, 1623); R.J. Zwi Werblowsky, *Joseph Karo: Lawyer and Mystic*, 2nd ed. (1977); and L.I. Newman (compiler and trans.), *The Hasidic Anthology: Tales and Teachings of the Hasidim* (1934, reissued 1987).

Gershom Scholem, *Sabbatai Sevi: The Mystical Messiah*, trans. by R.J. Zwi Werblowsky (1973; originally published in Hebrew, 1956), is a penetrating and comprehensive study of the great false messiah. Abraham Joshua Heschel, *God in Search of Man: A Philosophy of Judaism* (1955, reissued 1993), is a major work by a constructive theologian heavily influenced by Jewish mysticism. Moshe Idel, *Kabbalah: New Perspectives* (1998), emphasizes the experiential side of Jewish mysticism.

JEWISH MYTH AND LEGEND

The legends of the Talmud and Midrash are considered in the classic by Louis Ginzberg, *Legends of the Jews*, trans. from German by Henrietta Szold and Paul Radin, 2nd ed., 2 vol. (2003), also available in a 1-vol. abridgment (1961). The *Midrash Rabbah* has been translated and edited by H. Freedman and Maurice Simon, 3rd ed., 10 vol. in 8 (1983).

Compilations and studies of medieval myth and legend include Eleazar ben Asher ha-Levi and Jerahmeel ben Solomon, *The Chronicles of Jerahmeel*, trans. from Hebrew by Moses Gaster (1899, reprinted 1972); and Curt Leviant (ed. and trans.), *King Artus: A Hebrew Arthurian Romance of 1279* (1969, reissued 2003). Judeo-German (Yiddish) works on the subject include Moses Gaster (trans.), *Ma'aseh Book: Book of Jewish Tales and Legends*, 2 vol. in 1 (1934, reissued 1981). A study of Hasidic legend is Martin Buber (ed.), *Tales of the Hasidim*, trans. from German by Olga Marx, 2 vol. in 1 (1947, reissued 1991). Myths and legends of the Holy Land are treated in Dov Noy (ed.), *Folktales of Israel*, trans. from Hebrew by Gene Baharav (1963); Zev Vilnay, *The Sacred Land*, 3 vol. (1973–78); and Joshua Trachtenberg, *Jewish Magic and Superstition: A Study in Folk Religion* (1939, reissued 1987).

Index